The Chattering Mind

The Chattering Mind

A Conceptual History of Everyday Talk

SAMUEL McCORMICK

The University of Chicago Press   Chicago and London

The University of Chicago Press, Chicago 60637
The University of Chicago Press, Ltd., London
© 2020 by The University of Chicago
Published 2020
Printed in the United States of America

29 28 27 26 25 24 23 22 21 20   1 2 3 4 5

ISBN-13: 978-0-226-67763-7 (cloth)
ISBN-13: 978-0-226-67777-4 (paper)
ISBN-13: 978-0-226-67780-4 (e-book)
DOI: https://doi.org/10.7208/chicago/9780226677804.001.0001

Library of Congress Cataloging-in-Publication Data
Names: McCormick, Samuel, 1978– author.
Title: The chattering mind : a conceptual history of everyday talk /
    Samuel McCormick.
Description: Chicago ; London : University of Chicago Press, 2019. |
    Includes bibliographical references and index.
Identifiers: LCCN 2019024417 | ISBN 9780226677637 (cloth) |
    ISBN 9780226677774 (paperback) | ISBN 9780226677804 (ebook)
Subjects: LCSH: Kierkegaard, Søren, 1813–1855. | Heidegger, Martin,
    1889–1976. | Lacan, Jacques, 1901–1981. | Conversation—
    Philosophy. | Conversation—Philosophy—History.
Classification: LCC P95.45 .M367 2019 | DDC 302.34/6—dc23
LC record available at https://lccn.loc.gov/2019024417

FOR IRIS

Contents

Abbreviations in Text Citations

BH Martin Heidegger, *Becoming Heidegger: On the Trail of His Early Occasional Writings, 1910–1927*, ed. Theodore Kisiel and Thomas Sheehan (Evanston, IL: Northwestern University Press, 2007).

BOA Søren Kierkegaard, *The Book on Adler*, ed. and trans. Howard V. Hong and Edna H. Hong (Princeton, NJ: Princeton University Press, 1998).

BT Martin Heidegger, *Being and Time*, trans. John Macquarrie and Edward Robinson (Oxford: Blackwell, 1962).

C Aristophanes, *Clouds*, trans. Jeffrey Henderson (Cambridge: Loeb Classical Library, 1998).

CA Søren Kierkegaard, *The Concept of Anxiety: A Simple Psychologically Orienting Deliberation on the Dogmatic Issue of Hereditary Sin*, ed. and trans. Reidar Thomte (Princeton, NJ: Princeton University Press, 1980).

CD Søren Kierkegaard, *Christian Discourses*, ed. and trans. Howard V. Hong and Edna H. Hong (Princeton, NJ: Princeton University Press, 1997).

CI Søren Kierkegaard, *The Concept of Irony, with Continual Reference to Socrates*, ed. and trans. Howard V. Hong and Edna H. Hong (Princeton, NJ: Princeton University Press, 1992).

CL Sigmund Freud, *The Complete Letters of Sigmund Freud to Wilhelm Fliess, 1887–1904*, ed. and trans. Jeffrey Moussaieff Masson (Cambridge: Belknap, 1985)

COR Søren Kierkegaard, *The Corsair Affair and Articles Related to the Writings*, ed. and trans. Howard V. Hong and Edna H. Hong (Princeton, NJ: Princeton University Press, 1982).

CT   Martin Heidegger, *The Concept of Time*, trans. William McNeill (Oxford: Blackwell, 1992).

CUP 1   Søren Kierkegaard, *Concluding Unscientific Postscript to Philosophical Fragments*, vol. 1, ed. and trans. Howard V. Hong and Edna H. Hong (Princeton, NJ: Princeton University Press, 1992).

E   Jacques Lacan, *Écrits*, trans. Bruce Fink (New York: W. W. Norton, 2006).

EN   Aristotle, *Nicomachean Ethics*, rev. ed., ed. and trans. Roger Crisp (Cambridge: Cambridge University Press, 2014).

EPW   Søren Kierkegaard, *Early Polemical Writings*, ed. and trans. Julia Watkin (Princeton, NJ: Princeton University Press, 1990).

EUD   Søren Kierkegaard, *Eighteen Upbuilding Discourses*, ed. and trans. Howard V. Hong and Edna H. Hong (Princeton, NJ: Princeton University Press, 1990).

FR   Sigmund Freud, *The Freud Reader*, ed. Peter Gay (New York: W. W. Norton, 1989).

GA   Martin Heidegger, *Gesamtausgabe* (Frankfurt: Klostermann, 1975–).

GT   Gabriel Tarde, "The Public and the Crowd" (1901), in *Gabriel Tarde: On Communication and Social Influence*, ed. Terry N. Clark (Chicago: University of Chicago Press, 1969).

HJC   Martin Heidegger and Karl Jaspers, *The Heidegger-Jaspers Correspondence (1920–1963)*, ed. Walter Biemel and Hans Saner, trans. Gary E. Aylesworth (Amherst, MA: Humanity Books, 2003).

J   Søren Kierkegaard, *Judge for Yourself!*, in *For Self-Examination / Judge for Yourself!*, ed. and trans. Howard V. Hong and Edna H. Hong (Princeton, NJ: Princeton University Press, 1991).

JNB 1   Søren Kierkegaard, *Kierkegaard's Journals and Notebooks*, vol. 1, ed. Niels Jørgen Cappelørn et al. (Princeton, NJ: Princeton University Press, 2007).

JNB 2   Søren Kierkegaard, *Kierkegaard's Journals and Notebooks*, vol. 2, ed. Niels Jørgen Cappeløorn et al. (Princeton, NJ: Princeton University Press, 2008).

JNB 3   Søren Kierkegaard, *Kierkegaard's Journals and Notebooks*, vol. 3, ed. Niels Jørgen Cappeløorn et al. (Princeton, NJ: Princeton University Press, 2010).

JNB 4   Søren Kierkegaard, *Kierkegaard's Journals and Notebooks*, vol. 4, ed. Niels Jørgen Cappelørn et al. (Princeton, NJ: Princeton University Press, 2011).

JNB 5   Søren Kierkegaard, *Kierkegaard's Journals and Notebooks*, vol. 5, ed. Niels Jørgen Cappelørn et al. (Princeton, NJ: Princeton University Press, 2011).

JNB 6   Søren Kierkegaard, *Kierkegaard's Journals and Notebooks*, vol. 6, ed. Niels Jørgen Cappelørn et al. (Princeton, NJ: Princeton University Press, 2012).

JNB 7   Søren Kierkegaard, *Kierkegaard's Journals and Notebooks*, vol. 7, ed. Niels Jørgen Cappelørn et al. (Princeton, NJ: Princeton University Press, 2014).

JNB 8   Søren Kierkegaard, *Kierkegaard's Journals and Notebooks*, vol. 8, ed. Niels Jørgen Cappelørn et al. (Princeton, NJ: Princeton University Press, 2015).

JNB 9   Søren Kierkegaard, *Kierkegaard's Journals and Notebooks*, vol. 9, ed. Niels Jørgen Cappelørn et al. (Princeton, NJ: Princeton University Press, 2017).

LD   Søren Kierkegaard, *Letters and Documents*, trans. Henrik Rosenmeier (Princeton, NJ: Princeton University Press, 1978).

LHW   Martin Heidegger, *Letters to His Wife: 1915–1970*, ed. Gertrud Heidegger, trans. R. D. V. Glasgow (Cambridge: Polity, 2008).

M   Søren Kierkegaard, *The Moment and Late Writings*, ed. and trans. Howard V. Hong and Edna H. Hong (Princeton, NJ: Princeton University Press, 1998).

MGW   Ludvig Holberg, *Master Gert Westphaler; or, The Talkative Barber*, in *Seven One-Act Plays by Holberg*, trans. Henry Alexander (Princeton, NJ: Princeton University Press, 1950).

NSS   Bruno Latour, "Networks, Societies, Spheres: Reflections of an Actor-Network Theorist," *International Journal of Communication* 5 (2011): 804–5.

OWL   Martin Heidegger, *On the Way to Language*, trans. Peter D. Hertz (New York: Harper & Row, 1971).

P   Søren Kierkegaard, *Prefaces*, ed. and trans. Todd W. Nichol (Princeton, NJ: Princeton University Press, 1997).

PC   Søren Kierkegaard, *Practice in Christianity*, ed. and trans. Howard V. Hong and Edna H. Hong (Princeton, NJ: Princeton University Press, 1991).

PF   Søren Kierkegaard, *Philosophical Fragments*, ed. and trans. Howard V. Hong and Edna H. Hong (Princeton, NJ: Princeton University Press, 1985).

PPW   Martin Heidegger, "Why Do I Stay in the Provinces?" trans. Thomas J. Sheehan, in *Philosophical and Political Writings*, ed. Manfred Stassen (New York: Continuum, 2003).

PSC   Gilles Deleuze, "Postscript on the Societies of Control," *October* 59 (1992): 3–7.

S 1   Jacques Lacan, *Freud's Papers on Technique, 1953–1954*, ed. Jacques-Alain Miller, trans. John Forrester (New York: W. W. Norton, 1991).

S 2   Jacques Lacan, *The Ego in Freud's Theory and in the Technique of Psychoanalysis, 1954–1955*, ed. Jacques-Alain Miller, trans. Sylvana Tomaselli (New York: W. W. Norton, 1991).

S 3   Jacques Lacan, *The Psychoses, 1955–1956*, ed. Jacques-Alain Miller, trans. Russell Grigg (New York: W. W. Norton, 1993).

S 7   Jacques Lacan, *The Ethics of Psychoanalysis, 1959–1960*, ed. Jacques-Alain Miller, trans. Dennis Porter (New York: W. W. Norton, 1992).

S 11   Jacques Lacan, *The Four Fundamental Concepts of Psychoanalysis*, ed. Jacques-Alain Miller, trans. Alan Sheridan (New York: W. W. Norton, 1981).

S 19   Jacques Lacan, . . . *ou pire* (Paris: Seuil, 2011).

SD   Søren Kierkegaard, *The Sickness Unto Death: A Christian Psychological Exposition for Upbuilding and Awakening*, ed. and trans. Howard V. Hong and Edna H. Hong (Princeton, NJ: Princeton University Press, 1980).

SE   Sigmund Freud, *The Standard Edition of the Complete Psychological Works of Sigmund Freud*, ed. and trans. James Strachey (London: Hogarth, 1958).

SKS   Søren Kierkegaard, *Søren Kierkegaards Skrifter*, ed. Niels Jørgen Cappelørn et al. (Copenhagen: Gad, 1997–).

SS 1923 Martin Heidegger, *Ontology—The Hermeneutics of Facticity*, trans. John van Buren (Bloomington: Indiana University Press, 1999).

SS 1924 Martin Heidegger, *Basic Concepts of Aristotelian Philosophy*, trans. Robert D. Metcalf and Mark B. Tanzer (Bloomington: Indiana University Press, 2009).

SS 1925 Martin Heidegger, *History of the Concept of Time: Prolegomena*, trans. Theodore Kisiel (Bloomington: Indiana University Press, 1985).

SS 1926 Martin Heidegger, *Basic Concepts of Ancient Philosophy*, trans. Richard Rojcewicz (Bloomington: Indiana University Press, 2007).

SS 1930 Martin Heidegger, *The Essence of Human Freedom: An Introduction to Philosophy*, trans. Ted Sadler (London: Continuum, 2004).

SS 1935 Martin Heidegger, *Introduction to Metaphysics*, trans. Gregory Fried and Richard Polt (New Haven, CT: Yale University Press, 2000).

SS 1936 Martin Heidegger, *The Essence of Human Freedom: An Introduction to Philosophy*, trans. Ted Sadler (London: Continuum, 2002).

T   Plutarch, "On Talkativeness," in *Moralia*, vol. 6, trans. W. C. Helmbold (Cambridge: Loeb Classical Library, 2000).

TA   Søren Kierkegaard, *Two Ages*, ed. and trans. Howard V. Hong and Edna H. Hong (Princeton, NJ: Princeton University Press, 1978).

WES 1919 Martin Heidegger, *Towards the Definition of Philosophy*, trans. Ted Sadler (London: Athlone Press, 2000).

WS 1920–21 Martin Heidegger, *The Phenomenology of Religious Life*, trans. Matthias Fritsch and Jennifer Anna Gosetti-Ferencei (Bloomington: Indiana University Press, 2010).

WS 1921–22 Martin Heidegger, *Phenomenological Interpretations of Aristotle: Initiation into Phenomenological Research*, trans. Richard Rojcewicz (Bloomington: Indiana University Press, 2001).

WS 1924–25 Martin Heidegger, *Plato's Sophist*, trans. Richard Rojcewicz and André Schuwer (Bloomington: Indiana University Press, 1997).

Introduction

The Flight from Conversation

It's probably been a few minutes since you checked your phone—and maybe only a few minutes more since you sent your last text, tapped your last "like," or posted your last status update. Same here. But when was your last face-to-face conversation? When did you last speak with someone in person? My daughter left for school three hours ago, and I haven't spoken with anyone since. This is not uncommon, and not entirely unwelcome, thanks in part to the occasional chirping and buzzing of my phone. But even as I write these sentences, even with the self-reflection they afford, I am still uncertain how I feel about this state of affairs—an uncertainty which in turn provokes a mild yet marked unease.

In her best-selling book, *Reclaiming Conversation*, Sherry Turkle calls this uneasy shift from spoken discourse to digital talk "the flight from conversation."[1] With mobile devices in hand, lovers now send texts from room to room, friends and families now sit and dine and stare at screens together, and colleagues now spend meetings looking down, emptying their inboxes in unison. Many of us are even skilled enough to "phub," maintaining eye contact with one person while simultaneously texting someone else. Alone together and always elsewhere—this is how we experience the flight from conversation. In our rush to connect, we neglect to converse. But we also refuse to accept the consequences, anxiously hoping to rediscover intimacy on the internet. Is this a conversation? Was that a conversation? What, exactly, makes for conversation?

Scholars have been asking similar questions for well over a century. But it was not until the 1970s that they began to do so en masse. One group of inquirers emerged from North American departments of sociology and quickly came to be known as "conversation analysts." Armed with tape recorders and elaborate transcription codes, these sociologists-turned-communication-scholars were (and often remain) devoted to close analyses of naturally occurring talk in the immediate present, especially between ordinary speakers in face-to-face settings. Another group of inquirers emerged from French and German research programs with a keen interest in the literary history of conversation, especially as it found expression in early- and mid-modern letters, essays, memoirs, plays, novels, dialogues, treatises, and, of course, etiquette handbooks. It was the art of conversation as conceived and practiced by yesterday's educated elites, not the naturally occurring talk of ordinary citizens today, that intrigued (and often continues to fascinate) these literary historians.[2]

The social and historical gaps between these prominent lines of inquiry are worth noting. Conversation analysts rarely study ordinary language use before the postwar era, and literary historians rarely venture past the French Revolution in search of elite vernacular artistry. What happened to conversation—as a practice of everyday life and an object of learned concern—in the intervening century and a half? And what does this tell us about the flight from conversation today? Answering the first question and pressing toward the second are the primary tasks of this book.

A Usable Past

From Plato's contempt for "the madness of the multitude" to Kant's lament for "the great unthinking mass," the history of Western thought is riddled with disdain for ordinary collective life. But it was not until Søren Kierkegaard developed the term "chatter" (*snak*) that this disdain began to focus on the *communicative practice* of ordinary collective life. And not just any communicative practice: it was the average, everyday talk of modern mass society—in person and in print, among ordinary citizens and educated elites, with varying degrees of deliberateness and unawareness, and always in a certain state of excess—that caught his attention.

The intellectual tradition inaugurated by Kierkegaard's work on chatter has been insufficiently traced. This book aims to provide such a tracing. It is at once a genealogy of learned discourse on the practice of everyday talk, and, at its furthest reaches, an effort to reclaim this genealogy as a crucial conceptual foundation for ongoing discussions of collective life in the digital age, where chatrooms have now given way to snapchats, and the flight from conversation shows no sign of abating.

In this sense, *The Chattering Mind* is less a history of ideas than a book in search of a usable past. It is a study of how the modern world became anxious about ordinary language use, figured in terms of the intellectual elites who piqued this anxiety, and written with an eye toward recent dilemmas of digital communication. As near as I can tell, it is the first book-length study to explain how a quintessentially unproblematic form of modern communication—not the art of conversation but the practice of everyday talk—became a communication problem in itself, notably one in need of philosophical commentary and now, in the algorithmic era, ongoing technological support.

In particular, the following chapters trace the conceptual history of everyday talk from Søren Kierkegaard's inaugural theory of "chatter" (*snak*) to Martin Heidegger's recuperative discussion of "idle talk" (*Gerede*), to Jacques Lacan's culminating treatment of "empty speech" (*parole vide*)—and ultimately, if only allusively, into our digital present, where small talk on various social media platforms has now become the basis for big data in the hands of tech-savvy entrepreneurs.

This is not to suggest that Kierkegaard, Heidegger, and Lacan anticipated today's digital media environments. Nor is it to suggest that their influence on these datascapes can or should be established in hindsight. To be sure, readers versed in Snapchat, Twitter, Facebook, Reddit, and the like will find many striking parallels between the communicative practices examined in this book and those characteristic of these social networks. My goal is neither to dwell on these parallels nor even to document their occurrence but, instead, to anticipate future studies that might pursue such lines of inquiry. In service to this objective, the following chapters attempt to provide the first robust account of a certain conceptual history in whose reflection a curious image of ourselves can now be seen.

Means without End

What, then, is everyday talk? To begin, we might define it as the ordinary, habitual, and frequently recursive kind of communicating that occurs in private and public settings alike. And we might add that it is what became of conversation after the industrial revolution. To be sure, the preindustrial world was lousy with everyday talk. Gossip, babble, mumbling, and nonsense were especially pervasive.[3] And the art of conversation survived well into the nineteenth century. Members of polite society continued to frequent discussion groups, remaining hyperattentive to the "clubbability" of those around them.[4] My point is simply that the social, political, economic, and technological aftermath of the industrial revolution allowed the practice of everyday talk to displace the art of conversation as the basic communicative protocol of modern life. Which is why the twentieth-century revival of *conversation* could only begin with philosophers: more than a familiar feature of mass-mediated democratic life, conversation had become its distant interpersonal horizon, accessible only at the level of the concept.

Chatter, idle talk, and empty speech were symptomatic of this modern industrial shift from conversation to everyday talk. And they were just some of the ordinary communicative practices that intrigued Kierkegaard, Heidegger, and Lacan. As we shall see, each way of speaking was a lodestar for the analysis of many other discursive forms—some ancient, some modern, and some only now coming to fruition. So many, in fact, that the conceptual history to be traced in this book not only complements existing scholarship on preindustrial forms of everyday talk but also contributes to the nascent conceptual history of several abiding linguistic phenomena, notably phatic communion (now often studied as "small talk"), social gossip (usually considered alongside "rumor" and "reputation"), and political talk (also known as "informal deliberation").

At the risk of putting too fine a point on this related cluster of terms, we could say that phatic communion allows for social bonding without information exchange; social gossip achieves the same result, but only by way of information exchange; and political talk capitalizes on both achievements, pressing phatic communion and social gossip into the service of public opinion and collective will formation.[5] At issue in this sequence of terms—a sequence which not only reflects their chronological treatment in twentieth-century social thought but also suggests their continued relevance to late-modern collective life—is a gradual instrumentalization of ordinary language use, from the means-as-ends structure of phatic communion, where everyday talk doubles as evidence of the social bonds it also seeks to establish, to the means-to-ends structure of political talk, where the social bonds of everyday talk are repurposed for deliberative democratic culture.

Kierkegaard, Heidegger, and Lacan were keenly aware of these means-ends structures, but they discovered something far more remarkable in the purposive range of everyday talk—a motivational ingredient that has since become endemic to life in the digital age. In chatter, idle talk, and empty speech, these iconic (and frequently iconoclastic) thinkers saw several worrisome forms of social bonding, information exchange, and opinion formation at work. And beneath these worrisome forms of communication and culture, they found a common linguistic structure. Chatter, idle talk, and empty speech were neither means-turned-ends like phatic communion nor means-to-ends like political talk but, instead, *means without end* like nothing they had seen before.

Like any way of speaking, everyday talk involves the use of language for purposes of rhetorical appeal, with speakers so shaping their speech as to court the interests of those spoken to. Implicit in any such appeal, however, is an impulse to prevent its completion, if only to prolong the moment of courtship itself and, with it, one's use of language. In chatter, idle talk, and empty speech, this motive takes precedence. Speakers frequently suspend the pursuit of attainable rhetorical advantage in order to prolong their own utterances—and for no other reason than to prolong their own utterances. In this sense, the primary purpose of everyday talk is in fact a *pure purpose*—what Kenneth Burke aptly describes as "a kind of purpose which, as judged by the rhetoric of advantage, is no purpose at all, or which might often look like the sheer frustration of purpose."[6] As we shall see, there are many mechanisms by which the purpose of everyday talk remains "pure," but their communicative functions are always the same, allowing ordinary language use to operate as a means without end—and now, in the digital age, as an endless stream of data to be aggregated, mined, and sold to the highest bidder.

A Reverse Turing Test

Examples of everyday talk as a means without an end abound in the work of Kierkegaard, Heidegger, and Lacan. Many of these examples are considered in the following chapters, but one in particular deserves mention here, at the outset of this study. "What is it to chatter?" Kierkegaard asked in the mid-1840s, just as monarchical rule was giving way to representative democracy in his native Denmark. "It is the annulment of the passionate disjunction between being silent and speaking."[7] To illustrate this talkative annulment, Kierkegaard offers the following anecdote:

I once visited a family with a grandfather clock that for some reason or other was out of order. But the trouble did not show up in a sudden slackness of the spring or the breaking of a chain or a failure to strike; on the contrary, it went on striking, but in a curious, abstractly normal, but nevertheless confusing way. It did not strike twelve strokes at twelve o'clock and then once at one o'clock, but only once at regular intervals. It went on striking this way all day and never once gave the hour. (*TA*, 80)

Just as the regular strokes of this grandfather clock allow it to continue keeping time without ever telling anyone what time it is, so also does chatter communicate nothing more than its dysfunctional yet enduring status as a means of communication. Its communicative function, like that of this grandfather clock, is nothing other than the ceaseless communication of this function. It remains a way of speaking, but one whose primary referent has become itself and whose sole purpose has become its own continuation.

"One who chatters [*snakker*] presumably does chatter [*snakker*] about something, since the aim [*Ønsket*] is to find something to chatter about [*at snakke om*]," Kierkegaard goes on to quip. With no aim or anchor other than itself, chatter becomes "a frivolous philandering among great diversities," in which one "chatters about anything and everything and continues incessantly" (*TA*, 99–100). Topics may range from anything to everything, but each is forfeited as soon as it is found, for there is always something new to discuss. All suffer the same fate because none is so alluring as the next. Hence, Kierkegaard's use of *Ønsket* above, from the Danish *ønske*, a verbal noun referring to objects of desire as well as the experience of desire itself. If the topical range of chatter is wide, allowing anything and everything to become an object of desire, it is because chatterers never stop ranging from topic to topic in search of something new to discuss, continually rehearsing the experience of desire itself. It is precisely here, in and as the endlessly recurring meantime between topics, that chatter sustains itself.

Is this the "curious, abstractly normal, but nevertheless confusing way" that chatter operates? Yes, but only in part. When chatter prevails, the disjunction between speech and silence is neither maintained nor abolished but, instead, lulled into an oddly subliminal state—into what Kierkegaard, in the lead-up to his analogy of the grandfather clock, depicts as "a sort of drawling, semi-somnolent non-cessation [*slæbende halvvaagen Uafbrudthed*]" (*TA*, 80; trans. modified). When chatter flits from topic to topic, ever in search of something new to discuss—and thus, as Peter Fenves shrewdly observes, with nothing to say in the meantime—it does so as *somniloquy*.[8] As a form of everyday talk, chatter is as curious, confusing, and abstractly normal as someone talking in their sleep. Just as the grandfather clock continued to keep time by striking once at regular intervals, but never once gave anyone the hour, there is something senseless, involuntary, and strangely automated about the quasi-communicative function of chatter.

Not surprisingly, preindustrial notions of "chatter" were animalistic and deeply gendered. Ancients attributed it to birds and women alike.[9] Medievals used the term to disparage idle or thoughtless talk of any kind, but continued to understand it primarily as the quick shrill sounds of birdsong. To chatter was, above all, to twitter. Early-moderns went on to note its involuntarism, assigning chatter to the noise of teeth rattling from cold or fright. After the industrial revolution, chatter began to sound mechanical as well. Kierkegaard was among the first social theorists to notice. And his analogy of the dysfunctional grandfather clock was just one of many similar attempts to depict the machinelike features of this curious way of speaking. Some of these depictions, as we shall see, would echo throughout the conceptual history inaugurated by his work, resonating with later discussions of repetition, automatism, and mechanicity in the works of Heidegger and Lacan. Others would fall by the wayside. But the primary concern that fueled these depictions would in many ways become our own—albeit it in inverted form.

What Descartes initially imagined, and Alan Turing later proposed to test—namely, whether and to what extent machines could communicate like humans—natural-language-processing engines like Apple's Siri, Google's Assistant, and Amazon's Alexa are now close to confirming. Kierkegaard had the opposite concern: Whether machines could ever learn to talk like humans was of less interest to him than the extent to which humans had already learned to talk like machines. Whatever else we mean by "the flight from conversation," it arguably began here, in the modern human tendency to talk like a machine. Long before the first chatbots appeared (think ELIZA, PARRY, and Racter), and long before they evolved into today's social bots (notably Twitter bots, Instagram bots, Facebook Messenger bots, and, coming soon, Snapchat bots), we were anticipating their arrival, heralding their automated loquacity with our own, and thus, for better and for worse, preparing ourselves for the reverse Turing test now posed by their existence.

The Challenge of Attunement

Everyday talk may be unwitting, habitual, involuntary, automated, recursive, and machinelike—and sometimes all at once. But these are not its only features. As Kierkegaard, Heidegger, and Lacan were all careful to insist, everyday talk is also the condition of possibility for alternate, more resolved ways of speaking, thinking, and being with others. All of these alternatives are discussed in the following chapters, but they also bear mention here, in the opening pages of this book, if only to underscore the common line of social thought that Kierkegaard, Heidegger, and Lacan brought to the study of everyday talk.

In the chatter of modern democratic culture, Kierkegaard found an *"examen rigorosum"* by which industrial-era individuals could be religiously educated and thus prepared to apprehend "the universal in equality before God." Heidegger followed suit, albeit with less religiosity, insisting that the discursive forms of authentic existence are, in truth, "modifications" of those that constitute average everydayness. Like Kierkegaard before him, Heidegger believed there is always something about ordinary language use that cannot itself be understood as "ordinary." Lacan carried this argument even further, using analytic theory and technique to show that the resistive, egocentric practice of empty speech is, in fact, an opportunity structure for its opposite, a transformative mode of discourse he fittingly calls "full speech" (*parole pleine*).

All of which suggests that prevailing interpretations of these social theorists are at best incomplete and at worst incorrect. Kierkegaard, Heidegger, and Lacan were all convinced and committed to showing that there is more to everyday talk than alienation, inauthenticity, and the corruption of modern selves. As they saw it, ordinary language use was the proving ground, not the killing field, of genuine subjectivity.

But what does this line of thought mean for everyday talk in digital age, when so much of today's chatter, idle talk, and empty speech now occurs online, in virtual assemblies established and maintained by the mobile internet? In anticipation of more conclusive remarks in the final pages of this book, I would like to suggest that logging off, powering down, and stowing away are intuitive but ultimately misguided reactions to our much-bemoaned flight from conversation. Techno-skeptic maneuvers of this sort are not only rash and unrealistic but also increasingly unnecessary, thanks in part to clever screen-time reduction apps like Moment, Offtime, Breakfree, Space, Forest, Off the Grid, AppDetox, and the like—all of which transform the experience of overconnection into an occasion for copresent talk.

This is not to suggest that conscientious app designers are eager (or even able) to revive the early-modern art of conversation. But it is to suggest that many of the best solutions to overconnection in the digital age might await discovery in the experience of overconnection itself. It is still too soon to say what these solutions might be, but not too soon to preserve their possibility. The present may be blind to what the future will value, but with this insight comes an invaluable way of seeing the world around us—a way of seeing well-attuned to what Kierkegaard, Heidegger, and Lacan all understood as the challenge of attunement itself.[10]

Talk and Thought

Methodologically, this book resonates with several approaches to intellectual history. As a conceptual history of modernity's basic communicative practice—everyday talk—it is closely allied with the German tradition of *Begriffsgeschichte*, which prides itself on the diachronic study of fundamental terms (*Grundbegriffe*) in the development of contemporary social life. As a conceptual history of everyday talk anchored in the work of social theorists who were deeply invested in specific schools of thought—namely, Christian anti-philosophy, hermeneutic phenomenology, and post-Freudian psychoanalysis—it also intersects with the "Cambridge School" of linguistic contextualism, which seeks to understand the ideas of individual thinkers in relation to, but not necessarily in terms of, broader discursive formations. And because the schools of thought in which Kierkegaard, Heidegger, and Lacan participated are predominantly theoretical, and thus defined by the technical discourse and curricula vitae of intellectual elites, the following chapters further resonate with scholarship on the history and rhetoric of philosophy in general, and the history and philosophy of communication in particular—but with an important twist.

The central concept of this book has always been a marginal concept in the history and philosophy of communication. Even in the works of Kierkegaard, Heidegger, and Lacan, everyday talk rarely receives direct attention, much less sustained conceptual development, often appearing only in the periphery of other key terms in their well-known social theories. Part of the challenge of this book, then, is to excavate a series of passing references to a marginal concept in the history and philosophy of communication—and to do so in a way that not only illuminates their secret systematicity but also, more importantly, integrates this hidden structure into a conceptual narrative with evident bearing on our present. Excavation, illumination, integration—all suggest that the methodological challenge of this book is as much to find as it is to fathom the conceptual history of everyday talk.

Thankfully, chatter, idle talk, and empty speech are not the only conceptual clues available to us. In addition to theorizing various forms of everyday talk, Kierkegaard, Heidegger, and Lacan had much to say about attendant modes of everyday thought. Hence, *The Chattering Mind*. With this title, I mean to highlight the connection between everyday talk and everyday thought in their philosophies of communication. In Kierkegaard's existentialist critique of chatter, Heidegger's phenomenological account of idle talk, and Lacan's psychoanalytic treatment of empty speech, we see a recurring emphasis on the habits of mind that condition and ensue from everyday talk. Too numerous to list here, these habits of mind range across the characterological spectrum, but frequently verge on disorienting psychological states like distraction and preoccupation, delusion and deceit, projection and abstraction. All of these disorientations (and several more) are discussed in the following chapters.

More noteworthy at this point, in the context of this brief methodological statement, are the populations in which these habits of mind tend to proliferate. As Kierkegaard, Heidegger, and Lacan well note, ordinary speaking subjects are particularly vulnerable to garrulous lines of thought. But they are not alone. Educated elites are also prone to chattering minds. And because the chattering minds of educated elites are often shrouded in technical jargon and byzantine arguments, they are often more difficult to identify than those of ordinary speaking subjects. Kierkegaard, Heidegger, and Lacan were especially skilled at detecting these learned concealments and disclosing their persuasive artistry. So skilled, in fact, that the conceptual history to be traced in this book is not limited to their own elite theoretical reflections on the practice of everyday talk. On the contrary, it also includes a subtle yet sustained critique of the elitist belief that theoretical reflection is somehow impervious to everyday talk.

―――――

I have divided this book into three parts, each comprised of three chapters. Part 1 focuses on Kierkegaard's development of "chatter" (*snak*), paying special attention to the concept's literary and philosophical origins, its early entanglement with the social arithmetic of modern democratic culture, and its corresponding annex of mid-nineteenth-century religious discourse. Part 2 explores Heidegger's work on "idle talk" (*Gerede*) and a host of related terms, notably "babble" (*Geschwätz*), "scribbling" (*Geschreibe*), and "everyday discourse" (*alltägliche Rede*). It shows how his development of these terms in the early 1920s not only served as a biting social critique of the modern university system in which he was struggling to secure a professorship, but also, more importantly, provided the conceptual basis for an early Heideggerian spectrum of discourse that would eventually culminate in the existential analytic of *Being and Time*. Part 3 considers Lacan's elusive notion of "empty speech" (*parole vide*) alongside its linguistic counterpossibility, "full speech" (*parole pleine*), reading both terms against the backdrop of his momentous 1955 return to what is arguably the founding moment of psychoanalysis: Freud's iconic 1895 dream of Irma's injection. By way of conclusion, the final pages of this book return to the individuating potential of chatter, idle talk, and empty speech, suggesting that all of these communicative practices are, at root, techniques of self-cultivation. Thanks to the network revolution of late-modernity, which has increasingly transformed small talk into big data, I conclude that we are uniquely poised to embrace, advance, and even radicalize these techniques.

PART ONE

Chatter

ONE

Barbers and Philosophers

Public Debuts

It is hard to say when Kierkegaard's authorship began. He often dated his emergence as an author to the 1843 publication of *Either/Or*, leaving commentators to ponder the import of two earlier works: a literary review, *From the Papers of One Still Living* (1838), and his master's thesis, *The Concept of Irony* (1841). By way of an introduction to his myriad reflections on chatter (*snak*), I would like to suggest that Kierkegaard's authorship began years prior to any of these works, in the midst of an 1836 newspaper polemic on freedom of the press in Denmark's fledgling democracy. It was here, in the conservative political pages of *Copenhagen's Flying Post*, that Kierkegaard made his debut as an author. And it was here, at the start of his blisteringly productive career, that he began to explore the role of "chatter" in the modern world.

In the early months of 1836, Denmark's first liberal newspaper, *The Copenhagen Post*, published a series of articles on freedom of the press. Among them was an anonymous defense of the free press written by one of the country's leading liberal reformers, Orla Lehmann. Freedom of the press is essential to freedom of the people, he argued, and among the basic freedoms enjoyed by the press is the freedom to make stylistic errors, especially when these errors occur in service to breaking news. Much to Lehmann's frustration, Danish readers disagreed. Their demand for timely news coverage was matched only by their distaste for hastily chosen words and expressions. "If anything of common interest occurs without being mentioned by journalism—then that is wrong," Lehmann groaned. "If it is certainly mentioned but not exactly in the way in which each had thought it should be mentioned, then that is wrong, too." The best way forward, he surmised, is for journalists to prioritize up-to-the-minute news coverage over stylistic quibbling about "every single little word." In short, "What [Johannes] Hage recommends: [do] not bother too apprehensively about the tiresome *qu'en dira-t-on* [what will people say about it], but trustfully follow the path dictated by honor and conscience."[1]

Kierkegaard's reply to Lehmann, published under the pseudonym "B," appeared a few days later. It was everything the liberal reformer loathed: witty, precious, comically wrought, and scrupulous in its mockery of specific words and phrases. Before Lehmann could respond to B, however, another pioneering figure in Denmark's liberal movement rushed to the former's aid—the same outspoken political author mentioned in his article's conclusion: Johannes Hage. Like Lehmann, Hage had little patience for wordy critiques of the free press, and B's attack on Lehmann was a case in point: heavy on "mockery and witticisms" but light on "discussions about reality"—so much so, Hage complained, that the basis for B's critique remains completely obscure. Is it that Lehmann writes about "the press in general," instead of limiting his remarks to *The Copenhagen Post*? Or that, "against unjust critics, [he] recommends what we once said—not anxiously to pay attention to gossip [*Folkesnak*]?" Or could it be something else entirely? Perhaps, Hage speculates, B's critique is driven by a "petty, egotistical motivation . . . to glorify one's own little self" (*EPW*, 142–44).

Kierkegaard welcomed the opportunity to clarify his position. A week later, again under the pseudonym B, he explained that the problem with Lehmann article is also the problem with *The Copenhagen Post*: both display "a certain gadding about in ideas, a certain, if I may say so, intellectual vagrancy." If the clumsy prose of these liberal elites was now under attack, it was precisely for this reason, for "the unclearly expressed is also the unclearly thought" (*EPW*, 15). Thankfully, Kierkegaard goes on to tease, there is an utterly unambiguous word for confusion of this sort: "nonsense [*Sniksnak*]" (*EPW*, 17). And it is akin, not opposed, to the "gossip [*Folkesnak*]" bemoaned by Lehmann and Hage. To illustrate this kinship between the nonsensical form and gossipy function of their work, Kierkegaard then unleashes an ironic series of references, quoting Hage paraphrasing Lehmann paraphrasing Hage's advice that fellow journalists ignore "gossip [*Folkesnak*]" (*EPW*, 15). Lehmann and Hage are not just clumsy writers and vagrant thinkers trafficking in nonsense (*Sniksnak*), Kierkegaard suggests. They are also fundamentally confused about the nature of their work, which more closely resembles gossip (*Folkesnak*) than journalism, especially when it claims otherwise—and all the more so when it does so with pompous French expressions like "*qu'en dira-t-on.*"

When Lehmann finally managed to post a reply, it was only to admit that, like Hage, he was still struggling to grasp the substance of B's critique. "I have tried to the best of my understanding to find out what Mr. B's opposition to the attacked article actually consists of in *reality*, but I am, of course, far from being sure that I have seen the point," he confessed. "On the whole the attack seems chiefly to be only the vehicle for a number of more or less suitable jokes," and thus little more than "a stylistic exercise in the humoristic manner." More than a clever example of "journalistic literature," B's critique was a trifling break with the genre: "The author's intention is not to give information about anything but only to amuse" (*EPW*, 158).

Kierkegaard was hardly surprised by Lehmann reply, especially given Hage's earlier confusion. And he was eager to say as much in his final counterattack:

It has not surprised me at all that both Mr. Hage and Mr. Lehmann have assumed that my articles were merely to amuse, for the form certainly clashes with the solemn, funereal style one generally finds in *The Copenhagen Post*. This [paper] can therefore say with Gert Westphaler, "I do not believe that any person, not even my enemies, will say that I at any time have engaged in chatter [*Snak*] . . . I carry on purely political and foreign discourse not to be found in many books and worth its weight in pure gold."—And regarding its dispute with me, this paper can add, "Is it not incomprehensible that such a scoundrel as Jørgen Glovemaker dares to despise my speech [*Tale*] and turn up his nose at it." (*EPW*, 34; trans. modified)

With this final rhetorical flourish, Kierkegaard underscored his central argument against Lehmann and Hage: Only by dismissing B's critique as a pretentious exercise in idle amusement can these writers maintain the basic pretense of their own work, namely, the delusion that their "journalistic literature" is somehow more serious and significant.

In so doing, however, Kierkegaard also accomplished something else—something crucial to the conceptual history of everyday talk. By ending on the topic of Gert Westphaler's dispute with Jørgen Glovemaker, he referred Danish readers to the modern literary origin of *snak*—a point of origin to which Kierkegaard would return, again and again, in later critiques of this ordinary communicative practice. Like Gert Westphaler, the talkative barber in Ludvig Holberg's popular 1722 comedy, Lehmann and Hage sorely underestimated their opponent's discourse and grossly overvalued their own. If they were nettled by Kierkegaard, much as Gert Westphaler was nettled by the silence of Jørgen Glovemaker, it was not because he turned up his nose at their work, heedless of its journalistic excellence, but because he continued to look down his nose at it, accurately perceiving their work for what it was: chatter (*snak*).

With this allusive mashup of literary past and political present, Kierkegaard introduced readers to the communicative practice that would concern him for years to come—a way of speaking whose subsequent theorization, as we shall see in this chapter, frequently occurred with reference to Holberg's talkative barber. With Gert Westphaler as his guide, Kierkegaard ranged across the history of Greek, German, English, and Danish literature and philosophy, recovering analogous modes of speaking, thinking, and being with others in the works of Aristophanes, Plato, Aristotle, Plutarch, Shakespeare, Schopenhauer, Hegel, the Brothers Grimm, and a host of lesser-known but particularly nettlesome Danish contemporaries—all of whom, and with just as rangy an approach, receive attention in this chapter. Many of the themes in his 1836 newspaper polemic also recurred along the way, allowing him to further characterize chatter as nonsense, gossip, cliché, confusion, delusion, bombast, self-indulgence, and the like. But many more characterizations sprang up in turn, allowing Kierkegaard to associate chatter with noise, wind, sewage, babble, birdsong, wordplay, witticism, gimcrack, compulsion, automation, mechanicity, repetition, distraction, deception, abstraction, antiphony, derangement, logorrhea—indeed, the list goes on, further expanding the range of this chapter.

It was also here, at the bitter end of this public debate with two of Denmark's most outspoken reformers, that Kierkegaard finally introduced himself to Danish readers. Beneath his reference to Holberg's well-known play, where readers expected to find another "B," he printed his name instead: "S. Kierkegaard." It was the first signed text in one of the nineteenth century's most prolific intellectual careers. Years before publishing any of the anti-philosophical tomes that would eventually bring him fame, Kierkegaard's work as an author was underway—and with it his work on chatter.

Runaway Jaw

Ludvig Holberg was best known for the one-act comedies he wrote in the early 1720s, all of which, much to the delight of Danish audiences, were written and performed in the national tongue. Among these comedies was *Master Gert Westphaler; or, The Talkative Barber*—the same popular comedy that Kierkegaard cleverly cited at the end of his 1836 newspaper polemic. As we shall see, this was more than a passing reference to one of Denmark's most well-known literary works. Over the next decade, Holberg's talkative barber would become a familiar touchstone in Kierkegaard's emerging theory of *snak* and, in many ways, a key figure—second only to Socrates—in his outspoken critique of speculative idealist thought. Tracing these connections through Kierkegaard's work and drawing out their hidden conceptual structures are the primary tasks of this chapter.

That the passage Kierkegaard quotes in his final critique of Lehmann and Hage shows Gert Westphaler refusing to classify his discourse as *snak*—a move which recurs in other Holberg comedies, as we shall see in chapter 3—would have brought a smile to the lips of many Danish readers. For if there was one thing they knew about Master Gert, it was his proclivity for *snak*. Variations on this term appear on every page of Holberg's play, and almost always in reference to Gert's rambling discourse. Of central concern to everyone in the play, including Gert, is his inability to hold a conversation with anyone at all, including himself, without diverting from the topic at hand, distracting all involved with tedious, long-winded, and hilariously tangential monologues—and always on the same few subjects, as Holberg demonstrates in the play's opening scene:

PERNILLE [the maid]. Everybody has a weak point, and Master Gert's weakness is to bore good people to death with useless chatter [*Snak*].

HENRICH [a visiting servant]. What can he chatter about so much [*snakke saa meget om*]? Does he know a lot?

PERNILLE. He has three or four subjects to chatter about [*at snakke om*]. The first is an old bishop in Jutland, called Arius, who was persecuted because of a book he had published. The second is the counts palatine in Germany, the third is the Turk, and the fourth a trip he made from Harslev to Kiel. So that whatever you begin to talk about with him [*at tale med ham om*], in a jiffy he's up to his ears in the middle of Turkey or Germany.

HENRICH. That's a strange weakness.

19

PERNILLE. Suppose somebody says "It's nice weather today," he will answer: "I had this kind of weather once when I left Harslev." And then he'll jabber away about the whole journey till he's hoarse, so that if you dragged him from the house by the hair he wouldn't stop holding forth about his trip till he had got to Kiel. That's how he falls into chatter [Snak] every time . . .[2]

Most of the key themes in Holberg's comedy, especially those on which Kierkegaard would later dwell, are readily apparent in this opening dialogue. As Pernille claims and Henrich confirms, Gert's talent for chatter is a weakness of sorts. Later in the play, Gert attempts to explain: "We who have been abroad often have a kind of disease or obsession [Syge eller Orm], or whatever you like to call it, and we must tell everyone what we've heard and seen in foreign countries, so as to show we haven't always stayed home" (MGW, 36). More than a communicative disorder, Gert suffers from a "chatter disease [Snakke-Syge]" (MGW, 25; trans. modified). The clinical structure of this curious disease is an uncontrollable and strangely obsessive urge to transmit information to others. Uncontrollable because it typically overwhelms Gert's own intentions: "I often get chatting like that against my will [saadan Snak mod min Villie]" (MGW, 41; trans. modified). And obsessive because, once the urge to inform has overpowered his will to converse, Gert is unable to stop talking until each and every detail has been aired: "When I begin a speech I must finish it. That's my nature. Nothing annoys me more than when someone hears the beginning of my speech and won't stay till the end" (MGW, 30–31). So compulsive is Gert's urge to chatter that, as Pernille later quips, "I believe if you sewed up his mouth, he'd learn to talk through his nose" (MGW, 25).

Kierkegaard was fascinated by this characterization. Consider, for instance, his July 1848 exchange of letters with a friend:

I am sure you will easily remember that excellent passage in Holberg in which Pernille says of Gert W. that if one sewed his mouth shut, he would teach himself to speak with his nostrils. How splendid! It is so descriptive, so graphic, for when a person closes his mouth and tries to speak anyway, then his cheeks become inflated, and one cannot help but get the impression that words will have to escape through his nostrils. Furthermore, there is infinite vis comica [comic strength] in this "to teach himself how to" with his nostrils. . . . And suppose he succeeded, succeeded beyond all expectation, and instead of speaking with only one mouth could now speak with two—since he has, after all, two nostrils. What joy! Not even the inventor of that machine with which one writes and makes copies at the same time, in other words, with which one may write in duplo, could be as happy as G. W.

would be—although it would be horrible for the neighborhood if this infinitely garrulous [*snaksome*] person were now to have, as we speak of a double-barreled rifle, a double-barreled mouth with which to speak.

To which his friend replies:

Your commentary on the two nostrils is excellent, and I only regret that I received it a week too late, for it was just a week ago that I read part of Gert W. aloud one evening here, and I might then have plowed with your heifer and quite frightened the audience with the terrible prospect that Monsieur Gert might get a double mouth, so that he could commence with the second when the first grew tired. Consider also what an advantage it would be for those "Harslevian *Nobles venetiens*" or those crazy fellows in Frankfurt, if every jaw were hitched to such a team; it would be a run-away jaw, some kind of live espringal.[3]

As Kierkegaard and his correspondent both suggest, there is something mechanical about Gert's chatter. In particular, there is something automated about its commencement and almost robotic about its progression, such that, were someone to sew his mouth shut, this would only serve to displace its operation and double its output. Which is why Kierkegaard compares Gert's nose-turned-mouth to a pantograph—an early-modern drafting instrument that, through a series of parallel mechanical linkages, allows the movements of one pen to produce identical movements in another, effectively duplicating whatever is being drawn, traced, or written. It is also why the added comparison of Gert's nose-mouth to a double-barreled rifle was intriguing to Kierkegaard's friend, who carried this analogy even further, likening Gert's nose-turned-mouth to an espringal—a two-armed, torsion-powered artillery device, reminiscent of a Greco-Roman ballista, designed to hurl stones, bolts, and other missiles at one's opponents.

Together, these comparisons suggest that Master Gert's nose-turned-mouth is a *repeating machine,* graphically setting the stage for subsequent treatments of the communicative practice on which he relies—and not just by Kierkegaard. As we shall see, Heidegger had much to say about the repetitive functions of "idle talk," and Lacan paid equally careful attention to the mechanical aspects of "empty speech." Kierkegaard and his friend could not have anticipated these conceptual extensions, which makes their correspondence all the more interesting. The former's image of a double-barreled rifle, especially when coupled with his earlier mention of the pantograph, implies that sewing Gert's mouth shut would allow him to say numerous things at the same time, resulting in *simultaneous* repetitions of chatter. And the latter's image of the espringal, which could launch identical missiles back-to-back, implies that doing so would also allow Gert to say the same thing numerous times, resulting in *sequential* repetitions of chatter. In both instances, the gist of Pernille's comment remains: Any attempt to negate Gert's chatter would only serve to redouble it. Even and especially when he is prevented from speaking, Gert remains "a run-away jaw."

Master Gert vs. Mister Mouth

As Holberg's play progresses, Gert's run-away jaw becomes increasingly problematic, largely on account of repeated failures to woo his fiancée. Every opportunity for courtship becomes an occasion for Gert to chatter instead, and every outpouring of chatter further jeopardizes his prospect of marriage. Realizing this, Gert eventually decides to change his chattering ways—or at least to hold them at bay for a time:

(Master Gert alone)

MASTER GERT. Now, Master Gert, the question is whether you can stand the test or be a rascal for the rest of your life. I'm sure I can easily stop chatting [*snakke*] about learned matters for one hour. *(Puts his fist against his mouth.)* Hark'ee, Mister Mouth, you'll be terribly unlucky if you talk about anything but love this evening, and briefly about that. But when I think about it, it's dreadful that a person should be disliked just because he speaks learnedly. Still I must put up with this; all my happiness depends on it. But I hope to hold my own, unless someone drives me to chatter [*Snak*]. I can't deny that when somebody asks me about things that I know well, I get the greatest pleasure in the world to explain them. But I must train myself so as to resist that temptation. (*MGW*, 46; trans. modified)

As a test of his newfound resolve, Gert asks the local notary to play the part of his fiancée: "Pretend to be the young lady and ask me about some strange thing or other, to see if I can control myself. It's so hard for me to hide my talent, especially when someone gives me a reason for talking [*at tale*]." The notary begins by asking Gert about current events, then quickly pivots to the barber's trip from Harslev to Kiel—a topic which, as we shall see, caught Kierkegaard's attention as well:

NOTARY. Haven't you read the papers?
GERT. I'faith I have.

NOTARY. Is there anything new in them?

GERT. No, except—No, that's true; I haven't read the papers since I went abroad.

NOTARY. Have you been abroad, Master Gert?

GERT. I once went from Harslev to Kiel, and I'll never forget that trip. There was a hatter with us—*(Striking his mouth.)* Will you be quiet, you brute?

NOTARY. What were you going to say about the hatter?

GERT. Nothing except that he was a scoundrel, not worth talking about.

NOTARY. You're doing very well. (*MGW*, 47)

Emboldened by this rehearsal, Gert then asks the notary to fetch his fiancée. After the notary departs, however, Gert continues to struggle with his oral opponent, "*muttering to himself and hitting his mouth.*" This ongoing conflict between Master Gert and Mister Mouth comes to a head in the play's final scene, when Gert, in a desperate effort to court his fiancée, attempts but ultimately fails to resist the prodding inquiries of her maid and uncle:

GOTTARD. So, you've been abroad, Master Gert?

GERT. Oh, nothing very special.

PERNILLE. Well, I seem to have heard you went to Kiel once.

GERT. That's quite right. A few years ago I went from Harslev to Kiel, and I'll never forget that trip. We had with us—*(He stops and puts his handkerchief into his mouth.)*

GOTTARD. Who was with you?

GERT. *(with his handkerchief in his mouth).* No one.

GOTTARD. Hark'ee, sir, if you only talk [*taler*] about your journeys and tell stories, I can't see how anyone can blame you for that.

PERNILLE. I'faith, nor do I.

GOTTARD. And I'll scold my brother for being offended about it.

GERT. Thank you very much. But, excuse me, I have an errand with the young lady.

GOTTARD. For my part, Pernille, I must say there are certain things in the papers that I'd pay to have explained. I've often read about the Tories and the Whigs in England, but I don't know why no one in all the town can give me any information about them.

MASTER GERT *(who during this speech has been making love to Leonora* [his fiancée], *pricks up his ears and says):* I could tell you about them if I had time.

GOTTARD. I'm very doubtful about that, Monsieur, as no on in this town understands its properly.

GERT. Bad cess to you if I haven't it at my fingertips.

GOTTARD. Oh, I have a rough Idea about it. I know the Tories are the people who cut off King James's head.

GERT. You're all wrong, Monsieur. It's quite different. But I'll explain it to you later. First I've got to—

GOTTARD. Ha, ha! I can see you don't understand it. The Tories are those who killed the king. I know that, of course, but I wish I knew something about the others.

GERT. No, that's not right, Monsieur. There are four main parties in England: Tories, Whigs, Mennonites, and Anabaptists—. (*MGW*, 49)

And with that, the talkative barber embarks on a lengthy monologue about English political history, not realizing that Mister Mouth has once more prevailed until well after his fiancée has left the room: "Gracious heavens! Here I am chatting away [*snakker*] again. Where is the young lady?" (*MGW*, 50; trans. modified).

Notice how Gert's struggle unfolds in the foregoing passages. Initially, he attempts to reason with his mouth, merely threatening it with his fist. Then, in his exchange with the notary and immediately thereafter, Gert begins to insult his mouth and to act on his earlier threat, repeatedly striking it with his fist. And by the end of the play, in response to Gottard and Pernille, Gert has stuffed his handkerchief into his mouth, effectively jamming the oral machinery on which his chatter depends—much as one might jam the mechanical linkages of a pantograph, the cocked hammers of a double-barreled rifle, or the torsion-stretched arms of an espringal. Although Kierkegaard does not dwell on this aspect of Holberg's play, the relationship between automated speech and its ability to jam would remain a key theme in the conceptual history inaugurated by his work, finding decisive expression, as part 3 of this book demonstrates, in Lacan's treatment of "empty speech."

Also worth noting in the foregoing passages is the intense enjoyment Gert derives from chatter. He openly acknowledges this at the start of his struggle with Mister Mouth: "I can't deny that when somebody asks me about things that I know well, I get the greatest pleasure in the world to explain them." And he further specifies the extent of this pleasure in the play's final scene, breaking off an intimate sexual encounter with his fiancée in order to inform her maid and uncle about the history of English politics. This may be why, in the standard English translation of Holberg's comedy, Gert's fiancée and her maid do not depict his *Snakke-Syge* as a "chatter disease" from which he suffers but, instead, as a "love of talking" that precludes him from "making love [*at tale om Kiærlighed*]" (*MGW*, 25). As Pernille later warns Leonora's father, "Your daughter, instead of going to the bridal bed, will get a lecture from him at night" (*MGW*, 40).

Much of what Gert enjoys about chatter is the quality of information it allows him to convey. Hence, the excerpt Kierkegaard quoted to Lehmann and Hage at the end of their newspaper polemic: Gert is convinced that the contents of his discourse are "worth their weight in gold." If Holberg's talkative barber is not yet wealthy as a result of his talking, it is largely due to personal misfortune: "I'm unlucky in this town. If I lived in another place, I could earn money by talking" (*MGW*, 30). Part of the problem, Gert suspects, is that people in his hometown are ignorant of the learnedness with which he speaks. Although "there are some good folk who appreciate it," most are just "fools who know nothing" (*MGW*, 36, 37). Some are so ignorant that they more closely resemble animals than humans, Gert continues, likening his interlocutors to "swine" endowed with "donkey ears" who "don't think any more than a horse or a sheep" (*MGW*, 30, 37).

Everyone else in town is just jealous of his learned eloquence. "They see when I'm together with people I'm the only one who talks. The others would like to speak too but they can't, and so they don't care to hear me talk," Gert reminds himself in another smug reflection. Why else does Jørgen Glovemaker—the "scoundrel" with whom Kierkegaard identifies in his authorial debut—envy Gert more than anyone else? "Of all the people in this town, he's the one who would most like to get a word in, but he can't talk about politics when I'm there because he knows I'll be ready to argue with him at once, as I understand politics better than he does" (*MGW*, 37). Suffice it to say, the pleasure Gert derives from chatter is matched only by the pride he takes in this way of speaking.

Instead of ignorance and jealously, Gert believes his chatter should be met with admiration. "You are hated just because you do something they ought to love and respect you for," he assures himself after his fiancée suggests that her cat is a more fitting audience for his chatter, "for she understands it as well as I do" (*MGW*, 33). Enough love and respect to warrant compensation, Gert adds, returning to a familiar theme: "They blame me here in town for talking too much, but I don't talk nonsense [*Slidder Sladder*]. All I talk about is politics and the news. They ought to pay me for that." Instead, his ignorant and envious neighbors "only want to eat and drink and play checkers or cards" (*MGW*, 41). All of which leads Gert to conclude that it is his audience, not his chatter, which lacks value: "I won't open my mouth again; the people here are not worth it" (*MGW*, 33).

Many in town would have welcomed Gert's silence. But none were so fortunate. Throughout Holberg's play, the garrulous barber's pride and joy is shown to result in the townsfolk's pain and suffering. What Gert calls learnedness, they chide as idiocy. What he deems pertinent, they find pointless. And what he holds to be invaluable, they deride as insignificant. Interestingly, no one is more outspoken on these topics than Gert's mother:

One day after another goes by with your confounded chatter [*Snak*] that's not worth two-pence. D'you think anyone wants to know what you did on your trip to Kiel, how many taverns you went into on the way, how many girls' knees you felt in each tavern, and how many pipes of tobacco you smoked? You know there's a lot of people in town who have gone much farther in the world: Anders Christensen has been three or four times to Bordels and Ruin in France, and away off to Trebizond or Cattesund, but he doesn't talk nearly as much about his trips.

To which Gert replies, in typical fashion:

I'faith I don't just tell trifles about my trip to Kiel, how many quarts of ale I drank, and how many pipes of tobacco I smoked, but a lot of things that are worth listening to. You can see if they are trifles, Mother, if you'll let me go over the whole journey quickly—

"Oh, go to Jericho with your chatter [*Snak*]!" his mother interjects, abruptly ending the scene (*MGW*, 28).

All of the townspeople's complaints are on display in this tense interaction. Foremost among them is their complaint about the excessive quantity of Gert's chatter. He and his neighbors might disagree on the qualitative worth of his discourse, but no one, not even Gert, denies that its quantity is undue. "I admit, dear lady, that at times I chatter [*snakker*] too much," Gert confesses to his fiancée, echoing his mother's earlier reproach. And he finds himself muttering the same to himself a moment later, after his fiancée, angered by another bout of loquacity, leaves the room: "I admit I chattered [*Snak*] a little too much to the young lady" (*MGW*, 36–38; trans. modified).

These two aspects of Gert's chatter—its disputed worth and undeniable excess—conspire against him throughout the play. His unwavering confidence in the quality of his discourse, especially when contrasted with the repeated frustrations of his interlocutors and the failed marriage arrangement in which these frustrations culminate, more closely resembles a tragic mix of hubris and self-ignorance than a comic display of routine foolishness. His chatter may derive from an obsessive urge to inform, but it is driven by a narcissistic delusion of grandeur. And the excessive quantity of his talk only makes matters worse, suggesting that the overwhelming pleasure Gert derives from discussing matters "till the end" is, in fact, a perverse commitment to hermetically sealed and horribly repetitive anecdotes, all of which divert from more pressing issues and, in so doing, defer any attempt to address them. All of which suggests that, when Mister Mouth prevails over Master Gert, delusion and distraction are sure to follow. Let us consider both states of mind, for they are central to Kierkegaard's understanding of chatter.

Traveler's Logorrhea

In the wake of his 1836 newspaper polemic, while sifting through "Literature on the Wandering Jew," Kierkegaard took note of "the adventurer's peculiar loquacity [*Snaksomhed*]." Talkativeness of this sort, he argues, is proof that "the person in question has not understood what he himself relates" and is thus akin to "*alazonia*"—a misnomer for the Greek *alazoneia*, meaning quackery, imposture, and, above all, false pretension.[4] From Aristophanes to Shakespeare, the *alazon* was often depicted as a wandering vagrant crossed with a swaggering windbag— someone who confidently yet cluelessly purports to be more than they are and, as a result, is routinely compelled to abandon dubious listeners in search of more naive audiences. Like Gert Westphaler, the *alazon* is at once pompous, incompetent, and ignorant of both character flaws. And like the Wandering Jew, who "could talk for a week without being any the worse for it," they are both proficient chatterers (quoted in *JNB* 1, 403).

Kierkegaard does not explore these connections, but the resonance he notes between excessive pride and excessive talk, as we shall see, receives ample scholarly attention in Martin Heidegger's early discussions of *Gerede*. Of more pressing concern to Kierkegaard, especially as his work on chatter develops, is the deluded sense of adventure to which loudmouths like Gert Westphaler cling. At best, Gert's excessive chatter about his trip to Kiel is a testament to his self-ignorant talent for distraction. "Who does not know of that talkative barber, the tale of whose journey was in inverse relation to his journey, which was very short: from Haderslev to Kiel. As soon as one mentions Gert W., one thinks immediately of that journey," Kierkegaard writes in the marginalia of *Prefaces*. "But this is precisely the great thing in Holberg's conception of G., that he has allowed him, like many a genius, to mis-

understand himself and to lay most weight on the trivial and accidental above the essential."[5] At worst, however, Gert's excessive talk about
his insignificant trip is symptomatic of a serious mental disorder: "It
is unquestionably derangement when that garrulous [*snaksomme*] man
talks continually about himself and his little journey," Kierkegaard
goes on to argue in *Christian Discourses*.[6]

Along the way, Gert's long-winded chatter about his short inland
journey helped Kierkegaard distinguish his own humble commitment
to existential inwardness from the boastful conduct of systematic
thinkers, especially those with speculative idealist pretensions. From
the standpoint of speculative thought, the inwardly reflective individual appears to be "a laggard who has seen nothing of the world and
who has undertaken only an inland journey within his own consciousness and consequently gets nowhere, whereas every systematician is
experienced in an altogether different way and has been 'to the back
of the beyond in both Trapezunt and in R—'" (*P*, 44). Nothing could be
further from the truth. As the "existence-tasks" of inwardness teach all
who undertake them, "change in the external is only the diversion that
world-weariness and life-emptiness clutches at."[7] Whether it compares
to a short inland journey by the town's barber or a trip to Trapezunt
and beyond by the town's most traveled resident, the result of systematic speculation is the same. From the vantage point of inwardness, it
amounts to little more than distraction.

What speculative thinkers gain in intellectual range, they often
forfeit in the realm of lived experience. "One traipses through all the
sciences and spheres and yet does not live," much as charlatan poets,
"merely in order to entertain their readers, ramble around in Africa,
America, and, devil take them, in Trapezunt and R—," a reference to
the world travels of Anders Christensen, the townsman who, according to Gert's mother, has traveled twice as far but does not say half
as much as her son (*CUP* 1, 287). To such an extent that systematic
speculators not only stray from the path of wisdom but also lose sight
of reality itself:

Suppose that the speculator is not the prodigal son . . . but the naughty child who
refuses to stay where existing human beings belong, in the children's nursery and
the education room of existence where one becomes an adult only through inwardness in existing . . . Suppose that the speculative thinker is the restless resident who,
although it is obvious that he is a renter, yet in view of the abstract truth that, eternally and divinely perceived, all property is in common, wants to be the owner, so
that there is nothing to do except to send for a police officer, who would presum-

ably say, just as the subpoena servers say to Gert Westphaler: We are sorry to have to come on this errand. (*CUP* 1, 214)

In Gert's overweening pride and talent for distraction, Kierkegaard sees a remarkable parallel to the speculative thinker's woefully abstract sense of truth and restless approach to its acquisition. In particular, he sees the self-proclaimed learnedness of the former as a pointed admonition of the latter: "Gert could talk about anything, knew a great deal, and was so very perfectible that he perhaps could have managed to know everything," Kierkegaard gibes. Fluency, omniscience, and perfectibility—these are the delusions of grandeur that conspire against Gert and his speculative successors, inviting them to channel their excessive pride into even more excessive chatter, and often to the detriment of all involved, themselves especially. But there was "one thing he did not manage to know," Kierkegaard adds, again with an eye toward his speculative idealist peers—namely, "that he himself was a *Schwatzer* [*sic*]."[8] In order to understand this kinship between Holberg's talkative barber and Kierkegaard's learned peers—a kinship which, in turn, provides a unique point of access to Kierkegaard's renowned critique of the present age and, with it, his most thorough account of chatter—we must first determine how, exactly, each of these erudite figures qualifies as a *Schwätzer*. And in order to make this determination, oddly enough, we must return to the Greeks.

Communicable Disease

Kierkegaard rarely used German terms in place of *snak*. When he did, however, it was *Geschwätz*, meaning "babble," that appealed to him. This may be why Theodor Haecker, in his decisive 1914 edition of Kierkegaard's "Critique of the Present Age," translated *snak* as *Geschwätz*, encouraging generations of German intellectuals to misunderstand Kierkegaard's radical philosophical notion of chatter as a conservative social critique of babble. Kierkegaard did not pull *Geschwätz* from thin air, of course. He encountered it in a variety of German texts, ranging from philosophical works to religious sermons to children's stories. But his primary sources seem to have been German translations of a single Greek text: Plutarch's essay "Concerning Talkativeness." In place of *adoleschia*—the Greek word for "aimless speech" on which Plutarch and many of his predecessors relied—Kierkegaard's German translations read *Geschwätz*.

This may be why the young Heidegger, after studying Haecker's translation of Kierkegaard's "Critique of the Present Age," not only integrated *Geschwätz* into his emerging philosophy of communication but also, as we shall see in chapter 5, traced the meaning of this term to Greek discussions of *adoleschia*. That Lacan would eventually follow suit, likening the free associations of his patients to the *adoleschia* of ancient Greeks, makes this triangulation of *snak*, *Geschwätz*, and *adoleschia* in Kierkegaard's work an especially curious turning point in the conceptual history of everyday talk—and one we cannot ignore. In order to account for this triangulation of Greek, German, and Danish terms, we must follow Kierkegaard's lead, if only for a moment, returning to Greek discussions of *adoleschia*.

The ancient world was lousy with *adoleschia*, and Plutarch was not the first to notice. Aristophanes and Xenophon attributed this aimless way of speaking to philosophers like Socrates; Isocrates and Plato tried to pin it on the sophists; and Aristotle, Theophrastus, and Plutarch's contemporary, Dio Chrysostom, noted its occurrence throughout the citizenry.[9] Although it is beyond the scope of this chapter to address each of these nuanced accounts, it is important for us to explore those which directly influenced Kierkegaard's theory of chatter. Foremost among these influential texts was Plutarch's essay "On Talkativeness" and Aristophanes' well-known comedy *Clouds*.

Given his keen interest in the *Snakke-Syge* of Gert Westphaler, Kierkegaard must have been intrigued by Plutarch's characterization of *adoleschia* as a disease. "It is a troublesome and difficult task that philosophy has in hand when it undertakes to cure garrulousness [*adoleschian*]," his essay on talkativeness begins. "For the remedy, words of reason, requires listeners; but the garrulous [*adoleschoi*] listen to nobody, for they are always talking. And this is the first symptom of their ailment: looseness of the tongue becomes impotence of the ears."[10]

Barbers are especially vulnerable to this disease, Plutarch continues, "for the greatest chatterboxes [*adoleschotatoi*] stream in and sit in their chairs, so that they are themselves infected with the habit." To illustrate this occupational hazard, he recalls two talkative barbers, both of whom seem to have caught Kierkegaard's attention. The first is designed to amuse: "It was a witty answer, for instance, that King Archelaüs gave to a loquacious [*adoleschou*] barber, who, as he wrapped his towel around him asked, 'How shall I cut your hair, Sire?' 'In silence,' said Archelaüs" (T, 509A). The close connection between *snak* and *Geschwätz* is readily apparent in Kierkegaard's reading of this passage. In one journal entry, he aptly describes the theme of Plutarch's essay as *"Snaksomhed."* In the next, he quotes from the German translation of this particular anecdote, where "loquacious barber" appears as *"geschwätzigen Barbier."*[11]

More suggestive still is the second talkative barber described in Plutarch's essay:

It was a barber also who first announced the great disaster of the Athenians in Sicily, having learned it in the Peiraeus from a slave, one of those who had escaped from the island. Then the barber left his shop and hurried at full speed to the city,

> Lest another might win the glory
> of imparting the news to the city,
> and he come second.

A panic naturally arose and the people gathered in assembly and tried to come at the origin of the rumor. So the barber was brought forward and questioned; yet he did not even know the name of his informant, but referred the origin to a nameless and unknown person. The assembly was enraged and cried out, "Torture the cursed fellow! Put him on the rack! He has fabricated and concocted this tale! Who else heard it? Who believed it?" The wheel was brought and the man was stretched upon it. Meanwhile there arrived bearers of the disastrous news, men who had escaped from the slaughter itself. All, therefore, dispersed, each to his private mourning, leaving the wretched fellow bound on the wheel. But when he was set free late in the day when it was already nearly evening, he asked the executioner if they had also heard "how the general, Nicias, had died." Such an unconquerable and incorrigible evil does habit make garrulity [*adoleschian*]. (T, 509A–C)

Note the similarities between this garrulous barber and Gert Westphaler. Much as Master Gert suffers from a "chatter disease" characterized by an obsessive urge to inform and narcissistic delusions of grandeur, Plutarch's barber is unable to control, much less to curb, his glory-seeking impulse to report what he has heard—even after being tortured for it.

Also worth noting here are the connections Plutarch suggests between rumor-spreading, news-reporting, and talkative barbers. Kierkegaard makes a similar observation in his unfinished *Book on Adler*, to be discussed in chapter 3, almost certainly in reference to this ancient anecdote: "The person who does not have the opportunity of keeping up with the times by means of newspapers can very well be satisfied with the barber, who formerly, when people as yet did not have newspapers, was also what newspapers are now."[12] This is neither a compliment to barbers nor a celebration of newspapers. As Kierkegaard goes on to explain in his literary review of *Two Ages*, about which more in the following chapter, much of what passes for news in the modern era began as an offhand comment overheard by a "loquacious [*snaksom*] barber" (*TA*, 23). Again, it is difficult to ignore the parallels between the loquacious barber in Plutarch's anecdote, who incited panicked rumors about the great disaster of the Athenians, and the garrulous barber in Holberg's play, whose extensive claims against spreading rumors are, in fact, the primary subject of "town gossip" (*Folkes Snak*) (*MGW*, 35). Both fail to realize that the chatter disease from which they suffer is also, in effect, a communicable disease they spread to others.

Between the ancient barber and the modern journalist is the literary reviewer. "He rushes more swiftly through the streets than that barber who gave his life in order to be the first to bring the news of the victory at Marathon," Kierkegaard quips, inadvertently conflating Plutarch's anecdote with the legend of the runner from Marathon, who died after delivering news of victory to Athens. "His shout causes more sensation than when the one who first catches a glint out at sea shouts loudly throughout the whole fishing village: Herring!" (*P*, 15). In other words, Kierkegaard continues,

The book has come out. The reading public is gathered in the synagogue for mutual entertainment. "Have you read the book?" No, not yet, but I have heard that it is not great. "Have you read the book?" No, but I paged through it a little at Reitzel's book shop; if only I knew who the author is. "Have you read the book?" No, but I am eager to see it and already have promises in three places for the loan of it. There are variations on these and similar themes while the hubbub and noise increase, because empty barrels make the greatest sound and the synagogue, like the church bell, has—a tongue and an empty head. (*P*, 16)

Strewn throughout this cacophonous crowd are observant literary reviewers: "By their watchful gaze, their restless glances, their outstretched necks, their perked up ears, one easily identifies them." And the tasks of each are always the same: to listen carefully to "the public's gossip [*Bysnak*]" and, wherever possible, to amplify it in "chatter [*Snak*]" of their own. "When he has heard what he wants, he then rushes home and while the empty gossip [*den tomme Passiar*] is still rattling in his head, he writes a review," thereby occasioning more empty gossip and, in turn, more tawdry reviews. In this sense, the literary reviewer is not "a police inspector in the service of good taste" but, instead, "the acting water inspector who takes care that the wastewater flows freely and without obstruction. Everything is thereby completed in itself; the water comes from the public and flows back into the public." And so the cycle continues: "If only the chatter [*Snakken*] can be set in motion, then all is well" (*P*, 16–19; trans. modified; cf. *BOA*, 264).

How are we to understand this shift in imagery from reverberant containers of various sorts—empty heads, noisy barrels, church bells, bustling synagogues—to circular flows of wastewater? Again, Kierkegaard seems to have Plutarch in mind. If the first two symptoms of *adoleschia* are "looseness of the tongue" and "impotence of the ears," the pseudo-medical terms that Plutarch invents to describe these symptoms—*asigesia* and *anekoia*—point readers in a gastrological direction, encouraging them to understand the inability to remain silent as "diarrhea of the tongue" and the inability to listen as "constipation of the ears" (T, 512C, note a). A few sentences later, Plutarch confirms this crude account, effectively setting the stage for Kierkegaard's critique of literary reviewers: "While others retain what is said, in talkative persons [*adoleschon*] it goes right through in a flux [*diarreousin*]; they go about like empty vessels, void of sense, but full of noise" (T, 502D–E).

But there is more at stake in Plutarch's pseudo-medical discourse than a vulgar adaption of the ancient proverb about empty vessels making the loudest noise. Although *asigesia* and *anekoia* were coined by Plutarch and remain difficult to translate, *diarreousin* descends from the Greek verb *diarrhein*, which carries several clear meanings. When applied to vessels like barrels, *diarrhein* means "to flow through." When used in connection to news reports, it means "to spread about." And when considered epidemiologically, it refers to "the wasting away of a diseased body." Together, these definitions suggest that, as the *snak* of barbers, reviewers, and other *adoleschon* flows through the *Bysnak* of their neighbors, readerships, and other audiences—and vice versa—the communicable disease from which they all suffer gradually spreads throughout the populace, and always to its detriment. To engage in chatter is, for Plutarch and Kierkegaard alike, to emit a collective *rheuma*—the sickening communicative discharge of an already suffering civic body.

Wagging Tongues

If the mouth is the opening from which chatter pours, the mind is the cavity left vacant as a result. Plutarch clearly suggests as much in his pathologization of *adoleschia*, but it was Aristophanes' ridicule of Socratic dialogue that inspired Kierkegaard to develop this aspect of *snak*. In *Clouds*, Aristophanes portrays Socrates as an arch-sophist and chief pedagogue in an educational cult known as the "Thinkery," where students in search of fame and fortune pay to learn the arts of subtle reasoning and persuasive speaking, or, as Aristophanes chides, "hair-splitting" and "tongue twisting."[13] Among these students is Strepsiades, whom Socrates convinces to forsake all gods save those of the Thinkery: namely, "the Void, the Clouds, and the Tongue" (*C*, 424–25; trans. modified). Only later, in the play's final scene, does Strepsiades realize the error of his ways: "Forgive me for taking leave of my senses because of their babbling [*adoleschia*]," he begs Hermes, ultimately deciding, on Hermes' advice, to "burn down the house of the babblers [*adoleschon*]" (*C*, 1476–1492; trans. modified).

Aristophanes' hilarious depiction of Socrates as a babbling, cosmos-crazed sophist had a lasting impact on the philosopher's reputation in Athens, which is partly why Plato struggled to separate Socratic dialogue from aimless *adoleschia* and its sophistic counterpart. Although Socrates playfully acknowledges his weakness for "true babble [*alethos adoleschian*]" in *Theaetetus* (195c), he prefers to avoid this way of speaking all together: "I do not believe anyone who heard us now, even if he were a comic poet, would say that I am babbling [*adolescho*] and talking about things which do not concern me," he declares in *Phaedo* (70b–c; trans. modified). Nor could anyone justifiably reduce his talk to that of a "babbling sophist [*adoleschen sophisten*]," Plato adds in *Statesman* (299b; trans. modified; cf. *Republic* 488e).

Kierkegaard was eager to bolster Plato's defense of Socrates in his 1841 dissertation, *The Concept of Irony*. He even went so far as to quote the same passage from *Phaedo*—albeit with *snak* in place of *adolescho*.[14] But he was also more willing than his Greek predecessor to attribute *adoleschia*—and, by extension, *snak*—to the sophists. Privileging the *adoleschen sophisten* of the *Statesman* over Plato's tandem effort to separate *adoleschikou* from *sophisten* in the *Sophist* (225d–e), Kierkegaard insists that the sophists were famous for their self-indulgent "loquacity [*Snaksomhed*]"—a busily pretentious and consistently hyperbolic way of speaking whose "empty noise and unsatiating gorging" was "a matter of seeing something from the front, from behind, of chattering [*snakke*] up one side and down the other" (*CI*, 210, 18, 208). Just the opposite, in other words, of Socratic dialogue: "If the Sophists had an answer for everything, then [Socrates] could pose questions; if the Sophists knew everything, then he knew nothing at all; if the Sophists could talk without stopping, then he could be silent—that is, he could converse" (*CI*, 210). The closer sophistic chatter comes to Socratic conversation, the more it results in something else entirely: "eccentric antiphonal singing, in which everyone sings his part without regard to the other and there is a resemblance to conversation only because they do not all talk at once" (*CI*, 34). As we shall see, these distinctions between deceptive chatter and philosophical inquiry, as developed by Plato and extended by Kierkegaard, would become a central theme in the modern conceptual history of everyday talk.

And all, at least to start, in contrast to Aristophanes' depiction of Socratic dialogue. But challenging this depiction is not the primary reason Kierkegaard returns to *Clouds* in his dissertation on *The Concept of Irony*. What captivates him about this play is neither the garrulous form nor the sophistic function it assigns to Socratic dialogue, but the vacuous system of belief to which it connects this way of speaking. In "Socrates' urging Strepsiades not to believe in the gods but only in the great empty space and the tongue," Kierkegaard sees "a perfect designation of the boisterous twaddle [*larmende Snak*] that is apropos of nothing and reminds me of a line in the Grimm's *Irische Elfenmärchen*, where reference is made to people with an empty head and a tongue like a tongue in a church bell" (*CI*, 151).

How are we to account for this abrupt shift from Greek drama to German literature? Recall the foregoing shift from Plutarch's essay on talkativeness to Kierkegaard's critique of literary reviewers. While the recurring image of the empty head indexes the conceptual history of *adoleschia* from Aristophanes to Plutarch, that of the tongue in a church bell further integrates this history into Kierkegaard's already intermingled notions of *snak* and *Geschwätz*. The *larmende Snak* that Socrates' *adoleschia* calls to mind is that of the "loquacious wife" (*geschwätziges Weib*) in a Grimm brothers' tale, who is described as having "a tongue as busy with a head as empty as the great bell of the church steeple."[15]

Apart from these allusive passages, church bells rarely appear in Kierkegaard's work. But each time they do, it is again in reference to *snak*, again in keeping with its connections to *adoleschia* and *Geschwätz*, and again in anticipation of later work on this vacuous way of speaking. In a romantic 1835 flourish, Kierkegaard disparaged church bells as unnatural and thus ungodly calls to prayer, which turn worshipers away from "the true house of God, where heaven's arch forms the church ceiling, where the roar of the storm and the gentle zephyr take the place of the organ's bass and treble, where the warbling of the birds forms the congregation's hymns of joy," luring them into "the stone church where the pastor's voice is repeated in an echo from the roof-vault" (*JNB* 1, 12). A few years later, in the wake of his 1836 newspaper polemic, he complained that, "as in the fairytale, the liberals have a tongue and an empty head like the tongue in a church bell."[16] And in 1841, the same year in which he broke off his engagement to Regine Olsen, he bemoaned the role of a nearby church bell in their early courtship: "I can still recall and hear its dull strokes. At the appointed time the signal sounded in the middle of the sitting room small talk [*Dagligstue-Passiaren*], and the evening whisperings began."[17] In literature, philosophy, religion, politics, and love alike—all themes which would capture Kierkegaard's attention in subsequent discussions of *snak*—the tongues of church bells wag for the worse.

Windbags, Windsucks, and Hegelian Gert Westphalers

A year before his death, Kierkegaard found himself enthralled by another German term: *Windbeutel*. "It is an excellent word, and I envy the Germans it," he admits in his journal. "We Danes do not have the word, nor is that to which it refers characteristic of us Danes. It simply does not lie in the Danish national character to be a windbag." This is not to suggest, of course, that Kierkegaard and his contemporaries were impervious to the "windbaggery [*Windbeutelei*]" of their neighbors to the south. On the contrary, in keeping with "the age-old relationship between the Germans and the Danes," they were deeply influenced by it, resulting in "a different fault, a *complementary* fault," Kierkegaard goes on to confess. "And the Danish language does have a word for this fault, a word that the German language perhaps lacks, the word: windsuck [*Vind sluger*]." In short: "A German to make wind and a Dane to swallow it."[18]

The windiest of these German windbags, at least according to Kierkegaard, were the speculative idealists who emerged after Kant, which is why, in the same journal entry, he recalls Schopenhauer's critique of this philosophical tradition. "Here lies the origin of that philosophical method that arose immediately after Kant's teaching, that consists in mystifying, impressing, deceiving, throwing sand in the eyes and being a windbag," Schopenhauer grumbled. In Fichte, Schelling, and Hegel, we see "three notorious sophists" whose "windbaggery and charlatanism" set the stage for an abstract speculative movement that "the history of philosophy will one day refer to under the rubric of 'Period of Dishonesty'" (quoted in *JNB* 9, 720). Kierkegaard could not agree more. Schopenhauer's treatment of German idealism as "windbaggery and charlatanism" at once jibed with his earlier coupling of *snak* with sophistry and yielded fresh insight into his own speculative surroundings: "If [Schopenhauer] has had to deal with windbags, I have had to deal with windsucks" (*JNB* 9, 394–95).

Much of this idealist wind blew in from Hegel. And much of it, Hegel encouraged his Danish windsucks to believe, had been blowing for millennia. "Hegel was—presumably of necessity—a windbag, and—of necessity—the result of 6,000 years of world history," Kierkegaard snarks (*JNB* 9, 395). And this is where things get interesting: If Hegel is the preeminent German windbag, and his windbagging (*windbeuteln*) is the culmination of world history, then his attendant Danish windsucks are not just Hegelian disciples but also, as Kierkegaard is careful to specify, "Hegelian Gert Westphalers." Notice how he arrives at this conclusion:

The absolute method, Hegel's invention, is already a difficult issue in logic—indeed, a brilliant tautology that has been at the service of scientific superstition with many signs and wonderful deeds. In the historical sciences it is a fixed idea, and because the method promptly begins to become concrete there—since, after all, history is the concretion of the Idea—Hegel certainly has had occasion to display a rare scholarship, a rare ability to shape the material, in which through him there is turmoil enough. But it has also prompted the learner's mind to become distracted, with the result that he—perhaps precisely because of his respectfulness and his admiration for China and Persia, the thinkers of the Middle Ages, the philosophers of Greece, the four world-historical monarchies (a discovery that, just as it did not escape Gert Westphaler, has also agitated the glib tongues [*Snakketøi*] of many later Hegelian Gert Westphalers)—forgot to examine whether there has now appeared at the conclusion, at the end of that enchanted journey, that which was constantly promised at the beginning, that which was, after all, the primary issue, that which all the world's glory could not replace, the only thing that could make up for the misplaced tension in which we were kept—the correctness of the method.[19]

This crucial excerpt from *Philosophical Fragments* went through two earlier drafts, each of which was progressively sharper in its satire of Hegelian thought and influence. Consider, for instance, one of Kierkegaard's alternate introductions:

There is a phrase that, simply uttered, pierces the soul with awesome solemnity; there is a name that, simply uttered together with the phrase from which it is inseparable, makes the child of the age take off his hat and bow down, even someone who does not know the man: *the absolute method and Hegel*. The absolute method—this phrase is *einhaltsschwer* [weighty in substance], and yet it passes, as the poet says, from *Munde zu Munde* [mouth to mouth], but in every mouth it is equally weighty in substance. Nowadays the absolute method is at home not only in logic but also in the historical sciences. O worldly eminence, what a fraud you are—exclaimed the beggar who had envied that rich lord, until he discovered that His Lordship walked on crutches—just as the absolute method does. (*PF*, 205)

In this early draft, Kierkegaard suggests that the *Snakketøi* of Denmark's "Hegelian Gert Westphalers" yield little more than philosophical gossip—a kind of scholarly hearsay in which worshipful windsucks solemnly spread Hegel's arrogant thoughts from "mouth to mouth," heedless of the fact that the arrogance implicit in these thoughts is a deceptive overcompensation for their underlying intellectual weakness. On this point, Kierkegaard is particularly strident: "To have to take refuge in wordplay and witticisms, to cram holes with blotting paper, to have to parade with tinsel and be silent about its not hanging together properly—oh, this is a high price to be the absolute method" (*PF*, 200). Or, as he puts in the next draft, inverting his earlier anecdote about the beggar and the rich lord: "To have to take refuge in wordplay and witticisms and evasions, to have to help oneself along by half-untruths, to have to beg all through life merely to become the absolute, which does not begin *bittweise* [by request], to have to be silent about its not hanging together properly—oh, this is a high price!" (*PF*, 206).

Had Kierkegaard published any of these attacks on Hegel's absolute method, he would have incurred the wrath of many Danish thinkers—and he knew it. To speak out against "the logical gimcrackeries [*Snurrepiberier*] whereby it is supposed to be the object of pious fetish-worship" was nothing short of "philosophical high treason against Hegel" (*PF*, 206). But it was almost worth it to Kierkegaard, for the rhetorical effects of Hegel's wordplays, witticisms, evasions, half-untruths, logical gimcrackeries, crammed argumentative holes, and tinseled academic parades were nothing short of sophistic.

The sophistry of Hegel's absolute method is readily apparent in the historical sciences, Kierkegaard argues, where it distracts readers with learned tales of enchanted journeys through world-historical monarchies and, in so doing, causes them to neglect basic conceptual and methodological questions: What, exactly, is the Idea? And is world history truly its concretion? In service to questions of this sort, Kierkegaard invites readers to consider a hypothetical scenario: "Suppose it happened—and why should it not happen—that the thought that is to be pointed out in the concrete remained unclear but that the concrete was itself so rich, so variegated, that it captivated the soul so that the learner or the reader, rejoicing in this delight, forgot the thought, was not enraged with the one who really had deceived him, but even considered himself very indebted to him" (*PF*, 203).

The *locus classicus* of this deceptive technique, according to Kierkegaard, is Hegel's *Philosophy of History*—a series of lectures in which the great idealist attempts to track the development of human freedom (absolute spirit) through four progressively more advanced historical periods: Asian civilization (infancy), Greek democracy (adolescence), Roman statehood (adulthood), and German bureaucracy (maturity).

In the *first case*, for example, he speaks about China. Who would not be happy to know something about China? He amazes us with his learning; one is overwhelmed by all the new things to be learned and thanks him—if one is numbered among those who previously really did not know anything in particular about the subject and among those who in their rejoicing over it forget that this subject is not at all what they were supposed to find out. Another reader, however, is by chance very familiar with the Chinese and discovers that there is an error. This is made known, and there is a controversy. One is curious, reads both sides, finds out something new—and forgets even more what it is that one really wants to find out.—In the *second case* he speaks about Oriental philosophy, Greek, Jewish, etc. One acquires an indescribable amount of information, but unfortunately not what one seeks and what one as philosopher should achieve. (*PF*, 204)

The deceptions of such historiography are multiple. Hegelian Gert Westphalers are not just amazed by the philosopher's historical erudition, distracted by the amount of information it yields, and thus deterred from asking basic philosophical questions about "the correctness of the method." As time goes on, their *Snakketøi* compound these deceptions, causing subsequent generations of windsucks to mistake the clever transmission of historical data for the rigorous practice of philosophical inquiry. "Soon everyone who knows anything or knows how to talk about it will becomes a philosopher," Kierkegaard laments, anticipating Heidegger's later assault on the discipline of philosophy itself. "All unite in dragging men's minds down into multiplicity and, thus immersed, into forgetfulness of what is the philosopher's business and occupation." When all is said and done, "after every means of diversion has been employed to disturb the reader and bribe the judge," the history of any given philosophical quandary will be little more than a "long-winded report on what others have thought about it," a report which scholars will continue to pass from mouth to mouth in reciprocal acts of deceptive windbagging and deceived windsucking. What began as a method for concentrating thought will have become "an instrument of distraction, nothing but an instrument of distraction" (*PF*, 205).

Poorly Provisioned Parrots

Hegel was not the first man of exceptional learning to deploy this instrument of distraction. Nor was he the first to do so in an arrogant, long-winded account of world-historical change. Nor was he even the first to track this change through four world-historical monarchies.

While holding his fiancée in his arms, Gert Westphaler whispers into her ear about the fourth and final great monarchy of the world, and the seven electoral princes who prolong its existence in order to delay the end of history: "There have been three already, the Phrygian, Elamite, and Mesopotamian, and this is the last. When the electoral princes fall, the world will come to an end too, according to the Sibylline oracle, so they're very careful, as soon as one electoral prince dies, to choose another straight off, so that the world won't come to an end, and this has gone on continuously from the time of the Emperor Augustus, the famous emperor who founded the fourth and last monarchy at the request of the Sibyl" (*MGW*, 32). And so Gert continues, regaling his fiancée with amorous tales of taxation, papal rule, and cardinalate procedure, until she politely interjects, inviting him "to tell the rest of the story to my cat" (*MGW*, 33).

As the editors of *Søren Kierkegaards Skrifter* well note, Gert's lengthy historical account echoes that of the prophet Daniel, who interpreted one of Nebuchadnezzar's dreams along similar monarchical lines (Daniel 2:36–45). In this sense, Holberg's talkative barber is not just a windbag but also, at least in this instance of chatter, a windsuck as well. Add to this Kierkegaard's claim that Master Gert was the "first discoverer" of the "productive idea of the four world-historical monarchies" (*P*, 103), and the plot thickens further, suggesting that Hegel's pursuit of this idea was not an elaborate act of windbagging disguised as rigorous philosophical inquiry; rather, it was a loutish, third-hand bout of windsucking disguised as an elaborate act of windbagging disguised as rigorous philosophical inquiry. And all to the detriment of his Danish disciples, whose solemn mouth-to-mouth recitations of his third-hand lectures on *The Philosophy of History* followed suit, amounting to echoes of echoes of echoes.

Kierkegaard has a name for this iterative way of speaking: *Eftersnakken*. Its best translation is also the most derisive: "parroting." After

Hegel "come the parrots [*Eftersnakkerne*], who despite their survey of world history unfortunately lack all contemplation," Kierkegaard complains in *The Concept of Anxiety*. They know as much about world history as "that noble youth knew about raisins, who, when asked in the test for a grocer's license where raisins come from, answered: We get ours from the professor on Cross Street."[20] Kierkegaard's use of the Danish word *Professor* in this passage may have been a garbling of the similar-sounding *Provisor*, meaning "provisioner" (*CA*, 250, n. 34). In light of the foregoing analysis, however, this is doubtful. Hegel was the German professor whose windy thoughts provided Danish *Eftersnakkerne* with their quasi-learned provisions.

Among these poorly provisioned parrots was the jurist Carl Weiss, whose 1838 essay "On the Historical Development of the State" reiterated Hegel's idea of four world-historical monarchies and splashed onto the Danish intellectual scene in a much-discussed issue of *Perseus: Journal of the Speculative Idea*. Also appearing in this issue was an essay titled "The Logical System," by Denmark's foremost Hegelian scholar, Johan Ludvig Heiberg, whose urbane, aristocratic conservatism would eventually come to typify Golden Age Denmark, inspiring some of Kierkegaard's most biting social critiques in turn.[21] Much to Kierkegaard's surprise, Heiberg began his essay by highlighting several "imperfections in detail" in Hegel's system and ended it by noting "how far the previous presentation differs from the Hegelian etc." And much to Kierkegaard's amusement, Heiberg's fellow *Eftersnakkerne* were impressed. After reading "The Logical System," F. C. Sibbern could only conclude that Heiberg, at long last, was beginning to "go beyond Hegel" (quoted in *P*, 183–84, n. 157). Kierkegaard, of course, arrived at a different conclusion:

I have read philosophical treatises in which nearly every thought, almost every expression, was from Hegel. After having read through them, I have thought: Who, now, actually is the author? Hegel, I have then said to myself, is the author; the one who has written the treatise is his reporter [*Referent*] and as such he is dependable and accurate. This I could understand. But see! This was not the way it was; the author was a man who had gone beyond Hegel. Here my understanding came to a halt; the author says: I have gone beyond Hegel. If the article could speak, it would probably say: What chatter [*Snak*]! (*P*, 57)

In style and substance alike, Heiberg's *Eftersnakken* is inseparable "to a hair" from that of Hegel. Hence, Kierkegaard's use of *Referent* in the above passage, from the Latin verb *referre*, meaning "to carry back."

Like that of a middling academic tutor, whose output amounts to "a parroting echo's [*eftersnakkende Ecchos*] routine reproduction of what has been said," the primary philosophical contribution of Heiberg's essay is merely to return Danish readers to Hegel's own work (*CUP* 1, 72). And yet, paradoxically, the author purports to have "gone beyond Hegel." Chatter, indeed!

At issue here, Kierkegaard suggests, is a latent identity crisis, the symptoms of which are at once hilarious and disturbing. That "those who have gone beyond Hegel but nevertheless are Hegelians" fail to sense the paradox of their position makes their mouth-to-mouth *Eftersnakken* utterly ridiculous.[22] "Those who have gone beyond Hegel are like people who live out in the country and who must always give their address as 'via' a larger town," Kierkegaard jests. "In these cases the addresses read 'To Mr. X via Hegel'" (*JNB* 2, 100). But it also makes their *Eftersnakken* deeply disturbing, for it suggests that the anxiety of influence behind their delusions of grandeur is so profound that they are unable, or at least unwilling, to observe the contradiction between the underlying Hegelian structure of their work (which they do not appear to understand) and their overweening claims to have "gone beyond Hegel" (which their scholarship in no way does).

This may be why Kierkegaard, in his *Postscript* to *Philosophical Fragments*, contrasts "the scholar's elevated calm" with "the parroter's [*Eftersnakkendes*] comical thoughtlessness" (*CUP* 1, 22). And it is almost certainly why, in the abovementioned critique of Heiberg's essay, he uses the term *snak*. As Kierkegaard sees it, the relationship between the deluded chatter of Danish Hegelians and their thoughtless parroting of Hegel's work is one of container and thing contained. When authors like Heiberg proudly claim to have surpassed the Hegelian sources to which their scholarship nevertheless refers readers, Kierkegaard sees a remarkable form of duplicity at work: tedious *Eftersnakken* cloaked in pretentious *snak*, and all without the slightest bit of self-awareness.

The Age of Distinctions

If Heiberg and his fellow parrots are "Hegelian Gert Westphalers," it is not just because the information they transmit derives from Hegel, who in turn seems indebted to Holberg's talkative barber. It is also because the manner in which they transmit this information—glib tongues (*Snakketøi*) spreading quasi-learned gossip (*Eftersnakken*) in deluded bouts of chatter (*snak*)—closely resembles the peculiar communicative deficit of Master Gert. To be sure, Kierkegaard was amused by "the ingenious notion of world history from the point of view that there are 4 world-historical monarchies." But his amusement was nourished by a deeper interest in the way it passes from mouth-to-mouth in Denmark: "This idea has been taken up now in our time and one hears it everywhere, and at times it is spoken of in such a way that one would think Geert W. to be the source" (P, 104). Make no mistake, the way of speaking at issue here is chatter.

When Kierkegaard bemoans the systematicians of his day, particularly those with speculative idealist leanings, it is this curious mashup of Hegelian thought and Westphalerian chatter that he means to indict. In issuing this indictment of nineteenth-century Danish scholars, however, he also means to recall the era of learned culture that preceded them—an era whose commitment to radical thought and decisive action, as the next chapter demonstrates, Kierkegaard wished to renew:

The age of making distinctions is past. Like so much else it has been vanquished by the system. In our time whoever in a scholarly way clings to making distinctions— the craving of his soul is for something that has long since vanished. The age of making distinctions is past, that productive idea of the four world-historical monarchies reduces everything to the appropriate moment, whether this idea in its historical progress and immanent movement overcomes everything that rises up, or whether, more reminiscent of its first discoverer, Geert Westphaler, in the pathos of conviction it assimilates everything to itself in the course of chitchat [*Passiarens*]. (P, 103)

The heading for this excerpt from Kierkegaard's journal reads "Inter et Inter," the literal translation of which is "between and between." Kierkegaard probably borrowed this phrase from the Latin proverb *Distingeundum est inter et inter*, meaning "It is necessary to distinguish between notions that need to be distinguished." And he probably encountered this proverb in two of the nineteenth-century novels that sat on his bookshelf. The first is Eichendorff's *Memoirs of a Good-For-Nothing*, where one student musician says to another, "*Distinguendum est inter et inter*," adding "*quod licet Jovi, non licet bovi!*"—"what is permitted to Jupiter is not permitted to the ox." The second is Hoffman's *Life and Opinions of Tomcat Murr*, where Father Hilarious advises Kreisler against the donning of monastic robes: "I feel comfortable in my habit and wouldn't shed it at any price, but *distinguendum est inter et inter!*"[23] Thus, in choosing "Inter et Inter" as the heading for this journal entry,

Kierkegaard suggests that the distinctions in question are twofold, interrelated, and somehow reminiscent of the classic socio-historical separation of ostentatious pride from artful humility. Making sense of this suggestion and marking its relevance to Kierkegaard's work on the chatter of barbers and philosophers are the final tasks of this chapter.

A clue to its significance arrives in the epigraph to *The Concept of Anxiety*, which mirrors the above journal entry—but only to a point:

> The age of making distinctions is passed. It has been vanquished by the system. In our day whoever loves to make distinctions is regarded as an eccentric whose soul clings to something that has long since vanished. Be that as it may, yet Socrates still is what he was, the simple wise man, because of the peculiar distinction that he expressed both in words and in life, something that the eccentric Hamann first reiterated with great admiration two thousand years later: "For Socrates was great in 'that he distinguished between what he understood and what he did not understand.'" (*CA*, 3)

When read alongside each other, these parallel tributes to "the age of making distinctions" suggest that the first "Inter" in Kierkegaard's mysterious Latin heading refers to the distinction between the assimilating chatter of the present age and the eccentric wisdom of the previous era, while the second "Inter" refers to the distinction between those whose learned discourse has come represent each period. Champions of assimilating chatter, as we have seen, include ancient barbers, Greek sophists, Gert Westphaler, Hegel, and the latter's Danish parrots. And champions of eccentric wisdom, as the foregoing epigraph suggests, include Socrates, Hamann, and, by association, Kierkegaard himself. If indeed these groups are distinct, what, exactly, divides them?

Recall the tradition of chatter that Kierkegaard allows us to trace from antiquity to the eighteenth century. In the delusions of ancient barbers, the deceits of their sophistic peers, the distractions of Master Gert, the windbagging of German idealists, the windsucking of their Danish parrots, the gossip-mongering of modern journalists and literary reviewers—to say nothing of the prattling publics inspired by each and every one of these figures—Kierkegaard reveals several different kinds of *snak*, ranging in form and function from noise to nonsense, cliché to bombast, wordplay to witticism, tangent to reprise, gossip to gimcrack, diversion to duplicity, tedious anecdote to absurd abstraction, abrupt interjection to endless logorrhea. The rhetorical motives for *snak* are equally diverse, he further suggests, ranging in aim and origin from mechanical impulse to perverse enjoyment, conceptual confusion to chronic distraction, mental derangement to communicative disease. And yet, at each step of the way, Kierkegaard calls our attention to a particular state of mind: prideful knowledge coupled with profound self-ignorance. Barbers and sophists, windbags and windsucks, journalists and reviewers—all suffer from delusions of grandeur.

As we have seen, Kierkegaard describes this ailment as *alazoneia*. In so doing, he not only revives ancient Greek disdain for quackery, imposture, and false pretense; more importantly, he reappropriates the classic literary distinction between the *alazon* and the *eiron*. This distinction, as Martin Heidegger would later note in his critique of academic *Gerede*, came to legibility in Aristotle's *Nicomachean Ethics*, where the *alazon* is depicted as a braggart and the *eiron* as a self-depreciator. In the *alazon*, Aristotle sees a self-gratifying impostor who purports to be more than he truly is. In the *eiron*, he sees the inverse: an artist of humility skilled at appearing to be less than he truly is.[24] In this sense, both character types stray from sincere expressions of their own individual merits. But each does so in a different way: While the *alazon* traffics in excess and exaggeration, temporarily misleading others but continually deluding himself about his personal worth, the *eiron* thrives on deficiency and understatement, regularly deceiving others about his personal worth but never losing sight of this deception.

Learned culture has always been rife with both personality types— at least since Plato's *Republic*, where the sophistic *alazon* Thrasymachus squares off against the philosophical *eiron* Socrates. While Thrasymachus says more than he seems to know, Socrates seems to know more than he says. All of which, of course, infuriates the former: "What balderdash is this that you have been talking," Thrasymachus exclaims at one point in the dialogue, pouncing on Socrates and another interlocutor. "I won't take from you any such drivel." He was "like a wild beast," Socrates later recalls in a cunning display of *eironeia*. "And I, when I heard him, was dismayed, and looking upon him was filled with fear, and I believe that if I had not looked at him before he did at me I should have lost my voice." Much to Socrates' surprise, of course, he did not lose his voice: "Thrasymachus, don't be harsh with us. If I and my friend have made mistakes in the consideration of the question, rest assured that it is unwillingly that we err." If these errors and mistakes come across as drivel and balderdash, "it is our lack of ability that is at fault. It is pity then that we should far more reasonably receive from clever fellows like you than severity." To which Thrasymachus replies with a sardonic laugh: "Ye gods! here we have the well-known irony [*eironeia*] of Socrates" (*Republic*, 336b–37a).

Kierkegaard knew this section of the *Republic* well, and he often mimicked its portrayal of Socratic *eironeia*, especially in polemical works designed to underscore and, wherever possible, to undermine the *alazoneia* of his Hegelian peers. Consider, for instance, his culminating screed in *Prefaces*. "Philosophy cannot be indifferent to whether it is actually understood or not, and yet it can learn this only through the obtuseness of the one involved, because the one who is sagacious does not let it show," Kierkegaard explains. "My purpose, then, is to serve philosophy; my qualification for this is that I am obtuse enough not to understand it, indeed still more obtuse—obtuse enough to betray that." If sagacity belongs to the "worldly wise," who are skilled at concealing the fact that they "do not completely understand the very much that philosophy says in our times," Kierkegaard's self-proclaimed obtuseness is twofold, and thoroughly ironic: like his more sagacious peers, he does not understand the philosophy of his times; unlike them, however, he does not know how to conceal this non-understanding (P, 51).

The philosophy of his times had of course blown in from Germany. "Hegelian philosophy has now thrived for several years here at home. If this philosophy, after having explained everything, now advances and explains itself, what a splendid prospect," Kierkegaard continues, again in the spirit of Socrates. "I do not deny that Hegel has explained everything. I leave that to the powerful minds who will also explain what is missing" (P, 56). What Kierkegaard asks of these powerful minds is something far simpler: "I seek instruction" (P, 55). And he is not too proud to beg for it:

I plead, I plead for an explanation, an explanation, note well, that I can understand, because it would scarcely help me if there were to be an explanation that explains everything in Hegel, but in such a way that I cannot understand it. Give me the explanation; I will take it *à tout prix* [at any price]. Toss it to me with a shrug of the shoulders; I will still give thanks for it. Since we now have many philosophers here at home who zealously and successfully have comprehended this philosophy, the consequence for me is the happy prospect of the desired instruction. (P, 56)

Well, almost any price: "I will endure anything, suffer anything, do anything if only I may succeed in becoming initiated," Kierkegaard assures his Hegelian peers, just so long as it does not "require of me that I must explain to others what I myself do not comprehend" (P, 55). Like Socrates before him, Kierkegaard is determined to maintain the distinction between what he does and does not understand—and, by extension, what he is able to explain and what he can only parrot.

That so many of Denmark's powerful minds have already "gone beyond Hegel" might make this simple request for basic instruction a difficult one to grant, Kierkegaard admits, in which case he would be willing to settle for "a little telegraphic notice where they have arrived," especially if this notice could be sent "in the form of a categorical definition in order that it can, if possible, be understandable to me" (*P*, 57). Clearly, Heiberg was not the only learned traveler on Kierkegaard's mind. Like Master Gert's long-winded chatter about his short inland journey, Heiberg's claim to have surpassed Hegel raises the question of where, exactly, Heiberg now finds himself. Kierkegaard knew this question, like his request for instruction, would probably go unanswered. Surely, no one who has "gone beyond Hegel" would deign reply to "a laggard who has seen nothing of the world and who has undertaken only an inland journey within his own consciousness and consequently gets nowhere," he muses. "They cannot possibly find it worth the inconvenience of making a to-do [*at gjøre nogen Ophævelse*] over such a traveler, all the less likely since they make a big to-do [*gjøre saa mange Ophævelser*] over 'nothing'" (*P*, 44).

As the translator of this oblique passage well notes, Kierkegaard's combination of *gøre*, meaning "to make" and "to render," and *ophæve*, meaning "to nullify" and "to repeal," is a play on Hegel's *Aufhebung*, meanings of which range from "cancellation" to "suspension" to "sublation" to "preservation" to "transcendence." And his reference to "nothing" in this passage functions similarly, playfully alluding to the notorious *Nichts* of Hegelian ontology. When read alongside each other, however, these clever expressions point elsewhere. More than a play on Hegel's philosophy, they constitute a piercing critique of his Danish parrots, whose work simultaneously lays claim to the absolute method and fails to live up to its rigorous intellectual standards, yielding little more than deliberative fuss and prolonged commotion about their own trifling concerns.

To this extent, the "nothing" at the center of their *Eftersnakken* more closely resembles the "noting" at work in Shakespeare's *Much Ado About Nothing* than the *Nichts* at the root of Hegel's philosophical system. In the late sixteenth-century, "nothing" and "noting" were near-homophones, and the latter often meant "eavesdropping," "overhearing," and, crucially, "gossiping" about what one had heard. To note nothing was to spread rumors about something of no importance. In this sense, the big to-do about "nothing" in which Danish Hegelianism culminates is not an absolute philosophical *Aufhebung* in the spirit of Hegel but, instead, a "learned jumble" of *Eftersnakken* inspired by other *Eftersnakkerne*—"a ditto genuinely speculative mediation of what every Tom, Dick, and Harry, geniuses, and assistant professors have thought and written" (*CUP* 1, 99).

Two years after *Prefaces* appeared, Kierkegaard was still waiting to receive notice from Heiberg and his traveling Hegelians. And he continued to suspect that it would never arrive. But he also had a better understanding of why it might not. Behind his peers' outspoken claims to have "gone beyond Hegel," Kierkegaard was beginning to detect a certain social sagacity, not unlike the worldly wisdom he wryly admired in *Prefaces*, which knows how to conceal its own ignorance. "There surely have been some who simply have not cared very much about understanding Hegel but have certainly cared about the benefit one has by *even going beyond* Hegel," Kierkegaard goes on to rib (*CUP* 1, 370). If only he were not so obtuse. Then perhaps he, too, could enjoy this social benefit: "I stress a certain honesty that forbids me to parrot [*eftersnakke*] what I am unable to understand and bids me—something that in connection with Hegel has long caused me pain in my forsakenness—to renounce appealing to him except in particular cases, which is the same as having to relinquish the recognition one gains by the affiliation, while I remain what I myself admit is infinitely little, a vanishing, unrecognizable atom, just like every single human being" (*CUP* 1, 622).

Hence the basic distinction between the *eiron* and the *alazon*. What the former realizes about them both, the latter cannot bear to admit to himself: Knowledge of the world, like the life of its possessor, is always limited. And when human understanding reaches the outer limit of knowledge, beyond which only non-understanding endures, the *eiron* sees something more: not an occasion for speculative chatter but, instead, an opening for ironic instruction. Yet another reason why *The Concept of Anxiety* begins with Kierkegaard quoting Hamann quoting Plato's account of Socrates: "He distinguished between what he understood and what he did not understand." Where the worldly wisdom of the *alazon* ends, the eccentric wisdom of the *eiron* begins, and always with a wink—the same wink that began Kierkegaard's work as an author years prior, in his 1836 newspaper polemic against Lehmann and Hage.

TWO

Fuzzy Math

A Lost Count

When Plato depicted music and astronomy as kindred sciences—one for the ears and one for the eyes—it was the Pythagorean theory of the harmony of the spheres that he had in mind (*Rep.* 530d). According to Pythagoras, the quality of life on earth is determined by a numerically precise yet wholly imperceptible cosmic harmony, the pitches and intervals of which are in turn determined by the orbital hums of other celestial bodies. Aristotle was less convinced than his mentor: How could music of any sort, much less that of enormous stars and planets, be inaudible to the human ear? Because "the sound is in our ears from the very moment of birth and is thus indistinguishable from its contrary silence, since sound and silence are discriminated by mutual contrast," the Pythagoreans claimed. "What happens to men, then, is just what happens to coppersmiths, who are so accustomed to the noise of the smithy that it makes no difference to them." Aristotle minced no words in reply: "Absurdity" (*De Cael.* 290b–291a).

Kierkegaard's well-known nostalgia for "the age of revolution" and his corresponding lament for "the present age" are both decedents of this ancient debate. Notice how he depicts each era in his 1846 literary review of the novel *Two Ages*. "The age of revolution is essentially passionate and therefore essentially has *culture*," and the strongest testament to the essential culture of the revolutionary spirit is "the tension and resilience of the inner being" of those who advance its cause (*TA*, 61). It is tempting to interpret this tense and resilient inner being as an antecedent to Kierkegaard's much vaunted "single individual" (*den Enkelte*). But it has more to do with a certain mode of collective life, notably one in which subjective passions for shared ideas allow for a "unanimity of separation" between community members:

When individuals (each one individually) are essentially and passionately related to an idea and together are essentially related to the same idea, the relation is optimal and normative. Individually the relation separates them (each one has himself for himself), and ideally it unites them. Where there is essential inwardness, there is a decent modesty between man and man that prevents crude aggressiveness. . . . Thus individuals never come too close to each other in the herd sense, simply because they are united on the basis of an ideal distance. (*TA*, 62–63)

Heidegger would later describe this form of human togetherness as "*Dasein*-with" (*Mitdasein*), contrasting it with deficient modes of solicitude like "Being for, against, or without one another, passing one another by, not 'mattering' to one another."[1] And Lacan would further unearth its sociological structure in his early formulation of "intersubjectivity" (*intersubjectivité*) and subsequent critique of intersubjective descent into the imagined symmetry of dual relations. For Kierkegaard, however, the model for collective life of this sort was neither conceptual nor sociological but, instead, *musical.* "The unanimity of separation is indeed fully orchestrated music," he explains. And not just any kind of orchestrated music: "The harmony of the spheres is the unity of each planet relating to itself and to the whole. Take away the relations, and there will be chaos" (*TA*, 63).

Much to Kierkegaard's frustration, chaos of this sort typifies the present age. When a revolutionary age goes awry, it is because subjective passions have been removed, but shared ideas remain in place. When the present age goes awry, however, it is because subjective passions and shared ideas are both missing. At issue here are two distinct forms of social turmoil: "If individuals relate to an idea merely *en masse* (consequently without the individual separation of inwardness), we get violence, anarchy, riotousness; but if there is no idea for the individuals *en masse* and no individually separating essential inwardness, either, then we have crudeness" (*TA*, 63). What the first group experiences as *mass society*, the second group further devolves into *crass society*. In order to understand the role of chatter (*snak*) in the present age, we must resume our inquiry here, in the midst of this crucial yet often over-looked distinction between mass society and its crass successor.

The music of mass society may not be orchestrated like that of revolutionary culture, but it is musical nonetheless. "The gay and lively songs of conviviality that unite friends," "the dithyrambic songs of revolt that collect the crowds," "the sublime rhythms of religious fervor that under divine supervision muster the countless generations to review before heavenly hosts"—all are characteristic of mass society (*TA*, 63). And all are noticeably absent from its crass offspring. Far from the lively songs, dithyrambic chants, and sublime rhythms of mass society, and thus twice removed from the orchestrated harmonies of revolutionary culture, the music of the present age has been crudely reduced to "the mechanical counting of the beat [*den tillærte Tællen af Takten*]" (*TA*, 62). All that remains of its melodic predecessors, Kierkegaard concludes, is their basic unit of time—a regular and repetitive pulse of sound emitted from their beat levels.

But even this pulse of sound is increasingly drowned out in the present age, where the mechanical racket of modern counting procedures tends to be louder than any historic beat levels. Hence, the alliterative "t . . . t . . . t . . . t" of *den tillærte Tællen af Takten*. In crass society, the collective harmonies of the past are not only reduced to pulses of sound but also, paradoxically, replaced by the automated rhythms of the counting operations that purport to represent them. To be sure, *den tillærte Tællen af Takten* never misses a beat. But the only beat it ever seems to count is that of its own "t . . . t . . . t . . . t." Crass society may have lost the count of earlier collective beats, but it has not lost the beat of its own mechanical count, which is why its count is always, to some extent, *a lost count*. It not only strays from the collective rhythms of earlier times, but also fails to notice their disappearance from the present age, oddly mistaking the mechanical sounds of modern life for the social harmonies of previous eras.

Chatter is the linguistic medium in which this lost count proceeds. As we shall see in this chapter, it is the dysfunctional mode of *telling* (*at fortælle*) that accompanies modernity's automated mode of *tallying* (*at tælle*). And common sense (*Forstandighed*) is the collective habit of mind that allows this tally telling to continue without interruption, straying ever further from the passionate inwardness of essential culture. "Instead of joy there is a kind of sniveling discontent, instead of sorrow a kind of sullen, dogged tenaciousness, instead of enthusiasm the garrulous common sense of experience [*en snaksom Erfarings Forstandig-hed*]." Where elaborate communal harmonies once burst forth, saturating the soundscapes of revolutionary culture and mass society alike, automated exchanges of "gossip and rumor [*Bysnak og Rygte*]" now take place, structured and sustained by commonsense counting procedures that are mathematical but not musical, sonorous but not harmonious, omnipresent but rarely noticed (*TA*, 63).

Which brings us back to the Pythagorean smithy. Just as copper-smiths are so accustomed to the sound of their own hammering that they no longer distinguish it from silence, the present age is so accustomed to the garrulous common sense of experience that it no longer separates this chatty mode of existence from quieter ways of speaking, thinking, and being with others. Yet another way in which *den tillærte Tællen af Takten* operates as a lost count: Like the collective beats of the past, which it continually purports to represent but completely fails to track, the chattering count of crass society is at once incessant and, for this reason, imperceptible. If the harmony of the spheres is the ambi-ent music of life on earth, analogous to the environmental noise of a coppersmith's shop, the chattering count of crass society is the back-ground noise of the present age, a low-grade mechanical grate that par-adoxically sets the tone of the era.

Mean Values

The shift from revolutionary culture to mass society to crass society is, at root, subtractive. In revolutionary culture, individuals are directly inspired and collectively moved by shared ideas. In mass society, pas-sionate inwardness is absent, but shared enthusiasm remains. And in crass society, both are sorely missing: "No one has anything for him-self, and united they possess nothing, either: so they become trouble-some and wrangle" (*TA*, 63). Coming to terms with this quarrelsome social order, where individuals "shove and press and rub against each other in pointless externality," resulting in "turmoil and commotion that ends in nothing," is the basic objective of Kierkegaard's literary review of *Two Ages*.

Along the way, he introduces readers to a term whose influence would ripple through modern social theory for generations to come, finding especially pointed restatement in the early works of Heideg-ger and Lacan. "Individuals do not in inwardness turn away from each other, do not turn outward in unanimity for the idea, but mutually turn to each other in a frustrating and suspicious, aggressive, leveling reciprocity" (*TA*, 63). It is here, in the "mutual reflexive opposition [*gjensidige Reflexions-Modstand*]" of leveling reciprocity, that Kierkegaard discovers the basic social condition of the present age. And it is here, in the midst of this discovery, that he finds an occasion for its critique:

The coiled springs of life-relationships, which are what they are only because of a qualitatively distinguishing passion, lose their resilience; the qualitative expression of difference between opposites is no longer the law for the relation of inwardness to each other in the relation. Inwardness is lacking, and to that extent the relation does not exist or the relation is an inert cohesion. . . . Instead of the relation of inwardness another relation supervenes: the opposites do not relate to each other but stand, as it were, and carefully watch each other, *and this tension is actually the termination of the relation.* (*TA*, 78)

Unlike the passionate individuals of previous eras, whose tense, resilient, and distinct inner lives allowed for qualitative expressions of difference and mutual opposition, members of today's crass society, with inner beings drained of qualitatively distinguishing passions and (thus) collective lives incapable of sustaining difference and opposition, can only stand around, arms folded, like "courteous peers keeping a careful eye on each other" (*TA*, 78). To be a member of crass society, in other words, is to be an agent of surveillance society.

To illustrate this curious feature of modern life, Kierkegaard notes the difference between today's democratic citizen and yesterday's royal subject—a timely comparison in mid-1840s Denmark, when representative government was on the rise and public demand for a national constitution had reached a fever pitch. Unlike the typical royal subject, "who cheerfully does homage to his king and now is embittered by his tyranny," average democratic citizens remain apathetically removed from their sociopolitical surroundings. To be a citizen in the modern era is not to take part in a pluralistic society but, instead, to remain apart from social relations of every sort. No longer passionately engaged in existing forms of human togetherness, the modern citizen is *"an outsider"* looking in and passing judgment on the prospect of human togetherness itself. "The citizen does not relate himself in the relation but is a spectator calculating the problem," Kierkegaard claims. "They do not essentially relate to each other in the relation, but the relation itself has become a problem in which the parties like rivals in a game watch each other instead of relating to each other, and count [*tæller*], as it is said, each other's verbal avowals of relation as a substitute for resolute mutual devotion in the relation" (*TA*, 79; trans. modified).

How are we to understand this asocial game? In their otherwise exhaustive commentary, the editors of *Søren Kierkegaards Skrifter* admit to being flummoxed: "Determining what is meant has not been possible."[2] And yet it is precisely here, in this puzzling reference at the center of Kierkegaard's literary review, that the fundamental insight of his social thought begins to shine through, allowing for a radical rereading of what is arguably among the nineteenth century's most prescient statements on the dilemmas of modern democratic life. In service to this radical rereading, I would like this suggest that there are three ways to interpret Kierkegaard's comparison of modern life to an asocial game. As we shall see, each brings us one step closer to the most rigorous account of chatter in his authorship, but only one allows us to access the conceptual interiors of this account.

The first interpretation extends from chapter 1 of this book, recalling the garrulous barber at the center of Holberg's influential comedy, whose long-winded chatter about his short inland journey is analogous to the "verbal avowals" mentioned above, in which abstract talk about "the relation of inwardness to each other in the relation" becomes a substitute for the development of any such relation. When a crass society becomes a surveillance society, "the relation will not develop, but there is talk [*snakker*] about it," Kierkegaard notes (*TA*, 64). And the social effects of this empty talk are deadening: "It is one thing to save one's life by the enchantment of story-telling as in *A Thousand and One Nights*," he continues, throwing the narrative style of Master Gert into sharp relief. But "it is something else again to shut oneself out from the enchantment of enthusiasm over an idea and the rebirth of passion—by talkativeness [*Snaksomhed*]" (*TA*, 64). In the verbal avowals of the present age, Kierkegaard hears the final gasps of essential culture.

The second interpretation of modernity's asocial game is well-worn by secondary scholars, heavily indebted to the spectral imagery of Kierkegaard's broader social critique, and readily captured in the following excerpt from his literary review: "In this state of indolent laxity, more and more individuals will aspire to be nobodies in order to become the public, that abstract aggregate ridiculously formed by the participant's becoming a third party. That sluggish crowd which understands nothing itself and is unwilling to do anything, that gallery-public, now seeks to be entertained and indulges in the notion that everything anyone does is done so that it may have something to gossip [*at snakke*] about" (*TA*, 94).

We have seen gossip of this sort before. Recall, once more, Holberg's talkative barber, whose outspoken claims against the spreading of rumors are, in fact, the primary topic of town gossip; or the literary reviewers of the present age, whose journalistic skill consists in attending to public gossip and, wherever possible, amplifying it with chatter of their own; or the Hegelian parrots of Kierkegaard's day, whose wagging tongues spread philosophical hearsay throughout Danish culture. Whether we begin with the hapless prattle of deluded barbers, the clever chatter of modern reviewers, or the arrogant windsucking of second-rate scholars, the result is always the same: a suspicious, spiteful, and ever-surveilling rumor culture in which "superiority is kept down by contemptibleness and contemptibleness kept down by itself." According to Kierkegaard, this is "the quittance of nothingness" that allows individuals to become nobodies, nobodies to be abstracted and aggregated into gallery-publics, and gallery-publics to engage in self-indulgent gossip about anything and everything that one of their hollowed-out constituents might say or do. Gossip-mongering of this sort, he concludes, is "the basest kind of leveling, because it always corresponds to the denominator [*Divisor*] in relation to which all are made equal" (*TA*, 95–96).

Miss the numerical rhetoric of this final remark, which in turn recalls the counting, calculating, and aggregating procedures mentioned above, and we miss the third interpretation of modernity's asocial game. When a crass society becomes a surveillance society, communing with others (*at medtælle*) gives way to telling others about community (*at fortælle*), and the latter, in turn, succumbs to something else entirely—a way of living apart from others as well as oneself, in which communing and communicating alike have been reduced to "counting and counting [*tælle og tælle*]" (*TA*, 92). At issue here is neither the displacement of concrete action by vacuous speech (the first interpretation above) nor the reduction of lived experience to idle entertainment (the second interpretation above), but the *underlying numerical structure* of both modern social developments. When surveillance society prevails, individuals begin counting each other's statements, calculating their combined meanings, and aggregating the results, as well as themselves, in an abstract social sum known as the gallery-public. As a totalizing entity, the gallery-public is in turn thought to be logically superior to any and all of its constitutive elements, and thus fit to serve as their denominator—a numerical figure of their total population in terms of which the statistical value of each can be expressed.

With no inward relation to themselves and no outward relation to others, qualitatively distinct individuals become discretely numbered quantities (numerators) of uniform social parts (denominators). In other words, they become *fractions*, from the Latin *fractus*, meaning "broken." In this shift from qualitative distinction to quantitative uniformity, Kierkegaard sees a certain kind of social equality at work and, with it, a troubling new conception of the individual. "The trend today is in the direction of mathematical equality, so that in all classes about so and so many uniformly make one individual," he explains, alluding to the social statistics of the day—specifically, scientific efforts to calculate "the average man" and his equally middling values.[3] "Nowadays we understand that so and so many people make one individual, and in all consistency we compute numbers [*tæller man sig sammen*] (we call it joining together, but that is a euphemism) in connection with the most trivial things," he continues. "For no other reason than to implement a whim, we add a few pieces together [*tæller man sig nogle Stykker sammen*] and do it—that is, we dare to do it" (*TA*, 85; trans. modified; cf. *BOA*, 230–31). To be an individual in previous eras was to be a distinct person, and sometimes even to become a person of great distinction; to be an individual in the present age, however, is to be "a fraction in something utterly trivial" and wholly subject to the era's statistical whims (*TA*, 85).

Chatter is the way of speaking that allows all of this social arithmetic to occur. As the foregoing discussion suggests, it is at once the linguistic entity that individuals count and calculate (quantification), the discursive structure of the gallery-public in which these counts and calculations are amassed (aggregation), and the communicative practice by which individuals-turned-nobodies are further divided from themselves and each other, allowing for statistical expressions of self and society (denomination). Understanding and explaining these mathematical functions, all of which are integral to the chattering count of crass society, are the primary tasks of this chapter.

Educated or Destroyed

In the social arithmetic of modern public life, with its statistical push toward mathematical equality, Kierkegaard saw the conditions of possibility for another, more profound form of egalitarianism. Before delving into his critique of the former, we should consider his development of the latter. And before doing this, we should pause, if only for a moment, to recall the political and cultural circumstances in which Kierkegaard undertook both projects.

In the decade leading up to his literary review of *Two Ages*, absolutism gradually lost its grip on modern Denmark. Democratic elections of town councils began occurring in the mid-1830s; by the early-1840s, the range of representative government had grown to include counties and parishes; and in 1846, the same year in which Kierkegaard published his literary review, farmers in search of land reforms and social equality joined forces with urban liberals in search of a national constitution. Two years later, members of this political coalition, inspired by the European revolutions of 1848, marched to Christiansborg Palace and petitioned the king for a constitution. In the summer of 1849, the king acquiesced, providing Denmark with one of the most inclusive political franchises in the modern world.

While its farmers and politicos were hacking away at absolutism, Denmark's literati were clinging to the aristocratic ideals of the *ancien régime*. In the half-century leading up to the Constitution of 1849—an era of lavish creativity known as "Golden Age Denmark"—learned culture was limited to a narrow but highly influential group of educated elites, many of whom ranked highly in the absolutist bureaucracy and thus found themselves safely encircled by the medieval walls of Copenhagen. With little incentive to challenge royal authorities, and even less cause to leave the city, students, professors, priests, and upper-level civil servants were largely removed from the political transformations of their time.

Among these well-educated urbanites, no one garnered more attention than the Danish Hegelian we discussed in chapter 1: Johan Ludvig Heiberg. In addition to presenting himself as Denmark's leading philosopher, Heiberg saw himself as the nation's foremost poet and playwright. In opposition to mounting demands for freedom of speech and the liberty of the individual, Heiberg called for a society in which members of the public would attend to Golden Age elites in quiet, collective deference. More than constitutional guarantees, he argued, Danish citizens were in need of stricter aesthetic and philosophical imperatives.

Not surprisingly, Heiberg and Kierkegaard disagreed on how best to navigate the public and its problems. Heiberg called for a rigid social hierarchy in which Golden Age elites could regiment and refine the opinions of atomized individuals. In exchange for their deferent attention, he offered members of the public intellectual and cultural tutelage. Kierkegaard was less nostalgic for the *ancien régime*. In place of outmoded aristocratic hierarchies between learned and popular cultures, he encouraged Danish citizens to augment their demand for equal rights with another, more profound sense of egalitarianism. In the abstract social arithmetic of modern public life, Kierkegaard saw the opportunity structure for a renewed and deeply religious sense of essential culture, one free from nostalgia for the aristocratic standards of earlier times but also less encumbered by the statistical sensibilities of modern life. "The bleakness of antiquity was that the man of distinction was what *others could not be*," Kierkegaard explains. "The inspiring aspect [of the modern era] will be that the person who has gained himself religiously is only what *all can be*" (*TA*, 92).

With this emphatic comparison, Kierkegaard pits himself against the intellectual and cultural elitism of Heiberg and his Golden Age disciples. "It will no longer be as it once was, that individuals could look to the nearest eminence for orientation," he argues. "That time is now past. They either must be lost in the dizziness of abstract infinity or be saved infinitely in the essentiality of the religious life." In other words, "individuals have to help themselves, each one individually" (*TA*, 108). With this triangulation of freedom, equality, and responsibility—individual freedom from established figures of authority (be they ruling monarchs or educated elites), unconditional equality before God, and personal responsibility for the development of moral values—Kierkegaard makes a decisive break with educated elites like Heiberg. As Bruce H. Kirmmse well notes, he is "throwing down the gauntlet to all 'educated' political and cultural opinion, espousing a sort of divine egalitarianism in which existing notions of Dannelse [character-forming education] are worthless and in which only the simple integrity of the individual before God—which is available to everyone—has any worth."[4] No one—not even Kierkegaard—had the right to regiment and magisterially refine modern Danish citizens.[5]

By disavowing aristocratic conservatism, Kierkegaard hoped to help average Danish citizens realize their ecumenical promise as modern individuals, namely, "apprehension of the universal in equality before God." And he hoped to help them do so in the midst of modern democratic life, even and especially where the push of social statistics and the pull of mathematical equality were strongest. Rather than attempting to halt or hinder the leveling reciprocity of modern public life, Kierkegaard invites readers to treat it as an "*examen rigorosum*"—a rigorous social examination by means of which "every individual, each one separately, may in turn be religiously educated" (*TA*, 87). The risks of this learning process could not be overstated; but nor could its re-wards. Notice how Kierkegaard develops this point, at once connecting and opposing the religious education of modern individuals to the ab-stract social arithmetic of the present age:

If the individual is not destroyed in the process, he will be educated by this very abstraction and this abstract discipline (in so far as he is not already educated in his inwardness) to be satisfied in the highest religious sense with himself and his relationship to God, will be educated to make up his own mind instead of agreeing with the public, which annihilates all the relative concretions of individuality, to find rest within himself, at ease before God, instead of counting and counting [tælle og tælle]. (TA, 92)

Several of these themes—religious inwardness before God, self-certainty over public opinion, individual repose in the face of social arithmetic—take center stage in the following chapter. What matters here, on the cusp of a radical new reading of Kierkegaard's literary re-view, is his insistence that religious education is implicit in, not de-tached from, modern democratic public culture—the same public cul-ture on which he would also lavish critical attention. As we shall see in parts 2 and 3 of this book, Heidegger and Lacan shared this view of modern life. Both were just as critical of mass society as they were convinced that it entailed its own counter-possibility. In keeping with Kierkegaard's *examen rigorosum*, they believed there was more to mass society than alienation, inauthenticity, and the corruption of mod-ern selves.

Dialectical Fraud

From liquor consumption to suicide rates, the modern era seeks to enu-merate, aggregate, calculate, and statistically encode every aspect of lived experience. What troubles Kierkegaard about this social arith-metic is not the wide range of entities on which it operates, but the narrow habit of mind on which it relies. "If we had statistics on the use of prudence [*Forstand*] from generation to generation as we have them on the consumption of liquor, we would be amazed to see the enormous quantity used these days," he quips. "Not even a suicide these days does away with himself in desperation but deliberates on the step so long and so sensibly [*forstandigt*] that he is strangled by cal-culation [*Forstandighed*], making it a moot point whether or not he can really be called a suicide, in as much as it was the deliberating that took his life. A premeditated suicide he was not, but rather a suicide by means of premeditation" (*TA*, 68–69). In this lethal strand of *Forstandighed*—translations of which range from "sanity" to "reasonableness" to "computation" to "common sense"—Kierkegaard sees the deliberative artistry of the present age at work: "Its technical skill consists in letting matters reach a verdict and decision without ever acting" (*TA*, 69). And in this technical skill, he finds damning evidence of the era's fuzzy math.

In order to grasp the *Forstandighed* of the modern era, the fuzzy math on which it relies, and the chattering count in which both find expression, we must follow a faint yet fascinating trail through Kierkegaard's middle authorship, a trail of critical social thought initially blazed in *Philosophical Fragments*, further developed in *The Concept of Anxiety*, and frequently retraced in his literary review of *Two Ages*—and one which has eluded scholarly comment ever since. On this road less traveled through some of Kierkegaard's most rigorous works, the social arithmetic of the present age merges with its oddly indecisive deliberative skill, and their merger yields unprecedented access to the inner conceptual mechanics of chatter.

The easiest place to pick up this trail is near its end, in another frequently glossed excerpt from Kierkegaard's literary review—an excerpt whose careful rereading is long overdue:

Morality is character; character is something engraved (χαρασσω), but the sea has no character, nor does the sand, nor does abstract common sense [*Forstandighed*], either, for character is inwardness. As energy, immorality is also character. But it is equivocation [*Tvetydighed*] to be neither one nor the other, and it is existential equivocation [*Tvetydighed*] when the qualitative disjunction of these qualities is impaired by a gnawing reflection [*Reflexion*]. An uprising motivated by passion is elemental; a disintegration motivated by equivocation [*Tvetydighedens*] is a quiet and busy sorites going on day and night. . . . No one is carried away to great exploits by the good, no one is rushed into outrageous sin by evil, the one is just as good as the other, and yet for that very reason there is all the more to chatter [*at snakke*] about, for equivocation [*Tvetydigheden*] is titillating and stimulating and has many more words than are possessed by joy over the good and the loathing of evil. (*TA*, 77–78; trans. modified)

In antiquity, *charasso* had literary and economic import. It meant to inscribe documents and to stamp coins. But its primary significance was military. To *charasso* was to sharpen, to make pointed, to furnish with notches or teeth, often resulting in a pointed stake known as a *charax*, which was typically used to fortify the entrenchments of a palisaded camp (*charakōma*). To have character, Kierkegaard suggests, is not just to be stamped, inscribed, and engraved with moral or immoral values, but also to be entrenched, fortified, and thus protected against any attempt to obscure or erode the qualitative distinction between these values. The problem with sands, seas, and abstract common sense is not that they lack existential depth, but that the depths they sustain are too shifting and porous to hold any characterological pales in place.

Hence, the repeated use of *Tvetydighed* above, from the Danish *tvetydig*, meaning *equivocal*. In stressing this term, however, Kierkegaard suggests something more nuanced. As nineteenth-century Danes well knew, *tvetydig* is a calque of the German *zweideutig*, which is itself a composite of the words "two" (*Zwei*) and "interpretation" (*Deutung*)—and thus, as we shall see in part 2 of this book, the lexical source of what Heidegger would later describe as "ambiguity" (*Die Zweideutigkeit*). To be *tvetydig* is, in this sense, to be of *two minds*. When Kierkegaard claims that people who equivocate between good and evil are "neither one nor the other," this is what he means: They are neither entirely good nor entirely evil but, instead, a murky and partial characterological mix of both qualities. When *Tvetydighed* begins to dissolve the qualitative disjunction of good and evil, it does so by reducing their relationship from a dichotomous "either-or" to an indeterminate state between "neither-nor" and "both-and." What once inspired decisive actions, good and evil alike, now elicits only gnawing reflection.

When the distinction between good and evil succumbs to gnawing reflection, the classic law of thought on which it depends also perishes. Yet another key difference between revolutionary culture and its crass grandchild: "The age of revolution is essentially passionate; therefore it has *not nullified* [*hævet*] *the principle of contradiction* and can become either good or evil," Kierkegaard writes. "And whichever way is chosen, the *impetus* of passion is such that the trace of an action making its progress or its taking a wrong direction must be perceptible. It is obliged to make a decision" (*TA*, 66). In contrast, "the present age is essentially a sensible [*forstandige*] age, devoid of passion, and therefore it *has nullified* [*hævet*] *the principle of contradiction*" (*TA*, 97). What agents of revolutionary culture pursued with fierce devotion—difficult choices and decisive actions—members of crass society now use common sense and gnawing reflection to avoid entirely, effectively melding both habits of mind into a doubly *tvetydig* mode of thought: "The creative omnipotence implicit in the passion of absolute disjunction that leads the individual resolutely to make up his mind is transformed into the extensity of prudence-reflection [*Forstands-Reflexionens*]" (*TA*, 97).

When *Forstandighed* and *Reflexion* intersect, resulting in *Forstands-Reflexionens*, the principle of contradiction is not simply nullified. As Kierkegaard is careful to suggest with his emphatic use of the Danish *hævet* above—from the verb *at hæve*, meaning *to break off* and *to raise up*, *to eliminate* and *to elevate*—the principle of contradiction is at once canceled and sustained in the present age. In other words, it is *sublated*. That *hæve* is also the root of *ophæve*—the same verb that Kierkegaard, as we saw in the previous chapter, uses to deride his Hegelian peers, insisting that they "make a big to-do [*gjøre saa mange Ophævelser*] over 'nothing'"—further suggests that the sublation in question is structurally akin to the well-known *Aufhebung* of Hegelian dialectics. Two years after this critique appeared, in the spring of 1846, when his literary review of *Two Ages* was ready for publication, this suggestion had become a pronouncement: "Hegelian philosophy sublates [*hævet*] the law of contradiction" (*CUP* 1, 304; trans. modified). All of which suggests that, when Kierkegaard bemoans existential equivocation, gnawing reflection, and their contribution to abstract common sense, it is their underlying Hegelian dialectic that he means to indict. In the prudence of the present age, individual and collective passions for absolute disjunction are sublated in *"a tension of reflection [Reflexions] that lets everything remain and yet has transformed the whole of existence into an equivocation"*—in short, *"a dialectical fraud"* (*TA*, 77).

In order to circumvent this dialectical fraud, we must first detect its operation. But this is no mean feat. "Force can be used against rebellion, punishment awaits demonstrable counterfeiting, but dialectical secretiveness is difficult to root out," Kierkegaard warns. "It takes relatively more acute ears to track down the muffled steps of reflection stealing down the furtive corridors of ambiguity and equivocation" (*TA*, 80). In search of clues, he recalls the modern penchant for social equality, integrating his earlier critiques of leveling reciprocity, social arithmetic, and negative community into a single, coherent argument against its pursuit: "The dialectic of the present age is oriented to equality, and its most logical implementation, albeit abortive, is leveling, the negative unity of the negative mutual reciprocity of individuals." Again, Kierkegaard is struck by the mathematics of this process: "Just as one calculates [*beregner*] the diagonal in a parallelogram of forces, so also can the law of leveling be calculated [*beregne*], for the individual who levels others is himself carried along, and so on" (*TA*, 86; trans. modified). But again, calculations of this sort are difficult to make, especially in times of dialectical secretiveness: "Leveling is a quiet, mathematical, abstract enterprise that avoids all agitation," he reminds readers. "If an insurrection at its peak is so like a volcanic explosion that a person cannot hear himself speak, leveling at its peak is like a deathly stillness in which a person can hear himself breathe, a deathly stillness in which nothing can rise up but everything sinks down into it, impotent" (TA, 84). Secretiveness, muffled steps, furtive corridors, deathly stillness—all suggest that the fuzzy math of modernity's prudence, reflection, equivocation, leveling, and the like is as difficult to discern as it is to describe. And yet, as we shall see, this is precisely what Kierkegaard allows us to do with his critique of the present age.

Primitive Accumulation

If the dialectical fraud of modern life consists of quiet social arithmetic, it culminates in an almost lethal state of individual weakness. And this, according to Kierkegaard, is its greatest numerical ruse. In the negative unity of crass society, he sees "a union of people who separately are weak." More precisely, he sees "an evasion, a dissipation, an illusion, whose dialectic is as follows: as it strengthens individuals, it vitiates them; it strengthens by numbers, by sticking together, but from the ethical point of view this is a weakening" (TA, 106). Whatever else the dialectical fraud of modernity entails, its structure remains, at root, *mathematical*. And the ideological expression of this structure is a shared belief that society strengthens individuals by numbers.

To illustrate the error of these numerical ways, Kierkegaard recalls the historic shift from premodern logics of opinion formation, which consistently empowered the few over the many, to more recent "large-scale surveys" of public opinion, which now purport to upend this traditional social hierarchy: "Formerly the ruler, the man of excellence, the men of prominence each had his own view; the others were so settled and unquestioning that they did not dare or could not have an opinion. Now everyone can have an opinion, but there must be a lumping together numerically in order to have it. Twenty-five signatures to the silliest notion is an opinion" (TA, 106). Just as twenty-five signatures do not constitute an opinion, holding the same opinion as twenty-five people is not the same as acting on it—individually or collectively. Nor does chatting about this opinion bring anyone closer to decisive action. Just the opposite, in fact, which is why Kierkegaard finds "the garrulous experience of common sense" so dangerous.

When public opinion becomes the subject of chatter, it does not inspire concrete action; instead, it suspends the human capacity for action in the abstract experience of common sense, thereby eliciting more chatter, further suspensions, and so on. Once this garrulous cycle is underway, the prospect of decisive action becomes increasingly remote, the vitality of public life begins to recede, and the social arithmetic of the modern era sets in. Notice how Kierkegaard depicts this process: "Certain phrases and observations circulate among people, partly true and sensible, yet devoid of vitality, but there is no hero, no lover, no thinker, no knight of faith, no great humanitarian, no person in despair to vouch for their validity by having primitively experienced them. Just as in our business transactions we long to hear the ring of real coins after the whisper of paper money, so we today long for a little primitivity" (TA, 74–75).[6]

In the meantime, our capacity for decisive speech and action withers. Bold talk becomes "a profitable industry," in which we "fabricate and make up and renovate and buy up in bulk old and new witticisms." And daring conduct follows suit:

A young man today would scarcely envy another his capacities or his skill or the love of a beautiful girl or his fame, no, but he would envy him his money. Give me money, the young man will say, and I will be all right. And the young man will not do anything rash, he will not do anything he has to repent of, he will not have anything for which to reproach himself, but he will die in the illusion that if he had had money, then he would have lived, then he certainly would have done something great. (TA, 75)

In word and deed alike, the dialectic of modernity is not anchored in primitive experience but adrift in primitive accumulation. Strength in numbers—of people, of opinions, of witticisms, of financial resources—this is the era's false consciousness and, as Kierkegaard is careful to suggest throughout his literary review, the origin of its fuzzy math.

With no capacity for decisive conduct, the leveling of all becomes the life of each. In place of qualitative disjunctions underwritten by the principle of contradiction, modern democratic subjects learn to live with and within a dialectical flux of anything and everything that accumulates incessantly but ultimately amounts to nothing: "a little resolution and a little situation, a little prudence and a little courage, a little probability and a little faith, a little action and a little incident." All of which, when taken together, amounts to "a muddled confusion of everything with everything" (TA, 67, 131). Much as the either/or between good and evil slips into a liminal state between neither/nor and both/and, where "the one is just as good as the other, and yet for that very reason there is all the more to chatter [*at snakke*] about," the meaning of modern life becomes completely undecidable and, for this reason, wholly subject to the era's endless talk—so much so that Kierkegaard himself struggles to determine whether it consists in "a garrulous continuation or a continued garrulity [*en snaksom Fortsættelse eller en fortsat Snaksomhed*], a participial or infinitive phrase in which the subject must be understood or, more correctly, cannot be located at all because, as the grammarians say, the meaning does not make it clear for the simple reason that it lacks meaning" (*TA*, 67).

What it lacks in meaning, the chatter of modern life makes up for in variety. "Talkativeness [*Snaksomheden*] gains in extensity: it chatters [*at snakke*] about anything and everything and continues incessantly" (*TA*, 97). Even with "a great deal to chatter [*at snakke*] about," it never stops searching for more to discuss. "One who chatters [*snakker*] presumably does chatter [*snakker*] about something, since the aim is to find something to chatter [*at snakke*] about," Kierkegaard quips (*TA*, 99). More, more, more—and for no other reason than the pursuit of more—this is how chatter operates in the modern world. And with damning numerical effects on our ability to converse: "The less ideality and the more externality, the more the conversation [*Samtalen*] will tend to become a trivial enumerating [*Opramsen*] and name-dropping, references to persons with "absolutely reliable" private information on what this one and that one, mentioned by name, have said, etc., a garrulous [*snaksom*] confiding of what he himself wants or does not want, his plans, what he would have said on that occasion, what girl he is courting, why he is still not ready to get married, etc." (*TA*, 99; trans. modified). Suffice it to say: When conversation succumbs to chatter, talking with others (*at tale*) becomes a tallying of their opinions (*at tælle*). Public gossip and personal confession alike are enumerated and exchanged in trifling yet extensive lists, all of which seem to end with the same refusal to conclude: *et cetera*.

Crass society may begin in a state of subtraction, where subjective passions and shared ideas are both absent from lived experience, but its operational logic quickly moves in the opposite direction, increasingly relying on addition instead. And yet, as Kierkegaard is careful to insist, the social arithmetic of modern life not so simple. For in the present age, "all adding is subtracting, and the more one adds the more one subtracts" (*TA*, 103). So also when it comes to chatter: the more one gossips about anything and everything, the further one strays from essential conversation; and the further one strays from essential conversation, the less coherent one's speech and action become:

> The same man can say the most contradictory things, can coolly express something that, coming from him, is the bitterest satire on his own life. The remark itself is very sensible [*forstandig*], would go over very well at a meeting as part of a discussion that fabricates something in much the same way as paper is fabricated from rags. But the sum-total of these comments does not amount [*tilsammen*] to personal human discourse [*Tale*] as can be carried on even by the simplest man who is limited in subject [*tale*] but nevertheless does speak [*taler*]. (*TA*, 103–4; trans. modified)

As more *tælle* becomes less *tale*, the tragic irony of the present age becomes readily apparent: When the principle of contradiction succumbs to the dialectical fraud of *Forstands-Reflexionens*, and the chattering count of modernity begins, the only qualitative disjunctions that remain are those which divide individuals from themselves. Unlike "that constant number three Socrates speaks of so beautifully, which would rather suffer anything than become a number four or even a very large round number" composed of "all sorts of things," members of crass society are content to become anything and everything other themselves, and thus nothing at all, if only doing so will allow them to enjoy strength in numbers (*TA*, 97). But the strength they enjoy by sticking together is no greater than that of paper fabricated from rags.

What interests Kierkegaard about this remarkable tolerance for self-contradiction is neither the mass of calculating nobodies it yields nor the massive nothingness in which their calculations culminate, but the numerical sleight of hand by which the former seems to disappear into the latter. Of primary concern to him in his fierce attack on the social arithmetic of modern life is not the mathematical process of addition, whereby local singularities (quantities) are combined into more general orders of significance (sums), but the *numerical rhetoric of chatter* by which these more general orders of significance are made to appear superior to any and all of their discrete elements. Which brings us to the central question of his 1846 literary review, a question which has gone unanswered since its publication: How, exactly, does the collective no-thing of the present age—the gallery-public—come to seem greater than the sum of its constitutive no-ones?

In order to begin answering this question, we must first rephrase it, paying special attention to the way in which Kierkegaard anticipates its asking. Recall, once more, his repeated use of *Tvetydighed* in the passage with which this discussion began. As we have seen, the Danish *tvety-*

dig is a calque of the German *zweideutig*, meaning "equivocal." In German, the opposite of *zweideutig* is *eindeutig*, meaning "clear," "distinct," and "conclusive"—in brief, "unequivocal." As the prefixes *ein-* and *zwei-* well indicate, however, the structure of the relationship between these German terms is, in essence, *numerical*. To be *zweideutig* is to be of two (*Zwei*) minds, but to be *eindeutig* is to be of only one (*Eins*). And this is where things get interesting, for beyond *zweideutig*, there is no "*dreideutig*." Instead, we find the German *mehrdeutig*, whose prefix signals an indeterminate multiple: "more" (*mehr*). And beyond *mehrdeutig* we find something even stranger: *vieldeutig*, the prefix of which simply means "a lot." But the simplicity of this meaning belies the complexity of its being. To be "a lot" is to be at once singular and plural, and thus qualitatively distinct from either numerical category. If something is *vieldeutig*, it is a collective noun—or at least akin to one. It is impossible to understand Kierkegaard's use of *Tvetydighed* apart from this increasingly ambiguous count: *one* interpretation, *two* interpretations, *more* interpretations, *a lot* of interpretations. Which is another, more precise way of asking the question above: How is it possible for a count of any sort to proceed from a single unit (one) to an increasing multiple (two and more) to a collective entity (a lot)? It is easy to track the *quantitative* shift from one unit to two or more of the same kind; but when, exactly, does the *qualitative* shift from "more" to "a lot" occur?

Never, Kierkegaard claims. No quantity, however great, is sufficient to constitute a qualitative shift of this sort. Hence, each of the foregoing examples: no amount of public commentary is sufficient to constitute a personal pronouncement; no amount of gossip is sufficient to constitute a conversation; no amount of money is sufficient to constitute a hero; no amount of wit is sufficient to constitute a primitive experience; no amount of signatures is sufficient to constitute a public opinion; no amount of good and evil is sufficient to constitute someone's character; no amount of deliberative artistry is sufficient to constitute a decisive action; no amount of social statistics is sufficient to constitute essential culture; no amount of verbal avowals is sufficient to constitute a devoted relationship; no amount of common sense is sufficient to constitute a pivotal decision; no amount of pointless externality is sufficient to constitute passionate inwardness; and no combination of any of the above—"a little resolution and a little situation, a little prudence and a little courage, a little probability and a little faith, a little action and a little incident"—is sufficient to make a meaningful life in the modern era.

This is precisely why Kierkegaard, in the middle of the passage with which we began this discussion, characterizes the *Tvetydighed* of the present age as "a quiet and busy sorites going on day and night." With a single word, *sorites*, from the Greek *soros*, meaning "heap," he cuts to the ideological core of modernity's troubling social arithmetic. Behind the collective habit of mind he bemoans as *Forstandighed* and the cumulative mode of speech he derides as *Snaksomhed* is the same numerical paradox—a paradox that has stalked Western thought since antiquity, only to overtake it in the modern era: *the paradox of the heap*.

The Problem with Hereditary Sin

Eubulides of Miletus was known for his paradoxes. Some, like his paradox of the liar, quickly gained fame: "If someone says she is lying, is she telling the truth?" Others, like his paradox of the horns, were rightly forgotten: "What you have not lost, you must have. But you have not lost horns. Therefore, you must have horns." Others still, like his paradox of the heap, gradually seeped into Western thought: "Does a single grain of sand constitute a heap? No. Do two grains of sand constitute a heap? No. But a heap of sand is going to appear sooner or later, so where do you draw the line?"

Kierkegaard's 1846 description of the present age as "a quiet but busy sorites going on day and night" was informed by years of reflection on the paradox of the heap. Consider, for instance, his 1844 critique of long-winded attempts to prove the existence of God: "So long as I am holding on to the demonstration (that is, continue to be one who is demonstrating), the existence does not emerge, if for no other reason than that I am in the process of demonstrating it, but when I let go of the demonstration, the existence is there," he explains in *Philosophical Fragments*. This act of letting go may seem like a "diminutive moment [*lille Øieblik*]," especially when compared to the lengthy demonstration from which it breaks, but it also requires careful consideration, since it is structurally akin to a religious "*leap* [*Spring*]." Only when suspended by a leap of faith can a demonstration of the existence of God succeed, for "the existence itself emerges from the demonstration by a leap" (*PF*, 42–43).

Lest anyone miss his point, Kierkegaard goes on to recite a quipping exchange between the Stoic Chrysippus and the Skeptic Carneades:

Chrysippus was trying to determine a qualitative limit in the progressive or retrogressive operation of a sorites. Carneades could not grasp the point at which the quality actually made its appearance. Chrysippus told him that one could pause for a moment in the reckoning [*Tællingen holde et Øieblik inde*], and then, then—then one could understand [*forstaae*] it better. But Carneades replied: Please, do not let me disturb you; you may not only pause but may even lie down and go to sleep—it will not make any difference. When you wake up, we shall begin again where you stopped. (*PF*, 43; trans. modified)

In order to make sense of this anecdote, we must retranslate its central phrase. To *Tællingen holde et Øieblik inde* is not just to "pause for a moment in the reckoning." More precisely, it means *to stop the count in an instant*. At issue in this exchange between Chrysippus and Carneades is not the qualitative effect of the former's argument but its underlying mathematical structure. Or, at least, this is how Kierkegaard sees it, as indicated in an earlier draft of this anecdote, beneath which he cites W. G. Tennemann's rendition of Carneades' final remark: "As far as I am concerned, he said, you may not only rest but sleep, too. What good does it do you? There will follow another who wakes you with the question: 'At what number do you stop?'" None of this numerical rhetoric was lost on Kierkegaard: "In other words, Carneades disputed the thesis that two magnitudes are just as great as an equal third—if one is going to draw a conclusion from it. He is clearly right about this, for the thesis is only a tautology, since three mathematical magnitudes that are absolutely equal are not three but are the same magnitude" (*PF*, 191).

It was here, in his first sustained commentary on the numerical structure of sorites reasoning, that Kierkegaard began to develop his critique of mathematical equality in the present age. And it was in the midst of this development that he also noticed the kinship between ancient rhetorical techniques of sorites reasoning and the modern speculative practice of dialectical thought. Note, for instance, another argument he develops in *Philosophical Fragments*. When attempting to distinguish contemporaneous disciples of certain philosophical movements from their later-day counterparts, Kierkegaard argues, it is easy to slip into fruitless dialectical debates about the meaning of "contemporary" and, soon thereafter, into pointless sorites reasoning:

A sorites would eventuate only if to be contemporary [*Samtidig*, literally "at the same time"] were made dialectical in the bad sense [*dialectisk i slet Forstand*], by showing, for example, that in a certain sense [*Forstand*] no one at all was contemporary, for no one could be contemporary with all the factors, or by asking when the contemporaneity ceased and when the noncontemporaneity began, whether there was not a *confinium* [border territory] of haggling in which the talkative understanding [*pratende Forstand*] could say: to a certain degree etc. etc. All such inhuman profundity leads to nothing or in our time may lead to being considered genuine speculative profundity, since the despised sophism has become the miserable secret of genuine speculation (only the devil knows how it happened), and what antiquity regarded negatively—"to a certain degree" (the mocking toleration that mediates everything without making petty distinctions)—has become the positive, and what antiquity called the positive, the passion for distinctions, has become foolishness. (*PF*, 90–91; trans. modified)

Like the grinding social arithmetic of leveling reciprocity, which at once relies on and results in "the garrulous experience of common sense," the dialectical fraud of sorites reasoning finds expression in a talkative, haggling *Forstand* that continually seeks to reduce passionate human distinctions to meaningless degrees of separation.

If it seems like Kierkegaard is moving fast, it is because he is. But not without purpose: "We shall be as brief as possible, for we are speaking not historically but algebraically, and we have no desire to divert or fascinate anyone with the enchantments of multiplication" (*PF*, 91). Again, the original Danish is revealing: *Vi tale jo ikke historisk, men algebraisk, og ønske ikke at adsprede eller bedaare Nogen ved Mangfoldighedens Tryllerier.* To speak algebraically about sorites reasoning (*at tale algebraisk*) is not to participate in its algebraic count of blurred distinctions (*algebraiske tal*) but, instead, to break its garrulous dialectical spell on the diversity of lived experience (*Tryllerier* deriving from *trylle*, meaning "to do magic," and *Mangfoldighedens* meaning, quite literally, "manyfoldedness"). To demystify the sorites of the present age is not just to halt its tedious quantitative progression from one degree of separation to the next, but also to reawaken the ancient passion for qualitative distinctions of every sort—the same passion for distinctions that Kierkegaard, as we have seen, frequently bemoaned as lost to modernity, especially in the mid-1840s.

From ancient Greek thinkers to modern speculative philosophers, Kierkegaard detects the same intellectual wager: At some point in the quantitative development of a sorites argument, they venture, a qualitative shift in the matter at hand will occur. As the foregoing illustrations suggest, Kierkegaard was unwilling to join in this gamble. This became abundantly clear a few days after *Philosophical Fragments* appeared, when *The Concept of Anxiety* was published. As its convoluted subtitle suggests, *The Concept of Anxiety* is a sustained reflection on the Christian notion of hereditary sin. Fittingly, the book opens with a radical reconception of "the first sin." And crucial for our purposes, it does so by revealing the fuzzy math of the sorites reasoning that informs dogmatic accounts of this key moment in Christian lore:

That the *first* sin signifies something different from *a* sin (i.e., a sin like many others), something different from *one* sin (i.e., no. 1 in relation to no. 2), is quite obvious. The first sin constitutes the nature of the quality: the first sin is the sin. This is the secret of the first, and is an offense to abstract common sense [*abstrakte Forstandighed*], which maintains that one time amounts to nothing but many times amounts to something, which is preposterous, since many times signifies either that each particular time is just as much as the first or that all of the times, when added together [*tilsammen*], are not nearly as much. It is therefore a superstition when it is maintained in logic that through a continued quantification a new quality is brought forth. (*CA*, 30)

Not surprisingly, Kierkegaard has Hegel in mind. He even calls him out by name in the next sentence. But he also qualifies this indictment with a footnote, positioning Hegel in a broader tradition of misguided thought. From Greek sophists to German idealists, clever thinkers have convinced each other that new qualities can emerge by way of quantitative determination. And they continue to do so, Kierkegaard notes in a particularly jabbing passage:

It is indeed a logical and ethical heresy to wish to give the appearance that sinfulness in a man determines itself quantitatively until at last, through a *generatio aequivoca* [descent without mating], it brings forth the first sin in a man. But this does not take place any more than Trop, who by being a master in the service of quantitative determination, could thereby attain a degree in jurisprudence. Let mathematicians and astronomers save themselves if they can with infinitely disappearing minute magnitudes, but in life itself this does not help a man to obtain his examination papers. (*CA*, 31)

As the English translators of this passage well note, Trop was a popular character in one of J. L. Heiberg's vaudeville plays, where he is depicted as a perpetual student of jurisprudence, but one always on the verge of receiving his law degree. "I can at any time obtain a testimonial to the fact that I have almost been close to taking my law examination," Trop hilariously declares at one point in the play (quoted in *CA*, 233, n. 21). Hilarious because, if time spent studying jurisprudence were sufficient to constitute a Juris Doctor, preparing for one's law exam would be equivalent to taking it, and the latter the same as passing it. The only distinction between each of these momentous achievements would be its *numerical position* in the broader sequence of events, or, a Kierke-gaard snarls, "its serial number" (*CA*, 31).

Reasoning such as Trop's more closely resembles myth than logic. And its mode of speech more closely resembles small talk than serious dialogue. Kierkegaard is explicit: "When the understanding [*Forstanden*] takes to the mythical, the outcome is seldom more than small talk [*Passiar*]" (*CA*, 32). Notice how this pointed philosophical critique emerges from the logical warren of his earlier statement on hereditary sin, hooking into his broader critique of chatter-infused *Forstandighed*:

Sin comes into the world as the sudden, i.e., by a leap [*Springet*]; but this leap also posits the quality, and since the quality is posited, the leap in that very moment [*Øieblik Springet*] is turned into the quality and is presupposed by the quality and the quality by the leap. To the understanding [*Forstanden*], this is an offense; *ergo* it is a myth. As a compensation, the understanding invents its own myth, which denies the leap and explains the circle as a straight line, and now everything proceeds quite naturally. The understanding chatters [*snakker*] fantastically about man's state prior to the fall, and, in the course of this small talk [*Passiarens*], the projected innocence is changed little by little into sinfulness, and so there it is. The lecture of the understanding may on this occasion be compared with the counting rhyme [*Børneremse*] in which children delight; one-nis-ball, two-nis-balls, etc., up to nine-nis-balls, and tennis balls. (*CA*, 32; trans. modified)

In *Philosophical Fragments*, Kierkegaard suggests that the best way to undermine a sorites argument is to halt its quantitative progression from premise to premise, or, as he specifies, to stop its count in an instant (*Tællingen holde et Øieblik inde*). Embracing this diminutive moment (*lille Øjeblik*), he claims, is equivalent to a leap of faith (*Spring*). Here, in *The Concept of Anxiety*, he takes this argument a giant step further, integrating its key terms into a broader conceptual opposition between the sudden leap of a new quality into existence (*Øieblik Springet*)—an existential event he later dubs "the qualitative leap" (*det qualitative Spring*)—and the chattering, nonsensical count of the understanding (*Forstandighed*), which relies on the fuzzy math of sorites reasoning to argue that qualitative change issues from quantitative accumulation. Nothing could be further from the truth, Kierkegaard concludes. Just as one cannot count tennis balls into existence, no quantity, however abundant, is sufficient to constitute a new quality. Any claim to the contrary is either child's play (*Børneremse*) or, worse still, small talk (*Passiar*).

And yet, as we have seen, modern democratic subjects continue to believe there is "strength in numbers." If the contradictions inherent in this belief go unnoticed by ordinary citizens and speculative philosophers alike, it is because all are prone to become "thoughtlessly embroiled in noisy chatter [Snak] about one or another imposing, prodigious idea." Instead of striking out on their own in search of essential culture, "they unite in an unshakable faith that in union there is strength, a faith as marvelous as that of the alehouse keeper who sold his beer for a penny less than he paid for it and still counted on a profit, 'for it is the *quantity* that does it'" (CA, 67–68; trans. modified). Foolishness of this sort, backed by the fuzzy math of sorites reasoning and bolstered by the small talk of mass society, is precisely what Kierkegaard derides as "the garrulous experience of common sense"—a numerical delusion so widespread that "no one gives it a second thought" (CA, 68; trans. modified). No one, that is, save Kierkegaard.

P⊋{{*n*+1},{∅}}

At the center of *Tvetydighed* is the Danish verb *tyde*, meaning "to interpret." And at the center of its German prototype *Zweideutigkeit* is the verb *deuten*, also meaning "to interpret." *Tyde* and *deuten* both derive from the same Proto-Germanic root, *þiudijaną*, which in turn seems to have resulted from the collective noun *people* (**þeudō*) intermingling with a series of collectivizing verbs, particularly *to notice, to hearken*, and *to regard in a friendly manner* (**tew*). To *þiudijaną* was not just to interpret others. It meant to connect, engage, associate, and join with them. In addition to making assessments, it involved forming attachments. In this sense, *þiudijaną* was at once the operation and the result of coming together as a group, a collective, a community.

Somewhere along the way, as the Proto-Germanic *þiudijaną* careened toward the modern Danish *Tvetydighed*, communal life became a counting game. When Kierkegaard derides the public as an "abstract aggregate," it is this counting game that he means to indict. In modern democratic public culture, he sees neither groups, nor collectivities, nor even communities. Where organic forms of human togetherness once thrived, yielding qualitative disjunctions of every stripe, a lifeless quantitative accumulation of human equivocations now prevails, resulting in an abstract numerical mass that, through the optics of sorites reasoning, somehow manages to appear greater than the sum of its parts.

In keeping with the rest of his prescient 1846 critique of the present age, Kierkegaard's depiction of the public as an "abstract aggregate" was informed by subtle and sustained reflections on the underlying numerical structure of this phenomenon. Nowhere is this more apparent, or more apparently overlooked, than in the paragraphs leading up to his well-known depiction of modern public life. Reading these paragraphs anew, in light of the foregoing analysis, is the final task of this chapter.

Kierkegaard begins by defining the public as "an all-encompassing something that is nothing." Of particular concern to him is the tension between "something" and "nothing" in this abstract aggregate. As he goes on to explain, the public is "a colossal something" and, simultaneously, "a monstrous nonentity." It is "the entity that is supposed to include everything" and, paradoxically, "an abstract void and vacuum." Or, as Kierkegaard quickly summarizes, repeating himself for good measure, the public is "all and nothing" (*TA*, 91, 93). What are we to make of these apparently conflicting attributes? How can the public be something and nothing, an all-encompassing colossus and a nonexistent monstrosity?

At first glance, Kierkegaard seems to assuage this difficulty. The public is all-encompassing and nonexistent because it includes "all the people together," but only when they behave as "unsubstantial individuals" (*TA*, 91). If the public can be something and nothing simultaneously, it is because it is comprised of somebodies-turned-nobodies. But there is more to its "all and nothing" than meets the eye. In addition to all of the somebodies-turned-nobodies in a given era, the public includes something else, something in excess of this totality—a surplus of sorts that causes it to continue counting but also, somehow, amounts to "nothing." Again, Kierkegaard is thinking mathematically. When he claims that the public is "all and nothing," he means *the public = all + nothing*.

Notice how this equation takes shape in his literary review. "Little by little this public increases its numbers," gradually approaching the sum of all somebodies-turned-nobodies in a given era (*TA*, 136). Even after calculating this social sum, however, the public is forced to continue counting, for there is still something more for it to count, a remainder of sorts that requires further calculation but ultimately amounts to "nothing." In this sense, the public cannot help but outnumber its own totalizing count. On this point, Kierkegaard is outspoken: "The public is a corps, outnumbering all the people together [*Publikum er et Corps, talrigere end alle Folk tilsammen*]"—to such an extent that "even all the nations assembled together at one time and even all the souls in eternity are not as numerous [*talrige*] as the public" (*TA*, 91, 101). It is easy to account for the public's running tally of somebodies-turned-nobodies. It has the structure of an expansive set: {$n+1$}. But how are we to understand the supernumerary function of the public's count, that aspect of its numerical structure which exceeds the social aggregate {$n+1$} by adding "nothing" to the public's "all"?

Recall Aristotle's work on substance (*ousia*), notably his argument that wholes are greater than the sum of their parts. "In all things which have a plurality of parts, and which are not a total aggregate [*soros*] but a whole [*holon*] of some sort distinct from the parts, there is some cause of unity," he contends (*Met.*, 1045a). To discover this cause of unity is to discover that "in virtue of which the matter is a definite thing"—namely, "the substance of the thing." In hopes of clarifying the difference between the unity of a whole (*holos*) and the totality of an aggregate (*soros*), Aristotle invites readers to consider the difference between a single syllable (*ba* is his example) and the letters of which it is composed (in this case, *b* and *a*). "The syllable is some particular thing; not merely the letters, vowel and consonant, but something else besides." And this "something else besides" is just that: not another element of the thing in question but "the primary cause of its existence" (*Met.*, 1041b).

By defining the public as "all and nothing," Kierkegaard suggests that, in addition to all of the somebodies-turned-nobodies in a given era, the public is comprised of *something else besides*—a something else which is nothing at all but nevertheless extends its count beyond any given social aggregate, thereby causing the public to outnumber its own running tally. To be sure, this something-qua-nothing exceeds the total aggregation of somebodies-turned-nobodies in a given era. But it does not escape the counting procedure by which this abstract aggregate is formed. The something-qua-nothing that the public adds to its collection of somebodies-turned-nobodies is not separate from but *subject to* the mathematical operation by which it arrives at this social sum. In this sense, the "nothing" added to its "all" is not a distinct substance that causes the public to exist as a *holos*; rather, it is another unsubstantial element in the already vacuous count that defines it as a *soros*, which is to say, a *heap*.

This is why Kierkegaard insists, again and again, that the public is not a particular thing, much less a unified whole. "The public is not a people, not a generation, not one's age, not a congregation, not an association, not some particular persons, for these are what they are only by being concretions," he stresses in his literary review. Instead, it is a "mirage," a "phantom," a "fairytale," a "nonentity," an "abstraction," a "vacuum," a "void" (*TA*, 90–93). All of which suggests that, when Kierkegaard derides modern democratic public culture, he is not bemoaning life in a new communal whole but signaling the emergence a new hole in communal life itself. What appears to be a novel form of collective life is, in fact, a further subtraction from its already depleted state, the result of which is not a new community but, as Kierkegaard plainly states, a "negative community" (*TA*, 90). Plainly stated, because, much to his frustration, this social void remains hidden from most of its modern inhabitants. In order to determine how this concealment occurs, and the role of chattering common sense in its continuation, we must finish what Kierkegaard started, fully excavating the numerical structure of modern public life.

If the "all" in "all and nothing" refers to the total aggregation of somebodies-turned-nobodies in a given era, citizens of nations and souls in eternity alike, how does the addition of "nothing" to this calculation allow the public to outnumber its result? And what, exactly, is this supernumerary element that somehow counts for nothing? If the public outnumbers its own totalizing count, it might be because, in addition to this count, *the public includes itself.* If this were true, the fuzzy math of "all and nothing" would be obvious: the public would be equivalent to $\{n+1\}$ plus the public itself, which is to say, nothing at all—an abstract categorical surplus that, strictly speaking, "does not exist." In which case, it would amount to an abnormal set—namely, a collection of entities that includes itself as one of its members. To avoid "illegitimate totalities" of this sort, twentieth-century mathematicians would eventually develop the following axiom: "Whatever involves *all* of a collection must not be one of the collection."[7] Kierkegaard would have welcomed this prohibition against "illegitimate totalities," and he might have extended its jurisdiction to include the gallery-public, but his 1846 literary review predated it by more than half a century, so he had to develop another line of attack.

Channeling Aristotelian thought and anticipating modern set theory, Kierkegaard advances the following argument: If the public appears greater than the sum of its parts, it is not because it amounts to a substantial whole, but because it includes an indeterminate "something else" in its already vacuous count, thereby exceeding its sum of "unsubstantial individuals," but only by *one number*. In this sense, the expansive social set $\{n+1\}$ is not equivalent to the public but among its proper subsets. All of the somebodies-turned-nobodies in a given era are included in the public, but the public also includes something else—a something else which is paradoxically more and less than all of them combined. By what number, then, does the public exceed this proper subset? Because it amounts to "nothing," the number by which the public exceeds this social sum can only be *zero*. If the public = all + nothing, and the "all" in this formulation refers to the expansive set {*n*+1}, the addition of "nothing" to this calculation does not change its end result. Only in the present age, when the fuzzy math of sorites reasoning infuses the empty talk of mass society, empowering "the garrulous experience of common sense" over every other mode of existence, does {*n*+1}+0 appear greater than {*n*+1}.

But the fuzzy math of modern life is not so simple. When the public adds "nothing" to its running tally of "all," it surpasses this total aggregation by *an excess of one that amounts to zero*. In this sense, the number by which it exceeds all of the somebodies-turned-nobodies in a given era is neither one nor zero but, instead, *a forming-into-one-of-zero*. "Mirage," "phantom," "fairytale," "nonentity," "abstraction," "vacuum," "void," and "nothing" are all formations of this sort. Each is a proper name sutured to something purely indeterminate: *the being* (one) *of nothingness* (zero).

If the "all" of Kierkegaard's "all and nothing" is equivalent to the expansive set {*n*+1}, its corresponding "nothing" is equivalent to what Alain Badiou would later theorize as the empty set {Ø}.[8] Together, these two sets constitute the public, allowing us to issue a precise mathematical definition of this modern social phenomenon: $P \supsetneq \{\{n+1\},\{\varnothing\}\}$. Which reads: As "all and nothing," the public is a proper superset comprised of two equally proper subsets—one including all of the somebodies-turned-nobodies in a given era, and another including just one entity, an entity which is actually not one and thus more closely resembles the one of a nonentity, the supernumerary trace of something which, relative to the public's "all," amounts to "nothing."

That Kierkegaard often widens the public's already expansive subset {*n*+1} to include everything, in addition to everyone, is crucial in this context. Only when the "all" of modern public life shifts from everyone to everything does the meaning of its corresponding "nothing," and thus the significance of the empty set {Ø}, become apparent. As Kierkegaard sees it, the jurisdiction of the public's count is not limited to citizens of nations and souls in eternity. As "all-encompassing," the public includes beings of every sort. What begins as the sum of everyone, quickly becomes a running tally of everything. Again, Kierkegaard is explicit: "The public becomes the entity that is supposed to include everything" (*TA*, 91). And it is precisely here, in this shift from everyone to everything, that the public's "all" becomes entangled with a lingering "nothing." For if its counting procedure extends to *everything*, then the only thing which eludes its totalizing grasp is *nothing*. Beyond the public's count there is nothing because, in the public, everything is counted.

Hence the mathematical formulation above: $P \supseteq \{\{n+1\},\{\emptyset\}\}$. The "nothing" of the public's empty subset $\{\emptyset\}$ is not included in the "all" of its expansive subset $\{n + 1\}$. Just the opposite: The nothing named by $\{\emptyset\}$ is excluded from the everything contained in $\{n+1\}$. In keeping with Kierkegaard's earlier discussion of the shift from revolutionary culture to mass society to crass society, the relation of the public's empty subset to its expansive subset is not additive but *subtractive*. If the being of nothingness named by $\{\emptyset\}$ is to be included in the definition of the public, it must be according to this errant and estranged relation to the being of the public's totalizing count. Hence, the comma between $\{n+1\}$ and $\{\emptyset\}$ in $\{\{n+1\},\{\emptyset\}\}$. In the public's empty subset, we see the glaring presence of something that is structurally removed from its running tally of everyone and everything, an incandescent being-nothing that avoids being-all but also manages to elude non-being.

If the sum of the public's counting procedure amounts to everyone and everything, the only entity that exceeds this totality, and thus the sole referent of "nothing" in Kierkegaard's definition, is the entity which establishes and maintains this sum, namely, *the counting procedure of the public itself*. If this were not the case—which is to say, if the operation of the public's count were included in its result—the structure of this count would be inseparable from its effect, and both, by definition, would become others to themselves. Since this does not occur, the following conclusion arises: *The "nothing" which the public adds to its "all" is the counting procedure by which it arrives at this total aggregation*. What the expansive set $\{n+1\}$ fails to include, in other words, is *the operation of inclusion itself*, namely, the mathematical law that defines the being of its "all" as a set—a set whose jurisdiction is determined by the braces on either side of $n+1$. That the empty set $\{\emptyset\}$ can also be written $\{\}$ is not inconsequential here, for the braces which define $\{n+1\}$ as the expansive set of "everything" are the very same which define $\{\emptyset\}$ as the empty set of "nothing."

That all of these braces are also equivalent to those which define the public as the proper superset $\{\{n+1\},\{\emptyset\}\}$ further suggests another conclusion—a conclusion which cuts to the numerical core of Kierkegaard's social critique: *The public is the proper superset that includes what its running tally of everyone and everything cannot—namely, the counting procedure that secures and sustains this total aggregation*. This is why the public is so difficult to define, even for Kierkegaard. *It is at once the operation of a count that, relative to its result, amounts to nothing, and the result of a counting operation that applies to everything except itself.* In this sense, the being-nothing that allows the public to surpass its being-all is not just the result of a forming-into-one-of-zero, whereby names like "mirage," "phantom," "fairytale," and the like are sutured to the being of nothingness. It also marks a forming-into-one of the *operation* that allows for the encompassment of everyone and everything, an operation rendered null and void by the emergence of this total aggregation.

Taken together, these conclusions suggest another still: What defines the public as $P \supsetneq \{\{n+1\},\{\emptyset\}\}$ is also what defines its "all" as the expansive subset $\{n+1\}$ and its "nothing" as the empty subset $\{\emptyset\}$—namely, the braces that signal the forming-into-one of each collection. With each $\{\}$, the counting procedure of the public recurs, gradually emerging from the calculated shadows of an expansive subset comprised of $n+1$ beings, entering into the harsh numerical light of an empty subset comprised of $\emptyset$ alone, and ultimately encompassing both of these subsets in the broader superset $\{\{n+1\},\{\emptyset\}\}$—the operational result of a forming-into-one whose mathematical structure mirrors that of its already structurally twinned subsets.

If $P \supsetneq \{\{n+1\},\{\emptyset\}\}$ shows the operational result of the public's count, the braces that recur throughout this formulation reveal its operational logic. When the public adds "nothing" to its running tally of "all," thereby outnumbering its own totalizing count, it does so by *repeating* the operation by which n+1 becomes $\{n+1\}$, effectively subjecting this operation to itself. Hence, $\{\emptyset\}$. When the void point $\emptyset$ appears in the empty set $\{\emptyset\}$, the operation of forming-into-one that is excluded from the public's expansive set of $n+1$ beings—and thus forced to wander through this running tally in subtracted form, as its errant cause and a-structural effect—becomes the unique member of another subset determined by the very same procedure.

On its own, $\{n+1\}$ suggests that the fuzzy math of the modern public life is expansive. But this is misleading, for the public is more and less than an expansive set of $n+1$ beings. To suggest otherwise would be to reduce the public to one of its parts, thereby recapitulating the era's fuzzy math, albeit in inverted form: Instead of a whole that is greater than the sum of its parts, the public would become a whole that is *the same* as one of its parts, and thus less than the sum to which this part contributes. With the addition of the empty set $\{\emptyset\}$, and its subsumption alongside $\{n+1\}$ in the broader superset $\{\{n+1\},\{\emptyset\}\}$, this metonymic fog quickly clears, allowing for another, more penetrating insight into modernity's fuzzy math: The operational result of the public's running tally may seem to be expansive, but the counting procedure that sustains this mathematical sleight of hand, at once structuring this expansion and slipping into its numerical shadow, is in fact *recursive*.

Tælle Tale

If the fuzzy math of the modern era finds expression in "the garrulous experience of common sense," it originates in the numerical slippage between structure and effect, operation and result, in modern public culture—a numerical slippage well-captured in the equation $P \supsetneq \{\{n+1\},\{\varnothing\}\}$. Let us attempt to summarize these findings and, atop this summary, to take a final look at the theory of chatter developed in Kierkegaard's literary review.

Only by including $n+1$ in the expansive set $\{n+1\}$ can the public stabilize its running tally of everyone and everything in a given era, allowing it to culminate in a total aggregation of these entities. But only by excluding the forming-into-one of $n+1$ beings from this ensuing totality, effectively subtracting the operation of the public's count from its end result and thus rendering this operation null and void, can the public generate the remainder of "nothing," which proves that its account of "everything" is indeed complete.

And yet, in order for this evidence to appear, the public must subject the being of its nothingness to the same stabilization procedure that caused it to emerge in the first place—namely, the stabilization procedure that the public applied to its running tally of everyone and everything. What follows is a forming-into-one of the forming-into-one that counts for nothing in the expansive set $\{n+1\}$. This is not just a repetition of the counting procedure that is excluded from the public's total aggregation of everyone and everything; it is also a repetition that begets another just like itself, since it not only begins this procedure anew but also includes it in another set, simultaneously identifying this procedure as the void point $\varnothing$ relative to the expansive set $\{n+1\}$ and including this void point in the empty set $\{\varnothing\}$.

As "the entity that is supposed to include everything," the public has no choice but to tally the being-nothing of this empty set *alongside* the being-all of its expansive counterpart, a tally which, in turn, requires yet another stabilization. Hence the superset $\{\{n+1\},\{\varnothing\}\}$. As we have seen, $\{\{n+1\},\{\varnothing\}\}$ signals the forming-into-one of two subsets, resulting in a collection comprised of the forming-into-one that structures the expansive set {n+1} but is excluded from its result, and the forming-into-one that simultaneously marks this exclusion as the void point Ø and includes it in the empty set {Ø}.

Like Gert Westphaler, who would learn to speak through his nostrils if someone sewed his mouth shut, thereby doubling his output of chatter, the public is a *repeating machine* whose forming-into-one always seems to beget another. This is precisely how this abstract aggregate manages to exceed its already expansive set of n+1 beings, thereby appearing greater than the sum of everyone and everything in a given era, and thus authorized to serve as a *holos* above and beyond the totality of each and every *soros* in its jurisdiction. To this extent, P⊋{{n+1},{Ø}} is more than a precise mathematical definition of Kierkegaard's "gallery-public." It also provides an accurate and long-overdue account of the sorites reasoning on which members of this negative community rely, effectively serving as the *matheme* for their chattering common sense.

From this vantage point, the question at the heart of Kierkegaard's literary review almost leaps from the page: How does the fuzzy math of modern public life contribute to the garrulous experience of common sense, and how does the latter, in turn, find repeated expression in the former? "Paralogistically," Kierkegaard notes in passing, further revealing but still not quite exposing the fundamental link between loquacity and common sense, *Snaksomhed* and *Forstandighed*, in the abstract aggregate he derides as "a quiet but busy sorites going on day and night" (*TA*, 91, 78). What are we to make of this passing remark?

In Greek, *para-* means "beside" and "alongside." But it can also mean "aside from," "beyond," and, to this extent, "amiss" and even "abnormal." As we shall see in chapter 5, the ancient Greek notion of *logos* is even more complicated. In addition to "reason," *logos* means "speech." When Aristotle defines the human being as a *zoon logon echon*, he means that we are animals in which talking and thinking are inseparably linked. To talk and think paralogistically is thus to do so illogically, by means of unsound reasoning, often relying on logical fallacies and invalid arguments. If sorites reasoning is the paralogistic habit of mind that underwrites modern public life, chatter is the paralogistic way of speaking in which its fuzzy math unfolds, allowing quantitative accumulations of human equivocation to appear greater in quality than the sum of their equivocating human parts.

This is why Kierkegaard wavered between *at snakke* and *at raisonere* in early drafts of his literary review, especially in the much-discussed paragraph beginning, "What is it *to chatter?*" (*TA*, 97). As his English translators well note, *at raisonere* did not simply mean "to reason." In mid-nineteenth-century Denmark, it also meant "the dissipation of reason in verbosity, loquacity, garrulity." Dissipations of this sort apparently occurred with enough frequency to warrant the proper noun *Raisonneur,* meaning "one who uses his mouth" (*TA*, 173n72). Recalling his earlier depiction of Gert Westphaler as a babbling know-it-all (*Schwätzer*), Kierkegaard suggests that the mouth of the *Raisonneur* always serves the same purpose: "the loquacious man chatters about anything and everything conceivable [*den Raisonnerende raisonnerer om alt Muligt*]" (*TA*, 103; trans. modified). In other words, *he talks as the understanding thinks,* "giving utterance to reflection [*Reflexionens*]" as it slips into "abstract thought," and to abstract thought as it races from topic to topic, yielding "a profusion of things to speak about [*det Mangfoldige at tale om*]" (*TA*, 97, 130, 103).

When Kierkegaard insists that he is speaking algebraically, with "no desire to divert or fascinate anyone with the enchantments of multiplication [*Mangfoldighedens Tryllerier*]," it is the mathematical structure of this profuse, entrancing slurry of *Snaksomhed* and *Forstandighed* that he is attempting to reveal and, in so doing, to render inoperative (*PF*, 91). Where the modern mind "chatters about everything conceivable [*alt Muligt at snakke*] and continues incessantly," Kierkegaard hears the paralogos of the present age at work—a way of speaking, thinking, and being with others whose underlying structure, as we shall see in subsequent chapters, more closely resembles numerology than numerical logic (*TA*, 97).

Hence, the appearance of *talrigere* in his 1846 depiction of the public as "a corps, outnumbering all the people together" (*TA*, 91). *Talrigere* is an extension of the adjective *talrig,* meaning "numerous." And *talrig,* in turn, derives from the noun *tal,* meaning "figure," "amount," "digit"—in short, "number." That *tal* is also the root of *tælle,* meaning "to count," should come as no surprise. But we cannot stop here, for the social effects of these lexical ties are profound. When the public outnumbers its expansive count of everyone and everything, it does so automatically, almost militarily, as a corps, and thus in strict keeping with its *modus operandi* as "the entity that is supposed to include everything" (*TA*, 91). As we have seen, however, the structure of this *talrigere* does not serve as an extension of the public's counting procedure. Like Holberg's image of Master Gert with his mouth sewn shut and chatter spewing from nostrils—an image which, in turn, reminded Kierkegaard and his friend of pantographs, double-barreled rifles, and live espringals—the mathematical structure of the public is not extensive but *recursive*. When "nothing" is added to the public's "all," thereby causing it to outnumber its own totalizing count, the paralogos of this abstract aggregate shifts from counting alone to what Kierkegaard, at the outer limits of his own social thought, can only describe as "counting and counting [*tælle og tælle*]" (*TA*, 92). If the public is more numerous (*talrig*) than everyone and everything combined, it is not simply because it exceeds this total aggregation, but because it does so by *repeating* the count that allows it to secure and sustain this totality. And not just once, but multiple times! As we have seen, the public is a forming-into-one of two operations that follow the very same logic: the forming-into-one that structures the expansive set $\{n+1\}$ but remains excluded from its result, and the forming-into-one that simultaneously identifies this excluded operation as the void point $\varnothing$ and includes it in the empty set $\{\varnothing\}$.

We have seen this recursive count before. In $P \supseteq \{\{n+1\},\{\varnothing\}\}$, we find the precise mathematical expression of what Kierkegaard initially described as "the mechanical counting of the beat [*den tillærte Tællen af Takten*]" (*TA*, 62). At the start of this chapter, I interpreted this alliterative phrase to mean the following: Modernity gradually reduces the collective harmonies of previous eras to their beat levels and eventually replaces these beat levels with the automated rhythms of its own newfangled count—a self-referential calculating procedure that nevertheless purports to represent these collective rhythms. With the addition of $P \supseteq \{\{n+1\},\{\varnothing\}\}$, we can now say this as well: In the *tælle og tælle* of modern public culture, well-represented by the iterative braces in $\{\{n+1\},\{\varnothing\}\}$, the counting procedure of *tillærte Tællen af Takten* doubles as its own sociological result. In the paralogistic talk and thought that allow the public to function as $\{\{n+1\},\{\varnothing\}\}$, the chatter of the modern mind can be seen for what it is: Nothing more than the "t . . . t . . . t . . . t" of its own *tillærte Tællen af Takten*—a numerical recursion of consonants without syllables, parts without wholes, and quantities without qualities. This is why the count of modernity is always, to some extent, *a lost count*. When revolutionary culture gives way to mass society, mass society gives way to crass society, and crass society gives way to surveillance society, the only thing left for the modern era to count is the effaced structure of its own count.

That *tal* is also the origin of the Danish *tale*, meaning "to speak," is of equal importance here. As we have seen throughout this chapter, the garrulous experience of common sense, with all of its *Snaksomhed* and *Forstandighed*, is a paralogistic outgrowth of the secret affinity between speaking and counting, *tale* and *tælle*. It is what happens when *tale* becomes *tælle* and the latter, in turn, begins to speak. What bothers Kierkegaard about this conflation of speaking and counting is not just the mindless social chatter in which it finds expression, but also the chattering collective mind in which these expressions culminate—a false consciousness of sorts that would soon become our own, in which talking counts more than doing and numbers speak louder than words.

THREE

Preacher-Prattle

Sermonic Pain

For much of his life, Kierkegaard longed to become a rural pastor. In November 1840, he enrolled in the Royal Pastoral Seminary. In January 1841, he delivered his first sermon. And by February 1846, he was ready to commit: "It is now my idea to be trained to become a pastor. For a number of months I have prayed to God to help me along, for it has long been clear to me that I ought not to continue as an author, which is something I want to be entirely or not at all. That's also why I haven't begun anything new while reading the proofs [of *Postscript*], except for the little review of *Two Ages*, which is, once more, a concluding piece" (*JNB* 2, 415; trans. modified). But it was not meant to be. In November 1846, Kierkegaard began to doubt his decision. Two months later, he was ready to abandon the prospect of a rural parsonage all together. "The wish to become a priest someday out in the country has always appealed to me and has been in the background of my soul," he confides in his journal. But it had always been "an idyllic wish," the primary purpose of which, Kierkegaard now realized, had been to make his "strenuous existence" as an author more bearable (*JNB* 4, 107).

The breaking point came in May 1851, when he delivered a lengthy Sunday sermon on "The Changelessness of God" at Copenhagen's Citadel Church. Before, during, and after the sermon, Kierkegaard was miserable. "Beforehand I suffered greatly from every sort of strain, as is always the case when I have to use my physical person." From the pulpit, "I spoke in such a weak voice that people complained about being unable to hear." And the following day, "I was so weak and exhausted that it was frightful." As the week progressed, "I became weaker and weaker," he continues. "Then I became really sick. The lamentable, tormenting pain that constitutes the limit of my person began to rear up in fearsome fashion, something that had not happened to me in a long, long time." The harsh reality of his idyllic dream could no longer be ignored: "I felt that it went against the whole of my being."[1]

It was time to renew his authorship—but also to reenvision it. "My task is that of inward appropriation, and there is a great deal of the poet in me," Kierkegaard went on to console himself in the same tortured journal entry. After his Sunday sermon, however, he suspected there was also something more in him, something beyond the poetic impulse of his earlier work, something profoundly religious in need of further pursuit. "Something new has been born within me, for I understand my task as an author differently; it is now dedicated in a quite different way to straightforwardly advancing religion" (*JNB* 8, 371).

Four years later, Kierkegaard remained committed to this task. But weakness, exhaustion, and tormenting pain had returned once more. In September 1855, he collapsed several times—first at a party, then at home, and finally in the street. When he arrived at Royal Fredrick's Hospital, he claimed death was near and welcomed its arrival. "He considers his illness to be fatal" and his passing "necessary for the cause," the medical examiner reported. "Were he to go on living, he would have to continue his religious battle, but then people would tire of it. Through his death, on the other hand, his struggle will retain its strength, and, as he believes, its victory."[2]

Victorious or not, the struggle was real. And it did not begin in May 1851, when Kierkegaard finally woke from his idyllic dream of a rural parsonage, dedicating himself anew to the task of religious writing. In the years leading up to this momentous turn of events, he lavished critical attention on the religious life of his era. Of particular concern to him was the "preacher-prattle" (*Præstesnak*) of his contemporaries—a pseudo-Christian way of speaking characterized by hasty expression, bustling loquacity, busy trifling, esthetic dabbling, probabilistic talk, revisionist chatter, and endless digressions of what Kierkegaard bemoans as religious gibberish, fetishistic twaddle, and philosophical rigmarole. With these wayward forms of speech come several errant lines of thought, notably psychosocial flurries of alarm, anxiety, impatience, confusion, absentmindedness, equivocation, delusion, and spiritual dizziness. Tracking this priestly paralogos through Kierkegaard's middle work, with special reference to his unpublished *Book on Adler*, is the primary task of this chapter. In so doing, I hope to cut several new lines of inquiry through his authorship, yielding fresh insight into his imbricated philosophies of modern religion, mass society, and everyday talk.

Logos vs. *Lalia*

Kierkegaard's 1851 sermon on "The Changelessness of God" was an exegesis of his first and arguably most beloved biblical passage: James 1: 17–21. He began by reading the text aloud, then paraphrasing it for his listeners. Crucial for our purposes is his gloss on verse 19: "Let everyone be 'quick to hear,' that is, not listen to fast and loose talk, but listen upward, because from *above* there is always only good news," Kierkegaard summarizes. And let everyone be equally "'slow to speak [*langsom til at tale*],' since the chatter [*Snak*] we human beings can offer, especially about the here and now and in all haste, most often can only make the good and perfect gifts less good and perfect."[3] To further illustrate the hasty, transient *snak* of humankind, Kierkegaard contrasts it with God's serene capacity to remain silent: "Why do you think he is so quiet? Because he is serenely aware that he is eternally changeless. Someone who was not eternally sure of himself, sure that he is changeless, could not remain quiet in that way; he would rise up in his power; but only the eternally Changeless One can be that quiet. He takes his time and that he can of course do. He has eternity, and eternally he is changeless" (*M*, 274). For everyone else, there is little hope. At best, we can become "quick to hear" gospel truths of this sort. On this point, James is clear: Only when listening for "the word of truth" (*logo aletheias*) do we stand a chance of becoming "slow to speak" (*bradys eis to lalēsai*). What intrigued Kierkegaard about this sensory contrast between hearing and speaking is the linguistic difference it implies: The quiet *logos* of God is fundamentally distinct from the boisterous *lalia* of humankind. Hence, the shift from *tale* to *snak* in Kierkegaard's exegesis of verse 19. As he well knew, *lalia* is another Greek word for "chatter," comparable in form and function to *adoleschia*—and thus akin to many of the communicative practices we discussed in chapter 1.[4]

But there is more at stake in this contrast between the quiet *logos* of God and the boisterous *lalia* of humankind than a simple opposition between the silence required to hear the former and the clamor of the latter that prevents this from occurring. Like most conceptual distinctions, this one harbors a secret affinity—an affinity that proves integral to Kierkegaard's conception of religious discourse (*religieuse Taler*) and its fallen sibling, preacher-prattle (*Præstesnak*). In order to document this affinity, we must continue reading Kierkegaard's sermon, retranslating several key terms as we go.

When Kierkegaard stresses the tranquil silence of God, the Danish word on which he relies is *stille*, meaning "to put," "to place," and even "to lay down." The silence implicit in *stille* is that of something static, placid, and at rest. That God can remain completely silent is a function of his ability to remain completely still. Instead of rising up to quell the hasty *snak* of humankind, he "sits absolutely still [*sidder Ganske stille*] and looks, without a change of countenance, almost as if he did not exist" (M, 274). The logic here is simple: If God is able to keep quiet, it is because he is able to keep still; and if he is able to keep still, it is because he remains eternally changeless.

This does not mean God "takes his time," as the standard English translation of Kierkegaard's sermon suggests. Just the opposite, in fact. As the original Danish well indicates, God neither takes his time nor keeps it for himself. Instead, he gives it to us unconditionally, allowing us to use it as though it were our own. In this light, the passage following Kierkegaard's praise of divine stillness glimmers anew:

He gives time [*giver Tid*], and that he can of course do. He has eternity, and eternally he is changeless. He gives time [*giver Tid*], he does it deliberately. Then comes the accounting of eternity, in which nothing is forgotten, not one single idle word that was spoken, and eternally he is changeless. That he gives time [*giver Tid*] in this way can, however, also be mercy, time for turning around and reformation. But how terrible if this time is not used in this way, because then the foolishness and light-mindedness in us must instead wish that he would be promptly on hand with the punishment rather than that he gives time [*giver Tid*] in this way, ignores it and yet is eternally changeless. (M, 274; trans. modified)

In this sense, the difference between divine *logos* and human *lalia* is irreducible to simple dichotomies between silence and speech, stillness and tumult, forbearance and haste. Instead, it is a matter of *time*. Foremost among "the good and perfect gifts" quietly delivered from above, only to be made "less good and less perfect" by boisterous chatter below, is time. The problem is not that we squander this gift, effectively wasting God's time. Nor is it that we foolishly wish to be punished for this offense as promptly as we commit it. Rather, it is that, in all our chatter about the here and now, we forget that we have received this gift and, in so doing, lose track of time itself. God gives us time to use as we see fit, but we cannot find time to recall this gift.

All of which further suggests that the crucial conceptual difference between the *logos* of God and the *lalia* of humankind is not the volume at which each is expressed but the *rate* at which each should be heeded. The quiet *logos* of God should be welcomed without delay, but the boisterous *lalia* of society should be deferred indefinitely. More often than not, however, the opposite occurs. Because we are quick to join in the boisterous *lalia* of society, it is difficult for us to hear, much less to heed, the quiet *logos* of God. And even when we do have ears to hear the quiet *logos* of God, we are often tempted to filter it through the boisterous *lalia* of society, effectively subjecting "the divine Word" to "the opinions of men."[5]

Kierkegaard saw these dilemmas as reciprocally constitutive of modern religious life. In the present age, congregants are wont to chatter and are thus deaf to God; and the pastors who purport to lead them, even and especially when attempting to heed the word of God, cannot help but mediate it through congregational chatter, inadvertently redoubling the latter's harmful effect on essential Christian practice.

In 1846, Kierkegaard wrote a book on each way of speaking. The impatient chatter of today's congregants is symptomatic of "the garrulous commonsense" attacked in his literary review of *Two Ages* and discussed in the previous chapter. And the priestly habit of mediating divine *logos* through human *lalia* became the centerpiece of another literary review, one which Kierkegaard belabored until his death, ultimately deciding, and for good reason, to forgo its publication: *The Book on Adler.*

The Unemployed Messiah

Adolph Peter Adler was one of Kierkegaard's first classmates, and the boys got along well. As their educations progressed, however, they grew apart. By the early-1840s, there was little left of their former friendship. Adler had become a zealous Hegelian pastor, and Kierkegaard had emerged as an anti-Hegelian Christian thinker. Matters came to a head in the summer of 1843, when Adler visited Kierkegaard in Copenhagen, insisting that he had received a direct revelation. "Adler made it clear to Kierkegaard that he viewed him [Kierkegaard] as a sort of John the Baptist in relation to himself, who, since he had received the direct revelation, was the genuine Messiah," Hans Bløchner notes, recalling the faint smile on Kierkegaard's face as he informed him of this visit. Then Adler read aloud from a small volume of *Studies* he had recently published, varying the pitch and volume of his voice throughout: "Some of it he read in his ordinary voice, the rest in a strange whisper." When Kierkegaard questioned the validity of what he had just heard, suggesting that it did not amount to a direct revelation, Adler replied, "Then I will come to you again this evening and read all of it you in *this* voice (the whisper), and then you shall see, it will become clear to you."[6] Kierkegaard was amused, to say the least.

In July 1843, the Hegelian pastor went a step further, publishing a collection of his own *Sermons*, in the preface to which he not only recounted his direct revelation but also claimed divine inspiration:

In December of last year, I had almost completed a work that I had wanted to call "Popular Lectures on Subjective Logic." It was my own thought that had immersed itself in itself and with a superficial knowledge of the Bible had undertaken to explain creation and Christianity.

One evening I had just given an account of the origin of evil; then I perceived as if in a flash that everything depended not upon thought but upon spirit, and there existed an evil spirit. The same night a hideous sound descended into our room. Then the *Savior* commanded me to get up and go in and write down these words:

The first human beings could have had eternal life, because when thought joins God's spirit with the body, then life is eternal; when the human being joins God's spirit with the body, then the human being is God's child; so Adam would have been God's son. But they sinned. Thought immersed itself in itself without the world, without the body. It separated the spirit from the body, the Spirit from the world. And when the human being himself, when thought itself separates the spirit from the body and the spirit from the world, the human being must die in the world and the body become evil. And what becomes of the spirit? The spirit leaves the body. But God does not take it back. And it becomes his enemy. And where does it go? Back into the world. Why? It is angry with the world, which abandoned it. It is the evil spirit. And the world itself created the evil spirit.

Then Jesus commanded me to burn my own works and in the future to keep to the Bible.

As for the sermons from no. VI to the end, I know that they were written with Jesus' collaborating grace, so that I have been only an instrument. (quoted in *BOA*, 339–40)

A month later, Adler's ecclesiastical superiors asked him to resign. The pastor refused. So they suspended him from his office. By April of the following year, the bishop of the diocese was eager to make a final decision in the matter, so he addressed several questions to the suspended pastor, the first two of which, along with Adler's replies, bear mention here. "Do you acknowledge having been in an excited and confused state of mind when you wrote and published your *Sermons* and so-called *Studies*?" No, Adler replied. Since both texts can be shown to contain "meaning and coherence," it is clear that neither was composed in an excited or confused state. "Do you perceive that it is fanatical and wrong to expect and to follow such presumably external revelations as, for example, those you described in the preface to your *Sermons*?" No, Adler replied again. "That there was a rescue in marvelous ways—as I have described in the preface to *Sermons*—is for me a fact that I cannot deny. Even if my *Sermons* and *Studies* are regarded only as a child's first babbling [*lallende*], lisping, imperfect voice, I nevertheless believe that the words testify that an event through which I was deeply moved by faith did occur" (quoted in *BOA*, 343–45).

No sooner had Adler issued these replies than he decided to publish them all, along with the bishop's questions and related correspondence, resulting in an 1845 collection titled *Papers Concerning My Suspension and Dismissal*. Also included in this volume was his final letter to the bishop, an epistolary "overture" in which Adler, desperate to reach "an agreement with the authorities," seemed to walk back several of his earlier statements (*BOA*, 347–48). And all to no avail. In September 1845, the bishop replied with a rescript from the king. Adler was officially discharged from his office as pastor.

Not surprisingly, Kierkegaard followed these events carefully. He thought Adler should have complied with the church's initial request for his resignation. And he felt the king was justified in his final decision to remove Adler from office. But it was not until June 1846, when Adler simultaneously published four more books, none of which seemed related to his religious experience or its ecclesiastical aftermath, that Kierkegaard's interest was piqued. What began as an amusing visit from an overwrought childhood friend and quickly devolved into a public dispute with church officials now became the central theme of a new book project on Kierkegaard's desk, the subtitle of which left no question of his stance on the whole affair: "The Religious Confusion of the Present Age Illustrated by Magister Adler as a Phenomenon."

Trembling Impatience

The specifics of Adler's revelation—evil bodies, evil spirits, evil worlds, and the like—were of little interest to Kierkegaard. But its scholarly style immediately caught his attention: "Christ speaks almost like an assistant professor," Kierkegaard jests. "The words cited are exactly like a section heading." But Adler was serious—and this mattered. "In that preface he most solemnly announces that he has had a revelation in which a doctrine has been communicated to him by the Savior" (*BOA*, 52–53). There was nothing laughable about this part of Adler's religious experience.

Even so, Adler should not have been so quick to publish. Jesus may have ordered him to transcribe a new doctrine, but he did not order him to publish it in the preface to one of his own books, much less to claim it as a source of divine inspiration. Why did the pastor do this? Kierkegaard's answer is simple: Adler was confused. He mistook his lyrical genius as a Hegelian scholar for the religious authority of a Christian apostle. And he should have known better. In particular, he should have known the Bible better. "The whole confusion has its basis in his having no education in Christian concepts, no schooling that stands in a relation to his subjective state of being deeply moved, while on the other hand he quite seriously has found repose and satisfaction in the Hegelian volatilization of concepts" (*BOA*, 121). That Adler also saw his retreat to Hegel as an occasion to break with Hegel, even going so far as to burn all of his Hegelian texts, made his religious-philosophical confusion ironic as well. "Even his break with Hegel is by no means Christianly qualitative," Kierkegaard scoffs. "The break itself is a kind of Hegelianism" (*BOA*, 121).

Adler would have fared better without an advanced degree in philosophy. But he could have done without his advanced degree in theology as well: "If Magister Adler had been a layman (lawyer, physician, military officer, for example), it perhaps would have gone somewhat better for him. After being deeply moved by a powerful religious impression, he would then, in view of not being a theologian, have sought quiet [*Ro*] in order to become fully conscious of himself, sought schooling with teachers of Christian orthodoxy, and in this way he perhaps would have succeeded in attaining the necessary proportionality before he began to express himself" (*BOA*, 115–16). Silence first, expression second—this would have been Kierkegaard's advice. But not just any kind of silence: In addition to keeping quiet, Adler should have remained still. Hence, the Danish *Ro* above, meaning "rest," "repose," and "composure." Quiet was not enough; Adler needed quietude. But he decided to go public instead. And not just once, but several times: first in his collection of *Studies*, again in Kierkegaard's living room, and then, much to the detriment of his career as a pastor, in the preface to *Sermons*. Adler was not just noisy; he was restless. Instead of remaining calm, he became boisterous.

Whether Adler's religious experience was truly a direct communication from God was less important than the fact that he presented it as one in the preface to *Sermons*. On Kierkegaard's reading, this was evidence that his old schoolmate did not understand the Christian concept of direct revelation, much less the responsibilities entailed therein. To receive a message from God and then rush it to print was not just hasty but also reckless, for "what in him is truth can become for others the greatest corruption." Immediately after receiving a direct revelation, the recipient should "close himself off from everyone else, so that no uncircumspect utterance, no undietetic uncircumspection would ruin the whole thing in loquacity [*Snaksomhed*]," Kierkegaard warns. Instead of engaging in hasty chatter, one should "take time to settle in the pause of silence (*in pausa*)" (*BOA*, 166; cf. 249).

Why did Adler neglect to stop, *in pausa*, between the inner experience and outward expression of his so-called revelation? Because, at some level, he knew he was confused—and not just about the Christian concept of revelation. Was the voice that woke him in the night actually that of Jesus, or could it have been that of Adler's own mind— the same mind which had already "immersed itself in itself" and, earlier that evening, allowed him to perceive "in a flash" the basic insight of the new doctrine he would later transcribe? It was difficult for Adler to say, and this difficulty was apparently more than he could bear. Instead of faith, humility, and quiet resolve in the face of religious paradox, Adler became doubtful, irresolute, and increasingly chatty, eventually developing "a nervous tremor that in trembling impatience can neither hold on to anything nor beneficially give up anything." After his religious experience, Adler could neither remain silent nor say anything meaningful. He was too nervous, too impatient, and all to such an extent that it seemed to be this jumble of emotions, not Adler himself, which rushed to expression, causing the pastor to appear overwrought, fanatically confused, and nearly deranged. "Impatience says: the sooner the better, and the nervous impatience, bordering almost on insanity, says: If only it does not cease, if only the pressure within me does not vanish . . . seize it, seize it, seize it while it is foaming"

(*BOA*, 166–67). Adler may have been quick to hear the divine word, but the rate at which he rushed it to print was even swifter. The *logos* of God was no match for his own *lalia*.

Kierkegaard sensed his old friend's pain, but he also saw hasty expression as antithetical to Christian practice. Any "collision of the eternal and temporal in the moment, in the present, is a dreadful tension that can all too easily become sleeplessness, and all too easily insanity," he admits. "But it is certainly also terrible to give birth to wind because of sheer busyness [*Travlhed*]" (*BOA*, 166–67). The wind to which Kierkegaard refers is, of course, chatter. When *Travlhed* overwhelms religious experience, *Snaksomhed* is sure to follow. Adler was quick to speak, and thus guilty of *snak*, because he was preoccupied with the here and now, wrapped up in a moment of religious intensity for which his misunderstanding of Christian theology and overcommitment to Hegelian thought had poorly prepared him. What James warned against in his epistle to early Christians, and Kierkegaard later explained in his sermon on "The Changelessness of God," might well have been dubbed the Adler Phenomenon: *Let everyone be slow to speak, lest hasty chatter about the here and now corrupt the good and perfect gifts we have received from God, not least of which is the gift of time.*

The Premise-Author

In Adler's hasty chatter, Kierkegaard saw a certain human tendency at work—a tendency which had recently become trendy among his contemporaries. "Instead of making up their minds as individuals, each person for himself, about what they want *in concreto* before they begin to express themselves, they have a superstitious idea of the benefit of prompting a discussion," he gripes in the opening pages of his *Book on Adler*. "They have a superstitious idea that the spirit of the age, although individuals separately do not know what they want, would be able by its dialectic to make clear what it is they actually want" (*BOA*, 10–11).

Authors of this sort are authors in name alone. Because they write in hopes that readers will provide the conclusions they lack, their arguments amount to little more than premises. For this reason, Kierkegaard dubs them *premise-authors*.

The premise-author is the opposite of the essential author. The latter has his perspective. The most woeful confusion inevitably appears when people become momentary and then in turn superstitiously put all their trust in the moment—what indeed is the moment in the next moment! In his particular production the essential author is continually behind himself; he is certainly striving, but within a totality, not toward the totality. He never raises more doubt than he can explain. His A is never greater in scope than his B. He never draws upon the uncertain. In other words, he has a definite life- and world-view that he follows. (*BOA*, 13)

Essential authors can write *behind* themselves because they always grasp the significance of their authorships *before* picking up their pens to work on any particular project. And they can be said to *follow* specific life- and world-views for the same reason: The work of determining these views always *precedes* that of any given literary task. Essential authors never lose perspective because they always already have one. And they never give in to the heat of the moment because they always manage to keep it at a distance, holding every here and now in the same deep perspective. Not so with premise-authors. They cannot work behind themselves because they are always *getting ahead* of themselves. Instead of writing from their own perspectives, presenting readers with predetermined life- and world-views, they write *in search* of these perspectives, hoping readers will do the work of establishing these views for them.

This is why the work of the premise-author amounts to chatter. Recall Kierkegaard's quip in his other 1846 literary review: "One who chatters [*snakker*] presumably does chatter [*snakker*] about something, since the aim is to find something to chatter [*at snakke*] about" (*TA*, 99). To this extent, chatter is always already ahead of itself, and thus doubly removed from essential speech, since it not only lacks something meaningful to discuss but also limits its search for topics to mere trivialities. "Chattering [*Snakken*] gets ahead of essential speaking," Kierkegaard plainly states. "But the person who can speak essentially because he is able to keep silent will not have a profusion of things [*Mangfoldige*] to speak about but one thing only, and he will find time to speak and to keep silent" (*TA*, 97). When chatter prevails, we cannot find time for silence; but neither can we find time to speak. We only seem to have enough time for more chatter.

This, of course, is the fundamental difference between essential authors and premise-authors. What the former have, the latter lack: time to quietly determine something meaningful to discuss—and by extension something worthy of public debate—well before they pick up their pens. The only thing premise-authors have time to discuss is their pressing need of something to discuss. They have nothing to communicate beyond this need. And in this sense, they not only have nothing to communicate but also no need to communicate at all. Notice how Kierkegaard arrives at this conclusion: "Insofar as the essential author can be said to have a need to communicate himself, this need is entirely immanental, an enjoyment of the understanding to the second power, or it becomes for him a consciously undertaken ethical task. The premise-author has no need to *communicate himself*, because essentially he has nothing to communicate; indeed he lacks precisely the essential, the conclusion, the meaning in relation to the presuppositions. He has no *need to communicate* himself; he is the *one who is in need*" (BOA, 14).

Anyone inclined toward premise-authorship should set down his pen instead. Kierkegaard is categorical: "Everyone must be silent insofar as he [sic] does not have an understanding to communicate" (BOA, 15). All too often, however, the opposite occurs. Instead of holding still and remaining silent, premise-authors begin to write. And instead of remaining focused, their writings tend to meander, ranging across a profusion of topics. As we saw in chapters 1 and 2, and as subsequent chapters will further demonstrate, meandering of this sort is a basic feature of chatter. Which is again why Kierkegaard struggled to determine whether it consists in "a garrulous continuation or a continued garrulity [*en snaksom Fortsættelse eller en fortsat Snaksomhed*], a participial or infinitive phrase in which the subject must be understood or, more correctly, cannot be located at all because, as the grammarians say, the meaning does not make it clear for the simple reason that it lacks meaning" (TA, 97, 78, 131, 67).

How are we to understand "the subject" in this crucial passage? Is it a speaking subject, a subject of speech, or perhaps, given the grammatical tilt of this passage, a speaking subject who has become a subject of speech? Kierkegaard does not say, and his use of the Danish *Subjectet* here yields little insight. According to Peter Fenves, the missing subject to which Kierkegaard refers is a meaningful topic of discussion—the same meaningful topic of discussion that chatterers, in their tireless pursuit of something to discuss, continually defer. To this extent, Fenves echoes Kierkegaard: What distinguishes chatter from other modes of speech is its unique ability to *say nothing*. Unlike the classic rhetorical canon of delivery, which is premised on the ability of speech to convey something, *chatter delivers nothing*. It is a way of speaking whose object of communication is also, paradoxically, an abyss of communication.

As Fenves sees it, this is among its most remarkable achievements. By using speech to avoid communication, chatter inadvertently gives voice to a communicative void.[7] This is not to suggest that it withdraws from language, resulting in meaninglessness. Nor is it to suggest that it fails to communicate, resulting in unintelligibility. Rather, it is to highlight chatter's unique ability to communicate a *specifically linguistic nothingness*. "The vehicle of communication, language as structure and act, remains in operation, but it no longer *works*, for whatever it carries is somehow 'nothing,'" Fenves explains. "Utterances are neither garbled nor indecipherable nor meaningless; rather they have become, for all their clarity, idle vehicles, vehicles without content, vehicles in which 'nothing' is said."[8]

If chatterers have nothing to say, it is not because they are unable to communicate, but because what they communicate cannot be said. It is the medium of speech itself, in its "pure and endless mediality," that finds expression in their discourse.[9] To this extent, the missing subject of speech that continually incites additional bouts of chatter is also a speaking subject whose linguistic agency is continually sequestered by language itself. On this point, Fenves is adamant: "When chatter takes place, language itself, and not an 'existing' subject, speaks."[10]

We have heard this speech before. Recall, for instance, the "run-away jaw" of Holberg's talkative barber. As we saw in chapter 1, Gert Westphaler suffers from a "chatter disease," the clinical structure of which is an obsessive urge to transmit information that frequently overwhelms his own conscious intentions. Hence, the dramatic struggle between Master Gert and Mister Mouth at the end of Holberg's play. Only by stuffing a handkerchief into his mouth, effectively jamming the oral machinery on which his chatter depends, can Master Gert finally stem its flow, thereby reasserting himself as an intending subject—but never to such an extent that he regains authority as a speaking subject as well. When Gert begins to chatter, language speaks through him, not the other way around. And the only way he can resist this garrulous condition is by foregoing speech entirely, inadvertently forfeiting the very agency he hoped to regain from language.

What, then, do premise-authors lack? If they lack a meaningful subject of discussion, it is because they lack a coherent life- and worldview; and if they lack these, it is because they lack something even more basic: *a rigorous sense self.* When Kierkegaard insists that the premise-author "does not have an understanding to communicate," he does not mean that such authors are devoid of understanding. Rather, he is attempting to show that the understanding they convey to others is, in fact, a profound misunderstanding of themselves. The understanding they lack is always, to some extent, *self-understanding.* And this, according to Kierkegaard, is precisely what drives them to hasty publication. In exchange for premises strewn throughout their work, these authors hope to receive conclusions from the public—a literary transaction which proves that they are not as they appear. "One who needs the public or discussion in order to find understanding is not an author," Kierkegaard scowls. Instead of instructing the public with care, composure, and clever artistry, the premise-author "rushes at the public" in the heat of the moment, only to become its most impoverished student. "If he needs the public in order to find clarity and meaning in the matter, then of course the public knows more than he does, then of course he is a learner," specifically someone who "needs the public for its instruction and information, for its forbearing indulgences, for its most gracious applause with the air of connoisseurs, for its money, for its honors" (*BOA*, 14, 17).

Adler was certainly a premise-author, but not of the common sort. Instead of publishing many premises, he issued only one—namely, his outspoken belief that his subjective experience was in fact a direct revelation. But saying is not believing, and Adler's "revelation-fact" was no exception. "He himself seems to have become somewhat doubtful about what this revelation-fact really means," Kierkegaard suspects. "He himself seems to make it manifest that he does not understand himself in his being exceptionally favored in this way" (*BOA*, 18). In this sense, Adler's confusion was manifold from the start: He not only misunderstood his subjective experience as an objective event, and the latter as an occasion for immediate publication; he also failed to grasp the relevance of both misunderstandings to his work as a pastor, foolishly inviting readers to settle this matter for him. To this extent, Adler's uncertainty was strangely decisive, firmly establishing his revelation-fact as that of a premise-author. "By not understanding himself in it," he changed "the fact into a premise, into a miscellaneous announcement, into an inexplicable something about which one futilely seeks the explanation from him" (*BOA*, 18). Kierkegaard had experienced this futility personally in the summer of 1843, when Adler visited him in Copenhagen with news of a direct revelation. After *Sermons* appeared, it would be the bishop's turn to seek an explanation from the overwrought pastor.

Bustling Loquacity

Not everyone with a revelation-fact becomes a premise-author. And Adler might well have avoided this fate, quietly turning inward with his religious experience, much as an essential author would have done.

But he rushed at the public with news of a direct revelation instead. The irony of this gesture was completely lost on Adler, but Kierkegaard detected it immediately: "To foist on the public a revelation-fact and then himself to not know finally what is what, what he himself means by it, is to characterize himself as a premise-author, because it is thundering in the most terribly loud tones and then basically expecting that the surrounding world will come to his aid with the explanation as to whether he has actually had a revelation or not" (*BOA*, 22–23). This was a lot to ask of readers—and on a topic about which there should have been no question.

Initially, Kierkegaard thought Adler was arrogant, and his arrogance an overcompensation for deep uncertainty. But Adler was no *alazon*. For better and for worse, there was more to his thundering preface than the self-important bluster of someone compensating for profound self-ignorance. It was Adler's nervous preoccupation with a religious experience he did not understand, not the curious features of this religious experience itself, which drove him to hasty expression in the preface to *Sermons*; and it was this hasty expression which, in turn, gave him even more to fret about, eventually costing him his pastorate. His busyness begot chatter, and his chatter begot more busyness—to such an extent that Kierkegaard saw fit to coin a new term: "bustling loquacity" (*travl Snaksomhed*).

It was Adler's bustling loquacity, as much if not more so than his underlying confusion, that drew Kierkegaard to his work. But it was the intimate connection between his bustling loquacity and the era's trend toward premise-authorship that inspired to Kierkegaard to write a book about these discursive phenomena. As he saw it, the preface to Adler's *Sermons* was "a bitter epigram on the age" in need of careful interpretation:

In a tottering, irresolute, unsteady age, where in so many ways the individual is in the habit of seeking outside himself (in the sentiment of the surrounding world, in public opinion, in town gossip [*Bysnakken*]) what is essentially to be found only in the individual himself: decision—in such an age a man steps forth and appeals to a revelation, or, more correctly, he rushes out like one who is terrified, with frightful horror in his countenance, still shuddering from that moment of contact, and proclaims that a revelation has fallen to his lot. *Pro dii imortales* [Ye gods], there must certainly be help here, there must certainly be steadfastness here! Alas, he only resembles the age all too much. In the next moment he himself does not definitely know what is what [*veed han ikke selv med Bestemthed*]; he leaves it as such in abeyance. (*BOA*, 23)

Adler was startled by his religious experience, rushed to the public in search of answers, and, in so doing, forfeited his own capacity for judgment, allowing the whims of public opinion and the maunderings of town gossip to determine the import of his experience. To say that "he himself does not definitely know what is what," however, is to overgeneralize the state of confusion that brought Adler to this point. A better translation of *veed han ikke selv med Bestemthed* in the foregoing passage would be, "he does not know himself with certainty." As Kierkegaard's commentary on Adler's unwitting epigram continues to unfold, it becomes increasingly clear that this is precisely what he meant to suggest:

In those distant times when a man was vouchsafed lofty revelations, he used a long time to understand himself in this marvel before he began to want to guide others. That is, it can by no means be required of such a person that he must understand what surpasses human understanding, consequently understand the revelation, but he must understand himself in this, that it has happened to him, that it is the most certain of all that it has happened to him, and that, without any subsequent chatter [*Snak*], without any turning and twisting, it was and is and remains the revelation. Now, however, immediately the next morning one puts in the newspaper that one had a revelation last night. Perhaps one fears that the quiet [*stille*] solitary reflection (on what in the most extreme sense might very well alter a person's whole existence even if he never mentioned it to anyone) would lead one to the humbling but rescuing insight that it was an illusion, so one would drop the whole matter and would seek to become reconciled with God with respect to it, so one on lesser terms would truly become a teacher who knew how to teach others and to hold the highest infinitely in honor. Perhaps one fears this; on the other hand, perhaps one hopes that the announcement could prompt a discussion, the result of which could become that it now was certain that one had had a revelation, and that it was what the times demanded. In that case one could indeed maintain that one actually had had a revelation, relying upon the enormous sensation the announcement awakened, relying upon the acclamation with which one was hailed, not to mention how reassuring it was that several of the "really excellent journals we have" had expressed themselves in approval of it, and as a consequence public opinion sanctioned to the *n*th degree what, otherwise in the strictest, in the most isolating sense pertains to a particular individual, who with regard to this must unconditionally and exclusively seek certitude within himself. (*BOA*, 23–24)

Adler was not just nervous, impatient, and trembling with anticipation in the wake of his religious experience; he was also alarmed, horrified, and shuddering with terror. It was fear as much as confusion that made him quick to publish: fear of error and uncertainty, fear of silence and solitude, fear of humility before God—in short, fear of anything that might require private reflection and personal resolve. If the preface to his *Sermons* could meet with public approval and journalistic acclaim, Adler told himself, the sensation would likely become so enormous, so overwhelming, and so decisive that he could rest assured that his bewildering experience was, in fact, a direct revelation. For what match is the subjective experience of a single individual against "public opinion sanctioned to the nth degree"?

Once more, Kierkegaard is thinking numerically. And once more, he is taking aim at the fuzzy math of modern democracy. As we saw in the previous chapter, this fuzzy math finds decisive expression in social statistics, but it has the underlying numerical structure of sorites reasoning—a habit of mind at once anchored in the spurious belief that quantitative accumulation yields qualitative change and adrift in the false assumption that wholes are always greater than the sum of their parts. It was in pursuit of this chattering *Forstandighed* that we arrived at precise mathematical definition of the public: $P \supsetneq \{\{n+1\},\{\varnothing\}\}$. Along the way, we encountered several of its ideological outgrowths, not least of which is the modern conviction that there is *strength in numbers*—a conviction which indexes the expansive subset $\{n+1\}$ in the foregoing equation and is readily apparent in Kierkegaard's mistrust of "large-scale surveys" of public opinion. It is impossible to understand his scorn of "public opinion sanctioned to the nth degree" in *The Book on Adler* apart from this broader mistrust of democratic public culture—and all the more so given the footnote Kierkegaard appends to this scorn: "That is, since every newspaper writes in the name of the whole nation, a country acquires a fantastic population, which is just as many times greater than the actual population as there are mutually disagreeing papers" (*BOA*, 24). Fuzzy math, to be sure.

In his literary review of *Two Ages*, Kierkegaard figures these issues in terms of modern public culture. In his literary review of Adler's work, however, he figures them in terms of modern standards of authorship. When Adler attempted to incite a boisterous public discussion of his private religious experience, he not only fell into the literary trap of premise-authorship; he also stumbled into the religious dilemma of wishing for a public following beyond his congregation. To this extent, Adler was not just a premise-author. As Kierkegaard goes on to explain, he was "an adornment-author" as well—someone for whom "the main point and purpose of writing are to become noticed, recognized, praised." Adler was not writing as an apostle in service to new Christian doctrine; he was writing in search of public acknowledgment from as many readers as possible. It was "social esteem," not religious change, that the pastor sought (*BOA*, 260–61). Kierkegaard was hardly surprised, for Hegelian philosophers and Christian preachers often share the same vainglorious desire: "they all want to produce an effect, they all want their writings to win an extraordinary distribution and to be read, if possible, by all humankind" (*BOA*, 10). Adler was a perfect illustration of this. He even went so far as to prepare for the first run of *Sermons* to sell out: "The type remained set in the printing house, because he presumably expected that his *Sermons* would immediately require a new printing" (*BOA*, 241).

More than Adler wished to be understood, he expected to be "repeated again and again" (*BOA*, 12). This is why Kierkegaard argues that the public discussion he hoped to incite was little more than "town gossip" (*Bysnakken*). As we saw in chapter 1, the structure and effect of town gossip are the same: *repetition*. It was with this in mind that Kierkegaard depicted its garrulous purveyors as *Eftersnakkerne*. Adler was less a preacher in search of converts than a fanatic in search of parrots. His primary concern was no different from "the concern that usually plagues all busy, gadding people—to get some copycats, some adherents who agree with him, to get a society established that has its own seal" (*BOA*, 163). This was partly a result of his reliance on others for self-assurance: "He has no firm conviction at all but needs to have many people agree with him—so that his conviction can become convincing to himself." Which in turn suggests that "the nth degree" of public opinion Adler sought was equivalent to the greatest number of readers that *Sermons* could attract and influence. "To the degree to which many people listen to him, to the same degree he perceives that he has conviction, and to the same degree to which many people agree with him, to the same degree—he himself becomes convinced" (*BOA*, 100–01).

Adler's search for parrots was also symptomatic of the era. Public announcements like those in his preface to *Sermons* are wildly appealing "to all mediocre pates, all chatty people [*Snakkesalige*], all stuffed shirts, and therefore especially to the public," Kierkegaard laments (*BOA*, 146; trans. modified). In this sense, Adler's preface was no better than the response he hoped it would receive: he addressed Danish readers as a "chatterbox [*Snakke-Mester*]" and encouraged them to reply as "gossipmongers [*Sladder-Mestere*]." From his confused perspective, they were all part of the same "fabulous human mass," which he fully expected would bestir itself and take to "gabbing in the discussion-game" (*BOA*, 146–47).

Kierkegaard was stunned. This was the readership Adler hoped would settle the matter of his religious experience, providing him with a much-needed sense of self-certainty? If such a discussion-game were to begin, it would certainly be in response to Adler's bustling loquacity; but it would also come at his own expense, further subordinating him to this hasty way of speaking. If indeed there was an Adler Phenomenon, its axiom would have to stretch beyond the book of James: "The less time and self-mastery and perseverance a person has for wanting to understand himself, the more bustling loquacity [*travl Snaksomhed*] he has or, more correctly, the more he is in possession of bustling loquacity or, more correctly, is in the service of bustling loquacity" (BOA, 92–93).

Christian Wagers

The discussion-game Adler hoped to begin was, at root, *a numbers game*. In keeping with the modern doctrine of strength in numbers, Adler convinced himself that *more is better*. More publicity for his religious experience meant more assistance from others in determining its import to his work as a pastor; more assistance from others meant more town gossip about Adler himself; more town gossip about him meant more opportunities for religious parrots to emerge; and more religious parrots in flight meant more self-assurance for him to enjoy—or so Adler thought.

Much to Kierkegaard's chagrin, this line of thought was endemic to Adler's profession—the same profession Kierkegaard was still considering for himself at the time. In Christendom, numbers speak louder than words, and all the more so when they find expression in "preacher-prattle" (*Præstesnak*). Oftentimes, preachers rely on the fuzzy math we discussed in chapter 2, treating their congregations like religious publics. "Millions and millions of Xns, just as many Xns as there are peop," Kierkegaard glosses in his journal. "We are in Xndom, the country is Christian, we're all Xn. That's what's said. And when the priest speaks, on one Sunday he says that more and more people are becoming Xn—in Xndom, where everyone is Xn. On another Sunday it's that more and more are starting to fall away—in Xndom, where everyone is Xn." Fuzzy math of this sort is so pervasive among modern preachers that the religious community sustained by their prattle differs from the public in only one regard: "'Xndom' is a much more dangerous concept than 'the public.' It's a stage-setting that for the most part transforms all talk into drivel, even if what is said is otherwise well said."[11] Worse than the garrulous commonsense of the gallery-public as a whole is the preacher-prattle of Christendom in particular, Kierkegaard concludes.

More and more of everyone—this is the numerical rhetoric that Kierkegaard aims to indict, especially when it verges on imperialist claims that Christianity has "triumphantly conquered the whole world." Again, preacher-prattle is to blame: "We hear nothing but sermons that could more appropriately end with 'Hurrah' than with 'Amen,'" he complains. No wonder more converts to Christianity are attracting more converts to Christianity: "The majority are eager to be along when it is a matter of nothing more than celebrating and riding in the parade."[12] Like Adler, they adhere to the modern doctrine of strength in numbers.

With more converts come more priests, and with more priests, more numerical chatter. In addition to keeping a running tally of their congregants—right alongside running tallies of the nation's "sheep and ducks," Kierkegaard snipes—preachers now keep track of their own swelling numbers, again in hopes of demonstrating, once and for all, the triumph of Christianity in the modern world.

To illustrate this self-referential strand of preacher-prattle, Kierkegaard presents the following "Conversation":

A. Christianity simply does not exist.
B. What chatter [*snak*], how can Christianity not exist when there are 1,000 priests[?]
A. Yes, that's what the busybody [*Stundesløse*] says: How can I not have a great deal of business, I who employ 4 clerks and will soon have to take on a couple more[?] (*JNB* 8, 41; trans. modified. Cf. *JNB* 8, 140).

Readers would have been quick to recognize the busybody in question, recalling Holberg's three-act comedy about "The Fussy Man" (*Den Stundesløse*), which appeared just after his hilarious play about the garrulous barber we discussed in chapter 1. The main character, Fussy, is unemployed yet very busy, with a to-do list so long and varied that he only has time to lament how busy he is. He is too busy to complete any of his much-discussed tasks, but also too busy to realize that most of his unfinished business is utterly insignificant, with little if any bearing on his professional life. When others attempt to say as much, Fussy routinely dismisses their talk as "chatter [*snak*]" and replies with the numerical defense Kierkegaard outlines above—so often, it seems, that even Fussy's housekeeper is versed in the argument:

LEANDER. I don't understand what affairs a man can have who has no occupation.
FUSSY. I have so much business that I have no time to eat or drink. Pernille! He says I have no business. You can tell him about it.
PERNILLE. The master has ten men's work. It's his enemies who say he has no business. Besides me the master keeps four clerks; that alone proves he has plenty of business.[13]

In his *Book on Adler*, Kierkegaard takes this analogy between Fussy's four-clerk defense and Christendom's numerical chatter even further, using it to caution readers against another, more insidious strand of preacher-prattle. As he sees it, the "busy trifling" (*stundesløshed*) of his Christian peers finds decisive expression in their lofty sermons about "the eighteen hundred years" since Jesus walked the earth. The final testament to the triumph of Christianity, these preachers suggest, is neither their running tally of converts nor their running tally of priests but the fact that these tallies have be running for centuries.

Sometimes, prattling preachers use this historical fact to establish and maintain a vast spiritual distance between their congregations and the son of God, foolishly casting essential Christian practice into a "fantasy-twilight" where it quickly fades from daily life. More often than not, however, they use it to argue for the truth of Christianity and, in so doing, unwittingly undermine their own agenda: "The argument is made paralogistically from the eighteen centuries to the truth [*Sandhed*] of Christianity, by which brilliant and triumphant demonstration [*Beviis*] the truth of Christianity is unfortunately only undermined, since in that case it becomes true only as a hypothesis," Kierkegaard explains, indexing his critique of paralogistic talk and thought in his literary review of *Two Ages* (*BOA*, 36). Not surprisingly, he goes on to characterize this brilliant and triumphant line of demonstrative argument as a certain kind of chatter:

The eternal truth is just as true in its first moment as it is in its latest. Just as for God a thousand years is like one day, so also with an eternal truth, and it is impudence on the part of the thousand years to want to fancy itself to be something. The eternal truth does not become more true with the help of the thousand years, and neither does it become more obvious by their help that it is true. To say something like that is, as they say, to speak in spoonerisms or to chatter backward [*bakke snakvendt eller snakke bagvendt*]. (*BOA*, 36–37; trans. modified)

To further illustrate this curious strand of chatter, Kierkegaard recalls, once more, the bustling loquacity of Adler's preface, notably its implicit hope that public discussion of his religious experience might generate shared consensus regarding its significance and, in turn, personal conviction for the confused pastor. When someone "talks nonsense from time to time, there will be many who understand [*forstaae*] him. When there are many who understand [*forstaae*] him, the person who speaks in spoonerisms says: Now he has come closer to the truth than previously." But this, of course, is incorrect. "Because the thinker has abandoned the truth, there are many who understand [*forstaae*] him, that is, understand [*forstaae*] the untruth" (*BOA*, 37). This is precisely what happened when Adler went public with his religious experience. By subjecting the possibility of divine *logos* to the publicity of human *lalia*, he ensured that the only "understanding" available to him would be that of the *Forstandighed* which Kierkegaard, in his other 1846 literary review, stridently dismissed as "garrulous common sense."

Something similar happens when preachers speak in spoonerisms about the eternal truth of Christianity, attempting to justify it on the basis of centuries elapsed and worshipers recruited. "When someone speaks in spoonerisms, he thinks that the eternal truth has now become more obvious, more trustworthy. In other words, the eternal is not trustworthy enough; no, one thousand years and then a crowd!" As though eternal truth could be made more so by the mathematical process of addition. "What a preposterous inversion!" As Kierkegaard plainly states, there is nothing "mathematical" about the eternal truth of Christianity (*BOA*, 37).

Instead of being numerically precise, the eternal truth of Christianity is wholly paradoxical. And its central paradox is this: A changeless being entered into human existence, thereby riddling finitude with eternity. That many centuries have elapsed since this paradox emerged does not make it any less paradoxical. On the contrary, "it stands completely unaltered," impervious to "every impudent, importunate argument on the basis of the many years," Kierkegaard reminds his readers, clearly concerned that many of them, like Adler, no longer have "the time and patience and earnestness and the passion of thought" to recall this basic truth of Christian faith. "Whether the paradox existed for one thousand years or for only a half-hour makes no difference; it does not become more probable [*sandsynligt*] because it existed for one thousand years and not less improbable [*unsandsynligt*] because it lasted for only a half-hour" (*BOA*, 38).

It is only here, with the addition of probability (*sandsynlighed*) to his discussion of truth (*sandhed*), that the crux of Kierkegaard's claim against the numerical rhetoric of his priestly peers becomes fully apparent. When he insists that there is nothing "mathematical" about the basic paradox of Christianity or the religious truth in which it requires faith, he not only takes aim at religious appropriations of the modern belief that "more is better." More precisely, he targets the priestly use of more-is-better arguments to suggest that the truth of Christianity has somehow become more probable, and thus less paradoxical, over the centuries. Every triumphant tally of converts, clerics, and centuries points in this direction, adding to the erroneous belief that, with every passing year, the truth of Christianity becomes increasingly probable. Again, Kierkegaard has the era's fuzzy math in mind: "As soon as one begins to count [*at tælle*] the years, one begins to want to change the improbable into the probable" (*BOA*, 41). So much so that, "if one were to describe this entire orthodox apologetic endeavor in a single sentence, yet also categorically, one would have to say: Its aim is to make *Christianity probable*." All preacher-prattle about converts, clerics, and centuries serves this basic numerical purpose: to lure the primary paradox of Christianity into "the fussy officiousness of probability" (*BOA*, 39).

Hence, the lexical relationship between *sandhed* and *sandsynlighed* in Kierkegaard's original Danish. When the eternal truth of Christianity (*sandhed*) gives way to probabilistic talk of Christendom (*sandsynlighed*), the latter does not simply usurp the former, effectively taking its place in the era's religious imagination. Rather, as indicated by word *sandsynlighed* itself, which literally results from inserting *synlig* into *sandhed*, preacher-prattle about the *overt*, *visible*, and thus presumably *salient* features of religious life insinuates itself into the quiet, inward, and intensely personal pursuit of Christian truth. What bothers Kierkegaard about modern preacher-prattle, then, is not just its reliance on running tallies of converts, clerics, and centuries. More worrisome to him is the presentation of these tallies as *evidence* of Christianity's probable truth. At the risk of putting too fine a point on this concern, we might say that the difference between the *sandhed* of essential Christianity and the *sandsynlighed* of modern Christendom is the latter's penchant for observable and thus quantifiable signs (*syner*) of Christian truth, which its priestly purveyors mistakenly read as *proof* that the eternal truth of Christianity has become more demonstrable (*synlig*) and thus more probable (*sandsinlig*) over the centuries.

As we have seen, however, the religious effect of such preacher-prattle is just the opposite. Instead of showing that the truth of Christianity has become more probable and thus less paradoxical since Jesus walked the earth, this demonstrative line of argument sidesteps the issue of Christian truth entirely by reducing the primary paradox of Christianity and the leap of faith it demands to a series of scientific hypotheses in need of further testing, proof, and corroboration. Once again, the paralogos in question here amounts to sorites reasoning—a habit of mind which, as we saw in chapter 2, presumes that qualitative change can issue from quantitative accumulation. And once again, Kierkegaard's response is clear: No amount of modern *sandsynlighed* is sufficient to replace, much less to prove, the eternal *sandhed* of Christianity.

Epistemic Probability

Kierkegaard had been honing this argument for years. In *Philosophical Fragments*, he traces the issue of probability to an irreducible temporal gap between the historical period in which Jesus suffered and the present age in which would-be Christians laud his sacrifice. Irreducible, but not insurmountable, for to embrace the paradox of Christianity in a willingness to suffer as Jesus did is to become spiritually contemporaneous with him, thereby spanning the distance between his suffering and one's own in a profound leap of faith. As Kierkegaard is careful to insist, the structure of this trans-temporal leap is neither strictly eternal nor simply historical but, in keeping with the paradox of Christianity itself, an "eternalizing of the historical" that is also a "historicizing of the eternal." Together, these enfoldments of time prepare the way for "the *autopsy* of faith"—a personal and deeply private way of seeing one's relationship to God in and through which the believer becomes "eternally occupied with his historical existence" (*PF*, 61–62, 70).

All of this is muddled in Christendom. Instead of becoming spiritually contemporaneous with Jesus in reciprocal acts of suffering and faith, modern worshippers bemoan their comfortable historical distance from his personal abasement. And instead of following the lead of his apostles, they chatter wistfully about the glory they must have enjoyed as his immediate contemporaries, again lamenting their own historical remoteness (*JNB* 4, 240; *JNB* 7, 78). Kierkegaard sees this as another preposterous inversion of Christianity, and another opportunity to rib its modern adherents:

Only in one respect could I be tempted to regard the contemporary (in the sense of immediacy) as more fortunate than someone who comes later. If we assume that centuries elapsed between that event and the life of the one who comes later, then there presumably will have been a great deal of chatter [*Snak*] among men about this thing, so much loose chatter [*Snak*] that the untrue and confused rumors that the contemporary (in the sense of immediacy) had to put up with did not make the possibility of the right relationship nearly as difficult, all the more so because in all human probability [*Sandsynlighed*] the centuries-old echo, like the echo in some of our churches, would not only have riddled faith with gossip [*Sladder*] but would have eliminated it in gossip [*Sladder*]. (*PF*, 71; trans. modified)

The history of Christianity is a history of wistful chatter about the glory of being there with Jesus and his apostles—so much wistful chatter that quiet autopsies of faith have become nearly impossible. If Christendom is eager to celebrate the number of centuries it has endured since Jesus walked the earth, Kierkegaard is eager remind its priests and congregants that it has accumulated just as much loose historical chatter along the way, further separating them from essential Christianity with every passing year.

Later, in *Practice in Christianity*, Kierkegaard would define this chatter as "historical-talkative remembrance [*historisk-snaksom Ihukommelse*]," arguing that it only serves to make the era more ignorant of the religious past with which it is obsessed (*PC*, 9). The problem with "the garrulity of history [*Historiens Snaksomhed*]," especially when it comes to the life of Jesus, is the same as that of any other loquacious way of speaking: "when it gossips [*snakker*] about him [it] quite literally does not know what it is gossiping [*snakker*] about" (*PC*, 37; trans. modified). In *Philosophical Fragments*, however, Kierkegaard is more concerned with the rhetorical effect than the communicative structure of such chattering remembrance. Pastors and parishes alike may not comprehend the life of Jesus, but this does not mean any of them wish to remain ignorant of it. Which is precisely why their loose talk about Jesus and his apostles is so detrimental to Christian faith: The more they press for historical facts about his life, the further they stray from the religiosity of his basic teachings. "No matter how much one is educated up to the fact, it does not help," Kierkegaard explains. "On the contrary, especially if the one doing the educating is already himself well read along these lines, it can help someone to become a well-trained babbler [*Svatzer*] in whose mind there is neither a suggestion of offense nor a place for faith" (*PF*, 94).

Armed with "historical-talkative remembrance" and steeped in "the garrulity of history," these well-trained babblers are akin to all of the world-historical windbags and windsucks we discussed in chapter 1. Instead of meeting the absolute paradox of Christianity with faith or offense, they consider only what happened after its emergence, limiting their attention, once more, to the centuries between themselves and Jesus. Not surprisingly, the habit of mind they use to account for this temporal expanse resembles the haggling *Forstand* we discussed in chapter 2, allowing Kierkegaard to disclose yet another paralogistic application of the era's fuzzy math and sorites reasoning. Instead of culminating in social statistics, this quasi-religious habit of mind lends itself to *epistemic probability*—a way of thinking dedicated to the assessment of reasonable degrees of belief in propositions supported by evidence.[14]

Notice how Kierkegaard pits this way of thinking against the leap of faith, anticipating his later critique of preachers who argue by proof and probability—*Beviis* and *Sandsyndlighed*—for the truth of Christianity: "This generation is a long way from the jolt but, on the other hand, it does have the consequences to hold on to, has the probability proof [*Sandsynligheds-Beviis*] of the outcome, . . . has close at hand the probability proof from which there nevertheless is no direct transition to faith" (*PF*, 94). Were this not such a hindrance to the already difficult work of essential Christianity, Kierkegaard would make it the hilarious premise of a social drama fit for the Royal Danish Theater: "In order to come to the aid of humanity, a magnanimous person wants to use a probability proof to help humanity into the improbable" (*PF*, 94). But even this would fail to rouse Christendom from its fuzzy mathematical slumber, since the displacement of paradox with probability, the precondition of faith with a penchant for proof, has been "*naturalized* little by little" over the years, allowing epistemic probability to become the "*second nature*" of every modern worshiper (*PF*, 94–96).

Babble Dabble

Two years later, in his *Postscript* to *Philosophical Fragments*, Kierkegaard was still railing against epistemic probability. The truth of Christianity is not just paradoxical, he argues; it is also completely absurd. Rather than embrace this absurdity as "the dynamometer of faith," however, modern Christians attempt to rationalize it, effectively subjecting religious absurdity to probabilistic reason. With each attempt, the truth of

Christianity seems less and less absurd. "It becomes probable . . . more probable . . . exceedingly probable," Kierkegaard writes. So exceedingly probable that worshipers can "almost know, or as good as know, to a higher degree and exceedingly almost *know*" the truth of Christianity. "But *believe* it," Kierkegaard adds, "that cannot be done" (*CUP* 1, 211).

If the structure of Christian truth is faith, that of epistemic probability is understanding—and not just any kind of understanding. In line with much of his middle work, Kierkegaard uses the Danish term *Forstandighed* to describe the understanding at work in epistemic probability:

The sensible person, with his understanding of probability [*den Forstandige sig med Forstanden for i Sandsynligheden*], finds God where probability suffices and thanks him on the great festival days of probability when he has obtained a really good job and there is the probability of quick advancement to boot. And he thanks him when for a wife he finds a girl both beautiful and congenial, and even Councilor of War Marcussen says that it will be a happy marriage, that the girl has the kind of beauty that in all probability will last a long time and that she is built in such a way that in all probability she will bear healthy and strong children. (*CUP* 1, 232–33; trans. modified)[15]

And, and, and—this is exactly the kind of rambling, distracted, pedantic, and self-involved babble that the Greeks assigned to the *adoleschos*, that Kierkegaard later attributed to the *Schwätzer* and the *Raisonneur*, and that Heidegger and Lacan, as we shall see in subsequent chapters, further theorized in their own discussions of aimless, run-on speakers such as these.

Here, in *Postscript*, however, Kierkegaard is eager to connect the probabilistic maundering of "the sensible person" to that of "the well-trained babbler" he denounced in *Philosophical Fragments*, if only to suggest that average worshippers learn to speak this way from prattling priests, whose quasi-religious instruction he defines as *dabbling*. "As soon as the religious address casts a sidelong glance at fortune, comforts with probability, strengthens temporarily, it is a false teaching, is a regression into the esthetic and therefore is dabbling [*Fuskerie*]." *Fuskerie* descends from the Old Norse *fiska*, meaning "to fish," but its closest ancestor is the Danish verb *at fuske*, which has two basic meanings: "to swindle" and "to botch." Both are integral to Kierkegaard's critique of preacher-prattle: the poet who dabbles in the religious is a "bungler," and the priest who dabbles in the esthetic is a "deceiver" (*CUP* 1, 436). Obviously, the latter is of foremost concern to him. When priests "chatter esthetically [*snakker æsthetisk*]" about religious matters, they dabble in rhetorical appeals without regard for Christian practice, and these appeals, in turn, become "muddled up in talkativeness [*Snaksomheden*] and a lust for preaching" (*CUP* 1, 554, 490).

In order to understand how dabbling of this sort can be deceptive, we must recall the basic task of religious discourse (*religieuse Taler*) in Kierkegaard's middle work: *to uplift through suffering*. It is only through personal suffering, in the spirit of Jesus, that faithful Christians, in singular states of religious inwardness, can come to terms with themselves before God. "It is precisely in suffering that the religious breathes," Kierkegaard summarizes, recalling his earlier comments on the *examen rigorosum* of modern public life, "so that its absence signifies the absence of religiousness (*CUP* 1, 436–37). To be sure, preachers should be free to speak "widely and broadly on the world," and they needn't feel obliged to discuss religious suffering in every sermon. But all of their discourse, public and private alike, should hold the essential category of religious suffering in view, much as essential authors always grasp the substance of their authorships before picking up their pens to work on any particular project. "In whatever it says, however it skips around, whatever road it takes in order to catch people, however much it witnesses in monologue to the speaker's own existence, it must always have its totality-category present as a criterion, so that the experienced person promptly perceives the total orientation in the life-view of the address" (*CUP* 1, 235, 435). Otherwise, the religious speaker is no better than the premise-author—and their sermons are no more than bustling loquacity.

Religieuse Taler becomes *Præstesnak* when speakers lose sight of religious suffering, meander from topic to topic without focus, and then attempt to compensate for the resulting jumble of themes with increasingly dramatic rhetorical appeals (*CUP* 1, 435). In moments like these, religious address devolves into a "pastor's medley" of talking points, and the pastor becomes little more than "a poet-quack" (*CUP* 1, 439). The good news of salvation through suffering in the spirit of Jesus is lost in "a sad conglomeration of bits from every sphere"—a sad conglomeration to which pastors, sensing that their rambling discourse has failed to uplift struggling worshippers, then apply a "bourgeois-citified sugar coating" (*CUP* 1, 435, 482). Rather than address the topic of religious suffering, these poet-quacks attempt to console their listeners with "priestly drivel [*Præstesludder*] about a heavenly friend, the gentle doctrine of truth, the satisfying of deep longings, depth itself, and other such saccharine stuff, which the silk-clad priests serve up to their silk-clad listeners."[16] And all in service to worldly dialectics of fortune and misfortune, where the wages of Christian faith are not paid in personal suffering like that of Jesus but deferred with promises of future comfort bolstered by epistemic probability (see, for instance, *JNB* 9, 50). "The unfortunate person must not lose courage," pastors cry, for "there is, after all, the probability that 'with the help of God things will surely get better'" (*CUP* 1, 437). But not all at once, of course, lest our heavenly friend infringe upon the era's sorites thought: "little by little things will improve—indeed, this is probable" (*CUP* 1, 233).

At every step of the way, the religious chatter of these poet-quacks becomes increasingly dramatic, but also strangely vacuous. "His Reverence the pastor becomes most eloquent and gesticulates most vigorously, presumably because the religious category will not taste right, but it goes more easily by dabbling a bit in being a poet," Kierkegaard quips in *Postscript*—a quip made doubly ironic by the fact that the worldly dialectic over which the pastor frets is hardly a religious category, much less one worthy of Christian concern. But this is not the pastor's only esthetic device. When promises of future comfort fail to raise spirits and eloquent gesticulations no longer stir souls, today's dabbling preachers resort to another persuasive technique, distracting worshippers with any number of religious platitudes, all of which are so impossibly abstract that they preclude concrete action:

Preacher-prattle [*Præstesnakken*] is vapor off in the blue, whether the pastor is busily engaged [*travlt*] with vast world-historical visions and matchless hawk-eye views that are impossible to act upon, or he esthetically talks a lot of obscure nonsense [*snakker*] that is also impossible to act upon, or he describes imaginary states of mind for which the acting person vainly seeks in actuality, or consoles with illusions that the acting person does not find in actuality, or conjures up passions as they at most seem only to one who does not have them, or conquers dangers that are not there and leaves the actual ones unmentioned, conquers them by theatrical dynamics that are not found in life and leaves the dynamics of actuality unutilized. (*CUP* 1, 442; cf. *JNB* 7, 421)

In style and substance alike, the problem with such dabbling is clear: it distracts would-be Christians from the paradoxical truth for which they should faithfully suffer instead. In this sense, prattling pastors have much in common with garrulous barbers, speculative philosophers, and busybodies of every stripe. As we saw in chapter 1, Holberg's talkative barber is unable to hold a conversation with anyone, including himself, without straying from the topic at hand, distracting all involved with tedious, long-winded, and hilariously tangential monologues. And Hegelian thinkers are no better off, according to Kierkegaard, especially when it comes to their historical-conceptual writings, the primary effect of which is to impress readers with learned tales of enchanted journeys through world-historical monarchies and, in so doing, to avert serious methodological questions about the "correctness" of the absolute method itself. And who can forget Fussy, the unemployed yet terribly busy main character in the Holberg play mentioned above, who is perennially distracted from his long, varied, wholly insignificant to-do list by his own tireless kvetching about just how busy he is—as demonstrated, he claims, by the four clerks he employs. In each case, we see the same chattering mind at work—what it lacks in significance, it makes up for with diversion.

What makes the diversions of dabbling pastors especially dangerous is the close affinity they reveal between modern congregations and the era's gallery-public. As we saw in chapter 2, Kierkegaard defines the gallery-public as a spectral society inclined toward amusement and convinced that "everything anyone does is done so that it may have something to gossip about." When Sunday sermons devolve into theatrical performances, would-be Christians follow suit, becoming an especially gullible subset of modernity's spectacle society. "For a bagatelle, we gain admission to the pastor's dramatic performances, where we sit and observe what faith is capable of doing—not as believers, but as spectators" (*CUP* 1, 419). And we get what we pay for, Kierkegaard suggests, making clever use of the Danish *Bagatel*: not just a paltry performance for a paltry fee, but also, more deplorably, priestly folderol in exchange for our own.

The effect of this quasi-religious spectatorship is twofold. First, it sets the stage for the fuzzy mathematical claims discussed in this chapter. When entire congregations devolve into gallery-publics, individual congregants become particularly vulnerable to strength-in-numbers and more-is-better sermons on the triumph of Christianity, especially when these sermons are premised on running tallies of converts, clerics, and centuries. And second, it causes would-be worshippers to equivocate about the meaning of Christianity and its relevance to their everyday lives, a spiritual wavering of sorts whose expression, in keeping with the garrulous commonsense of the gallery-public, resembles the very preacher-prattle that spoke it into existence: "The whole crowd of experienced and commonsensical people [*Erfarne og Forstandige*], of tinkers and patchers, shows up and with the help of probability [*Sandsynlighed*] and grounds of comfort rivets the scraps or holds the rags together. Life goes on; advice is sought from the sagacious men of ecclesiastic or secular rank, and it all becomes a muddle [*Kludderie*]" (*CUP* 1, 443). When probabilistic talk of religious comfort passes from "well-trained babblers" on pulpits to "experienced and commonsensical people" in pews, the result is not an additional outburst of poetic quackery but, instead, a collective state of spiritual confusion, comparable in form and function to the *Tvetydighed* that Kierkegaard denounces in his 1846 critique of the present age.

Hence, the use of *Kludderie* above, from the Danish *klud*, meaning *rag*. As we saw in chapter 2, Kierkegaard likens public discussion and collective decision-making to the fabrication of paper from rags (*klude*), suggesting that the strength in numbers which modern democratic citizens enjoy is no greater than that of poorly crafted paper (*TA*, 103–4). In his unpublished *Book on Adler*, he adds biblical captions to this biting analogy: "'One does not put a new patch on an old garment or new wine into an old wineskin, lest the hole become larger and the wineskin burst'—and the very same thing will happen if by uncircumspect treatment in hasty busyness [*Travlhed*] the absolutely new point of departure is muddled [*kluddret*] into the old" (*BOA*, 249; cf. Matt. 9: 16–17; Luke 5:36–37). At the risk of creating a muddle of our own, we might summarize this allusive argument as follows, integrating several of Kierkegaard's key terms into a single statement: When confused pastors succumb to bustling loquacity, which in turn finds expression in esthetic dabbling and probabilistic talk, average worshippers in need of clear spiritual guidance become equivocating spectators at an overwrought theatrical performance—and consequently just as confused as the pastors who purport to lead them.

Maundering Equivocation

Adler was one of the era's confused pastors. And his primary confusion, as we have seen, was religious-philosophical: he mistook his lyrical genius as a Hegelian scholar for the religious authority of a Christian apostle. On Kierkegaard's reading, this was symptomatic of the era's ongoing effort to displace the paradoxical truth of Christianity with the epistemic probability of modern thought. Notice how he draws this connection, subtly pinning the blame on religious Hegelians like Adler: "The effort has been to make Christianity probable, comprehensible, to take it out of the God-language of the paradox and get it translated into the Low-German of speculative thought" (*BOA*, 40). In this sense,

Adler not only personified the religious confusion of the present age, but also gestured toward its regrettable origin in modern philosophy. Kierkegaard was quick to seize on both aspects of the Adler Phenomenon, if only to level his sights, once more, on the era's speculative thinkers, notably its Danish Hegelians.

That Adler could mistake his lyrical genius as a Hegelian scholar for the religious authority of a Christian apostle was in keeping with a more fundamental confusion—a confusion whose paralogos, as we have seen throughout this chapter, troubled Kierkegaard immensely. When Adler awoke to a hideous sound and a voice instructing him to write, he mistook his internal subjective experience for an external religious event, and the latter as a reason to declare that he had received a direct revelation. In making this announcement, however, he only added to his own confusion. But this also exposed the underlying clinical structure of his ailment. More than a Hegelian scholar posing as a Christian apostle, Adler was a "vacillating person" struggling to serve two masters: "He wants to be called by God in a special sense, and then he also wants to be called by the age, be what the times demand. He uses the cry 'I am called by God' as an interjection in order to get a hearing in the noisy crowd, and then he wants to convert his call from God into a call from public opinion" (BOA, 25). So which was it—the voice of Jesus or the lure of publicity—that woke him in the night and compelled him to write? Adler could not say.

To this extent, he not only personified the era's religious confusion and gestured toward its intellectual history. He also embodied the psychosocial link between this spiritual condition and its philosophical predecessor, adding illustrative captions to the liminal state that Kierkegaard described in his other 1846 literary review, which we further conceptualized in the previous chapter: *equivocation*. Just beneath the surface of Adler's religious-philosophical confusion was the shifting intellectual sand of the present age itself: "dialectical equivocation [*dialektisk Tvetydighed*]" (BOA, 19; trans. modified).

Notice how Kierkegaard presents this dilemma, integrating several familiar themes—aimless talk, muddled thought, gnawing reflection, common sense, dialectical fraud, and the like—into a summative critique of Adler's work: "On the whole Magister Adler may be regarded as a good example of the maundering in dialectical sense [*den Sluddervorrenhed i dialektisk Forstand*] that is so common in our day. One jumbles one thing into another, gives up one system as it is called and goes further, but at no point does one ever come to any decisive determination." The lesson to be learned from his "equivocating phenomena [*tvetydige Phænomener*]" is simple: "one must keep a sharp lookout," especially when Hegelians are about, for "equivocation speculates—in confusing [*Tvetydigheden spekulerer–i at forvirre*]" (*BOA*, 249–50; trans. modified).

This assumes, of course, that anyone even attended to Adler's equivocating work. Kierkegaard certainly had his doubts—and this was all he could say to Adler's credit. "One can fortunately say of him that he has not done very much harm," but only "because he has been completely ignored" (*BOA*, 258). Ignored by everyone, it seems, except his ecclesiastical superiors, several of whom not only read Adler's *Studies* and *Sermons* but also determined that these books posed a direct threat to the church—direct enough, it seems, to warrant the pastor's interrogation and ultimately his dismissal.

As we saw at the start of this chapter, the bishop of the diocese addressed several questions to Adler in response to *Studies* and *Sermons*. When asked if he had been "excited and confused" during the composition or publication of either book, Adler cited the "meaning and coherence" of both texts. Kierkegaard found this hilarious. How was the pastor's ability to satisfy "grammatical requirements" evidence of his calm and collected state of mind when writing or publishing either book? "Adler's reply is an answer to the question in neither one sense nor the other," Kierkegaard concludes (*BOA*, 56). Already, the pastor was beginning to equivocate.

Matters only grew worse as the interrogation proceeded. When asked to account for his claims of direct revelation and divine inspiration, Adler dodged this question as well. Instead of defending or abandoning his earlier claims, he redefined his religious experience as "a rescue in marvelous ways" by which he was "deeply moved," and then reduced his boisterous declarations of this marvelous rescue to "a child's first babbling, lisping, imperfect voice" (as quoted in *BOA*, 344–45). Both revisions gave Kierkegaard pause. First and foremost, they changed the topic. Rather than accounting for his earlier claims, Adler was attempting to mitigate them *ex post facto*, retroactively converting them into expressions far less offensive to the state church. What began as a series of decisive statements about direct revelation, divine inspiration, and new religious doctrine now became the tentative announcement of a marvelous yet rather vague spiritual awakening. This was neither a vindication nor a revocation of his earlier claims but, instead, the presentation of entirely new ones! Adler not only left the bishop's second question unanswered, much as he did the first, but also sought to alter the very conditions of its asking. After explaining "what a circle is," he now wants to explain "that it is a square," Kierkegaard chides. "This is no explanation; it is a new statement" (*BOA*, 266).

Not surprisingly, it also serves as preacher-prattle. And not just because Adler "allowed the first statement to stand and then loquaciously [*snaksomt*] said this and that about its not being anything new and about its not being exactly a revelation either but in a way some remarkable something or other" (*BOA*, 241). Indeed, there was more to his "turning and twisting" than a revisionist moment of volatile Hegelian "chatter [*Snak*]" (*BOA*, 23). This became especially clear when, after downplaying the religious import of his marvelous rescue, Adler likened his earlier claims of direct revelation, divine inspiration, and the like to "a child's first babbling, lisping, imperfect voice." In so doing, he not only offset the brazen claims of *Studies* and *Sermons* with less offensive remarks, but also affected a certain kind of "praiseworthy author-modesty," apparently in deference to his ecclesiastical superiors—a gesture which Adler seems to have hoped would return him to their good graces. Like most preacher-prattle, this deprecating rhetorical maneuver tapped into the self-indulgent, comfort-oriented *Forstandighed* of modern public culture. Or, at least, that is how Kierkegaard saw it: "An esteemed, cultured public that in its lack of categories has a most cherished preference for complimentary chatter [*Complimenet-Snak*] would certainly like it if there was nothing else in the way" (*BOA*, 68).

And like most preacher-prattle, this complementary chatter was an affront to essential Christianity. If indeed Adler had taken dictation for Jesus, written sermons at his behest, and thus become "an instrument" of divine *logos*, it was wholly inappropriate for him to diminish or dismiss his earlier pronouncements as childish, lisping, imperfect, or babbling. The final term in this diminutive series must have been particularly vexing to Kierkegaard, and all the more so given that "babbling" translates Adler's use of the Danish *lallende*, an obvious descendent of the Greek *lalia*. To deliver divine *logos* and then reduce it to childish *lalia* was not just inappropriate; it was blasphemous. And to do so in an effort to appease church officials, effectively sacrificing the new doctrine he initially claimed to receive from Jesus in hopes of retaining his job as a rural pastor, proved Kierkegaard's point: *Adler was playing the odds.*

Instead of suffering for his earlier pronouncements in fear, trembling, and faith that the voice he heard was in fact that of Jesus, Adler was using preacher-prattle to console church officials in hopes of securing his own future comfort. In the wake of his religious experience, he was all too quick to join in the boisterous *lalia* of society, rushing at the public with news of direct revelation, divine inspiration, and a new religious doctrine; and in the wake of his suspension from office, he seemed willing to go even further, hastily reducing the divine *logos* which compelled his actions to childish *lalia* of no concern to the church. What Kierkegaard would later warn against in his sermon on "The Changelessness of God," Adler readily displayed in response to the bishop's interrogation: a willingness to subject the word of God to public opinion, or, at least, to waver retroactively between the two, effectively reducing the rigorous practice of essential Christianity to the probabilistic reason of modern preacher-prattle.

PART TWO

Idle Talk

FOUR

Beginning More than Halfway There

Between Things

In 1916, Martin Heidegger published his obscure postdoctoral thesis on *The Doctrine of Categories and Signification in Duns Scotus*. A decade later, he published the book that would make him famous: *Being and Time*. In the intervening years, he published nothing at all—and his university career suffered accordingly. Twice he was denied professorships due to lack of publications, and even when he managed to secure a tenure-track appointment, largely on the basis of unpublished work, he was denied full pay for the same reason.

Heidegger conceived of "idle talk" (*Gerede*) and several related terms—notably "babble" (*Geschwätz*), "scribbling" (*Geschreibe*), and "everyday discourse" (*alltägliche Rede*)—during this decade-long period of scholarly silence and professional strife. This was not a coincidence. As we shall see, his initial accounts of these ordinary communicative practices not only paved the way for his renowned theories of speech and language in *Being and Time*; they also served as biting social critiques of the publish-or-perish prerogatives of the modern research university—the same prerogatives that stymied his early career and eventually compelled him to publish *Being and Time* well before the manuscript was complete. Documenting this amalgam of professional anxiety, social critique, and communication theory in Heidegger's early thought is the primary task of this chapter. Bringing some conceptual clarity to the key terms, core arguments, and methodological agendas he developed along the way is its ultimate goal.

To begin, consider the auspicious start of Heidegger's university career. From the winter semester of 1915–1916 to the summer semester of 1923, he was an unsalaried instructor at Freiburg University. And from 1919 to 1923, he also served as Edmund Husserl's teaching assistant. During this period, Heidegger taught a series of widely acclaimed courses and seminars. So widely acclaimed, in fact, that Husserl frequently tried and repeatedly failed to place his assistant in a tenure-track appointment. The eminent phenomenologist began by writing to Paul Natrop at Marburg University in February 1920:

In the last two years [Heidegger] has been for me an invaluable philosophical coworker. I have the very best impressions of him as a professor and philosophical thinker, and I place great hopes in him. His seminar meetings are as well attended as my own, and he is able to captivate beginners as well as advanced students. Moreover, his highly praised lecture courses—polished in form and yet profound— are very heavily attended (about 100 students). He has worked his way into phenomenology with the greatest energy, and he strives to lay the most secure foundations for his philosophical thinking. . . . I can now say that he is one of the most promising young men whom we have to look after (as regards his material plight, which he nonetheless bears lightheartedly. To use the Viennese expression, Heidegger is not a *Raunzer*, a whiner).[1]

Nothing came of Husserl's glowing letter. Acclaimed instructor or not, Heidegger lacked the requisite publications for a tenure-track appointment. But Husserl refused to give up.

Two years later, in February 1922, he wrote to Natrop again, offering a frank yet favorable assessment of Heidegger's scholarly progress:

Although Heidegger is developing strongly, one is unable to provide public documentation of his considerable talents, because he still chooses not to publish. It would not surprise me at all if an *uncommon* measure of energy and power were aborning in him. His *receptive* abilities are somewhat *underdeveloped*, and he is anything but tractable. He is *an entirely original personality*, struggling, searching for himself, laboring to forge his own solidly grounded approach. . . . Despite his dry lecture style, he exerts a strong attraction on beginning and advanced students alike through his original ideas, presented in a language that he himself has forged. (*BH*, 368–69)

Again, nothing came of Husserl's effort. Heidegger remained an unsalaried instructor at Freiburg University, in an ongoing state of "material plight."

So when Georg Misch at the University of Göttingen wrote to Husserl later that spring in search of candidates for an associate professorship in philosophy, inquiring about Heidegger in particular, Husserl leaped at the opportunity to recommend his teaching assistant. Again, he celebrated Heidegger's intellectual abilities: "the depth of his insight, the scope of his scholarship, his original style with a feel for the finest intellectual nuances inimical to all overbearing catchphrase and bombastic rhetoric, drawing all his insights from material thought through in the most concrete way." And again, he coupled this with praise of Heidegger's work in the classroom: "As a teacher, Heidegger is already well known beyond Freiburg. His impact is extraordinary, in view of the heavy demands that he imposes on the students who work with him. His phenomenological pro-seminar, in which nevertheless most of my advanced students tend to participate, has eighty-six persons registered in this semester. The usual number is generally between sixty and eighty. He could even venture to advertise a *four-hour* course on Aristotle—Interpretations—with success." Still, however, Husserl could not ignore Heidegger's lack of publications: "Beginning in autumn, the *Yearbook* will bring out a series of great treatises [by Heidegger]. . . . It is too bad that the newly planned publications are not already in print. For then there would be no question" (*BH*, 371–72). Misch seemed to agree. In the hiring proposal he submitted to the Ministry of Science, Art, and National Education, he and his colleagues praised Heidegger for his "strong philosophical talent" and "strong influence as a teacher of philosophy" but ultimately ranked him second due to his lack of "finalized literary achievements." The problem with Heidegger, Misch plainly stated, is that "his fame precedes his literary achievements" (*BH*, 341).

It was not until December 1922 that anyone other than Husserl was willing to take a risk on his eminently unpublished teaching assistant—and it was not much of a risk. The philosophical faculty at Marburg University nominated Heidegger for an untenured and woefully underpaid associate professorship. And like all of Husserl's letters of recommendation, the nomination Marburg addressed to the Ministry attempted to offset Heidegger's lack of publications with outspoken praise of his formidable intellectual strength and increasing renown as a teacher: "The novelties of his goals dictated a slow maturation, which also accounts for the fact that Heidegger has published nothing for years. That he has not stood still in this time is borne out by his prolific teaching activity, whose fruitfulness has been felt by students and colleagues far beyond the realm of the academic life of Freiburg" (*BH*, 343). The Minister of Science, Art, and National Education agreed: Husserl's teaching assistant was worth the risk.

When Heidegger joined the faculty at Marburg University in October 1923, his reputation as a revolutionary college instructor only increased, attracting students like Hannah Arendt, Herbert Marcuse, Hans-Georg Gadamer, Leo Strauss, and several other soon-to-be-illustrious scholars. Much to the frustration of his colleagues, however, Heidegger still refused to publish—and his career continued to suffer as a result. In the summer of 1925, for instance, the faculty met to consider Heidegger for promotion to full professor. No one doubted that his work in the classroom was impressive, but all agreed that his ongoing refusal to publish remained a problem. When skeptical faculty members asked, "which of Heidegger's writings have been published," his staunchest supporters could only reply that "there is a new and outstanding work by Heidegger but that, nevertheless, as with his earlier work, it has not yet been published."[2] Word of this dispute soon reached Husserl, and, once more, he rushed to Heidegger's defense:

His singular virtuosity as a teacher—the way his lectures seize the whole person and win people over by the seriousness of his philosophical views—must surely be well known among the colleagues at Marburg. In my view Heidegger is without a doubt the most significant of those who are now making their career. Absent some irrational fate or unforeseen occurrence, he is predestined to be a philosopher of the grand style, someone who can lead beyond the confusion and decadence of the present age. He has a host of original things to say, but for years now he has maintained his silence in order that he might publish only what is completely mature, conclusive, and compelling. All of this will be proven by the works he will be publishing in the very near future. (*BH*, 377)

The philosophical faculty at Marburg ultimately agreed with Husserl. In August 1925, they nominated Heidegger for promotion to full professor. Their recommendation centered on two of Heidegger's works in progress. The first was a much-anticipated book manuscript on Aristotle: "To be sure, this major work has not yet appeared in publication, but it has long been complete in repeatedly reworked form, and will soon appear." The second was "a systematic work of recent origin—now being printed—on 'Time and Being' [*sic*], which shows us yet another side of Heidegger, as an independent and constructive philosophical thinker" (*BH*, 344–45). Once again, Marburg's philosophical faculty was willing to take a risk on the eminently unpublished Heidegger.

This time, however, the Prussian Minister of Education disagreed. In January 1926, he denied their request that Heidegger be promoted to full professor. "While acknowledging Professor Heidegger's success as a teacher," the minister wrote, "it seems nevertheless inappropriate to transfer him the budgetary, Ordinary Professorship with the histori-cal significance of the Marburg position before an extensive literary accomplishment finds specific acknowledgement, demanding such ap-pointment, by members of the discipline" (*HJC*, 224). Works in prog-ress, brilliant or not, were insufficient for the advancement of Heideg-ger's career.

In response to this rejection—the latest and most pronounced in a series professional setbacks, all due to lack of literary accomplishment—Heidegger rushed his magnum opus to print well before the manuscript was complete. But even this proved insufficient. When Heidegger's colleagues replied to the minister in June 1926, appending the galley pages of *Being and Time* to their letter and imploring him to reconsider their request for Heidegger's promotion, the minister issued another, far more devastating rejection, insisting that Heidegger's forthcoming book was "inadequate" (*BH*, 379). The minister even declined to keep the galleys, returning them to Heidegger instead.

Husserl, ever Heidegger's advocate, could only offer his "deepest sympathy" and a few words of encouragement: "All this happens just as you are blessed with the great fortune of having in press the book with which you grow into what you are and, as you well know, have given your own being as a philosopher its first realization. Beginning with this book you will blossom into new dimensions. No one has greater faith in you than I, and I am sure nothing will drag you down into resentment" (*BH*, 379).

But it was too late. By the summer of 1926, Heidegger had already come to resent the profession whose publish-or-perish prerogatives continued to stymy his university career. And this resentment toward the discipline of philosophy fueled his early discussions of ordinary language use. Indeed, as we shall see, all of the key terms at play in these early discussions—*Gerede, Geschreibe*, and *Geschwätz*—took shape around issues of academic philosophy in the early-1920s.

"He Who Publishes Nothing"

Heidegger knew his refusal to publish was hindering his career. But he also thought refusal of this sort was requisite to philosophical inquiry in the early-1920s. "The old ontology (and the structures of categories that have grown out of it) must be rebuilt from the ground up—if this is taken seriously, it means grasping and directing one's own personal life in its basic intentions," he wrote to Karl Jaspers in June 1922, while Misch and his colleagues at Göttingen University, at Husserl's behest, were considering Heidegger for a professorship. In order to grasp and direct the basic intentions of one's own life, Heidegger continued, one must turn profoundly inward, away from the pedantic world of philosophical talk and text, even (and especially) at the risk of professional and financial ruin—and yet in such a way that one continues to embody the life of the mind, modeling for one's students, if for no one else, the hard work of "scientific research." On this point, ironically enough, Heidegger seemed eager to write:

To concretely and cleanly fulfill this task—solely as a pretask—indeed, merely to bring it to the basis of a clear formulation, requires a lot of work. When we earnestly, constantly, and livingly pursue this in respect to the question of the explication of the meaning of the being of life, as *the* object that we *are*, and with this every intimacy and every care—every agitation as caring in the broadest sense, then, out of inner respect for the object with which we go around philosophizing—we keep ourselves from saying something just to get published.

Either we are serious with philosophy and its possibilities as a principal kind of scientific research, or we understand ourselves as scientific persons of the worst deficiency—in that we gurgle on and on [*weiterplätschern*] in worn-out concepts and half-clear intentions, and we work only as required.

Should we grasp the first alternative, then we have chosen the danger of risking our entire external and internal existence for something whose success and result we are not able to see.

I have made it clear to myself without sentimentality that the decision in favor of this alternative comes into question only for the philosopher as a scientific investigator. There are things about which we do not speak and, in a pronouncement like this, only indicate. If it doesn't succeed in awakening such consciousness positively and concretely in the youth, then all chatter [*Gerede*] about the crisis of science and the like is just chatter [*Gerede*]. If it is not clear to us that we must live out such matters—in first developing them—in front of the youth, then we have no right to live in scientific research. (*HJC*, 34–35; trans. modified)

Anything less than this, Heidegger concluded, might make for "a fine livelihood," but it would amount to little more than "philosophical gurgling [*philosophischen Geplätscher*]" (*HJC*, 36).

Maybe so, Jaspers replied, but this did not free Heidegger from the professional and philosophical obligation to publish some of his scientific research. Quite the opposite, in fact: "I would like to read something new from you . . . because not only the inner, but also the outer, destiny of what we are talking about depends upon such publications—from you above all, since you already hold strong personal credit with many, and they only wait for *something to come of it*" (*HJC*, 37).

Heidegger was willing to meet Jaspers halfway. A few months later, when he learned he was a candidate for professorships at Marburg and Göttingen, he decided to dictate and deliver to both universities "a concrete orientation concerning my planned projects." In so doing, he hoped to secure "a *prominent* place" in their nomination letters—"presumably," he later quipped to Jaspers, "the famous second place." At the top of Göttingen's list, Heidegger went on to jest, would almost certainly be someone with extensive "*business trips*." And at the top of Marburg's would obviously be someone with "a lot paper."

Heidegger was proud that neither of these academic honors appeared on his curriculum vitae. Conference presentations and scholarly publications were inimical to his work as a rigorous scientific researcher. Indeed, as he explained to Misch in his application materials, philosophical inquiry should challenge "the narrow working context which originally belongs to the historical human sciences" by pursing an "explicitly rigorous and always concretely actualized bearing and development of the scientific consciousness." And the proper forum for this pursuit is neither a conference hotel nor an academic journal but, instead, the undergraduate classroom: "Such a consciousness does not get activated by speeches and pamphlets, which in the new [generation of] youth only breeds fatigue and exhaustion, but by bringing today's academic youth back from the excess of reflection and discussion to concrete and solid work on the matters themselves, on objective contexts that are given by scientific philosophy" (*BH*, 109).

Behind these bold pronouncements, however, Heidegger worried about his job prospects. It pained him to know that his avoidance of "speeches and pamphlets" continued to hinder his career, all but precluding the possibility of any philosophical faculty ranking him first in its hiring recommendation. "For myself, I would have to feel that such a ranking is a *disgrace*," he confessed to Jaspers in November 1922, "but, above all, I want peace for myself—one way or another. This being led on with half-prospects, bungling with recommendations, etc., brings you to a terrible state, even when you make up your mind not to get caught up in it" (*HJC*, 40). All of which suggests that, by the end of 1922, Heidegger was increasingly desperate for a tenure-track position but still unwilling to meet its basic academic requirements.

Much of this professional angst subsided in the summer of 1923, when he received Marburg's job offer. Heidegger saw the job offer as a vindication of his refusal to publish, and his adherence to this anti-disciplinary position only strengthened as a result. Refusing to engage in scholarly production became an even more pronounced feature of his philosophical agenda. "The fundamental reconstruction of philosophizing in the universities (i.e., in and with the sciences) will never be achieved by merely writing books," he proclaimed to Jaspers in July 1923, as he was preparing for his new position at Marburg. "Whoever still doesn't notice this and leads his pseudoexistence in the humdrum of today's busyness [*Betriebes*] does not know where he stands" (*HJC*, 47). For this reason alone, Heidegger went on to admit, and not without a little pride, "I still haven't printed anything, and I simply endure it when I am referred to as *he who publishes nothing*" (*HJC*, 46). More important to his work as a philosopher—and now more so than ever—was his work in the classroom:

I leave the world of books and literary goings-on, and fetch myself some young people—*fetch* means to treat them strictly, so that they are *under pressure* the whole week. Many can't endure it—the easiest kind of selection—many need two or three semesters to understand why I permit them nothing: no laziness, no superficiality, no bunk, no phrases, and, above all, nothing *phenomenological* . . . all of which demands *preparation*, that is, intensive involvement with the matter at hand, which is not half so comforting as writing book after book. (*HJC*, 47)

Even as a tenure-track professor, Heidegger was willing to forego the prospect of career advancement in service to what he viewed as a principled mode of philosophical inquiry. "As you see, I do not intend to become a genteel and cautious professor," he continued in his correspondence with Jaspers. "90 percent of my energy goes into teaching" (*HJC*, 46). It would take a few more years of material plight, and repeated failures to secure tenure and promotion, before Heidegger would be willing to devote any more energy to scholarly publication.

The Crisis of Learning

The academic obsession with "speeches and pamphlets" was a recurring theme in Heidegger's early lecture courses, especially those he delivered as Husserl's teaching assistant. It was here, in the lecture halls of Freiburg University, where he often expounded at length on the "philosophical gurgling" of his peers, that Heidegger first began to theorize everyday talk, gradually developing several key concepts in his early philosophy of ordinary language use. In the spoken discourse of his contemporaries, Heidegger heard *Gerede*; in their written discourse, he saw *Geschreibe*; and throughout it all, he discerned varying degrees of *Geschwätz*.

Even the transcripts of his first lecture course show Heidegger advancing these concepts. Prefiguring much of his work in the early-1920s—work which would eventually culminate in *Being and Time*—he begins the War Emergency Semester of 1919 by defining philosophy as a "primordial science" whose basic medium is "personal existence" and whose prime objective is "scientific consciousness." As he is equally careful to note, however, practitioners of this primordial science also must consider how their personal existence is rooted in various forms of collective life: "Every personal life has in all moments within its particular predominant life-world a relationship to that world, to the motivational values of the environing world, of the things of its life-horizon, of other human beings, of society." And the predominant life-world of modern philosophy, Heidegger continues, is the modern university system: "The life-context of scientific consciousness expresses itself objectively in the formation and organization of scientific academies and universities," where today's philosophers remain "connected to a community of similarly striving researchers with its rich relations to students."[3]

Like many of his contemporaries, Heidegger was deeply concerned about the state of higher education in the Weimar Republic, where so many other social, political, and economic institutions were already in acute states of crisis. Much to his alarm, these crises had begun to impinge on academic culture, causing scholars and students alike to question the nature of their chosen disciplines. "Every field of study was affected," Fritz K. Ringer explains. And they were all affected in the same way: "After announcing a crisis in their discipline, speakers tended to follow immediately with an attack upon the overspecialization and positivism of the nineteenth century." Everyone around Heidegger seemed to agree that the university system required a "spiritual renewal," and that this renewal should consist in "a reintegration of scholarship, cultivation, and weltanschauung."[4]

Not surprisingly, this commitment to spiritual synthesis over academic specialization, intellectual wholeness over disciplinary compartmentalization, found its way into the "speeches and pamphlets" of the academic community: "In examining the German academic pamphlet literature of the Weimar period, one is struck, above all, by a frantic sense of engagement. Addresses at German universities were traditionally designed to relate the specialized concerns of the speakers to the moral, philosophical, and political problems of the day; but the determination to derive salutary lessons from scholarship had never been quite as pronounced as it was during the 1920s. After 1921, the professors tried harder than ever to show that they were not mere specialists and that their work had elevating implications."[5]

Many of these addresses and publications trafficked in the same buzzwords. When scholars spoke and wrote about "the idea of the university," they rarely did so without stressing the need for "wholeness" and "synthesis" in the "worldviews" of higher education—terms which became increasingly ideographic as the "spiritual renewal" of the German university progressed. "Arguments and ideas which had once been stated with a modicum of precision were transformed into automatic associations," Ringer notes. "The academic literature of the 1920s reflected visions, unconscious semantic preferences, and mental habits, not just factual propositions or formal arguments." More than a spiritual renewal, the revival of learning in Weimar Germany was "a semantic disease." So much so that, as Ringer well summarizes, "the German language itself was affected by the passions of the day. Words became emotional stimuli. They trailed ever larger clouds of implicit meanings. Audiences were trained to respond to an expanding circle of vaguely antimodernist and antipositivist allusions."[6]

Even Heidegger's trusted friend, Karl Jaspers, seems to have suffered from this semantic disease. Although he was critical of existing attempts to reform the university, disparaging them as "the activities of prophets and apostles," Jaspers shared the reformers' worries about the increasing specialization of the disciplines, the growing division between individual research programs, and the apparent inability of the German professorate to connect the mission of higher learning to the "whole of life"—enough, at least, to join in the conversation. "Today, a philosophical weltanschauung is longed for again, and the fragmentation of the disciplines . . . is not felt to be the ultimate and necessary condition," he declared in 1923. "The idea of the university . . . is urging us on from an epoch of splintering and dissolution toward a new gestalt, the creation of which is the joint task of today's teachers and students."[7]

Heidegger did not share his friend's passion for worldviews. Nor was he convinced that such an approach to higher education would provide students or scholars with meaningful access to "the whole of life." On the contrary, as Heidegger argues in his piercing 1919 review of Jaspers' much-discussed *Psychology of Worldviews*, philosophical worldviews of "life" cannot help but remain aloof from lived experience, largely on account of jargon-clotted communicative styles whose key terms are at once vague and vacuous, static and stultifying, rarified and utterly reifying:

Every attempt to understand life is forced to turn the surge and flux of the aforementioned process into a static concept and thereby destroy the essence of life, i.e., the restlessness and movement. . . . Apart from the fact that problems concerning meaning, concepts, and language are approached only from a very narrow perspective that focuses on objective, reifying concepts, these problems are allowed to remain on the level of a very crude and vague treatment, which contributes nothing toward that type of treatment in which one would attempt to define the fundamental sense of life and lived experience as a whole. And instead of using this "glut on the market" to provide oneself with an air of profound philosophy (such talk about ineffability easily gives the impression that one has actually gazed upon ineffable realms), it is high time that we found genuine problems to deal with. (*P*, 16)

It is difficult to separate this pointed attack on worldview philosophies of "life" from Heidegger's broader concern about the lifeworld of philosophical inquiry itself—a lifeworld whose conceptual rigor and methodological integrity were increasingly under assault by the muddled terms and vapid arguments of the university reform movement. When he defined philosophy as a "primordial science," its practice as "scientific research," its practitioner as a "scientific investigator," and its horizon as "scientific consciousness," Heidegger intended to combat this reform movement, laying waste to its insipid claims of "spiritual renewal." Consider a few more of his opening remarks to students during the War Emergency Semester of 1919:

The much discussed university reform is totally misguided, and is a total misunderstanding of all genuine revolutionizing of the spirit, when it now broadens its activities into appeals, protest meetings, programs, orders and alliances: means that are antagonistic to the mind and serve ephemeral ends.

We are not yet ripe for *genuine* reforms in the university. Becoming ripe for them is the task of a *whole generation*. The renewal of the university means a rebirth of genuine scientific consciousness and life-contexts. But life-relations renew themselves only by returning to the genuine origins of the spirit. As historical phenomena they need the peace and security of genetic consolidation, in other words, the inner truthfulness of a worthwhile, self-cultivating life. Only life, not the noise of frenetic cultural programs, is "epoch making." Just as the "active spirit" of literary novices is a hindering force, so also is the attempt, to be found everywhere in the special sciences (from biology to the history of literature and art), to summon up a scientific "worldview" through the phraseological grammar of a corrupted philosophy.

But just as the awe of the religious man makes him silent in the face of his ultimate mystery, just as the genuine artist lives only in his work and detests all art-babble [*Kunstgeschwätz*], so the scientific man is effective only by way of the vitality of genuine research. . . . This includes an analysis that clears away crude and continually disruptive misunderstandings and naïve preconceptions. (*WES* 1919, 4–5; trans. modified)

In this opening statement of the semester, Heidegger presented students with two options: they could either fall in line behind popular intellectual hacks and adopt "the phraseological grammar of a corrupted philosophy," or they could band together with him in a radical philosophical attempt to renew "genuine scientific consciousness." In the former's corruption, Heidegger saw a misguided and confused yet noisily programmatic effort to reform the university by way of babbling worldviews and naive preconceptions severed from lived experience—in short, "unscientific idle talk [*Gerede*]" (*WES* 1919, 37). In the latter's consciousness, however, he saw an outwardly quiet but inwardly honest mode of self-cultivation, a way of being in the world that was conceptually focused yet also intellectually wide-ranging—and all while remaining steeped in genuine life-relations. Students could choose lives of idle talk or lives of conceptual rigor, but they could not waver between.

By the end of the semester, these divergent lines of thought had become the basis for a sharp, methodological distinction between worldview philosophies of life and what Heidegger now described as the "communicative science of phenomenology." Consider, for instance, his final words of the semester, as recorded by one of his students:

Aim of phenomenology: the investigation of life as such. Apparent suitability of this philosophy for worldview. The opposite is the case.

Phenomenological philosophy and worldview are opposed to one another.

Worldview: this is bringing to a standstill. (Natrop maintains this against phenomenology.) Life, as the history of the spirit in its transcendental expression, is objectivized and frozen in a definite moment. Religious, aesthetic, natural-scientific attitudes are absolutized. All philosophy of culture is worldview philosophy. It freezes definite situations in the history of the spirit and wants to *interpret culture*. Worldview is freezing, finality, end, system. Even Simmel in his last works does not grasp life as such, i.e. he grasps the transcendental historical rather than the absolute historical.

But *philosophy* can progress only through an absolute sinking into life as such, for *phenomenology* is never concluded, only *preliminary*, it always sinks itself into the preliminary.

The science of absolute honesty has no pretensions. It contains no idle talk [*Gerede*] but only *evident steps*; theories do not struggle with one another here, but only genuine and ungenuine insights. The genuine insights, however, can only be arrived at through honest and uncompromising sinking into the genuineness of life as such, in the final event only through the genuineness of *personal life* as such. (*WES* 1919, 187–88; trans. modified)

In worldview philosophy, Heidegger saw a misguided attempt to freeze, reify, systematize, absolutize, and ultimately terminate lived experience in flourishes of babble and idle talk—*Geschwätz* and *Gerede*—masquerading as "transcendental expression." In stark contrast, he understood the "communicative science of phenomenology" as an honest, genuine, insightful, evident, and wholly uncompromising approach to lived experience—a mode of critical inquiry which privileges personal existence over philosophical pretense. Whatever else it meant to Heidegger at the start of his career, phenomenology had little room for aconceptual *Geschwätz* and even less for unscientific *Gerede*.

Wringing Necks

It would be wrong to interpret Heidegger's opposition between the "communicative science of phenomenology" and the "unscientific idle talk" of worldview philosophy as a recapitulation of Husserl's 1910 essay on "Philosophy as a Rigorous Science," which advocates for a complete break between scientific and worldview approaches to philosophy. As Heidegger realized in the early-1920s, Husserl's search for an objective, systematic mode of "transcendental phenomenology" suffered from the same procedural problem of worldview philosophy. By privileging the self-experience of the absolute subject over the lived experience of its mortal coil, Husserl could not help but lose sight of life itself as a concrete, historical mode of existence.

As Husserl's teaching assistant, and someone in search of a tenure-track appointment, however, Heidegger was reluctant to challenge his mentor directly. "We're on the way to achieving a genuine, simple & more elemental grasp of life—the creation of a new style—not according to programs, but to motives awakening from the innermost self," he wrote to his wife in January 1920. "This is what puts me such poles apart from Husserl today, &—simply to support us financially—I must now find the possibilities for going along with him without violent conflict or emphasis upon such conflict."[8] This is partly why Heidegger refused to publish anything in the early-1920s: Although he had "a clear position with respect to Husserl," and his position clearly diverged from the latter's transcendental phenomenology, Heidegger still hoped to secure "the offer of a chair" before making this position public. And in order for this to occur, he needed his mentor's assistance. By holding back his critique Husserl, Heidegger hoped "the little rogue" would finally "get me the title" (LHW, 91, 70).

It was not until his final year as Husserl's assistant, when he began to suspect that his candidacy for professorships at Göttingen and Marburg had failed, that Heidegger began to speak out against his aging mentor. In the final hour of his winter 1922–23 course on Husserl's *Ideas I*, for instance, Heidegger claimed to have "publicly burned and destroyed the *Ideas* to such an extent that I dare say the essential foundations for the whole [of my work] are now cleanly laid out. Looking back from this vantage to the *Logical Investigations*, I am now convinced that Husserl was never a philosopher, not even for one second in his life." With each passing day, "he becomes ever more ludicrous" (BH, 372). A few months later, Heidegger extended this critique into a new course that "strikes the main blows against phenomenology." As he reported to Karl Löwith, "I now stand completely on my own feet. . . . There is no chance of getting an appointment [with Husserl's help]. And after I have published, my prospects will be finished. The old man will then realize that I am wringing his neck—and then the question of succeeding him is out. But I can't help myself" (BH, 372). By the end of Heidegger's early Freiburg period, the professional resentment that Husserl would later caution him against was increasingly directed at Husserl himself.

There was more (and less) at stake in this Oedipal drama than Heidegger's fading prospect of a tenure-track appointment. From the auspicious beginning of his assistantship to its increasingly bitter end, Heidegger was struggling to articulate his own approach to phenomenology—and always in opposition to the *Geschwätz* and *Gerede* of other, more popular lines of thought. While planning a course on medieval mysticism in August 1919, for instance, he targeted popular accounts of religious experience: "The chatter [*Gerede*] about mysticism as the 'formless' is merely the sweet-talk [*beschwatzt*] of fundamentally unscientific methods of conceptually clever 'oppositions.' One [*Man*] reduces it to formulas, i.e., one [*man*] says nothing substantial and cannot, in clinging to a word and a dogma."[9] The following summer, in a lecture course on the *Phenomenology of Intuition and Expression*, he targeted Oswald Spengler and the "windy chatter" («*windigen Gerede*») of those he cites. "Spengler neither saw nor solved the problems of contemporary philosophy . . . but merely concealed them anew through a violent generalization," Heidegger jabbed. This, he felt, was why *The Decline of the West* had proven so popular: "The notorious ignorance and journalistic superficiality of today's educated crowd had to seize on Spengler's book, especially since it has starkly positive and easily accessible but no philosophical qualities."[10]

In the winter semester of 1921–22, Heidegger rerouted this attack on popular scholarship and its educated crowd through his ongoing critique of the university reform movement. Of particular concern to him was the degree to which this "spiritual" movement, by luring his colleagues into trite and trifling discussions of the German university, allowed "the ontological character of the university itself and its current state for us, with respect to its ontological structure," to become "covered over" (*verdeckt*). Anticipating his account of *Gerede* and *Geschreibe* in *Being and Time*, where both are shown to "close off" (*verschließen*) and "cover up" (*verdecken*) *Dasein*'s being-in-the-world, Heidegger invited students to consider whether and to what extent their other professors, in "making speeches" and "writing pamphlets," had actually contributed to the crisis of learning they were attempting to assuage.[11] If modern academic culture, as a specific mode of existence, now "lives and takes effect in a completely hidden and obstructed and concealed way [*ganz verdeckt und gehemmt und verborgen lebt und sich auswirkt*]," it was partly their fault, Heidegger argued (*WS* 1921–22, 58; trans. modified).

Heidegger's proposed solution was simple yet arresting, and could only be heard as a call to arms: "No grand reformative plans, claims,

loud demands, prior to actually 'being there,' 'having been there'—
accomplishments!" (WS 1921–22, 141). From students and professors
alike, he demanded a complete and utter commitment to the concrete,
historical experience of *factical life*—a commitment whose realization in scientific inquiry, he warned, would be directly opposed to the
"spiritual renewal" of academic culture, and thus open to public con-
demnation by university reform advocates. "Today we have become so
cunning, so richly gratified by dainty literary morsels and glossy maga-
zines, and so enervated by 'religious' whining that we cry down [*ver-
schreit*] such a pledge of life as stupidity and rate these cries [*Geschrei*]
as evidence of superiority and of the possession of 'spirituality'" (WS
1921–22, 53). In whining and crying of this sort, which thrives on public ridicule of quieter, more reticent approaches of life, we see an early
example of what Heidegger would later bemoan as "the loud idle talk
[*Gerede*] which goes with the common sense of the 'they'"—a fallen
way of speaking characterized by "jealous stipulations and talkative
fraternizing" (BT, 342, 344–45). And in the slick, glossy publications
that support this noisy way of speaking, we see an early illustration
of what he would later deride as a literary culture whose output "takes
the form of 'scribbling' [»*Geschreibe*«]" and whose audience "feeds upon
superficial reading" (BT, 212).

In the winter of 1921–22, however, Heidegger was more concerned
about the critical condition of the German university system than the
broader state of modern public discourse. He was particularly worried
about his own discipline, where the push for "spiritual renewal" in
teaching and research "belies its own peculiar fickleness that has no
roots" (WS 1921–22, 6). In their struggle "to keep up with the latest,"
Weimar philosophers were operating "without any serious knowledge"
of their primary topics. Instead of straining toward scientific consciousness in principled modes of critical inquiry, they were settling
for "an uncritical acceptance of the entire problematic of principles."
What made this "superficiality of thinking" so dangerous to the discipline of philosophy, Heidegger thought, was not just "the current
proliferation of metaphysical needs" that it unleashed but also, more
precariously, "the growing indifference to rigorous problematics" with
which it attempted to meet these needs (WS 1921–22, 21). Although he
makes no mention of *Gerede* or *Geshreibe* in this context, their effects
on the discourse of philosophy are pronounced: "People move in the
'externalities' of philosophy, in its 'concepts' . . . People give a hearing
to unverifiable and therefore suspect claims, currently circulating demands. The perversity extends so far that such empty mental labor is

extolled as a sign of the priority and superiority of philosophy over and against the sciences, a sign of the radicality of philosophy. Thus decline is announced as an excellence and is turned into a basic task, one that cannot even be surpassed" (*WS* 1921–22, 141).

In postures of intellectual superiority, Heidegger sees signs of conceptual emptiness; in pronouncements of academic excellence, he finds proof of methodological decline; and throughout it all, he notes the suppression of any and all attempts to say as much, especially in research programs that diverge from "the latest currently circulating demands." Nothing could be further from the task of philosophical inquiry, Heidegger laments. "Never was there such an 'unphilosophical' epoch as the present one." (*WS* 1921–22, 21)

"The Book!"

Heidegger begins his renowned 1921–22 lecture course on Aristotle by wondering what it means to study "past philosophy" today. In particular, he wonders how the history of philosophy, as a venerable line of research, sees itself. "This history looks upon itself as strict factual research," Heidegger gathers. Implicit in this scholarly self-regard, he adds, is a subtle disregard for other modes of thought, especially modes of thought in which questions of historicity arise: "For this 'exact' research, everything else counts as babble [*Geschwätz*], even the attempt to bring it itself to clarity in its own conditionality and standpoint" (*WS* 1921–22, 3; trans. modified). How is Heidegger using *Geschwätz* here? And how does this usage relate to his understanding of *Gerede*?

According to Heidegger, historians of philosophy disregard critical studies of their discipline's factical life because they misunderstand the nature of factical life itself. He describes this misunderstanding as an "erroneous tendency to overestimation, to a rash preconception and acceptance of philosophy as a matter of fact." And he abbreviates his argument for clarity: "facticity, becoming lost, becoming a matter of fact, presenting itself as a matter of fact" (*WS* 1921–22, 21). By documenting this conceptual confusion, Heidegger hopes to show that historians of philosophy are also prone to *Geschwätz*, especially when they level this accusation against scientific research on the historicity of their work. And by dispelling this conceptual confusion, he is attempting to show that *Geschwätz* of this sort is antithetical to rigorous scientific inquiry. "I may not, therefore, introduce just any objects and summon a great 'babble' [*ein großes »Geschwätz« vorführen*]," he tells his students

(*WS* 1921–22, 28; trans. modified). Nor may anyone else, he continues: To subject the history of philosophy to scientific-philosophical inquiry is to preclude the possibility of this inquiry ever becoming "a mere theme for the superficial babble [*Geschwätz*] of dilettantes and fools at cocktail parties" (*WS* 1921–22, 37; trans. modified).

Where others claim to encounter spiritual depths, Heidegger discovers only intellectual shoals. Like Kierkegaard before him, he finds the popular philosophy of his day to be lacking in substance what it accomplishes in style. Here, in the winter of 1921–22, he is eager to show how the intellectual historian's effort to reclaim "past philosophy" is equally problematic. To be sure, radical scientific research has much to gain from previous systems of thought; but it should not seek a "modernized renewal" of these earlier systems, for doing so would subject its practitioners to the very desire they must now traverse—namely, "the desire to say what is 'new.'" And with this, Heidegger begins to conceptualize *Geschwätz*:

The situation is all the more difficult today, now that everyone says everything, now that philosophy is so shrewd, so deep, and so comprehensive that everyone can take comfort and be assured of his own superiority in having already said this or that, which can be found in some book or other. As if it were a real accomplishment just to say something; especially today when anyone with a little cleverness and a capacity to speak and write, along with a convenient medium for the propagation and digestion of the newest in literature, can publish anything and even have it taken seriously! In such a time—or at any time whatsoever—can it really be someone's ambition to have already said something?

If someone, while "reading," should acquire the "impression" that this book was not dashed off yesterday evening on the basis of the "relevant" background literature and the circulating babble [*umlaufenden Geschwätzes*], and if he should thereby direct his comportment toward real understanding, then the main purpose will be achieved; anything further is beyond my power. (*WS* 1921–22, 145–46; trans. modified)

Shrewd thought, clever talk, and self-assured superiority throughout—students in Heidegger's winter 1921–22 lecture course would have recognized these themes and readily sensed the sarcasm in their instructor's voice. But they also would have heard something new in these comments, something which would soon begin to figure largely in Heidegger's social thought—namely, an emphasis on the modern desire for *novelty*, specifically an emphasis on the recursive desire to say something new simply in order to have said something new and, in having said something new, to rekindle the desire to say something new again, *ad infinitum*. Later, in *Being and Time*, Heidegger would define this circuitous lust for the new as "curiosity" (*Neugier*), a habit of mind that "seeks novelty only in order to leap from it anew to another novelty" (*BT*, 216). Here, however, he understands it as "babble" (*Geschwätz*), a way of speaking whose lust for novelty is characterized by delusions of grandeur and, above all, perennial states of distraction. This understanding of *Geschwätz* would stick with Heidegger throughout the 1920s.

When babblers settle on a specific topic, but this topic fails to generate rigorous philosophical discussion and thus to allow for "real understanding," another way of speaking often takes hold. In his winter 1921–22 lectures on Aristotle, Heidegger describes this focused yet facile way of speaking about certain topics as *Gerede*. And when this occurs in print, he characterizes it as *Geschreibe*. To illustrate these kindred modes of discourse, he invites his students to consider a topic of special import to him, his mentor, and his prospective employers in the early-1920s—namely, the projected book on Aristotle that these winter 1921–22 lectures were designed to introduce, the same book project whose prospectus Heidegger would later send to Göttingen and Marburg in hopes of securing a professorship.

Note, in particular, how he situates this unfinished book project in the broader discipline of philosophy. "The text is addressed only to those philosophers and researchers who are convinced that it is of prime importance in philosophy to see to it that one's own house is in order before travelling around the world," Heidegger explains, recalling Kierkegaard's critique of Gert Westphaler and his speculative successors. Since this "text" is still a work in progress, however, its author as well as its addressees should refrain from any "public discussion" of its contents (*WS* 1921–22, 143–44). From Heidegger's point of view, remaining silent about his unfinished book manuscript was a critical response to the *Geschreibe* of his peers, specifically "the degeneracy of the litterateurs, which is greater in philosophy than anywhere else." But it was also a defining feature of the broader research agenda at work in the book itself: "This consideration of principles, precisely in view of its own intention, should not show itself publicly to others while the concrete results are not yet available" (*WS* 1921–22, 144).

In order to advance his university career, however, Heidegger could not remain completely silent about this work in progress. At the very least, he needed to convince his colleagues that silence on this topic was justified. So he pleaded with them: "Should concrete results be demanded of the one who is submitting this 'program,' then his answer is first and foremost the plea to let lie the remarks contained in this installment until the genuine investigations 'arrive.'" And he praised them in turn: "Anyone who is willing to wait so long and to defer the discussion . . . is doing well, since too much is already being written as is" (*WS* 1921–22, 143–44). Heidegger even offered to share the spotlight with them: "It might be much better for these people, however, if they do not simply wait for *my* possibly forthcoming efforts but, instead, bring their own concrete investigations to bear on what has been said. Their own investigations will also be more familiar to them, and I myself will concede to each one the authorship and discovery of the self-evident truths he submits. That is a better way of filling the time while waiting for the appearance of my work, provided anyone finds it important to wait for that, which I do not believe" (*WS* 1921–22, 144).

Heidegger knew that many of his colleagues would not be swayed by these appeals. And he knew that some of his dubious peers would continue to engage in "public discussion" of his projected book on Aristotle—public discussion that, however sharply focused, would amount to little more than "idle talk about worldviews [*Weltanschauungsgerede*], which drags things in out of the blue and degrades phenomenology practically to the opposite of that which it genuinely is and that whereby it is—*knowledge!*"

This does not mean that Heidegger was opposed to intellectual discussion and debate. On the contrary, "I am certainly willing to participate in materially productive disputes." But there was nothing to be disputed at this point—no "genuine investigations" to be scrutinized, no "concrete results" to be questioned, and, above all, no scholarship to be discussed. This was reason enough, he thought, for everyone to remain silent about his book project: "It would be better for people to ignore this book than to scribble and gossip [*Geschreibe und Gerede*] about it in the usual vacuous way that has been rampant for so long." Even in the table of contents for his early lecture course on Aristotle, Heidegger was adamant: "No idle talk [*Gerede*] about the book!" (*WS* 1921–22, 145, xi; trans. modified).

Ruinant Factical Life

By the spring of 1922, Heidegger had formulated several key terms in his emerging philosophy of ordinary language use—and all while struggling to address several pressing issues in the German university system, notably issues of communicative practice and intellectual rigor in (and around) the discipline of philosophy. In the *Geschwätz* of his contemporaries, he discovered a garrulous state of *distraction*, where self-important speakers flit from novelty to novelty, ever in search of something new to discuss. In their *Gerede* and *Geschreibe*, he discovered an equally verbose yet slightly more focused communicative practice, an effusive state of *preoccupation* in which speakers and writers fixate on certain topics of discussion but never in such a way that allows for rigorous scientific inquiry.

Gerede, *Geschreibe*, and *Geschwätz* were all hindering the conduct of scientific research and, by extension, the cultivation of scientific consciousness. And they were all doing so by arresting the development of what Heidegger, in his first significant use of the term *Entschlossenheit*, calls "the resoluteness of the understanding" (*WS* 1921–22, 53). More than a barrier to his emerging research program, however, the arrested development of resolute understanding was its condition of possibility. In the *Gerede*, *Geschreibe*, and *Geschwätz* of his peers, he found a cluster of inauthentic communicative practices over and against which to define the resoluteness characteristic of genuine scientific inquiry:

This resoluteness is all the more certainly present the less it breaks out in speech and, instead, keeps silent [*schweigt*] and can wait. Because we are no longer able to bide our time and lie in wait for life in the genuine sense (not in the manner of a detective or one who snoops on the intellect), and because, instead, we want the matter [*das Geschäft*] to be sorted out with uproarious haste [*lärmender Eilfertigkeit*], we fall prey to surrogates of intellectual showmanship, or to an illusion of objectivity that actually dims our eyesight and constantly flees from the issues. (*WS* 1921–22, 53; trans. modified)

When *Geschwätz*, *Gerede*, and *Geschreibe* prevail, we are unable to remain silent and thus unable to wait and watch for factical life "in the genuine sense." Together, these trained incapacities blind us to the temporal particularity of lived experience, namely, "the basic historiological sense of facticity" (*WS* 1921–22, 103, 139). Heidegger refers to this impaired mode of existence as *ruinance*, from the Latin *ruina*, meaning "a collapse," "a tumbling down," and, put a bit more archly, "a fall." Prefiguring his later work on the absorptive experience of "falling" (*Verfallen*), Heidegger defines ruinance as an existential state of impatience, echoing Kierkegaard's disdain for busybodies like Adolph Peter

Adler: "Ruinance is an unwillingness to wait and an inability to wait" (*WS* 1921–22, 139). When ruinance prevails, we are always short on time: "Factical, ruinant life 'has no time' because its basic movedness [*Grundbewegtheit*], ruinance itself, takes away 'time.'" In other words, "it seeks to abolish the historiological from facticity" (*WS* 1921–22, 104).

Months later, in the October 1922 introduction to his much-anticipated book on Aristotle—the same introduction he culled from his lecture notes for *Phenomenological Interpretations of Aristotle* (*WS* 1921–22) and shared with prospective employers at Göttingen and Marburg—Heidegger returned to this topic, further indicating what he meant by the "basic movedness" of ruinant factical life. Of special concern to him was the ontologico-existential distinction between the proper originary experience of each unique lifetime and the restless public experience of average everyday life. In pursuit of this experiential difference—a difference which would eventually undergird his entire existential analytic—Heidegger introduced readers to several new terms in his quickly evolving social theory: "interpretedness" (*Ausgelegtheit*), "averageness" (*Durchschnittlichkeit*), "publicness" (*Öffentlichkeit*), and their generic pronominal subject, "everyone" (*das Man*).

Noticeably absent from this list of terms are *Gerede*, *Geschreibe*, and *Geschwätz*—all of the communicative practices that attend ruinant factical life. The absence of these terms is especially glaring in light of Heidegger's outspoken commitment to revealing the "*phenomenological hermeneutics*" of this fallen state: "Because of its tendency to lapse, factic life lives for the most part in what is inauthentic, i.e., improper, in what has been handed down to it, in what has been reported to it, in what it appropriates in averageness. Even that which has been developed originally as an authentic possession lapses into averageness and publicness. It loses the specific sense of its provenance out of its original situation and 'free floats' its way into the ordinaries of the 'everyone'" (*BH*, 166–67). Only later, after sensing that his essay had missed its mark, initially failing to earn him a professorship, did Heidegger realize the importance of ordinary language use to his existential analysis of ruinant factical life. Hence, the epigraph he eventually added to the essay, well over a year after sending its first draft to Marburg or Göttingen: "Life will find a way to escape even this critique by a flight into clichés and catchphrases" (*BH*, 155). *Gerede*, *Geschreibe*, and *Geschwätz* may not have appeared in the essay's original form, but their relevance to ruinant factical life was apparent throughout—even if only in the hindsight of ongoing professional strife.

A Specter in Disguise

All of the key concepts in Heidegger's October 1922 essay return in his summer 1923 lecture course on "the hermeneutics of facticity," and they are all anchored in the temporal particularity of ruinant factical life, which Heidegger now condenses into a single term: "the today" (*das Heute*). To study the interpretedness, averageness, and publicness of ruinant factical life, especially as these existentials contribute to the generic social category of the everyone, is to study *"the present of those initial givens which are closest to us."* Inquiry of this sort does not call for "wide-ranging and longwinded discussions which provide entertaining *portraits* of the so-called 'most interesting tendencies' of the present," Heidegger quickly adds, lest anyone mistake the existential analysis of "our time" for an idle celebration of the modern era. "What is crucial is that the today be lifted up into the starting point of analysis in such a manner that a *characteristic of being* already becomes visible in it."

The characteristic of being that concerned Heidegger in the summer of 1923 was the characteristic of being that would occupy him for years to come: "The theme of this investigation is facticity, i.e., our own *Dasein* insofar as it is interrogated with respect to, on the basis of, and with a view to the character of its being." And the character of *Dasein's* being to be studied by phenomenological hermeneutics was the characteristic "being-there of *Dasein*" itself—what Heidegger, at this point in his career, described as the "how of facticity" by which human beings move through the world, in varying degrees of self-disclosure.[12]

Which in turn brought Heidegger to ordinary language use. With a nod to Kierkegaard, he tells students that the basic movedness of *Dasein*—the existential medium in which it moves through the world, encountering itself at every turn—is *Gerede*:

It moves [*bewegt sich*] (a basic phenomenon) around in a definite mode of discourse about itself: *idle talk* [*das Gerede*] (technical term). This discourse "about" itself is the public and average manner [*die öffentlich-durchschnittliche Weise*] in which *Dasein* takes itself in hand, holds onto itself, and preserves itself. What lies in this idle talk [*Gerede*] is a definite comprehension which *Dasein* in advance has of itself: the guiding "*as what*" in terms of which it addresses "itself." This idle talk [*Gerede*] is thus the how in which a definite manner of *Dasein's* *interpretedness* [*Ausgelegtheit*] stands at its disposal. (*SS* 1923, 25; trans. modified)

If interpretedness, averageness, and publicness are the defining existential features of ruinant factical life, it is because they are, at root, effect structures of idle talk. And the same is true of their pronominal subject, *das Man*:

> Idle talk [*Gerede*] discusses everything with a peculiar insensitivity to difference. As this kind of averageness [*Durchschnittlichkeit*], the innocuous initial "givens" of the day which are closest to us and these givens as a for-the-most-part and for-most-of-us, publicness [*Öffentlichkeit*] is the mode of being of the "*every-one*" ["*Man*"]: everyone says that . . . , everyone has heard that . . . , everyone tells it like . . . , everyone thinks that . . . , everyone expects that . . . , everyone is in favor of . . . The idle talk [*Gerede*] in circulation belongs to no one, no one takes responsibility for it, every-one [*das Man*] has said it. (*SS* 1923, 26; trans. modified)

To further illustrate this circuitous mode of discourse, Heidegger directs students, once more, to the literary culture of the present age. "'One' even writes books on the basis of such hearsay [*Hörensagen*]," he scoffs (*SS* 1923, 26). And thus in opposition to the basic task of phenomenological hermeneutics: "Putting forth *questions*." According to Heidegger, modern literary culture has forfeited the key questions of human existence—the very questions he had been struggling to pose in precise philosophical terms—settling instead for "the common 'problems' of today which 'one' picks up from hearsay and book learning and decks out with a gesture of profundity." Much to his frustration, "questioning has today fallen out of fashion in the great industry [*Betrieb*] of 'problems'" (*SS* 1923, 4).

The effects of such industry are readily apparent in the "*educated consciousness*" of the present age, especially in "*the idle talk* [*Gerede*] *heard in the public realm from the average educated mind.*" But its causes are more difficult to discern and require further elaboration. Again, Heidegger begins by gesturing toward the modern university system. "An example: At a critical time when he was searching for his own *Dasein*, Vincent van Gogh wrote to his brother: 'I would rather die a natural death than be prepared for it at the university, . . .'" (*SS* 1923, 26; trans. modified). Had Heidegger continued quoting from this letter, students would have found the painter's pronouncement even more illuminating: "and I have occasionally had a lesson from a hay-mower [*hannekemaaier*] that seemed more useful than one in Greek."[13]

It would take another decade of thought before Heidegger realized the connection between respect for agrarian culture and his broader theory of ordinary language use. In his 1934 radio address "Why Do

I Stay in the Provinces?" he recalls the death of an elderly peasant woman who used to visit him at his cabin: "She spent the night of her death in conversation [*Gespräch*] with her family. Just an hour and a half before the end she sent her greetings to the 'Professor.' Such a memory is worth incomparably more than the most astute report by any international newspaper about my alleged philosophy." And all the more so, he adds, given the "condescending familiarity and sham concern" on display in "the literati's dishonest idle talk [*Gerede*] about 'folk-character' and 'rootedness in the soil.'" The "very loud and very active and very fashionable obtrusiveness" of these educated elites, especially in popular publications about Heidegger's work and condescending chatter about peasant existence, could not be further removed from the "robust language" of his elderly friend.[14]

In the summer of 1923, however, Heidegger remained focused on the German university system. With this quotation from Van Gogh, he hoped to indicate that the state of higher education since the painter's death had only grown worse: "*Today:* The situation of academic disciplines and the university has become even more questionable. What happens? Nothing. Everyone writes 'brochures' on the crisis in the academic disciplines, on the academic calling. The one says to the other: everyone's saying—as everyone's heard—academic disciplines have had it. Today there is already even a specialized body of literature on the question of how matters should be. Nothing else happens" (*SS* 1923, 27).

To be sure, Heidegger implicates all academic disciplines in the production of "*the average educated mind*" and, by extension, "*the idle talk [Gerede] heard in the public realm.*" But he is fiercely critical of two academic disciplines in particular. In order to retrieve the being-there of *Dasein* from the idle talk of *das Man*, we cannot limit our inquiries to research on the communicative practices of mass society, he argues. We must also trace these communicative practices back to the disciplinary formations from which they emerged. And according to Heidegger, we need look no further than modern departments of history and philosophy for these origins: "If the *Dasein* of today is to be brought into view from out of the initial givens of the today which are closest to us, we need to consult this idle talk [*Gerede*] which belongs to its publicness, in which it speaks especially of itself, in which it is thus there as an object in some manner. Such public talk [*Gerede*], educated consciousness, always derives from more original modes of dealing with the matters discussed. Two such modes in which we find some form of discourse about *Dasein* are *inter alia* historical consciousness and philosophy" (*SS* 1923, 38; trans. modified).

Heidegger's argument is readily summarized: While historians seek to objectify the past in hopes of addressing each of its moments subjectively (relativism), philosophers purport to overcome all subjectivity in hopes of providing an objective account of all beings (universalism). Implicit in these methodological differences, however, is the same impossible demand. Historical and philosophical modes of inquiry are both in hot pursuit of a transcendent vantage point from which to observe the totality of beings. And it is precisely here, in the strained academic discourse that accompanies this futile quest, that Heidegger aims to intervene. In the totalizing discourse of historians and philosophers, he finds the garrulous wellspring of *Dasein*'s "having-been-interpreted in the today" (*SS* 1923, 24). Here, at last, was the historiological dimension of ruinant factical life.

Not surprisingly, Heidegger is particularly concerned about his own discipline. But he is no longer content to bemoan "the noise and industry [*Lärm und Betrieb*] of philosophy" (*SS* 1923, 38). In addition to lampooning what passes for scholarship among "today's distinguished philosophers," he wants to show "how 'the idle talk' [*»das Gerede«*] about *Dasein* is circulating in it" (*SS* 1923, 46, 32; trans. modified). Throughout his lectures on *Ontology—The Hermeneutics of Facticity*, he does so by quoting from a recent essay by one of Dilthey's leading disciples, the philosopher-turned-psychologist Eduard Spranger: "All of us—Rickert, the phenomenologists, the movement associated with Dilthey—meet up with one another in the great struggle for *the timeless in the historical* or *beyond the historical*, for the *realm of meaning* and its historical expression in a concrete developed culture, for a *theory of values* which leads beyond the merely subjective towards the objective and the valid."[15] Heidegger first responds to Spranger by claiming that the psychologist's work is a "systematically conducted [*betriebene*] watering down of Dilthey's thought"—a biting scholarly attack, given Spranger's renowned start as one of Dilthey's leading students, as well as his pronounced commitment to advancing his teacher's program of inquiry (*SS* 1923, 11). Heidegger then amplifies this insult by asking to be excluded from the intellectual movement described in Spranger's essay: "As for the 'phenomenologists,' I ask to be exempted." What bothers Heidegger about this intellectual movement is the totalizing "All of us . . ." in which Spranger frames it, and the extent to which this totalizing turn of phrase not only opposes but also purports to overcome historical consciousness. "This disagreement is *the* public problem within today's interpretedness: 'All of us . . .'" (*SS* 1923, 34).

At the center of this public problem, Heidegger goes on to argue, is a wrongheaded, objectivist approach to philosophical inquiry. "Amid the snarl of worldviews putting forth their opinions and conducting their experiments, it brings the objective possibility of a more objective *agreement*, the 'All of us . . . ,' i.e., it makes present and offers to *Dasein* itself the prospect of the tranquil certainty and security of the general and unanimous 'yes, I agree'" (*SS* 1923, 50). But this tranquil consensus is in fact a ruse. The disciplinary motive behind Spranger's totalizing discourse is neither certainty nor security but, instead, a particular kind of intellectual spinelessness: "Spranger's 'all of us' is only a masking of uncertainty and insecurity: no one has seen it, no one believes it, each is too cowardly to admit it" (*SS* 1923, 80).

Make no mistake, the "no one" Heidegger detects in Spranger's "All of us" is the *everyone* that he conceptualizes and critiques throughout his summer 1923 lecture course. And the "yes, I agree" implicit in Spranger's "All of us" is a pointed illustration of the communicative practice on which the everyone relies: *Gerede*. Students would have easily made this connection between the *Gerede* of *das Man* and the "yes, I agree" implicit in Spranger's "All of us," especially in light of Heidegger's recent comment on the connection between *das Man* and *Dasein*. "This 'everyone' is precisely *the* 'no-one' which circulates in factical *Dasein* and haunts it like a specter," he explains. And *Gerede*, of course, is the guise in which this specter appears: "*Dasein* speaks about itself and sees itself in such and such a manner, and yet this is only a *mask* which it holds up before itself in order to not be frightened by itself. The warding off 'of' anxiety. Such visibility is the mask in which factical *Dasein* lets itself be encountered, in which it comes forth and appears before itself as though it really 'were' it; in this masquerade of the public manner of interpretedness, *Dasein* makes itself present and puts itself forward as the *height of living* (i.e., of industriousness [*Betriebes*])" (*SS* 1923, 26; trans. modified). As Heidegger sees it, *das Man* is a phantasmatic iteration of *Dasein*. It stalks authentic human being like an ephemeral yet revenant shadow. And *Gerede*, he suggests, is the talkative guise in which this shadow is cast, a generalizing mode of concealment in which *Dasein* appears before itself as *das Man*.

When Heidegger describes Spranger's "All of us" as "a masking of uncertainty and insecurity," it is this generalizing mode of concealment that he is attempting to illustrate. Just as the *Gerede* of *das Man* is a public masquerade in which ruinant factical life allows *Dasein* to hide from itself, so also is Spranger's "All of us" an overweening ideological front for the underlying intellectual cowardice of today's philosophers. In this sense, "even philosophy is in the open space of publicness,"

Heidegger concludes. "It makes itself present and puts itself forward in the public realm, making itself a topic of discussion, so as to contribute to the general talk [*Gerede*], give itself a foothold in life, and preserve itself in it" (*SS* 1923, 49). More than intellectual peers, Heidegger's colleagues were chattering minds.

More Impulses from Kierkegaard

As indicated throughout this chapter, Heidegger often uses the word "industriousness" (*Betriebsamkeit*) to signal his frustration with modern public life. If *Gerede* is the guise in which *Dasein* encounters itself as *das Man*, *Betriebsamkeit* is the illusion of modern public life on which *Gerede* thrives. But "industriousness" fails to capture the full meaning of *Betriebsamkeit* in Heidegger's early work. Throughout the 1920s, Heidegger frequently used the term to mean *busyness*, in the pejorative sense of appearing to be actively engaged when, in fact, one is merely wasting time. Much like Kierkegaard before him, who coined the term "bustling loquacity" (*travl Snaksomhed*) to account for modernity's confluence of tumult and chatter, Heidegger traced the origin of his era's *Gerede*, *Geschreibe*, and *Geschwätz* to the busyness of Weimar public life.

Hence, the foreword to his summer 1923 lecture course, where Heidegger reduces modern educated consciousness to "the pseudo-understanding of a bustling curiosity [*betriebsamen Neugier*], i.e., diversion from what is solely at issue in this course" (*SS* 1923, 4; trans. modified). Hence also the pride of place he later assigns to such bustle, among other basic phenomena of ruinant factical life: "Industry [*Betrieb*], propaganda, proselytizing, cliquish monopolies, intellectual racketeering" (*SS* 1923, 15; trans. modified). Much to Heidegger's frustration, the existential *busyness* of modern public life was part and parcel of the intellectual *business* in which he was struggling to secure a job.

But this did not stop him from attacking both industries. In order to critique the former, however, he decided to prolong his assault on the latter. Deconstructing the business of philosophy was, from Heidegger's perspective, a crucial first step in the broader existential analysis of modern busyness itself. Even the anti-philosopher Kierkegaard, from whom Heidegger claimed to receive "strong impulses for the hermeneutical expression presented here," came under fire: "What was basically in question for him was nothing but the kind of personal reflection he pursued [*betrieb*]" (*SS* 1923, 25). But it was the intellectual work of his contemporaries that most annoyed Heidegger. In their teaching and research, he saw "the great bustle [*Betrieb*] of philosophy." And in "the noise and bustle [*Lärm und Betrieb*] of [this] philosophy," he saw "an antsiness [*Betriebsamkeit*] generated from ignorance of subject matter" (*SS* 1923, 16, 38, 60; trans. modified).

This antsy philosophical ignorance was especially apparent in the subdiscipline of phenomenology:

Phenomenological research, which was supposed to provide a basis for scientific work, has sunk to the level of wishy-washiness, thoughtlessness, and summariness, to the level of the philosophical noise of the day, to the level of a public scandal of philosophy. The bustle [*Betrieb*] surrounding schools and their students has blocked the avenues of access for actually taking up phenomenology and doing it. . . . It is impossible to make out anything about phenomenology or obtain a definition of it from this philosophical industry [*Betrieb*]. The business is hopeless! All such tendencies are a betrayal of phenomenology and its possibilities. The ruin can no longer be halted! (*SS* 1923, 58; trans. modified)

Even and especially in the work of his closest colleagues, then, Heidegger found a glaring example of what ailed modern academic culture and, by extension, contemporary public life. In particular, he found a pointed illustration of the basic problem that his peers were unwittingly exacerbating—the same problem that his existential analysis was designed to address—namely, the era's "great industry [*Betrieb*] of 'problems.'" His critique was sweeping: "90% of the literature is preoccupied with ensuring that such wrongheaded problems [do] not disappear and are confounded still more and in ever new ways." If indeed there was a crisis of learning in Weimar Germany, the preoccupied scholarship of his fellow phenomenologists was largely to blame: "Such literature dominates the industry [*Betrieb*]—everyone sees and gauges the progress and vitality of academic disciplines with it." That this literature also provided its authors with "employment and livelihood" must have been particularly frustrating to Heidegger: "Perhaps called once to be the conscience of philosophy, [phenomenology] has wound up the pimp for the public whoring of the mind" (*SS* 1923, 37).

Holding Out and Holding Back

From the business of phenomenology to the busyness of the modern world, Heidegger saw the present age as a compounding state of

Betriebsamkeit in which academic text and everyday talk—*Geschreibe* and *Gerede*—were amplifying various forms and forums of "public chatter" (*öffentlichen Geschwätz*) (*SS* 1923, 63). And in the midst of all this noise and bustle, he was committed to remaining silent, even at the expense of his university career. Quietly refusing to practice philosophy "in a businesslike [*betriebsmäßig*] fashion" was integral to scientific research as Heidegger understood it in the early-1920s (*SS* 1923, 58). As we have seen, this principled scholarly commitment found early expression in the winter semester of 1921–22, when Heidegger claimed that biding one's time and lying in wait for factical life, in an anticipatory state of resolute silence, is the condition of possibility for genuine scientific inquiry. By way of contrast, he went on to indict the prevailing academic priority on "making speeches" and "writing pamphlets," as illustrated by the ruinant unwillingness and remarkable inability of his colleagues to keep quiet about his projected book on Aristotle. All of which clearly suggests that Heidegger's philosophical account and personal embodiment of reticent scientific inquiry was as much a critical response to the *Gerede*, *Geschreibe*, and *Geschwätz* of his colleagues as it was a defining feature of his budding existential analysis.

As we also have seen, Heidegger pursued this line of thought into the summer of 1922, doubling down on his commitment to resolute silence, even in the face of ongoing professional strife. Or, at least, this was how he explained his activities (or lack thereof) to Karl Jaspers: "Out of inner respect for the object with which we go around philosophizing—we keep ourselves from saying something just to get published." As his wife well knew, however, there were academic politics behind Heidegger's principled silence. Only by holding back his emerging research agenda—a research agenda which was "poles apart from Husserl"—could Heidegger rest assured of his aging mentor's support on the job market. "Simply to support us financially," he wrote to her, "I must now find the possibilities for going along with him" (*LHW*, 70). Confessions of this sort, which recur throughout Heidegger's personal correspondence, especially in the early 1920s, further indicate the nature and extent of his careerist commitment to resolute silence.

Not until the summer of 1923, after accepting Marburg's offer of an associate professorship, did Heidegger begin to speak out against his mentor, openly criticizing Husserl's research agenda in service to the development of his own. It was only then, in his final semester as Husserl's teaching assistant, that he also began to rethink his scientific-philosophical priority on resolute silence. By the end of the summer, remaining silent was more than a careerist maneuver embodied in a performative critique of modern academic culture. It was also an authentic mode of existence available to *Dasein*, and thus a basic object of inquiry for phenomenological hermeneutics itself. Nevertheless, as Heidegger's use of *Betrieb* throughout the summer semester showed, he remained highly critical of the *Gerede*, *Geschreibe*, and *Geschwätz* of the discipline in which he had finally managed to secure a professorship.

This shifting grammar of motives marks an important turning point in Heidegger's early thought. What annoyed him about the philosophical *Betrieb* of his colleagues was its uproarious haste. In criticizing this uproarious haste, however, he also discovered its reticent counter-possibility—an alternate way of speaking, thinking, and being with others that would occupy him for years to come. Accounting for this discovery, especially as it relates to the careerist conceptual work we have already discussed, is the final task of this chapter.

In pursuit of this alternate, more authentic mode of existence, Heidegger developed the neologism *Jeweiligkeit*—a conceptual fusion of the adjective *je*, meaning "each" and "every," and the verb *weilen*, meaning "to tarry" and, more poetically, "to while." As a phenomenon of lived experience, *Jeweiligkeit* describes the *awhileness* of any given being-there. It shows how *Dasein* is always, in each instance of its being-there, dwelling for a while in some particular time. More precisely, *Jeweiligkeit* indicates the *temporal particularity* in which *Dasein* is always, to some extent, "tarrying for a while, not running away, being-*there*-at-home-in, . . . being-*there*-involved-in" (*SS* 1923, 5). As John van Buren aptly notes, there are several ways to understand this lingering mode of existence. "The *Jeweiligkeit* of the be-ing (there) of facticity and, more concretely, of the be-ing (there) of human beings and the world refers to at least three dimensions: (1) the *particularity* or *individuality* of their 'be-ing there,' (2) their 'be-ing there' or 'whiling (there)' *at the particular time*, and (3) their 'be-ing there' or 'tarrying (there)' *for a while*" (*SS* 1923, 108, n. 9). Although the first and second of these dimensions would eventually take center stage in *Being and Time*, it was the third dimension of *Jeweiligkeit*—*Dasein*'s ability to linger for awhile somewhere—that occupied Heidegger's thought in the summer of 1923.

The problem with "the industry of 'problems'" in phenomenological research, departments of philosophy, the German university system, and modern public life more broadly, Heidegger suggests, is that it prevents anyone from remaining anywhere for any length of time. When the *Betriebsamkeit* of *das Man* takes precedent, the *Jeweiligkeit* of *Dasein* remains concealed. But coining and conceptualizing *Jeweiligkeit* was insufficient to bring the awhileness of *Dasein* out of hiding, Heidegger thought, for this neologism failed to specify *how*, in the midst of modernity's noise and bustle, *Dasein* could tarry for awhile on any given topic at any given point in its otherwise ruinant life. So he decided to couple *Jeweiligkeit* with several related terms, all of which derive from the German verb *halten*, meaning not only "to stop," "to linger," and "to last," but also "to hold," "to keep," and "to bear." Central among these kindred terms were those indebted to the verbs *aufhalten*, meaning "to hold out," and *enthalten*, meaning "to hold back."

Consider, for instance, Heidegger's cryptic 1923 statement on what it means to study the "peculiar kind of *movement* [*Bewegtheit*]" characteristic of *Dasein* (SS 1923, 51)—the same peculiar kind of movement that he previously described as the "basic movedness [*Grundbewegtheit*]" of ruinant factical life (WS 1921–22, 104) and later defined as the "basic phenomenon" that attends *Gerede* (SS 1923, 25):

It is mistaken to be out to participate in movement [*Bewegtheit*] as such—especially if this is done with a view to being able to see the movement of life and bring it into the forehaving of categorical explication as an object. We are able to see *movement* in an authentic manner only from out of a genuine "*sojourn*" [»*Aufenthalt*«] in which we hold out for a while at a particular time [*jeweiligen*]. Existential sojourn, in this sojourn—what is to be fixed on as standing still [*Stillstand*]? And thus the most important task: precisely winning a genuine sojourn and not just any kind—the sojourn *before* the *possibility* of leaping into the work of worried decision—not talked about, but it is constantly there [*ständig da*]. Motion [*Bewegung*] is visible in the sojourn and from out of this the possibility of countermovement [*Gegenbewegung*] as the genuine way to sojourn.

Sojourning and holding out [*Aufhalten beim*] in life itself, in the meaning of its being and of its being an object: facticity. Holding back [*Enthalten*] from a ruinous movement, i.e., being in earnest about the difficulty involved, actualizing the wakeful intensification of the difficulty which goes with this, bringing it into true safekeeping. (SS 1923, 84–85; cf. 51)

Holding out and holding back for a while in the midst of modern *Betriebsamkeit* is neither a busy nor cacophonous affair. Instead, it is a way of standing still (*stillstehen*) and remaining silent (*stillschweigen*) in the ruinous chop and garrulous flow of contemporary public life (*Bewegung*)—and thus akin to the silent stillness we discussed in the previous chapter. In the early-1920s, Heidegger saw these dual responses to the present age as critical moments in the same intellectual countermovement (*Gegenbewegung*). Recall, for instance, his July 1923 correspondence with Karl Jaspers: Anyone who believes that the future of philosophy consists in "writing books" and thus "leads his pseudoexistence in the humdrum of today's busyness [*Betriebes*] does not know where he stands," Heidegger declares (*HJC*, 47). Which is why "I still haven't printed anything, and I simply endure it when I am referred to as *he who publishes nothing*" (*HJC*, 46).[16] Holding back from modern *Betriebsamkeit* and holding out in pensive *Jeweiligkeit* were tandem commitments, as far as Heidegger was concerned.

The tie that bound these commitments together was also the line of inquiry which led Heidegger away from the *Gerede*, *Geschreibe*, and *Geschwätz* of his colleagues. Early in his university career, this often meant escaping to his hometown of Messkirch: "Here I really am quite free & far away from any surroundings that remind me of university & the philosophical business [*Philosophiebetrieb*] of the schools, of discussions & chatter [*Redereien*]," he wrote to his wife in August 1920 (*LHW*, 74). Later in life, it was the family cabin near Todtnauberg that provided him with refuge: "Professors & everything that goes with them—have come to seem so remote from me—& I don't feel the slightest need of their worries & machinations," he wrote to her in October 1932 from its remote confines in the Black Forest (*LHW*, 139).[17] In the intervening years, Heidegger routinely felt trapped: "I work all day long & wish to myself that the whole appointment business would come to an end," he groaned in the spring of 1923. "It's disgusting the way they're conjecturing, wangling & scheming around" (*LHW*, 91). Even among his closest friends, Heidegger's disgust for academic life was pronounced: "With Jaspers (& wife) there was much—too much—talk about the chair, & I've now realized how hopelessly stuck these people are, like many others, in the psychosis of 'professorships,'" with all of its "unbearable chatter [*unerträgliche Gerede*]" (*LHW*, 123). At this point, holding out and holding back, in a state of resolute silence, was as much a personal response to Heidegger's glib surroundings as it was a principled agenda for his philosophical work.

Later, in *Being and Time*, this balance would shift. But the opposition between resolute silence and unbearable chatter would remain. Channeling his early lecture courses, Heidegger would again theorize reticent philosophical inquiry as a counter-possibility implicit in "the loud idle talk [*lauten Gerede*] which goes with the common sense of the 'they' [*des Man*]" (*BT*, 342; cf. 208, 322). And again, *Betrieb* would find a prominent place in his critique: "*Dasein* is always ambiguously 'there'—that is to say, in that public disclosedness of Being-with-one-another where the loudest idle talk [*lauteste Gerede*] and the most ingenious curiosity keep 'things moving' [*»Betrieb« im Gang halten*], where, in an everyday manner, everything (and at bottom nothing) is happening," Heidegger explains, hearkening back to his winter 1921–22 lectures (WS 1921–22) on the "uproarious haste" of ruinant factical life. "But when *Dasein* goes in for something in the reticence [*Verschwiegenheit*] of carrying it through or even genuinely breaking down on it, its time is a different time and, as seen by the public, an essentially slower time than that of idle talk [*Gerede*], which 'lives at a faster rate'" (*BT*, 218–219; cp. 222, 239, 409). Decades later, in his postwar lectures on language, Heidegger would restate this opposition in even broader terms, carefully distinguishing between meaningful moments of silence in which nothing is spoken but much is said and meaningless torrents of speech in which much is spoken but nothing is said.[18] Realizing how slippery his thinking on this topic had become, he would even go so far as to quip—and only half-jokingly—that "to talk and write about silence is what produces the most obnoxious chatter [*Gerede*]" (*OWL*, 52).

In the early-1920s, however, when Heidegger was just beginning to formulate the philosophical distinction between remaining silent and chattering nonstop, both of these communicative practices remained entangled with his career prospects in an academic discipline whose publish-or-perish prerogatives were not his own. Like so many of the key terms in his early thought—*Dasein*, *das Man*, averageness, interpretedness, publicness, curiosity, idle talk, resoluteness, and the like—keeping silent did not begin as an abstract philosophical concept but, instead, emerged from a unique set of concrete historical circumstances, all of which, as we have seen, stemmed from Heidegger's flagging university career. It was his lived experience as an unpublished and thus unpromotable scholar in the German university system that inspired his critical commentary on the *Gerede*, *Geschreibe*, and *Geschwätz* of his chosen discipline and, more broadly, of the modern world itself. Waiting and watching, holding out and holding back, remaining silent and standing still—all of the counter-possibilities implicit in *Gerede*, *Geschreibe*, and *Geschwätz*—began as practical, careerist reactions to the "speeches and pamphlets" of his peers. Only later, from the relative security of Heidegger's first professorship, did they become principled philosophical approaches to the study of human *Dasein*.

FIVE

Ancient Figures of Speech

Reading the Newspaper

Heidegger had been teaching Aristotle for years. But it was not until he arrived at Marburg University in the fall of 1923, joining the philosophical faculty as an untenured and woefully underpaid associate professor, that he began to understand his Greek predecessor. Again, the lecture hall became a seedbed for Heidegger's thought. And none of his lectures proved more fertile than those of his renowned summer 1924 course on *Basic Concepts of Aristotelian Philosophy*. In order to account for Heidegger's philosophy of ordinary language use in the years between his assistantship to Husserl and his professorship at Marburg, we must begin here, in the summer session of 1924.

Heidegger opens the semester with a flourish of Aristotelian thought: "The being of human beings . . . has the *character of speaking* [*Sprechens*]." More specifically, it has the character of *speaking about*. And speaking about, Heidegger claims, has the basic function of *logos*. As such, any conceptual inquiry into the being of human kind must take its start from the inherent human propensity for *logos*. "We are always inquiring into the *logos*, into that speaking-about, and addressing of, the world, wherein concept and conceptuality are at home," he tells his students. "We are seeking the basis, the indigenous character, of concept formation in being-there itself. Concept formation is not an accidental affair, but a basic possibility of being-there itself."[1]

When Heidegger refers to the "indigenous character" of *logos*, he means the being-there of human existence—namely, the average, everyday, familiar lifeworld in and as which human beings exist. The being-there of *Dasein* is always a being-there with others: "The basic determination of its being itself is being-with-one-another." And the basic mode of being-there with others is speech: "This being-with-one-another has its basic possibility in speaking, that is, in speaking-with-one-another, speaking as expressing-oneself in speaking-about-something" (*SS* 1924, 71–72). In this sense, human beings are not just beings that speak. More precisely, they are beings that speak with others about the world.

According to Heidegger, this is what Aristotle meant when he described the human being as a *zoon logon echon*—an animal with speech. "We do not have a corresponding definition," he goes on to note. "At best, an approximately corresponding definition would be: the human being is a living thing that reads the newspaper. At first this may sound strange to you, but it is what corresponds to the Greek definition. When the Greeks say that the human being is a living thing that speaks, they do not mean, in a physiological sense, that he utters definite sounds. Rather, the human being is a living thing *that has its genuine being-there in conversation and in discourse [das im Gespräch und in der Rede sein eigentliches Dasein hat]*" (*SS* 1924, 74). In other words, the human propensity for *logos* is anchored in an ontological "ability-to-discourse [*Redenkönnen*]."

To realize this ability-to-discourse in the company of others is to communicate. And to communicate is always to present something to someone in a certain way, from a certain perspective—a perspective which, in turn, invites them to see it *as* a certain kind of thing. Thus, to communicate something to someone is always, to some extent, to *interpret* it for them. And if what one communicates is subject to interpretation, then it is also susceptible to *mis*interpretation. As the medium in which communicators actualize the human ability-to-discourse, *logos* not only reveals "the *mastery* of interpretedness" in the being-there of humankind, but also indicates "the *possibility of error* in being-there as thus characterized" (*SS* 1924, 187). And this, Heidegger concludes, is how being-there itself typically finds expression, in a discursive tangle of prevailing interpretations, attendant misinterpretations, and ever-present possibilities of error—the likes of which, as we shall see in this chapter, prove integral to his understanding of *Gerede* and its garrulous siblings.

Rhetorical Hermeneutics

Hence, the centrality of Aristotle's *Rhetoric* in Heidegger's summer 1924 lecture course. "Speaking in the mode of speaking-in-discourse [*Sprechens-in-der-Rede*]—in public meetings, before the court, at celebratory occasions—these possibilities of speaking are definitively expounded instances of customary speaking, of how being-there itself speaks. With the interpretation of the *Rhetoric*, one aims at how basic possibilities of the speaking of being-there are already explicated therein" (*SS* 1924, 75–76). In service to this interpretation, Heidegger recalls Aristotle's understanding of ethics. It has less to do with morality than with "the 'comportment' [*Haltung*] of human beings, how the human being is there, how he offers himself as a human being, how he appears in being-with-one-another." To illustrate this mode of public appearance, Heidegger then considers "the way that the orator speaks [*wie ein Redner spricht*]." There is "a comportment [*Haltung*] in the way he stands with respect to the matters about which he speaks" (*SS* 1924, 73; cf. 111f). *Speaker*, *speech*, and *spoken-about*—these are the terms with which Heidegger begins his reading of Aristotle's *Rhetoric*.

In ancient rhetorical theory, the visibility of an orator's comportment with regard to the topic at hand was thought to follow from a *decision* regarding how to best comport oneself with regard to this topic. In rhetoric, "the deciding factor lies in 'taking hold,' the *proairesis*" (*SS* 1924, 73). A *proairesis* is an act of deliberate choice in which someone decides to pursue a specific purpose, plan, or course of action. It is at once a political judgment and a policy choice. What interests Heidegger about decision-making of this sort is its condition of possibility. For if discourse presupposes decision, the latter in turn presupposes some sort of initial attunement to the matter at hand, specifically a preliminary, indigenous orientation toward the available means of addressing this matter. Only when aware of these available means of address are orators prepared to select, develop, and advance specific lines of argument—and, in so doing, to comport themselves with respect to the matter at hand.

Aristotle seems to have known as much. Recall his definition of rhetoric: "Let rhetoric be an ability, in each case, to see the available means of persuasion" (*Rhet.*, 1355b26–27). What interests Heidegger about this definition is the basic modality it assigns to rhetoric: *potentiality*. "Rhetoric is the *possibility* of seeing what is given at the moment, what speaks for a matter that is the topic of discourse [*Rede*], the possibility of seeing at each moment what can speak for a matter," he tells his students, translating in real time from Aristotle's Greek (*SS* 1924, 78). "It does not have to cultivate a definite conviction about a matter, to set it to work with others. Rather, it only sets forth a possibility of discourse [*eine Möglichkeit des Redens*] for those that speak, insofar as they are re-solved to speak with *peisa* [persuasion, obedience] as their aim." Before comportment, before oratory, before judgment, the art of rhetoric "cultivates a possibility for the one who wants to convince, a possibility that cultivates in itself the ability-to-see that which speaks for a matter" (*SS* 1924, 79). As an ability to see, a capacity for sight, the basic function of rhetoric is not to persuade others but to envision how such convincing might occur. In this sense, rhetoric is not the product of persuasive artistry but, instead, the practice which allows for such production.

This is not to suggest that rhetoric constitutes a *techne*. Unlike medicine, arithmetic, and other technical arts, knowledge of which is circumscribed by specific subject areas, "rhetoric has *no subject area* that can be demarcated in any way" (*SS* 1924, 79). At most, Heidegger explains, rhetoric "gives an orientation with regard to something," an orientation toward something which in turn can be "extracted" (*ent-nehmen*) from a particular set of circumstances and mobilized for purposes of persuasion. When Heidegger refers to "that which speaks for something," this is what he means: "that which speaks for something speaks for the conviction that the one discoursing [*der Redende*] wants to cultivate in others, with respect to this discourse [*dieser Rede*]" (*SS* 1924, 80).

The orator's desire to build conviction in others is integral to Aristotle's theory of rhetoric. But it also suggests something more profound: "In the *Rhetoric*, we have something before us that deals with speaking as a basic mode of the being of the being-with-one-another of human beings themselves, so that an understanding of this *legein* [saying, speaking, gathering] also offers the being-constitution [*Seinsverfassung*] of being-with-one-another in new aspects" (*SS* 1924, 80). Thus, rhetoric is not just attuned to the available means of persuasion in any given situation. More specifically, it is attuned to the "definite conduciveness" (*bestimmten Beiträglichkeit*) of these means of persuasion and, with it, their indication of the basic phenomenological structure of human togetherness: *logos*.

If speaking-with-one-another is the basic mode of being-with-one-another, and being-with-one-another is "the basic determination of the being of human beings," then rhetoric, in its attunement to "what one debates in life in a customary way, and the manner and mode of talking it through," is not just the art of *"knowing-the-way-around in everyday being-there"* but also, more fundamentally, *"the genuine understanding of being-there itself"* (*SS* 1924, 84, 92). Documenting this genuine understanding and bringing some conceptual clarity to its discursive form is precisely what Aristotle attempted to accomplish with his treatise on rhetoric, Heidegger argues. "Rhetoric is nothing other than the discipline in which the self-interpretation of being-there is explicitly fulfilled," he summarizes, repeating himself emphatically for good measure: *"Rhetoric is nothing other than the interpretation of concrete being-there, the hermeneutic of being-there itself.* That is the intended sense of Aristotle's rhetoric" (*SS* 1924, 75). At last, the centerpiece of Heidegger's projected but never published book on Aristotle was in place—along with the key conceptual scaffolding for his emerging philosophy of ordinary language use.

Eyes Wide Shut

Years later, in a crucial section of *Being and Time*, Heidegger would be content to echo the foregoing argument, leaving readers to ponder its relevance to his existential analytic. Aristotle's *Rhetoric*, he notes in passing, "must be taken as the first systematic hermeneutic of the everydayness of Being with one another" (*BT*, 178). In the summer of 1924, however, he was eager to explain why this is the case by showing students how, exactly, Aristotle's treatise opened the being-there of humankind to its first genuine understanding.

Heidegger begins by recalling the basic goal of persuasive artistry: "to cultivate, in speaking itself, *pisteuein* [trust, faith, compliance] with those to whom one speaks, specifically, about a concern that is up for debate at the time." More precisely, he adds, the aim of rhetoric is "to cultivate *doxa*." In antiquity, *doxa* referred to the external appearance of someone or something—specifically, to a true or false opinion, expectation, or supposition held by others about the external appearance of someone or something. Heidegger equips his students with a similar definition: *"doxa* is a definite manner of appropriating beings as they show themselves" (*SS* 1924, 81). To have a *doxa* with respect to these beings is thus to have a *view* of these beings. Whatever else the relationship between rhetoric and *doxa* entails, it remains, at root, a relationship governed by *sight*. Which is why Heidegger is intrigued by the orator's attempt to cultivate *pisteuein* in an audience:

Pisteuein is a "view" [*Ansicht*], *doxa*, on which speaking depends, and which, therefore, is presumably something that governs, or guides, the everydayness of being-there, the being-with-one-another of human beings. Being-with-one-another moves in definite, always modifiable views [*wieder modifizierbaren Ansichten*] regarding things; it is not an insight, but a "view" [*Ansicht*], *doxa*. It is a *doxa* regarding things, but not such that things which are brought to language are themselves thematically investigated. This *pisteuein*, "holding in a view" [*in einer Ansicht sich halten*] within being-with-one-another, is that upon which discourse [*Rede*] itself depends. (*SS* 1924, 81)

If rhetoric is a way of seeing the available means of persuasion in any given situation, and these means of persuasion are defined by their conduciveness to the cultivation of *pisteuein* in others, then the art of cultivating *pisteuein* in others consists in using the available means of persuasion in any given situation to access and adjust the "always modifiable views" of being-with-one-another. Or, put more succinctly, we might say that rhetoric is a way of *seeing, addressing,* and ultimately *modifying* the views of others in any given situation. It is at once dependent on *doxa* and dedicated to its manipulation.

Logos was the basic phenomenon, but not the basic determinant, of being-there in ancient Athens. For Aristotle and his contemporaries, the basic determinant of being-there was *doxa*'s more illustrious sibling: *endoxon*. According to Aristotle, *endoxa* are the "reputable opinions" at work in any given community, namely, the opinions "accepted by everyone or by the majority or by the wise—i.e., by all, or by the majority, or by the most notable" (*Top.,* 100b21–24). As Heidegger goes on to explain, these reputable opinions can refer to all sorts of things: "what is of the future, what has already happened, what is present, what is conducive, what is fitting and what is not fitting, the beautiful and the ugly"—in short, anything about which community members can share a point of view. In its dependence on *doxa* and commitment to its manipulation, rhetoric can be shown to *operate* on communal points of view, at once relying on them, referring back to them, and frequently attempting to revise them. This is because *endoxa* are always already, as Heidegger quips, "in *doxa*" (*SS* 1924, 88–89).

In *endoxa* and the various *doxai* they inform, Heidegger sees more than the communal building blocks of persuasive artistry. He also sees "the *basic phenomenon of everydayness*, the basic phenomenon that underlies this speaking itself," and thus the "definite conditions for how *logos* itself must be with respect to its *exhibiting-character*, its *concreteness*" (*SS* 1924, 90, 93). With an eye to this exhibiting-character, he at once recalls and extends his earlier definition of *doxa* as a governing or guiding "view" in the everydayness of being-there. "*Doxa* designates, first of all, the 'view of something,' but at the same time it means, for the most part, 'to have a view,'" he explains. "I do not seek first; I am not, at first, on the way to the ascertaining of the structure of a matter, but I am situated thus and so toward the matter" (*SS* 1924, 93). If rhetoric is a way of seeing the available means of persuasion in any given circumstance, *doxa* is the way of seeing that allows any particular circumstance to appear as "given" in the first place. It is the having-of-a-view that allows for the giving-of-a-circumstance. But it is also the having-of-a-view that allows any particular arrangement of entities and events to appear as a givable "circumstance," any particular cluster of entities and events to appear as a discernable "arrangement," and any particular thing in the world to appear as a distinct "entity" or "event." As a phenomenon of everyday life, *doxa* thus suggests that circumstances of every sort, and all of their various contours, are not sought but *found*. This is not to suggest, however, that we find certain circumstances ourselves. On the contrary, as Heidegger is careful to suggest, it means that *we always already find ourselves in certain circumstances*.

To illustrate this "being-situated," Heidegger likens *doxa* to an agreement of sorts between the viewer, the viewing, and the viewed. He starts by returning to the Greek notion of *phasis*, meanings of which range from "appearance" to "expression" to "utterance." Taken together, these meanings indicate that *phasis* is "a certain *legein*," Heidegger glosses. More precisely, it is "a certain *yes-saying* [*Ja-Sagen*] to that of which I have a view." The same is true of *doxa*, he adds. It is at once "a being-situated toward the matter" and, to this extent, "a certain yes-saying [*Ja-Sagen*]" with respect to this situatedness (*SS* 1924, 93). "This becomes clear when we translate *doxa* correctly: 'I am for maintaining that the matter is thus and so'" (*SS* 1924, 97).

How are we to grasp the "yes-saying" implicit in *doxa*? Heidegger's German is instructive here. *Ja-Sagen* relies on the German verb *sagen*, which in turn derives from Proto-Indo-European root **sekw-*, meaning "to say," "to see," and, interestingly, "to follow." At the risk of putting too fine a point on the *sagen* in *Ja-Sagen*, we might argue that it consists in *following what is said with one's eyes*. And yet even this would not be precise enough, especially given our discussion in the previous chapter of Heidegger's earlier attack on the cowardly "yes, I agree" implicit in Eduard Spranger's "All of us . . ." As students would have been quick to observe, there is a striking kinship between Heidegger's *Ja-Sagen* and the German figures of *die Ja-Sagerin*, "the yes-man," and, more suggestively, *der Jasager*, "the stooge." To have a *doxa* is not just to hold a preexisting viewpoint with respect to what someone says. More specifically, it is to hold this viewpoint *unreflectively, unquestioningly*, and often *regardless* of what someone says—in short, to follow what is said with one's eyes *closed*.

Incapacitating Falsehood

The condition of possibility for this peculiar way of having-a-view is familiarity, and the medium in which this familiarity is established and maintained is speech. "This familiarity regarding the world, and dealing and living in it, is borne by speaking as the peculiar exhibiting of that to which one is oriented," Heidegger argues. "At the same time, this familiarity is the mode in which views and orientations are cultivated. Views are cultivated, renewed, established, hardened in speaking." Even hardened views, however, are subject to change. "Having-a-view is thus *only* a view; it could also be otherwise." So also with the reputable views of the community. "*Endoxon* is the manner of being-oriented in which one is oriented toward beings *that can also be otherwise*. There is the possibility of the view being *revised*." This is why *doxa* cannot be understood as *episteme*. "With respect to beings that always are how and what they are, with regard to *episteme*, there is no revision. On the other hand, *revisability* belongs to *doxa* in itself; it is assumed of itself" (*SS* 1924, 93–95).

If *doxa* is subject to revision, it is because having-a-view is not a way of knowing. Instead, it is a way of seeing. "In *doxa*," Heidegger recalls, "I do not have the being itself, but rather an orientation in relation to it" (*SS* 1924, 96). And like any way of seeing in the realm of human togetherness, where contingency and plurality reign supreme, the orientation provided by *doxa* is at once subject to change and prone to range, varying in fit and fidelity to the matter at hand. "The being that is under discussion in everydayness," Heidegger explains, is "that which can simultaneously be more or less what it precisely is," depending on one's orientation. Yet another reason to distinguish *doxa* from *episteme*. "If I know definite information about something, it belongs to the sense of this knowing that what is known cannot be 'false,' cannot be *pseudes*, since in that case it would not be *episteme*." In *doxa*, however, truth and falsehood are equally possible. "In itself, *doxa* is true and false," Heidegger claims. "It could be thus, it could be otherwise" (*SS* 1924, 93).

In marking this strange simultaneity of truth and falsehood, Heidegger is not just confirming the well-known fact that opinions can be true or false. He is also linking this fact to his earlier claim that all opinions are also subject to change. If opinions can be true or false, and they are always subject to change, then "false" opinions can eventually become "true" opinions, and vice versa. This is because *doxa*, like rhetoric, thrives on potentiality. As Aristotle well knew, every potential to be or do is always also a potential *not* to be or do. If this were not the case, which is to say, if every potentiality (*dynamis*) was not always also an impotentiality (*adynamia*), "potentiality would always already have passed into act and be indistinguishable from it."[2] When Heidegger claims that *"doxa* is true and false," he is building on this logic. In particular—and this is the key point—he is suggesting that falsehood is *doxa*'s basic *potentiality*, and truth is its corresponding *impotentitality*. *Pseudos* is the Greek term he assigns to this capacity for falsehood. And *aletheia*, of course, is the Greek term he assigns to *the incapacitation of falsehood in manifestations of truth.*

Even at this early stage in his career, Heidegger is reading *aletheia* as an extension of the Greek verb *lethein*, meaning "to escape notice," "to remain unseen," and (thus) "to forget." Like the Latin *in-* and the Germanic *un-*, the Greek *a-* at the front of *aletheia* serves a privative function, effectively negating the verb to which it is attached. To be *alethes* is *not* to escape notice, *not* to remain unseen, *not* to slip into forgetting. Hence, Heidegger's early-Marburg translations of *alethes* as "unhidden," *aletheia* as "uncovering," and *aletheuein* as "to take out of hiddenness," "to make unhidden," and, more playfully, "to 'dis-cover' what was covered over"—all of which would eventually culminate in his coinage *enthergen*, meaning "to unconceal."[3] As *aletheia*, Heidegger suggests, truth at once presupposes and struggles to overcome its initial concealment in falsehood. It is simultaneously present in, disguised by, and resistant to *pseudos*.

Here, in his 1924 lectures on Aristotle, Heidegger is eager to stitch these notions of truth into a coherent line of inquiry accessible to his students. The *alethes* is "the unconcealable-being-that-is-there, which has the possibility of being conducive to *aletheuein*," he summarizes. And *aletheuein* is "a mode of being-in-the-world, such that one has unconcealed it there just as it is." Which in turn brings him to their collective goal that semester: "This *aletheuein* is the basic phenomenon toward which we are headed" (*SS* 1924, 81).

Rhetoric and *doxa* figure prominently in this summer course because both are fundamentally oriented toward the basic phenomenon of *aletheuein*. In its search for *pistis*, rhetoric cannot help but verge on *aletheia*. "*Pistis*, 'what is able to speak for a matter,' is speaking of the matter itself," Heidegger notes, improvising on Aristotle's treatise. "In speaking, the *alethes* should be exhibited, what is 'unconcealed' in the very way that the matter is, free of all determinations. And in particular, this *alethes* should be showing 'on the basis of the occurrences and circumstances that speak for the matter'—an *alethes* that is not opened up through *theorein*, but rather makes the true visible in what is probable" (*SS* 1924, 83). In this sense, rhetoric aims to cultivate a certain type of *doxa*: It aims to discover and develop what Heidegger calls "the right view of a matter" (*SS* 1924, 94).

In much the same way, *doxa* remains intrinsically, if only impotentially, oriented toward the *alethes*. But even this falls short of Heidegger's central argument. What is ultimately at stake in his recuperation of *doxa* is his unwavering belief that all opinions inherently lean toward truth. And by "truth," of course, he means *aletheia*. "*Doxa* must possess *orthotis* [soundness or correctness of apprehension and assertion], to which belongs 'direction' toward, 'being-directed' toward *aletheia*," he insists (*SS* 1924, 93). In other words, the view provided by *doxa* is always, to some extent, "directed to the *alethes*." And lest anyone misunderstand what he means by this, Heidegger quickly integrates his earlier definitions of both terms: "The view has the tendency to intend the being unconcealed in itself" (*SS* 1924, 96). *Doxa* may be a "yes-saying" (*Ja-Sagen*), and its possessor may resemble a "yes-man" (*Jasager*), but these are not its only characteristics: "A being-after something in the direction of the *alethes* is also found in *doxa*" (*SS* 1924, 98).

Nevertheless, the ways of seeing afforded by rhetoric and *doxa* tend to be cloudy. Though essentially inclined toward *aletheia*, they often remain shrouded in *pseudos*. Rhetoric may intend "the right view of a matter," but it frequently results in dissimulation. And *doxa* may conceive of "the being unconcealed in itself," but this conception usually remains just that: "a conception that, as conception, is likely false" (*SS* 1924, 96). As Heidegger sees it, the push of *pseudos* is always stronger than the pull of *alethia*.

Which brings us back to the opening topic of his summer 1924 lecture course: *speech*. As we shall see, rhetoric and *doxa* are at their best when contributing to the production of *Rede*—a localized, concrete strand of *logos* that is inclined toward authentic speech and true opinion, modes of being in the world that allow what is spoken about and thus seen to appear uncovered, unconcealed, just as it is. At their worst, however, rhetoric and *doxa* yield only *Gerede*—a dislocated, indeterminate strand of *logos* in which inauthentic speech and false opinion allow what is spoken about and thus seen to remain hidden, concealed, and disguised. Elaborating on these crucial differences and anticipating more nuanced distinctions to come are the tasks to which we now turn.

The Yes-Man Finds His Voice

If *logos* is the medium in which the interpretedness of being-there finds expression, *Gerede* is the fallen form of *logos* in which the *mis*interpretations indigenous to this interpretedness supersede. In characterizing these misinterpretations as "indigenous" to the interpretedness of being-there, Heidegger is attempting to demonstrate that *logos* is the mode and manner in which *all* conceptions of human being, even *false* conceptions of human being, are developed and deployed. "Insofar as this *logos* is that in which all that is conceptual occurs, *it* is also that which constitutes the *possibility of error* in being-there as thus characterized" (*SS* 1924, 187).

In order to grasp the meaning of *Gerede* in this context, we must first understand what Heidegger means by "error." As we have seen, he initially anchored this term in the Greek *pseudos*, from the verb *pseudein*, meaning "to deceive" and, more precisely, "to cheat by lies." Toward the end of his summer 1923 lecture course, however, Heidegger arrived at a more precise definition: All errors operate by "*leading astray [Irre-führen]*." When someone is purposely led astray, the result is known as *deception* (*Täuschung*). In their "being-deceived," we see the "dominance of the *false*, of the *pseudos*" (*SS* 1924, 187). But not all errors are intentional. Some are accidental. If intentional errors constitute deception, accidental errors result in *dissimulation* (*Verstellung*). And if lies are the origin of deception, *Gerede* is the origin of dissimulation. At issue in idle talk is not a form of deceit but, instead, as the German *Verstellung* suggests, a type of *disguise*. When idle talk prevails, speakers fail to see what their speech says, allowing matters at hand to remain obscure, hidden, and veiled—in short, *to remain concealed*.

In a conceptual flurry that would culminate in sections 33–35 of *Being and Time*, Heidegger attempts to explain how such dissimulation occurs: "The experienced and the seen is, for the most part what is *expressed* [*Ausgesprochenes*]. In expression, it is communicated to others, and through this *communication* [*Mitteilung*] comes into circulation: what is repeated [*das Nachgesprochene*]. In this speaking-around-us [*Sich-herumsprechen*], *idle talk* [*Gerede*], what is expressed increasingly loses its ground. Through this idle talk [*Gerede*], this being-further-spoken [*Weitergesprochenwerden*] without recourse to the expressed matter, idle talk [*Gerede*] comes to cover up and dissimulate [*zu verdecken und zu verstellen*] that which is genuinely meant. What is expressed carries in itself the possibility of *dissimulation* [*Verstellung*]" (*SS* 1924, 187; trans. modified). In this crucial passage, Heidegger not only describes how speakers lose sight of what they are saying. Nor does he simply allude to the mode and manner of concealment in which this losing-sight occurs. Of equal importance, he suggests, is the rhetorical trope on which *Gerede* relies—a trope which clearly connects his reflections on everyday talk to those of Kierkegaard before him: *repetition*.

As we saw at the start of this chapter, the basic determinant of human being is being-with-one-another, and the condition of possibility for being-with-one-another is speaking-with-one-another. Insofar as speaking with others also implies listening to others, some amount of repetition is unavoidable, especially when it comes to ordinary, face-to-face modes of communication. "All these modes of natural speaking-with-one-another carry in themselves the claim that the other does not merely take notice of something, but *takes* something up, *follows* something, *reflects* on something," Heidegger notes. "The other *repeats* [*wiederholt*] that which is spoken in such a way that in repeating [*Wiederholen*] he *listens* to it" (*SS* 1924, 72).

But listening is not the only horizon of such repetition. While intently listening to others, we also run the risk of unwittingly following their lead. In *Gerede*, this risk becomes a reality. What is taken up, followed, and reflected upon—in short, what is heard and thus repeated—is not some*thing* but, rather, some*one*. When *Gerede* surges forth, cults of personality follow.

Hence, *der Jasager*. In *Gerede*, the yes-man finds his voice. In its idolatrous circuit, the sociology of his "yes-saying," and with it the experience of *doxa* itself, becomes readily apparent: "In this structure of *doxa*, lies the possibility of its reaching a characteristic *authority and stubbornness*. One repeats the opinions to others [*Man spricht eine Meinung den anderen nach*]. Repeating [*Nachsprechen*] does not depend on investigating *what* is said. What is said is not decisive, but rather it is *he* who said it. Behind the authority of *doxa*, stand other people, who are peculiarly indefinite, whom one cannot get a hold of—*one* has the view [*man ist der Ansicht*]" (*SS* 1924, 102). Note the ambiguity of Heidegger's final remark: "*man ist der Ansicht.*" On first glance, he seems to be suggesting that the person who holds the *doxa* which the *Gerede* of *der Jasager* repeats is an indefinite being. When read in light of his earlier (and later) work on *das Man*, however, this final remark suggests something more nuanced: the "*one*" in question is not an unnamed individual but, rather, a *generic collectivity*. What the *Gerede* of *der Jasager* repeats is not the opinion of an unidentified someone but, instead, *the indefinite opinions of everyone*. In his "yes-saying," we see a garrulous deferral to *das Man*. What is unreflectively adopted and unquestioningly followed in his *Gerede* is nothing less (and nothing more) than the viewpoint of this generic collectivity.

In *Gerede*, Heidegger sees an average instance of speaking-with-one-another and, by extension, an average instantiation of being-with-one-another. "Average: the task of investigating the world is not posited," he glosses. "One does not have to investigate everything with regard to its concrete content; what others say about it is what one thinks about it" (*SS* 1924, 102). In this average failure to investigate the world, he finds another opportunity to stress the importance of familiarity in speaking-with-one-another, in being-with-one-another, and thus in any conception of the world. "All speaking is oriented toward bringing the questionable, the unintelligible, into a *definite familiarity*," he reminds his students. "Familiarity is the standard of intelligibility that *logos* possesses, that proceeds from the *endoxon* and returns to it" (*SS* 1924, 185).

Endoxon is the origin of familiarity, as well as its destination. But *Gerede* is the vehicle in and by which familiarity travels this circuit of shared opinion. In this sense, *Gerede* is not only groundless but also, paradoxically, *foundational*. None of this is lost on Heidegger. In idle talk, he claims to find "the basis, the indigenous character, of concept formation in being-there itself" (*SS* 1924, 71). On this point, he is adamant: "Idle talk [*Gerede*], the 'way in which one speaks about things,' is authoritative for the world-conception itself" (*SS* 1924, 192; trans. modified). Again, Heidegger walks his students through the logic of his argument: "*A definite sense of being guides* every natural interpretation of beings. This sense does not need to be made categorically explicit, and precisely when it is not, it possesses its genuine being and its authority. In *this* interpretation of being-there, being means *being-present, being-completed*. The being is not only there in its look; the being-character is itself explicitly there, in the sense of the explicitness of everyday seeing, considering, discussing" (*SS* 1924, 185). Echoing his lecture course of the previous semester, Heidegger describes this everyday mode of discussing as *Gerede*. In this average, ordinary way of speaking, he sees the indigenous character of being-there and, with it, the condition of possibility for world-conception itself.

"Opening One's Eyes"

Discovering the origin of interpretedness is not the same as developing what Heidegger calls "an *original interpretedness*." And yet, as he also contends, these two procedures are tightly interlaced. To illustrate this, he notes how, "Coming into the world, one grows into a determinate tradition of speaking, seeing, interpreting. Being-in-the-world is an already-having-the-world-thus-and-so." Another word for this immersive, multifaceted tradition, Heidegger continues, is "heritage."

When *Gerede* prevails, heritage becomes a site of false consciousness, or, as Heidegger calls it, "*prevailing interpretedness*." When *Rede* prevails, however, our heritage of false consciousness becomes a resource for genuine conceptuality, which is what Heidegger describes as "*original interpretedness*." In this sense, original interpretedness is not separate from prevailing interpretedness. Instead, it is "the proper possibility" of prevailing interpretedness. "Since the everyday can seize hold of heritage, it follows that being-there has the possibility of tearing heritage away from the everyday, and bringing it to an *original interpretedness*, that is, out of everydayness, and in opposition to it in the *hexis* to *appropriate* the conceptual *in the genuine sense*" (*SS* 1924, 186–89). The secret of false consciousness, it would seem, is its double life as an occasion for genuine conceptuality.

At stake in Heidegger's discussion of prevailing and original modes of interpretedness is a critical-historical method of philosophical inquiry capable of retrieving the latter from the former. The original, primary, and heretofore hidden contents of prevailing interpretedness "must be liberated from that which has been accumulated through idle talk [*Gerede*] and pointless discussion" (*SS* 1924, 189). As we know, Heidegger had been developing this retrieval technique for years. In the 1922 introduction to his projected book on Aristotle, for instance, he described the "object-field" of philosophical inquiry as the loquacious "how" of factical life—namely, the everyday talk in and by which various ways of being in the world are "handed down to it" and "reported to it" (*BH*, 167). But this object-field is difficult to discover, and even trickier to traverse, because philosophical inquiry has long remained entrenched in its own thoughtless, everyday heritage. "For the most part today, philosophy operates inauthentically within the *Greek* conceptuality," Heidegger explains. "The basic concepts have lost their original functions of expression, functions which were specially tailored to fit regions of objects experienced in a particular way." Even so, "some mark of their provenance still remains. These basic concepts still bear within themselves a part of the genuine tradition of their original sense" (*BH*, 168). As Heidegger saw it, Greek thought had become the false consciousness, and thus also the authentic conceptual horizon, of German philosophy.

Redeeming philosophical inquiry from its threadbare heritage of Greek conceptuality remained on Heidegger's research agenda in the summer of 1924, and it continued to inform his philosophical work for years to come. Ever since Plato and Aristotle brought in "the initial great harvest" of philosophical thought, he told students in the summer of 1930, "the history of philosophy has been threshing this harvest, and now it is only empty straw which is being threshed. So we must go out and bring the harvest in anew, i.e., we must come to know the field and what it is capable of yielding." But this is easier said than done in the present age, Heidegger warns: "We can only do this if the plough is sharp, if it has not become rusted and blunt through mere opinions, in idle talk and scribbling [*Gerede und Geschreibe*]. It is our fate to once again learn tilling and ploughing, to dig up the ground so that the dark black earth sees the light of the sun. We, who have for all too long unthinkingly taken the well-trodden roads."[4]

Part of the challenge, Heidegger realized in the early-1920s, is that the Greeks themselves also suffered from the kind of false consciousness that attends average, everyday ways of speaking. When he claims that "the Greeks lived in discourse [*Rede*]," this is what he means to suggest: They not only saw speech as "the genuine possibility of being-there" but also struggled against the tendency of being-there to become "*ensnared*" in ordinary language use. Proximally and for the most part, their sense of being-there remained "absorbed in the immediate, in fashions, in babble [*Geschwätz*]," Heidegger reports. "For the Greeks themselves, this process of living in the world, *to be absorbed* in what is ordinary, *to fall* into the world in which it lives, became, through language, the *basic danger of their being-there*" (*SS* 1924, 74).

Hence, the rise of sophistry. Notably, the Protagoras principle: "to discuss geometry with a geometer, even if one understands nothing about geometry, to guide the conversation in such a way that I conquer the other without knowledge of the matter discussed. Sophistry is proof that the Greeks fell prey to *the* language that *Nietzsche* once named 'the most speakable of all languages'" (*SS* 1924, 75). And yet it is precisely here, in the realm of sophistry, that any attempt to grasp its opposite—"genuine speaking, deliberating, concrete grasping," which is to say, "scientific research"—must take its start:

We must take measure of what it means to retrieve speaking from this alienation of Greek being-there, from conversation and idle talk [*Gerede*], to bring speaking to that place in which Aristotle can say that *logos* is λόγος οὐσίας, "speaking about the matter as to what it is." Aristotle stood in the most extreme opposition to that which was vital around him, to that which stood against him in the concrete world. One must not imagine that science had fallen into the laps of the Greeks. The Greeks were completely absorbed in the outward. At the time of Plato and Aristotle, being-there was so burdened with babble [*Geschwätz*] that it required the total efforts of them both to be serious about the possibility of science. (*SS* 1924, 75; trans. modified)

Later in this summer course, Heidegger recalls the ancient struggle to retrieve speaking from sophistry. And he does so using much of the same language above, notwithstanding a curious shift from *Geschwätz* back to *Gerede*—a shift which anticipates the almost complete disappearance of the former from Heidegger's later work, along with any mention of his indebtedness to Kierkegaard's notion of *snak*, which, as we saw in chapter 1, entered the German language as *Geschwätz*: "Only from this standpoint can one understand what was a strain for the Greeks, who were to a certain degree in love with *logos*: to work their way out toward a concreteness, from out of discussion and idle talk [*Gerede*]. Only thus can we understand that it is false when one holds Greece in general to be a fantastical place, as if things just fell into the lap of these distinguished men" (*SS* 1924, 176; trans. modified). Even Aristotle's definition of the human as "a being that speaks" was strained by *Gerede* and its everyday conceptual heritage. "This definition is not invented by Aristotle," Heidegger reminds his students. "He says explicitly that with this definition he repeats an *endoxon*, a *doxa*, that has authority in Greek being-there itself. Already before Aristotle, the Greeks saw the human being as a being that speaks" (*SS* 1924, 73). Indebtedness of this sort is also readily apparent in his treatise *On Rhetoric*, Heidegger adds. "Rhetoric, as a reflection on speaking, is older than Aristotelian *Rhetoric*. In Aristotle's works, there is also handed down to us the rhetoric *ad Alexandrum*. It does not come from Aristotle" (*SS* 1924, 78).

By returning to the Greeks, and to Aristotle in particular, Heidegger hopes to retrieve the interpretedness of concrete being-there from *Gerede* and render it conceptually intelligible in *Rede*, thereby paving the way for original and (thus) authentic philosophical discourse. But what, exactly, constitutes a discourse as original, authentic, and philosophical? If *Gerede* consists in the dependent, practical activity of "dealing" with beings in the world, and *Rede* consists in the codependent, political activity of "debating" with beings in the world, Heidegger understands authentic philosophical discourse as the independent, pre-theoretical activity of "exhibiting" beings in the world (*SS* 1924, 189). "It is related to bringing-to-seeing as a mode of fulfillment of looking-out as such," he explains. "It depends on seeing beings themselves, so to speak, through idle talk [*Gerede*] and through the theory that conceals the way of being of nature. The primary step is opening one's eyes, apprehending the fact of the matter in itself, and, on the basis of this fore-having, explicating what shows itself" (*SS* 1924, 194; trans. modified).

As we have seen, rhetoric and *doxa* are both anchored in visual metaphors. Rhetoric is a way of seeing the available means of persuasion in any given circumstance, and *doxa* is a preexisting point of view—a preview of sorts—allowing certain circumstances to appear as "given" in the first place. Here, in one of the final flourishes of his summer 1924 course on Aristotle, Heidegger attempts to anchor his project in another visual metaphor. In sharp contrast to the "yes-saying" of *der Jasager*, which consists in following the idle talk of *das Man* with eyes wide shut, the critical-conceptual method of philosophical inquiry at stake in Heidegger's project involves "opening one's eyes" to "what shows itself" in and through such idle talk. What are we to make of this metaphorical kinship between rhetoric, *doxa*, and philosophical inquiry?

Hidden Kings and Medicine Men

Recall Heidegger's discussion of *aletheia*. "What shows itself" is the *alethes*, and the *alethes*, in turn, is what occasions the basic phenomenon toward which Heidegger claims to be headed in the summer of 1924: *aletheuein*. By suggesting that his critical-conceptual methodology consists in "opening one's eyes" to "what shows itself," he invites students to consider the *identity* of the individual whose life consists in *aletheuein*—"a mode of being-in-the-world, such that one has unconcealed it there just as it is." Who is best able to apprehend the *alethes* when he opens his eyes and, in so doing, to adopt *aletheuein* as his mode of being?

Again, the connection between persuasive artistry, public opinion, and philosophical inquiry presents itself. Throughout his summer course on Aristotle, Heidegger suggests that rhetoric and *doxa* both have representative figures, and that each of these representative figures is characterized by a particular way of speaking. Rhetoric is the purview of the orator (*der Redner*) and typically culminates in localized discourse (*Rede*), while *doxa* is possessed by the stooge (*der Jasager*) and often yields little more than dislocated talk (*Gerede*). In its quest for *aletheia*, philosophical inquiry also cultivates a specific subject position and, with it, a characteristic way of speaking. Heidegger, again drawing on Aristotle, names this individual the *aletheutikos*.

The *aletheutikos* is someone whose identity consists in "having being-there with respect to discoveredness [*Entdecktheit*] at one's disposal, presenting oneself so that one's self-presentation and being with others is not a self-concealing [*Sichverbergen*], feigning [*Sichverstellen*], *presenting oneself as one is and as one thinks.*" Neither more nor less than who he is, "each speaks and behaves in the way he is," and thus lives his life in "the mode of being-able-to-be-there-unconcealed [*Unverborgen-da-sein-Könnens*]." When he opens his eyes, the *aletheutikos* sees "the disclosive being-oriented in being-toward-oneself and in being-toward-others." In other words, he sees *aletheia*. And when he opens his mouth, he "speak[s] about things, insofar as they are stripped of the look they have in immediate relations"—namely, the look they have when mired in *Gerede*. In speech and deed alike, the *aletheutikos* is "undisguised" (*unverstellt*). When he passes through the world, he does so in a state of "uncoveredness" (*Unverdecktheit*) (*SS* 1924, 176–78).

But this is an exceptional state, even for the *aletheutikos*. More often than not, he remains concealed from others as well as himself, appearing in speech and deed alike as someone more or less than he truly is. When the *aletheutikos* appears to be more than himself, truthfulness slips into boastfulness, transforming him into an *alazon*; and when he appears to be less than himself, truthfulness becomes buried in mock modesty, transforming him into an *eiron*. That both of these figures— *alazon* and *eiron* alike—played important roles in Kierkegaard's theory of chatter makes them worthy of consideration here, particularly in light of Heidegger's early academic career, which, as we have seen, set the stage for his nascent philosophy of ordinary language use.

To illustrate the *eiron*, Heidegger, like Aristotle and Kierkegaard before him, recalls the figure of Socrates, "who passes himself off as one who knows nothing yet knows more, indeed, than others" (*SS* 1924, 177–178; cf. *EN*, 1127b26). But he probably had himself in mind as well. By the mid-1920s, Heidegger was famous among university students. So famous, in fact, that Hannah Arendt, in her reflections on *Being and Time*, wondered "whether the unusual success of this book—not just the immediate impact it had inside and outside the academic world but also its extraordinarily lasting influence, with which few of the century's publications can compare—would have been possible if it had not been preceded by the teacher's reputation among the students, in whose opinion, at any rate, the book's success merely confirmed what they had known for many years." What distinguished Heidegger's fame from other, more visible instances of academic celebrity in the mid-1920s, Arendt went on to contend, is that "there was nothing tangible on which his fame could have been based, nothing written, save for notes taken at his lectures which circulated among students everywhere. These lectures dealt with texts that were generally familiar; they contained no doctrine that could have been learned, reproduced, and handed on. There was hardly more than a name, but the name traveled all over Germany like the rumor of the hidden king."[5] It would have been difficult for students in Heidegger's summer 1924 lecture course to imagine a more fitting example of the mock-modest man.

According to Aristotle, boastfulness is worse than mock modesty and thus more directly opposed to truthfulness. Heidegger builds on this opposition, pitting the braggart's obsession with public opinion against the *aletheutikos*'s commitment to revealed truth. "He sticks to speaking the sort of thing that universally enjoys reputation," Heidegger explains. Unlike the life of the *aletheutikos*, which involves speaking and acting "in the way he is," the life of the braggart consists in "making something up about oneself, so that one conceals [*verbirgt*] one's genuine being." In other words, the braggart is "not the sort who presents his being undisguisedly [*unverstellt*]" (*SS* 1924, 177). In this regard, he resembles *der Jasager*. While the former traffics in *endoxon* and the latter clings to *doxa*, both thrive on leading astray (*Irreführen*). To the stooge's hapless reliance on dissimulation (*Verstellung*), however, the braggart adds an overweening twist of deception (*Täuschung*). In place of *aletheia*, the braggart offers *pseudos*. And in this sense, he more closely resembles the sophist, who uses *doxa* and *endoxon* alike to deceive audience members, effectively rendering them stooges.

If Socrates embodies mock modesty, who personifies boastfulness? Aristotle does not say. Instead, he suggests that braggarts come in three kinds, each of which is defined by a specific purpose. Some boast for enjoyment, delighting in the production of falsehood itself; others boast in service to fame, claiming qualities that others are likely to praise; and others still boast for personal gain, pretending to have qualities that others are likely to value. From Aristotle's point of view, each of these objectives is more loathsome than its predecessor: To boast for enjoyment is "futile rather than bad," and to boast for fame is "not very much to be blamed," but to boast for financial gain is to advance something far "uglier." What makes the latter so despicable is not its pursuit of "qualities which are of value to one's neighbors" but the fact that "one's lack of [these qualities] is not easily detected." Which is why "the powers of a seer, a sage, or a physician" are always subject to doubt, Aristotle concludes (*EN*, 1127b9–20). More often than not, their powers are limited to self-aggrandizing deception.

Following Aristotle's lead, Heidegger does not attribute boastfulness to anyone in particular. For better and for worse, students in his summer 1924 course were left to wonder who, in the discipline of philosophy, might serve as its representative figure. Given Aristotle's indictment of seers, sages, and physicians in search of financial gain, and Heidegger's outspoken criticism of industrious, profiteering scholarship in the 1920s, however, students were well prepared to venture a few guesses. First and foremost in their minds would have been "the litterateurs" of the Weimar period. Even as early as the winter of 1921–22, in his first lectures on Aristotle, Heidegger was attempting to distinguish himself from these racketeering intellectuals. "I have no ambition to make discoveries and take out patents on them," he told students that semester. "Only litterateurs and corruptors of spiritual life, jealous and protective of their own little treasure troves, misuse philosophy in this way to feed their vanity" (*WS* 1921–22, 87). As we have seen, Heidegger often returned to this topic, notably in his summer 1923 lectures on the hermeneutics of facticity, reminding students that philosophical insights are "not mere cultural goods which lie around in books, provide a source of occasional amusement, or offer a possible employment and livelihood" (*SS* 1923, 51). "Beware of all this!" he warned. Phenomenology "is not simply to be picked up as a theme and treated in a businesslike fashion" (58).

Even (and especially) in the field of phenomenology, the pursuit of financial gain had begun to supplant the quest for philosophical truth. As we saw in the previous chapter, Heidegger believed that phenomenology had forfeited its authority as "the conscience of philosophy" in order to become "a pimp for the public whoring of the mind" (*SS* 1923, 37). No longer a school of thought, it had devolved into a "philosophical industry"—specifically one characterized by "propaganda, proselytizing, cliquish monopolies, [and] intellectual racketeering" (58, 15). In short, phenomenology had become "quackery" (60). Recalling Aristotle's indictment of seers, sages, and physicians in search of personal gain—not to mention Kierkegaard's subsequent critique of pseudo-religious "poet-hacks" and "Hegelian Gert Westphalers"—Heidegger likened the field of phenomenology to a self-aggrandizing, self-perpetuating, and woefully shamanistic enterprise. "We have today become so pithless and weak-kneed that we are no longer able to hold out in the asking of a question. When one medicine man cannot answer it, then one turns to the next. The demand increases the supply" (16).

Clearly, Heidegger did not wish to join their ranks. On the contrary, as we discovered in chapter 4, he often took it upon himself to challenge the "industriousness" of these medicine men. In this regard, the imagery of his 14 July 1923 letter to Karl Jaspers glimmers anew: "Much preaching must be wiped out (i.e., the various medicine men of today's philosophy must have their dreadful and pitiful handiwork exposed) in their own lifetime, so that they don't believe that God's kingdom has appeared today with them" (*HJC*, 47). Make no mistake: If Heidegger was "the hidden king" of German philosophy, these medicine men were his kingdom-come opponents.

Foremost among these medicine men of philosophy, as any student of Heidegger's in the 1920s well knew, was Edmund Husserl. Even at the start of his assistantship to Husserl, Heidegger was depicting him as an "old man" and his approach to phenomenology as "a sad state of affairs" (*BH*, 368). As shown in the previous chapter, these critiques became more pointed and pronounced during the final year of Heidegger's assistantship, when he began to suspect that Husserl's support was insufficient to secure him a professorship. It was in this context, near the end of his summer 1923 lecture course on the hermeneutics of facticity—the course in which he claimed to have struck "the main blows against phenomenology" (*BH*, 372)—that Heidegger wrote to Jaspers about the "medicine men" of contemporary philosophy. And it was here, immediately after his tirade against "their dreadful and pitiful handiwork," that he presented his most eviscerating critique of Husserl:

You already know that Husserl has been offered an appointment in Berlin. He behaves worse than a *Privatdozent* [unsalaried instructor] who mistakes the Ordinariat [full professorship] for eternal bliss. What is happening is shrouded in darkness. To begin with, he sees himself as *Praeceptor Germaniae* [Teacher of Germany]. Husserl is completely falling to pieces—if the pieces were ever together in the first place, which has lately become more and more questionable to me. He swings back and forth and talks trivialities, so that it would move one to pity. He lives with the mission of being the *founder of phenomenology*. No one knows what that is. Whoever is here for a semester knows what is wrong. He begins to perceive that people are no longer going along with him. He believes, naturally, that it is too difficult; naturally, no one understands the *mathematics of the ethical* (the latest!), even when he has advanced further than Heidegger, about whom he *now* says: Of course he must immediately give lectures himself and can't visit mine; otherwise, he would have advanced further. *This* is now supposed to redeem the world in Berlin. (*HJC*, 48)

Much to Heidegger's embarrassment, phenomenology had become a self-aggrandizing, shamanistic enterprise—and Edmund Husserl had become its boaster-in-chief. In keeping with his legendary status as "the hidden king" of German thought, Heidegger did not need to provide his students with an example of Aristotle's boastful man. Nor did he need to provide a character sketch of the intellectual braggart he had in mind. By the summer of 1924, they already knew this braggart by name.

The Babbler

A few months later, in his winter of 1924–25 course on *Plato's Sophist*, Heidegger introduced his students to another frustrating figure of everyday talk—a figure we have encountered before: *the babbler* (*der Schwätzer*). Neither honest nor duplicitous, boastful nor mock-modest, the babbler is a forlorn subtype of the orator (*der Redner*) who engages in argumentation and debate, but only in a rash and rambling manner—and only on trivial and trifling matters.

Even the deceptive words of the sophist take on "a serious character" when compared the "mere pedantic babble [*bloßes Bildungsgeschwätz*]" of *der Schwätzer*. At the very least, Heidegger quips, in a fleeting moment of praise for the sophist, "his speeches are concerned with some matter or other."[6] Indeed, "Gorgias was not a mere babbler [*bloß ein*

Schwätzer]."[7] If the *Rede* of the orator trumps the *Gerede* of the sophist, the latter, it would seem, trumps the *Geschwätz* of the babbler.

To illustrate the way of speaking characteristic of the babbler, Heidegger, like Kierkegaard before him, considers Plato's account of the *adoleschos*:

> The *adoleschos* is the babbler, used in the special sense of one who babbles pedantically about trifles. Meant here are those who do not pass a minute of their lives without philosophizing about trifles or speaking about them, who cannot even climb a mountain without pouring forth all their knowledge to their companion, indeed with the intention of provoking the other to a response and leading him into a debate. What is characteristic is that this sort of man speaks constantly and seeks ever new opportunities to set a dialogue in motion. (*WS* 1924–25, 212)

In this regard, the defining feature of the *adoleschos* is not the substance but the *style* of his discourse. Echoing his winter 1921–22 lectures on Aristotle, where he characterized *Geschwätz* as the garrulous pursuit of novelty for novelty's sake, Heidegger suggests that, when the *adoleschos* flits from topic to topic, ever in search of something new to discuss, his babble undermines the purposive, referential, and deliberative functions of *Rede*. Where the localized and concrete discourse of the orator was, a meandering and groundless way of speaking takes hold—one whose sole objective is a continuation of the discussion at hand.

In this regard, Heidegger also echoes Kierkegaard's account of chatter. "One who chatters presumably does chatter about something, since the aim is to find something to chatter about," Kierkegaard quips in a section of his 1846 literary review of *Two Ages* that captured our attention in chapters 2 and 3. With no aim or anchor other than itself, conversation becomes "a frivolous philandering among great diversities" in which one "chatters about anything and everything and continues incessantly" (*TA*, 99–100). Heidegger probably had this passage in mind when discussing *der Schwätzer*, especially given his familiarity with the prevailing German translation of Kierkegaard's "Critique of the Present Age," which, as we have seen, renders *snak* as *Geschwätz*.

But this is not where Heidegger turns after recalling Plato's *adoleschos*. Instead, he quotes Aristotle's student Theophrastus, who bolstered Plato's claim that the discourse of the *adoleschos* operates by "constantly bringing up new topics in order to draw the other into a dialogue":

> "*Adoleschía* is a mode of circumlocution in rambling and rashly chosen words [*eine Weise des Daherredens in weitläufigen Worten und unüberlegt*], and the *adoleschos* is,

e.g., a man who approaches someone he does not at all know (in a train or wherever) and gives him a long speech in praise of his own wife, or relates to him what he dreamt that night, or treats in detail what happened during the afternoon. After that, if the other is still listening, he goes on to say that people today are much worse than formerly, that the price of wheat on the market has risen, that there are many foreigners in town, that since the Dionysian festivals the sea has become navigable again (these are all obvious things), that if Zeus would send more rain it would be better, that the harvest will be such and such this year, and that in general life is difficult." (*WS* 1924–25, 212)

Of central import here is not the list of topics broached by the *adoleschos*—married life, a recent dream, current events, people today, market prices, foreign visitors, sailing conditions, weather patterns, the difficulty of life, and so on—but the mode and the manner in which this list unfolds. Again, Heidegger's German is instructive here. *Daherredens* derives from the verb *daherreden*, meaning "to chatter." But *daherreden* also lends itself to descriptions of people who *yap, rant, prate, talk without thinking*, and, put a bit more archly, *talk through their hats*. All of which, in turn, allows Heidegger to suggest that the babbler's choice of words is just as imprudent (*unüberlegt*) as their delivery is sprawling (*weitläufigen*).

For better and for worse, this is the closest Heidegger ever came to a formal definition of *Geschwätz*. But it is not the last time that this rash, rambling, trifling, and pedantic way of speaking would take center stage his early work—or in the conceptual history of everyday talk that continued to develop in its wake. Indeed, as we shall see in part 3 of this book, Lacan would have much to say about the perpetually discontinuous way of speaking that Kierkegaard theorized as *snak* and Heidegger later described as *Geschwätz*. And much of what he would have to say, in keeping with the work of his predecessors, would hook into Plato's earlier account of the *adoleschos*.

Modes of Concealment

Students who followed Heidegger from his summer 1924 course on Aristotle's *Rhetoric* to his winter 1924–25 course on Plato's *Sophist* would have noticed several through lines. Not least of these was their professor's sustained interest in the hidden connection between the *Gerede* of everyday life and the practice of philosophical inquiry. In the summer of 1924, Heidegger claimed that the goal of phenomenological research is to retrieve the interpretedness of concrete being-there from *Gerede* and render it conceptually intelligible in *Rede*, thereby paving the way for original, authentic modes of philosophical inquiry. By the winter semester of 1924–25, the hidden king was eager to develop and expand this claim.

He begins by repositioning *Gerede*, *Rede*, and philosophical inquiry in a broader, more sophisticated hierarchy of spoken discourse. Beneath the *Rede* of the orator, he places the *Gerede* of the sophist; and beneath the *Gerede* of the sophist, he locates the *Geschwätz* of the babbler. Above the *Rede* of the orator, he places the "speaking-through" of the dialectician (*Durchsprechen*); and above this speaking-through, he locates the "genuine speaking" of the philosopher (*echte Sprechen*). Crucial for our purposes are the idle talk of the sophist, the genuine speech of the philosopher, and the "speaking-through" of the dialectician, which traverses the former in search of the latter. In order to account for their curious relationship, however, we must first consider how Heidegger, at this stage in his emerging philosophy of ordinary language use, reinterprets the connection between idle talk and common opinion.

Once more, he anchors his discussion in Greek notions of truth and falsehood. "Truth, which for us is something positive, is for the Greeks negative as *aletheia*; and falsehood, which for us is something negative, is positively expressed by them as *pseudos*" (*WS* 1924–25, 11). And once more, he notes that the Greeks understood truth as the *unconcealment* of what otherwise remains shrouded in falsehood. "*Aletheia* means: to be hidden no longer, to be uncovered. This privative expression indicates that the Greeks had some understanding of the fact that the uncoveredness of the world must be wrested, that it is initially and for the most part not available. The world is primarily, if not completely, concealed" (*WS* 1924–25, 11).

But concealment comes in several forms. First and foremost is *ignorance*. In his December 1924 Cologne address, "Being-There and Being-True According to Aristotle," Heidegger described ignorance as "straightforward concealment" and chalked it up to "unfamiliarity with a region of being that for the first time gets revealed and made visible—or, to use a good German expression, *entdeckt* [discovered, uncovered]" (*BH*, 225). Back in Marburg, he and his students feasted on a more detailed account. The state of nature is initially and for the most part a state of ignorance, Heidegger claims. "Only in the immediate circle of the surrounding world, insofar as natural needs require," does ignorance give way to something like "disclosive knowledge" or, as he quickly specifies, "natural consciousness" (*WS* 1924–25, 11).

No sooner has natural consciousness emerged, illuminating the surrounding world, than human speech intervenes, returning the world to darkness. "That which in natural consciousness was, within certain limits, perhaps originally disclosed comes to be covered up again and distorted by speech." And by speech, of course, Heidegger means *Gerede*: "everyday *Dasein* moves in a double coveredness: initially in mere ignorance and then in a much more dangerous coveredness, insofar as idle talk [*Gerede*] turns what has been uncovered into untruth" (*WS* 1924–25, 11). He develops this argument more fully in the Cologne address: "Something that was already originally discovered once, and at one time had been a proper possession of someone who had original knowledge of it, submerges once more and thus becomes something that 'everyone' understands, 'everyone' repeats and says to others until it becomes 'valid.' What was brought forth once in an originary and creative manner now becomes uprooted. It loses its ground [*Boden*]. But it does so in such a manner as to retain its dominance as true knowledge" (*BH*, 225).

Note the parallels between this passage and the summer lectures that preceded it. Again, Heidegger shifts from the indefinite being of "someone" to the generic category of "everyone." Again, he emphasizes the stubborn, authoritative nature of everyone's talk. And again, he suggests that the prevailing trope of their everyday talk is repetition. By way of repetition, the *Gerede* of *das Man* not only produces "untruth" but also propagates this untruth until it becomes "valid"—so valid, in fact, that it can be mistaken for "true knowledge." Where natural consciousness was, in the proximal presence of something originally known, false consciousness finds its place, deracinating knowledge and thus allowing what was originally known to slip into forgetting. "This is the most dangerous kind of concealment," Heidegger concludes. When knowledge is uprooted from the known and allowed to drift through the discourse of *das Man*, "it presents itself as a self-evident truth that requires no further questioning" (*BH*, 225).

At this point, of course, Heidegger is no longer referring to original knowledge. Instead, he is speaking of common opinion. When the *Gerede* of everyone misappropriates the knowledge of someone, the state of nature in which natural consciousness first emerged—ignorance—surges forth anew as the second nature of common opinion. "One sees, one judges, one wishes, one has needs in the manner in which one talks, in the manner in which everyone speaks," Heidegger summarizes. "Therefore, the Everyone [*das Man*]: a curious phenomenon of the most immediate *Dasein* of the human being, one that governs an entire way of being [in the world], the way and manner in which the world is seen, judgmentally criticized, and questioned. The important thing is that we keep in mind that everyday *Dasein* sees the world and itself within common opinion, and maintains a definite opinion about them" (*BH*, 223–24). At issue here, Heidegger claims, is another mode of concealment from which *Dasein* typically suffers. "We have already met up with this hiddenness," he observes, recalling his summer 1924 lectures on *doxa*. "It is hiddenness by way of those common opinions within which everyday life operates. It is the concealment [*Verborgenheit*] by way of the specific ways of seeing in which everyday living moves" (*BH*, 225). In keeping with his earlier lectures on Aristotle, Heidegger reminds his audience that holding a view (*Ansicht*) is not the same as having an insight (*Einsicht*). Both are ways of seeing, but the former conceals what the latter discloses.

With common opinions come various concepts and propositions, all of which, when subjected to *Gerede*, tend to supplant truths with truisms. "Opinions rigidify themselves in concepts and propositions; they become truisms which are repeated over and over [*nachgesprochen*], with the consequence that what was originally disclosed comes to be covered up again" (*WS* 1924–25, 11).

To illustrate this process, Heidegger invites students in his winter 1924–25 lecture course to consider how propositions frequently emerge and recur in ordinary conversation:

To understand a preposition, I do not necessarily have to repeat [*nachsprechen*] it in each of its steps. Some days ago it rained, I can say, without presentifying to myself the rain, etc. I can repeat [*hersagen*] propositions and understand them without having an original relation to the beings of which I am speaking. In this peculiar confusion, all propositions are repeated [*nachgesprochen*] and thereby understood. The propositions acquire a special existence; we take direction from them, they become correct, so-called truths, without the original function of the *aletheuein* being carried out. We participate in the propositions, with our fellows, and repeat them uncritically [*spricht sie nach auf Treu und Glauben*]. In this way *legein* acquires a peculiar detachment from the *pragmata*. We persist in idle talk [*Gerede*]. This way of speaking about things has a peculiar binding character, to which we adhere inasmuch as we want to find our orientation in the world and are not able to appropriate everything originally. (*WS* 1924–25, 18; trans. modified)

Clearly, there is more at stake in this passage than the rhetorical function of *Gerede* and the correspondence theory of meaning it subverts. Underlying Heidegger's account is an important yet still unanswered question: If our adherence to and persistence in *Gerede* provides "an orientation in the world," one which presumably compensates for our inability "to appropriate everything originally," what is the source and substance of this incapacity? Are we unable to appropriate everything originally because the *pragmata* of the world are too many? Or is there something about us, as human beings, that remains inadequate to the task?

Talking Through

From the vantage point of everyday life, and thus through the optics of common opinion, the problem would seem to be our lack of time. But this is just an illusion. Indexing his previous critiques of philosophical industriousness (*Betriebsamkeit*), and thus also Kierkegaard's broader attack on modern busyness (*Travlhed*), Heidegger attributes this illusion to "the bad present of the everyday"—an experience of the here and now in which humanity "lives with its watch in its hand," and all watches appear to keep the same time. In the spirit of his earlier lectures on ruinance and the today, he defines the time of everyday life as "One"-time (*"Man"-Zeit*), namely, "the time in which *one* [*man*] is with one another."[8]

Not surprisingly, *Gerede* thrives on this "One"-time. And all of "that in which such idle talk [*Gerede*] maintains itself, all restlessness, all busyness, all noise, and all racing around" routinely finds expression in the same utterance: "I have no time" (*CT*, 14–15). With more time, we tell ourselves in the midst of such talk—which Heidegger further reduces to "babbling" (*Geschwätzigkeit*)—all the *pragmata* of world would be readily available to us (12; trans. modified). But again, this is just an illusion.

According to Heidegger, the fundamental barrier to our complete—and completely original—appropriation of the world is not our lack of time but, instead, our excess of speech. Words do not uncover things as they are in the world; instead, they uncover only those aspects of things which lend themselves to words. Even in the mode of *aletheuein*, this remains true: "*Alethes* means literally 'uncovered.' It is primarily things, the *pragmata*, that are uncovered. *To pragma alethes*. This uncoveredness does not apply to things insofar as they are, but insofar as they are encountered, insofar as they are objects of concern." And the medium in which things appear to us as objects of concern, Heidegger continues, is nothing other than the discourse in which we find ourselves "speaking about things" (*WS* 1924–25, 17). Thus, even when we are speaking about things in the mode of *aletheuein*, disclosing the world in a genuine and authentic manner, our words remain just that: *words*. On this point, Heidegger is equally pointed: "All the forms of *aletheuein* we saw in Aristotle, with the exception of *nous*, are determined by the character of the *meta logon*: they are carried out in discourse." And for anyone who may have missed his earlier lectures on Aristotle, he reiterates his main argument: "*Logos*, addressing something in speech, is our most immediate mode of carrying out *aletheuein*, whereas *nous*, pure perception, is as such not possible for man, the *zoon logon echon*" (*WS* 1924–25, 136). What allows us to uncover the *pragmata* of the world is also, ultimately, what keeps us detached from them: language use. Which is precisely why *Gerede* is so misleading: it purports to overcome this basic existential dilemma.

Between the blindness of *Gerede* and the pure perception of *nous* are three intermediate ways of speaking, each of which cleaves closer to the *alethes* than its predecessor: the "speech and counter-speech" of the orator (*Rede und Widerrede*), the "speaking-through" of the dialectician (*Durchsprechen*), and the "genuine speech" of the philosopher (*echte Sprechen*). Having already spoken at length about the *Rede und Widerrede* of the orator in his summer 1924 course on Aristotle, Heidegger wastes no time in his winter course on Plato introducing students to the *Durchsprechen* of the dialectician. Beyond the *Geschwätz* of the babbler, the *Gerede* of the sophist, and the *Rede* of the orator, he argues, is the *dialegesthai* of Platonic dialogue, which has "the specific comportment of inter-locution [*Durchsprechens*]" (*WS* 1924–25, 135). "Inter-locution" is a reasonable yet incomplete translation of *Durchsprechens*. By nominalizing the German verb *durchsprechen*, meaning "to talk through," Heidegger is attempting to suggest that the type of "discussing" (*dialegesthai*) typical in Platonic dialogue is not just something that occurs *between speakers*, and not just something occurs *by way of speech*, but also—in keeping with the Greek verb *dialegein*, meaning "to speak through"—something that operates by *passing through certain kinds of speech*.

What kind of speech does *dialegesthai* attempt to pass through? In order to begin answering this question, Heidegger asks students to recall the radical philosophical task that Plato inherited from Socrates: "To pass from *logos* as idle talk [*Gerede*], from what is said idly and hastily about all things, to genuine speaking [*durch des echte Sprechen hinderdurchzugehen*], to a *logos* which, as *logos alethes*, actually says something about that of which it speaks. *Dialegesthai* is a passing 'through speech' [*ein Hindurchgehen durch das Sprechen*], departing from what is idly said, with the goal of arriving at a genuine assertion, a *logos*, about beings themselves" (*WS* 1924–25, 135; trans. modified). And the *durch's* just keep coming: *dialegesthai* is not just a "speaking-through [*Durchsprechen*]" but also, more combatively, a "running-through [*Durchlaufen*]" of *Gerede*, Heidegger explains. It attempts "to cut through idle talk [*durch das Gerede hindurchzudringen*]" by "disclosing *in the mode of discussion* [*Aufdekens in der Weise des Durchsprechens*]" something beyond the garrulous purview of *das Man*. "This 'speaking-through' [*Durchsprechen*] begins with what people [*man*] first say about the matter, passes through this [*durch dieses hindurch*], and is directed to and finds its end in a speaking which genuinely expresses something about the theme, i.e., in genuine assertion, genuine *logos* [*über dast Thema eigentlich etwas aussagt, in der Aussage, im echten logos*]" (*WS* 1924–25, 11; trans. modified).

If *Gerede* is the idle and inauthentic *logos* through which *dialegesthai* attempts to pass, what is the genuinely expressive *logos* toward which *dialegesthai* aims? Again, Heidegger recalls the Greek *aletheuein*. "If we say that *logos*, here as *dialegesthai*, is disclosive [*aufdeckend*], and is taken in any case in this facticity, then that means that an *aletheuein* belongs to *logos*." This is not to suggest, of course, that every *logos* is also an *aletheuein*: "*Logos* itself, simply as *logos* does not constitute without further ado a carrying out of *aletheuein*, and . . . consequently *the uncovering within logos* [*das Aufdecken im logos*] is not indigenous to it as *logos*" (*WS* 1924–25, 135–36). On the contrary, when left to its own devices, *logos* does not become *dialegesthai* in service to *aletheia*. Instead, it remains mired in *Gerede* and committed to *pseudos*:

According to its original sense and according to its original facticity as well, *logos* is not disclosive [*aufdeckend*] at all but, to speak in an extreme way, is precisely concealing [*verdeckend*]. *Logos* is at first idle talk [*Gerede*], whose facticity is not to let things be seen [*sehen*] but instead to develop a peculiar self-satisfaction at adhering to what is idly spoken of [*was man so sagt*]. The domination of idle talk [*Gerede*] precisely closes off beings for the *Dasein* and brings about a blindness with regard to what is disclosed and what might be disclosive. (*WS* 1924–25, 135; trans. modified)

Note the tension between seeing and saying, *sehen* and *sagen*, in this passage. In *Gerede*, we have *sagen* without *sehen*: a great deal is said about all manner of things, but none are seen as they truly are in the world. Much as *der Jasager* follows what others say with his or her eyes closed, the *Gerede* in which his or her "yes-saying" finds expression remains blind to what *dialegesthai* attempts to disclose. In this sense, *Gerede* is antithetical to what Heidegger, following Aristotle, describes as *nous*. In *nous*, we have *sehen* without *sagen*: things are seen as they truly are in the world, but only insofar as they confound the speech of its inhabitants. If *Gerede* is a yes-saying, *nous* is a "saying nothing [*nichts zu sagen*]" (*WS* 1924–25, 289). Where the stooge goes blind, the theorist remains silent (*schweigen*).[9]

Dialegesthai is somewhere in between. Like its lesser siblings—*Geschwätz*, *Gerede*, and *Rede*—it remains anchored in *logos*. "*Dialegesthai* remains a matter of speech [*Besprechen*]; it *does not arrive at pure noein*. It does not have at its disposal the proper means to attain its genuine end, i.e., to attain *theorein*." More than any other way of speaking, however, *dialegesthai* aspires toward this objective. As it passes through the *pseudos* of idle talk, it presses ahead to the *aletheia* of genuine speech: "The pressing ahead must be such a speaking [*Sprechen*] that, by means of speeches pro and con [*Für- und Gegensprechen*], it leads more and more to what is being discussed [*wovon die Rede ist*] and lets that be seen [*sehen*]. *Dialegesthai* therefore possesses an *immanent tendency toward noein*, toward seeing [*Sehen*]. Yet insofar as the consideration remains in *legien*, and as *dialegesthai* continues on in speaking-through [*Durchsprechen*], such speaking-through can indeed relinquish idle talk [*Gerede*] but cannot do more than *attempt* to press on to the things themselves" (*WS* 1924–25, 136; trans. modified).[10] Thus, to summarize: *Gerede* tells all but shows nothing; *nous* shows all but tells nothing; and *dialegesthai* is the intermediate practice of linguistic show-and-tell. Equal parts *sagen* and *sehen*, the Platonic practice of "speaking-through" remains grounded in spoken discourse but ever-goaded by pure perception.

Rhetoric, Aristotle famously claimed, is the counterpart of dialectic. In his treatment of *dialegesthai*, Heidegger suggests that the opposite is also true. Just as the art of rhetoric culminates in the speech and counterspeech of the orator (the *Rede und Widerrede* of *der Redner*), so also does the practice of speaking-through involve speaking for and toward (*Für- und Gegensprechen*) what the discourse is about (*woven die Rede ist*). Add to this their mutual (if only metaphorical) investment in sight—rhetoric as a way of seeing and cultivating in others "the right view of the matter" (*SS* 1924, 94), and *dialegesthai* as a way of speaking that "leads more and more to what is being discussed and lets that be seen" (*WS* 1924–25, 136)—and the kinship between these *Arten des Sprechens* becomes even more apparent.

But this is as far as their likeness goes. As we have seen, the *Rede* of the orator operates on the common opinions circulated by idle talk. It is at once dependent on and dedicated to the adjustment of *doxa* as well as *Gerede*—not in an effort to show matters as they truly are in the world (*aletheuein*) but in hopes of shifting the worldly viewpoints from which others continue to misperceive them (*peitho*). Thus, as a way of seeing, rhetoric does not allow matters themselves to be seen. Instead, it shows the "modifiable views" (*modifizierbaren Ansichten*) from which these matters are commonly seen. In sharp contrast, the *Durchsprechen* of the dialectician obviates common opinion and idle talk, cutting through *doxa* and *Gerede* alike in a sustained (yet always incomplete) effort to arrive at the pure seeing of *theoria*, the pure perceiving of *nous*, and, ultimately, the "pure showing of the things themselves" (*BH*, 221). In its commitment to *echte Sprechen*—genuine speech about matters as they truly are—this effort can only be described as *aletheuein*. Unlike the orator, who settles for conviction, the dialectician continually strives toward truth.

Were we to map these kindred ways of speaking alongside those we have already discussed in this chapter, the result would be an early Heideggerian spectrum of discourse, ranging from the silence of the *theoros* to the babbling of *der Schwätzer* (table 5.1).

In his summer 1924 lectures on Aristotle, Heidegger suggested that the original and thus genuine philosopher is neither a boastful medicine man (like Husserl) nor a mock-modest intellectual star (like Socrates) but, instead, an *aletheutikos*—someone who, in speech and deed alike, presents himself exactly as he is and exactly as he thinks. The *bios aletheutikos* is a life lived in "the mode of being-able-to-be-there-unconcealed," Heidegger lauds. Implicit in this admirable mode of being in the world is a particular way of seeing the beings of this world. In the summer of 1924, Heidegger was still struggling to explain this way of seeing to his students: "It is related to bringing-to-seeing as mode of fulfillment of looking-out as such." At the same time, however, he was paving the way for his later work on the *Durchsprechen* of *dialegesthai*: "It depends on seeing beings themselves, so to speak, through idle talk [*durch das Gerede hindurch*]" (*SS* 1924, 189, 194; trans. modified). In his winter 1924–25 lectures on Plato, he solidified this connection, suggesting that the *bios aletheutikos* thrives on *dialegesthai* and the latter, in turn, consists in the twofold task of passing through the *pseudos* of *Gerede* and pressing forward in the *aletheia* of *echte Sprechen*.

This is how Heidegger came to understand original, genuine philosophical inquiry in the mid-1920s. "Philosophy faces the tasks, on the

Table 5.1. An early Heideggerian spectrum of discourse

	Linguistic practice	Communicative effect	Representative figure
Truth **(Aletheia)**	Silence (*Schweigen*)	Pure perception (*Noein*)	Theorist (*bios theoretikos*)
	Genuine speech (*echte Sprechen, logos alethes*)	Disclosive knowledge (*Aletheuein*)	Philosopher (Heidegger) (higher form of *bios aletheutikos*)
	Speaking-through (*Durchsprechen, dialegesthai*)	Thinking-through (*Dianoein*)	Dialectician (Plato), Mock-modest man (Socrates) (lower form of *bios aletheutikos*)
↑ ↓	Speech and counterspeech (*Rede und Widerrede*)	Persuasion (*Peitho*)	Orator (*der Redner*) (higher form of *bios politikos*)
Falsehood **(Pseudos)**	Idle talk (*Gerede*)	Deception (*Täuschung*)	Sophist (Gorgias), Braggart (Husserl) (lower form of *bios politikos*)
		Dissimulation (*Verstellung*)	Stooge (*der Jasager*) (higher form of *bios koinonikos*)
	Babble (*Geschwätz*)	Distraction (*Adoleschía*)	Babbler (*der Schwätzer*) (lower form of *bios koinonikos*)

one hand of breaking through for the first time to the matters them-selves (the positive task) and, on the other hand, of taking up at the same time the battle against idle talk [*Gerede*]" (*WS*, 1924–25, 11; trans. modified). And this, he began to realize, is precisely why we need the Greeks now more than ever: "We have to learn again what real philo-sophical research looks like, and in fact we have to learn this from the Greeks. The Greeks already carried out such research long before us. We do not need to 'take over' the Greeks. Rather, the outcome of our work will perhaps be very different from theirs; what remains the same, however, is the basic way of doing philosophical research" (*BH*, 231).

Hence, the return to Aristotle's rhetorical theory in *SS* 1924. But also the attempt to recover something beyond the art of rhetoric in *WS* 1924–25: namely, "the fundamental sense of Platonic dialectic." As a prelude to the pure sight of *theoria*, the pure perception of *nous*, and, by extension, the pure truth of beings themselves, "dialectic is not some sort of crafty operation of thinking but is in its very sense always al-ready a *wanting* to see [*Sehenwollen*]," Heidegger concludes. "Dialectic is not the art of out-arguing another [*Überredungskunst*] but has precisely the opposite meaning, namely of bringing one's partner in the argument to open his eyes and see [*den Mitunterredner zum Sehen zu bringen und ihm die Augen zu öffnen*]" (*WS* 1924–25, 137–38; trans. modified). In the summer of 1924, he claimed that the first stage of the *bios aletheutikos* involves "opening one's eyes." By the winter of 1924–25, he was also ready to mark its final step: What begins when we open our own eyes ends when it opens the eyes of another as well. Where *der Jasager* was, another *aletheutikos* must become.

SIX

The World Persuaded

Discoursing About or Discoursing Without?

When Heidegger joined the philosophical faculty at Marburg University, he was known among students and colleagues alike for his piercing interpretations of Greek thought. His summer 1924 lectures on Aristotle's *Rhetoric* and winter 1924–25 lectures on Plato's *Sophist* only added to this reputation. In the shadow of these celebrated lecture courses, however, he was working on another philosophical project, a book-length study that would soon bring him international fame: *Being and Time*.

The earliest draft of this 1927 masterwork—its "original form," according to Gadamer—was a July 1924 address to Marburg's theological faculty titled "The Concept of Time." In the months following this address, Heidegger expanded his speaking notes into a lengthy essay with the same title. Like all of his writings in the decade prior to *Being and Time*, however, this essay went unpublished. Nevertheless, in keeping with past practice, much of this essay found expression in the undergraduate classroom, where, in the summer of 1925, Heidegger delivered a series of lectures titled the *History of the Concept of Time*. In the first division of the main part of this lecture course, the hidden king of German thought presented the penultimate draft of division 1 of *Being and Time*—and with it a remarkable prelude to his first published account of idle talk (*Gerede*) and its garrulous siblings.

In Heidegger's 1924 address, "The Concept of Time," *Rede* appears only twice, and each time only in passing. In his lecture course, *History of the Concept of Time*, however, *Rede* takes center stage, much as it does in *Being and Time*. Again, Heidegger recalls the ancient Greek characterization of our species. By *zoon logon echon*, he explains, the Greeks meant that the human being is "a living being capable of discourse [*das reden kann*]." Any thorough account of human existence must start here, with a *"phenomenology of discourse [Phänomenologie der Rede]"* anchored in the Greek understanding of *logos*, Heidegger insists. And any thorough phenomenology of discourse must begin with "the *discourse* of everydayness" [*die Rede der Alltäglichkeit*]," he adds (*SS* 1925, 264, 261). Understanding what he meant by this in the summer of 1925 and then in *Being and Time*, particularly with reference to the other modes of discourse that occupied him during this period, are the primary tasks of this chapter.

In the discourse of everyday life, Heidegger claims to have discovered two basic modes of communication: one inclined toward authentic existence and another inclined toward inauthentic existence. In keeping with table 5.1 in the previous chapter, he suggests that the communicative trajectory from the discourse of everyday life (*Rede*) to the genuine speech of authentic existence (*echte Sprechen*) parallels the ancient conceptual pathway from rhetoric to dialectic. In the speech and counterspeech of rhetorical practice (*Rede und Widerrede*), Heidegger sees an impulse toward the speaking for and against that is characteristic of theoretical disputation (*Für- und Gegensprechen*) and, by extension, a push toward the speaking-through of dialectical inquiry (*Durchsprechen*)—the communicative practice well captured in the Greek *dialegesthai*, which, as we saw in chapter 5, "leads more and more to what is being discussed [*woven die Rede ist*] and lets that be seen" (*WS* 1924–25, 136).

Heidegger doubles down on this argument in his summer 1925 lecture course: "Discoursing [*Reden*] now has an emphatic function in being-with-one-another as the possibility of talking something through [*die Möglichkeit des Durchsprechens von etwas*]. And this talking something through easily takes the form of a dispute, a theoretical disputation. Discoursing and *logos* for the Greeks thus assume the function of theoretical discussion [*theoretischen Beredens*]. The *logos* accordingly gets the sense of exhibiting what is talked over [*Beredeten*] in its whence and what about" (*SS* 1925, 264–65; trans. modified). In this crucial passage, Heidegger not only recalls the kinship between rhetorical practice and dialectical inquiry, but also strengthens their relationship. Just as the *Durchsprechen* of theoretical disputation strives for *echte Sprechen* of disclosive knowledge, so also does the *Rede* of oratorical practice lean toward the *Durchsprechen* of theoretical disputation. Hence, his use of *Beredens* to characterize such disputation, and *Beredeten* to describe "what is talked over" when it occurs. Both terms derive from the verb *bereden*, meaning "to argue." But they also resonate with the German word for eloquence: *Beredtheit*. All of which further suggests that the communicative trajectory from everyday life to authentic existence is one in which the persuasive speech of the orator gives way to the speaking-through of the dialectician, and the latter, in turn, gives way to the genuine speech of the philosopher. Were we to chart this progression (again recalling table 5.1 in the previous chapter), it might look something like table 6.1.

Of central import to Heidegger in this progression from the *Rede* of rhetorical practice to the *echte Sprechen* of philosophical inquiry is what gets "talked over" along the way. In his summer 1925 lectures, he divides the communicative practice of talking-over into two structural moments: "the *about-which*" (*das Worüber*) and "the *said*" (*das Gesagte*) (*SS* 1925, 262). First and foremost, prior to any shift toward the *Durchsprechen* of dialectical debate and the *echte Sprechen* of philosophical inquiry, *Rede* is always discourse *about* some aspect of the world. "This about-which of discourse [*Worüber der Rede*] is purely and simply what is under consideration [*Angesprochene*], which as such is therefore always already there from the start, having the character of world," Heidegger explains. "This about-which of discourse becomes manifest insofar as something is said [*gesagt*] about something in every discourse." Hence the second structural feature of "what is talked over" in any given discourse: "the *said* as such" (*SS* 1925, 262).

To illustrate the difference between what is said in discourse (*das*

Table 6.1. The communicative trajectory from everyday life to authentic existence

	Way of speaking	Way of being
Authentic existence ↑ **Everyday life**	Genuine speech (*Echte Sprechen*)	Philosophical
	Speaking-through (*Durchsprechen*)	Dialectical
	Persuasive speech (*Rede*)	Rhetorical

Gesagte) and that about which discourse speaks (*das Worüber*), Heidegger invites students to contemplate a medium-sized dry good: "When I talk [*rede*] about a thing, for example, a chair, this thing is in itself, as it is on hand in the world, the about-which. When I say [*sage*], 'it is upholstered,' this being-upholstered of the chair is the said as such; it does not coincide with the chair. In what is thus said, the about-which is talked *over* [*besprochen*]; in talking anything over what is considered is talked over as well [*in jedem Besprechen von etwas ist das Angesprochene mitbesprochen*]" (*SS* 1925, 262).

Whenever "something is said about something," an about-which is at stake. If what someone says cleaves close to what she is speaking about, the about-which of her discourse will come into public view. Heidegger refers to this process as communication (*Mitteilung*). Building on *Basic Concepts of Aristotelian Philosophy*, where he likens communication to a "*talking-through* [*durchsprechen*]," he suggests that, when communication takes place, *Rede* edges toward *Durchsprechen*: "that about which it is, is *shared with* the other through [*durch*] what is said, through [*durch*] the said as such" (*SS* 1924, 43; *SS* 1925, 263). Later, in *Being and Time*, he would define communication of this sort as a "genuine" (*echt*) function of spoken discourse, even going so far as to merge discourse and communication into a single linguistic phenomenon: discursive communication (*redende Mitteilung*). In so doing, however, he would also abandon the through line between *Rede* and *Durchsprechen*, a through line on which he had been working for years, offsetting the medial preposition *durch* with its more immediate sibling *in*. "Discursive communication, in what it says [*in ihrem Gesagten*], makes manifest what it is talking about [*worüber sie redet*], and thus makes this accessible to the other party" (*BT*, 56; cf. 205). Here, in *History of the Concept of Time*, however, *durch* remains his operative term. *Rede* is at its best, Heidegger contends, when it speaks *through* what is said in order to arrive at that about which it speaks.

But communication of this sort is the exception, not the rule, of spoken discourse. Which is why Heidegger stresses the non-coincidence of the chair's being-upholstered (the said) and the chair itself (the about-which) in the foregoing excerpt from *History of the Concept of Time*. What is said in *Rede* is always to some extent *in excess* of that about-which it speaks. Hence, the stress on the "*be-*" in *besprochen* above. With this emphasis, Heidegger specifies the nature of this linguistic excess. Whenever "something is said about something," what is said cannot help but *overlay* that about-which it speaks, effectively *covering* this entity with language—much as a chair can be covered with upholstery. So much so, he notes, that speakers and audiences alike can *lose sight* of that about which they are attempting to communicate—and all while their discourse remains perfectly intelligible.

In other words, articulated discourse can be understood without an original being-with involved in what the discourse is about. This means that in hearing and subsequent understanding, the understanding relation-of-being to that about which the discourse is can be left undetermined, uninvolved, even emptied to the point of a merely formal belief in what the original understanding had intended. The matter being spoken of thus slips away with the absence of the understanding relation of being. But while the matter being talked about slips away, what is said as such—the word, the sentence, the dictum—continues to be available in a worldly way, along with a certain understanding and interpretation of the matter. The discourse is of course uprooted [*entwurzelt*] in the absence of right understanding, but it still retains an understandability. (*SS* 1925, 268–69; cf. *WS* 1924–25, 18)

We have encountered this uprooted, worldly way of speaking before. When the about-which slips away, but the said remains in circulation, we see idle talk (*Gerede*) at work. And when empty, uninvolved, wholly indeterminate ways of seeing follow suit, displacing original modes of understanding, we see its equally average sibling *doxa* at work as well. "Understanding becomes non-understanding," Heidegger explains, recalling his earlier work on true and false opinion. "This does not mean that there is no longer anything at all here; for this is absurd, inasmuch as discoveredness and so understanding always belong to *Dasein*. Rather, there is something more fundamental here than nothing, namely, pseudo-understanding [*Scheinverstehen*], a semblance of understanding, a look-alike, as though this incomprehension [*Unverständnis*] were still a genuine comprehension. There is in *Dasein* itself the possibility of bringing itself into deception [*Täushung*]" (*SS* 1925, 260). Orators who attempt to realize this possibility are not rhetors engaged in *Rede* but sophists trafficking in *Gerede*. To capitalize on the non-coincidence of word and world—what is said in discourse and that about which it speaks—is nothing short of deception, Heidegger insists. In the *Gerede* of the sophist, the talking-things-over (*besprechen*) inherent in every discourse and properly oriented toward the genuine speech of philosophical inquiry becomes a talking-*over*-things (*besprechen*) in service to a fallen form of eloquence (*Beredetheit*)—not the persuasive artistry of theoretical discussion (*theoretischen Beredens*), in which discourse strives toward truth (*aletheia*), but the duplicity of sophistic address in which discourse slips into falsehood (*pseudos*).

Heidegger did not develop this distinction between *besprechen* and *besprechen* in his summer 1925 lecture course. Nor did he pursue it further when revising these lectures for publication in Division One of *Being and Time*. Nevertheless, as a careful reading of *History of the Concept of Time* suggests, he certainly could have. And had he done so, the subtle difference between these two terms would have given way to a clear conceptual distinction, allowing the discursive tension between talking-things-over in *Rede* and talking-over-things in *Gerede* to become readily apparent. Consider, for instance, this embryonic passage from one of his summer 1925 lectures: "Genuinely enacted and heard, communication brings an understanding of being-with to fruition in what is talked over [*Besprochenen*]. Since the communication is being said in words, what is said is 'verbal' for the other, which means that it is available in a worldly way. The articulated is accompanied by an understanding in public, in which what is talked over [*Beredete*] does not necessarily have to be appresented as something on hand and handy" (*SS* 1925, 268). This passage is indicative of a broader trend in *History of the Concept of Time*. More often than not, Heidegger links *besprechen* to the genuine *Rede* of communication and *bereden* to the inauthentic *Gerede* of public life. So often, in fact, that when he shifts from *besprechen* to *bereden* in passages like the one above, he signals a shift from the proper communicative horizon of human speech to its irreducible, ever-present threat. "This public world advances its claims and demands, it is right in everything, not by virtue of an original relationship to the world and to *Dasein* itself, not because it might have a special and genuine knowledge of the world and of *Dasein*, but precisely by talking over [*beredenden*] everything while not going 'in the matters,'" he tells his students (*SS* 1925, 246). "The hearing of discourse is now no longer participation [*Teilnahme*] in the being of being-with-one-another involved in the matter being talked over [*beredeten*], for the matter itself now is no longer uncovered in an original way" (*SS* 1925, 269).

In moments like these, when talking-things-over (as *besprechen*) devolves into talking-over-things (as *bereden*), causing the participatory structure of communication (as *Mitteilung*) to collapse in turn, the deceptive eloquence of the sophist rears its head, allowing for a certain kind of *Gerede* that, had he pursued it further, Heidegger might have dubbed "*Berede*." But this coinage never occurred. Instead, students in his summer 1925 lecture course heard this: "*Dasein* in the everydayness of its being has allowed itself to be taken in by the world being talked over [*der beredeten Welt*]" (*SS* 1925, 267). In light of his earlier lectures on rhetoric in general and sophistry in particular, however, many probably heard this final remark—*der beredeten Welt*—as their professor almost certainly meant it: *the world persuaded*.

Lost Examples Regained

As we saw in chapter 5, the deceptive oratory of the sophist is just one type of idle talk. Another is the deceived discourse of those taken in by such sophistry. In his summer 1924 lectures on Aristotle, Heidegger described this latter way of speaking as a kind of "yes-saying" (*Ja-Sagen*) and, in so doing, encouraged students to envision its practitioner as a stooge (*Jasager*). By the following summer, in his lectures on the *History of the Concept of Time*, Heidegger was eager to collectivize this representative figure, suggesting that the modern world is effectively a world of stooges—a world in which the deceptive *Gerede* of the sophist is perpetually courting the deceived *Gerede* of the stooge.

As *Being and Time* would soon reveal, it was the idle talk of the world persuaded that peaked Heidegger's interest in the mid-1920s. Which is why most of what he says about *Gerede* in his summer 1925 lecture course also finds expression in section 35 of *Being and Time*. When words are "uprooted" from the world, allowing what is said in *Rede* (*das Gesagte*) to drift apart from that about which *Rede* speaks (*das Worüber*), the prospect of communication (*Mitteilung*) tumbles into the pitfall of hearsay (*Hörensagen*). "Hearing is now hearing *mere talk as talk* [*bloßen Geredetseins*]," Heidegger tells his students. "Things so heard and in a certain way understood can be passed along, and this process of passing along and repeating [*Weiter- und Nachreden*] now produces a growing groundlessness of what was originally articulated" (*SS* 1925, 269). Hearsay, repetitive speech, passing the word along, growing groundlessness—all of *Gerede*'s basic operations, as described in *Being and Time*, were on display in the summer of 1925.

Even *Geschreibe* received some airtime that summer. Although the term itself does not appear in the course transcript, its function as a kind of *Gerede* is readily apparent throughout. Not since Heidegger's early Freiburg lectures had the role of reading and writing in the cultivation of idle talk been so pronounced:

Idle talk [*Gerede*] is not restricted to oral communication in speaking; much more idle talk [*Gerede*] today comes from what is written. Repetitive talk here is not talking from hearsay but hearing and talking from what is picked up by reading. Such reading takes place characteristically without understanding the subject matter, but in such a way that the reader—there are purported to be such readers in the sciences as well—acquires the possibility of dealing with the matters with great skill without ever having seen them. Something being said here to some extent acquires an intrinsic authoritative character. That it is said at all and that something definite is said is sufficient to assume that what is said is true and to proceed to repeat it and pass it along on the strength of its being said. (*SS* 1925, 269)

More interesting than any of these parallels between *History of the Concept of Time* and *Being and Time* are the passages in the former that Heidegger did not include in the latter. Foremost among these are two illuminating discussions of idle talk in modern academic culture, both of which, in light of what we now know about Heidegger's early-career anxieties, bear repeating here. In the first of these excluded passages, he likens idle talk to the coinage and circulation of academic jargon:

Before the war, for example, we had a tendency to interpret *Dasein* in terms of "experiencing" and "lived experience." Everyone, philosophers included, talked about "experiencing" and "lived experience." The word has nowadays lost its preeminence; there is even a reluctance to use it at all. Nowadays we talk in its stead of the "questionability of existence" and "decision." It is already the fashion for existence to become "questionable." Everything is "decision" nowadays, but it remains open whether those who talk in this way have ever "resolved" themselves or will ever "decide," just as it is an open question whether those who talked of "lived experience" still in fact had the possibility of "experiencing" anything, or whether this possibility was rather not exhausted precisely because idle talk [*Gerede*] about it had begun. Catchwords and catchphrases are indices of idle talk [*Geredes*], which is a mode of being of *Dasein* in the Anyone [*Man*]. (*SS* 1925, 272)

Not since the winter of 1921–22, at the height of his own professional angst, had Heidegger so intently railed against the philosophy of "lived experience." And not since his critique of Spranger's "All of us . . ." in the summer of 1923 had he so overtly ridiculed the insecurity, uncertainty, and indecisiveness of scholars who unwittingly rely on buzzwords of this sort in their work. Even and especially in the field of philosophy, the epigraph of his 1922 essay on Aristotle—the same essay he sent to Marburg and Göttingen in hopes of securing his first professorship—remained applicable: "Life will find a way to escape even this critique by a flight into clichés and catchphrases" (*BH*, 155).

Much of this philosophical *Gerede* can be heard at academic conferences, Heidegger goes on to chide in another passage that did not appear in *Being and Time*:

Nowadays, one decides about metaphysics or even higher matters at congresses. For everything which must be done nowadays, there is first a conference. One meets and meets, and everyone waits for someone else to tell him, and it doesn't really matter if it isn't said, for one has now indeed spoken one's mind. Even if all the speakers who thus speak their minds have understood little of the matter, one is of the opinion that the cumulation of this lack of understanding will nevertheless eventually generate an understanding. There are people nowadays who travel from one conference to another and are convinced in so doing that something is really happening and that they have accomplished something; whereas in reality they have shirked the labor and now seek refuge in idle talk [*Gerede*] for their helplessness, which they of course do not understand." (*SS* 1925, 272–73)

It is difficult to find a more satirical portrait of academic life in Heidegger's work. Not even in the early-1920s, when his prospect of a professorship seemed ever remote, was Heidegger more outspoken in his distaste for disciplinary protocol. Nevertheless, common themes abound in this passage. Recall, for instance, his summer 1923 attacks on "philosophical industry" and the various "medicine men" whose "propaganda, proselytizing, cliquish monopolies, [and] intellectual racketeering" sustain it. Consider, also, his use of Aristotle the following summer to dismiss these medicine men as boastful sophists in search of loyal sycophants—pseudo-philosophers manipulating *doxa* in order to convert young scholars into simpleminded stooges. Here, in *History of the Concept of Time*, Heidegger seems eager to prepare his students for these academic deceits, telling them where and how conversions of this sort are likely to occur. Academic conferences are not arenas of thoughtful debate (*Durchsprechen*), much less seedbeds of philosophical inquiry (*echte Sprechen*), he claims. Instead, they are swamps of scholarly *doxa*, where the deceptive *Gerede* of sophistic thinkers, replete with catchwords and catchphrases, yields little more than the deceived *Gerede* of scholars and students turned stooges.

Equally troubling, Heidegger claims, is the false belief that if enough non-understanding occurs at these scholarly events, then an original understanding of the topics under discussion is sure to follow. As we saw in part 1 of this book, Kierkegaard likened assumptions of this sort to a kind of sorites reasoning in which quantitative accumulations are mistakenly thought to result in qualitative change. Heidegger extends his predecessor's insight—albeit in his own words: "Our sole concern here is to draw attention to a phenomenon, to a possibility which is constitutive of the structure of *Dasein*," he states in *History of the Concept of Time*. Shoring up the false belief that non-understanding at academic conferences can produce its opposite in the realm of philosophical thought is a "peculiar kind of idle talk [*Gerede*], which governs *Dasein* in being-with-one-another, [and] is a function of uncovering, but now in the remarkable mode of *covering up*." Indeed, "because of its inherent neglect to consider matters in an original understanding, idle talk [*Gerede*] is from the very beginning *in itself a covering up*. In communicating, idle talk [*Gerede*] puts a view [*Ansicht*], an opinion, in front of the matter which is disclosed or to be disclosed" (*SS* 1925, 273). When concealment of this sort occurs, the horizon of philosophical research (*alethia*) succumbs to the hazard of academic *doxa* (*pseudos*). Resisting this tendency is the primary stake in Heidegger's critique of the parasitic relationship between the idle talk of the scholarly stooge who accepts false *doxa* and the idle talk of the intellectual sophist who profits from this acceptance. This is precisely why he uses the same term—*Gerede*—to describe their communicative practices. "Ancient sophistry," Heidegger concludes, underscoring its relevance to the *Ja-Sagen* of academic conferences, "was nothing but this in its essential structure, although it was perhaps shrewder in certain ways" (*SS* 1925, 273).

Suffice it to say, contemporary academic culture is inhospitable to the *bios aletheutikos*. It not only uproots this authentic mode of being, but also effectively upends it. "With the emergence of certain ways of being attuned, of feeling, a disposition can develop which inverts a *Dasein* into an alien one," Heidegger argues. "The state of being familiar with oneself is turned upside down, so that one is no longer who he actually is." In the *Gerede* of intellectual sophists and scholarly stooges, where the *doxa* of what they say at professional conferences obscures the phenomena about which they purport to speak, Heidegger sees "*the deviation of Dasein from itself*—deviation from its authentic original disposition and disclosedness"—in short, deviation from the *bios aletheutikos* (*SS* 1925, 273–74).

The only remaining question is whether academic culture errs on the side of deficiency or excess in its reliance on idle talk. And even this, as we learned in chapter 5, is not much of a question. For every mock-modest thinker quietly working in the philosophical tradition inspired by Socrates—a tradition in which Kierkegaard and Heidegger clearly saw themselves—there are many more intellectual braggarts using slogans and buzzwords, at conferences and in print, to prolong the lineage of pseudo-philosophy extending from the sophistry of Gorgias to the phenomenology of Husserl. By the summer of 1925, Heidegger had secured a professorship in philosophy; but he was far from finished professing his disgust for this discipline.

Babbling *Bathos*

In idle talk, Heidegger found a linguistic accompaniment to the "pseudo-understanding" of which he spoke in *History of the Concept of Time*. Unlike communication, which allows interlocutors to *pass through* what is said in their discourse (*das Gesagte*) in order to arrive at that about which their discourse speaks (*das Worüber*), thereby setting the stage for original understandings, idle talk lures interlocutors into pseudo-communication, encouraging them to *pass along* what is said in discourse apart from that about which they purport to speak. If communication is a genuine function of *Rede* and effectively orients *Dasein* toward authentic existence, as Heidegger suggests, the pseudo-communicative practice of *Gerede* is its disingenuous sibling, ever luring *Dasein* in the opposite direction. As it reorients *Dasein* toward average everydayness, idle talk threatens to leave it completely disoriented in the realm of inauthentic existence.

In *Geschwätz*, this threat becomes a reality. Worse than the deceptive *Gerede* of the sophist, and worse off than the deceived *Gerede* of the stooge, is the distracted babbling of *der Schwätzer*. Adding to table 6.1 above, we can represent this fall from *Rede* to *Gerede* to *Geschwätz* as shown in table 6.2.

In *History of the Concept of Time*, Heidegger describes the babbler as "the man of many words." What makes his *Geschwätz* more dangerous than the *Gerede* of the sophist and the stooge is its remarkable ability to forestall discursive communication and, with it, any attempt to arrive at that about which *Rede* speaks. "Talking a lot [*Viel-Sprechen*] does not in the least guarantee that the about-which of discourse [*Worüber der Rede*] becomes manifest sooner and more fully. On the contrary, talking a lot not only can uncover nothing but can actually cover things up and reduce everything to incomprehensibility [*Unverständlichkeit*], to babble [*Geschwätz*]" (*SS* 1925, 267).

Like many passages in *History of the Concept of Time*, this one reappears in *Being and Time*, but with one important difference: in place of "incomprehensibility" (*Unverständlichkeit*) and its connection to "babble" (*Geschwätz*), Heidegger writes about "sham clarity—the incomprehensibility of the trivial [*Scheinklarheit, das heißt Unverständlichkeit der*

Table 6.2. The communicative spectrum between authentic and inauthentic existence

	Way of speaking	Way of being
Authentic existence ↑ **Everyday life** ↓ **Inauthentic existence**	Genuine speech (*Echte Sprechen*)	Philosophical
	Speaking-through (*Durchsprechen*)	Dialectical
	Speech (*Rede*)	Rhetorical
	Idle talk (*Gerede*)	Deceptive
		Deceived
	Babble (*Geschwätz*)	Distracted

Trivialität]" (*BT*, 208; trans. modified). What are we to make of this revision? Incomprehensibility and sham clarity—*Unverständlichkeit* and *Scheinklarheit*—are both in keeping with *History of the Concept of Time*. While the former refers to the "non-understanding" of which Heidegger spoke, the latter recalls his notion of "pseudo-understanding," which disguises non-understanding as its opposite, effectively presenting others with a "*semblance* [*Scheines*]" of original understanding (*SS* 1925, 260).

Which makes the shift from *Geschwätz* to *Trivialität* especially interesting. In the standard English translation of *Being and Time*, *Trivialität* appears as "the trivial" (*BT*, 208). In German literary culture, however, *Trivialität* also doubles as a term for *bathos*—the literary device by which attempts at sublime discourse lapse into ridiculous utterances, producing the rhetorical effect of anticlimax. In this sense, the literary device of *bathos* is an ironic take on its Greek namesake. In antiquity, *bathos* meant "depth," but it also suggested other dimensions, notably height, length, and breadth. If a thought or utterance possessed *bathos*, it was anything but shallow, ridiculous, or anticlimactic.

And this, of course, is precisely how babblers hope to appear before others. When they speak, they speak at length, and across a wide breadth of topics, all of which they purport to understand deeply. But the understanding evinced by their *Geschwätz*, as Heidegger repeatedly notes in his early lecture courses, is little more than a pseudo-understanding, behind which there lurks a more basic non-understanding of the topics under discussion. More so even than the *Gerede* of the sophist and the stooge, the *Geschwätz* of the babbler is a semblance of communication, or, in keeping with the foregoing discussion, a *pseudo-communication*.

"It Was No One"

As Heidegger suggests with his use of the word *Mitteilung*—a fusion of the German *mit* meaning "with" and *teilen* meaning "to share"—communication is a way of taking part in the world and thus sharing the world with others. "The understanding of communication is the *participation* [*Teilnahme*] in what is manifest," he explains in *History of the Concept of Time*. "All subsequent understandings and co-understanding is as being-with a *taking part* [*Teilnahme*]" (*SS* 1925, 263). When spoken discourse slips from *Rede* to *Gerede* to *Geschwätz*, however, the communicative prospect of taking part in the world with others (*Mitteilung*) gives way to the pseudo-communicative experience of standing apart from others in the world (*Abständigkeit*). Instead of concern for the shared world of which *Dasein* is a part, the fall from *Rede* to *Gerede* to *Geschwätz* results in "*Dasein*'s concern over being apart [*Abstand*]" from those with whom it nevertheless shares this world (*SS* 1925, 245).

Abständigkeit would eventually make its way into *Being and Time*, appearing alongside "averageness" and "leveling down" as a way of being characteristic of *das Man* and a basic constituent of what Heidegger calls "publicness" (*BT*, 164–65). But the standard English translation of this key term—"distantiality"—has blurred its otherwise stark contrast with *Mitteilung*. In the summer of 1925, this distinction was still clear: *Standing apart from others in the world conceals our being a part of the world with them.* At stake in the recovery of this distinction between *Abständigkeit* and *Mitteilung* is one of the most counter-intuitive insights of Heidegger's philosophy of communication—an insight which informs *Being and Time* but all too often eludes its readers. And with this added insight, as we shall see, comes another into his philosophy of ordinary language use.

Taking part in the world with others by way of communication is a condition of possibility for authentic selfhood, allowing for a certain kind of independence—a sense of autonomy *in the midst* of human togetherness. Heidegger describes this authentic state as "constancy of the self" (*Ständigkeit des Selbst*) and, more suggestively, as "self-constancy" (*Selbst-ständigkeit*). With the addition of this hyphen, he likens the sense of independence afforded by communication (*Selbständigkeit*) to an experience of existential stability (*beständigen Standfestigkeit*) in which *Dasein* not only stands on its own feet, firmly planted in the soil of human togetherness (*Bodenständigkeit*), but also, paradoxically, enjoys enough autonomy to make up its own mind, thereby arriving at a state of "anticipatory resoluteness" (*BT*, 369).

Implicit in the authentic possibility of *Ständigkeit des Selbst* and *Selbst-ständigkeit*, however, is their inauthentic counter-possibility: *Un-selbständigkeit* and, as Heidegger further specifies, *Unselbst-ständigkeit* (*BT*, 153, 166, 369, 370). The former term adheres to the German *un-selbständig*, meaning "dependent," and suggests a state of existential instability and irresolution in which *Dasein* is unable to stand on its own feet or make up its own mind. With the addition of another well-place hyphen, however, Heidegger allows this dependent way of being to stray from its adjectival origin. In keeping with the standard English translation of *Selbst-ständigkeit* as "self-constancy," we can translate *Unselbst-ständigkeit* as "unself-constancy" or, more elegantly, "constancy of the Unself." At issue here is not a simple inversion of *Beständigkeit* but, instead, a strange perversion of this existential state, whereby standing apart from others paradoxically increases—and increasingly solidifies—our dependence upon them. If *Mitteilung* concentrates *Dasein*, empowering interlocutors to become *autonomous together*, *Abständigkeit* scatters *Dasein*, allowing individuals to remain, as Sherry Turkle recently put it, *alone together*.

Heidegger assigns this heavily populated yet strangely isolated mode of existence to *das Man*, and he describes the inauthentic form of self-hood in which it culminates as *das Man-selbst*. "The Self of everyday *Dasein* is the *they-self* [*das Man-selbst*], which we distinguish from the *authentic Self*—that is, from the Self which has been taken hold of in its own way [*eigens ergriffenen*]. As they-self, the particular *Dasein* has been *dispersed* into the 'they'" (*BT*, 167). When Heidegger goes on to write about "the constancy of the Unself," it is the persistence of this they-self that he aims to recall. As John Macquarrie and Edward Robinson well note in their footnotes to *Being and Time*, *Unselbst-ständigkeit* refers to "the constancy or stability of that which is other than the Self—the non-Self, or more specifically, the they-self" (*BT*, 369, n. 2). Unlike "*authentic Being-One's-Self*," which always belongs to someone specific—and someone specifically committed to the *bios aletheutikos*—the inauthentic being of the they-self points to *no one in particular*, abstracting selfhood to such an extent that even staunch commitments to the *bios aletheutikos* cannot help but buckle under the doxastic weight of its counter-possibility. This is precisely what Heidegger means when he insists that "*Dasein*, as a they-self, gets 'lived' by the common-sense ambiguity of that publicness in which nobody resolves upon anything but which has always made its decision" (*BT*, 344). Where the *bios aletheutikos* was, the *bios koinonikos* becomes.

What the authentic self gains in the mutual understanding afforded by discursive communication with other people (*Verständlichkeit*), the inauthentic self forfeits to the common sense implicit in the idle talk of no one in particular (*Verständigkeit*). Instead of becoming someone rooted in the world of human togetherness, *Dasein* loses its footing in being-with-one-another, loses its voice in speaking-with-one-another, and, as a result, loses its authentic sense of self as a being-in-the-world. "Everyone is the other, and no one is himself," Heidegger writes in *Being and Time*, echoing his remarks in *History of the Concept of Time* and, before them, Kierkegaard's outspoken critique of the gallery-public. So much so that in everyday life "the agency through which most things come to pass is one of which we must say that 'it was no one.' The '*they*,' which supplies the answer to the question of the '*who*' of everyday *Dasein*, is the '*nobody*' to whom every *Dasein* has already surrendered itself in Being-among-one-another [*Untereinandersein*]" (*BT*, 165–66).

As Heidegger goes on to explain, however, the nobody in question is hardly "nothing at all." When mired in the common sense *Gerede* of *das Man-selbst*, and attempting to account for the conduct of this garrulous they-self, *Dasein* can certainly say, "it was no one." But it cannot also claim, in the same manner of speech, that "this 'they' is 'really' nothing" (*BT*, 165–66; cf. *SS* 1925, 247).

In order to make the leap from "it was no one" to "it was really nothing," *Dasein* must shift from idle talk to a way of speaking that we have yet to consider—a way of speaking whose theorization eluded Heidegger and, for this reason, now warrants careful attention. In order to grasp this elusive way of speaking, however, we must first come to grips with the reciprocity between average everydayness and authentic existence in Heidegger's early thought. It is to this preliminary task that we now turn.

Scales of Existence

Immediately following his discussion of idle talk, curiosity, and ambiguity in *Being and Time*, Heidegger begins to excavate the existential structure of average everydayness on which they depend. Everyday life, he explains, is a mix of alienation (*Entfremdung*), self-dissection, (*Selbst-zergliederung*), subjective entanglement (*Verfängnis*), and existential turbulence (*Wirbel*)—all of which contribute to the human condition he initially theorized as "ruinance" and now, in *Being and Time*, redefines as "fallenness [*Verfallen*]" (*BT*, 222–23).

Which raises an important question for Heidegger: "Can *Dasein* be conceived as an entity for which, in its Being, its potentiality-for-Being is an *issue*, if this entity, in its very everydayness, *has lost itself*, and, in falling, 'lives' *away from itself*?" Yes, he concludes, for "in falling, nothing other than our potentiality-for-Being-in-the-world is the issue, even if in the mode [*Modus*] of inauthenticity" (*BT*, 223–24). On this point, he is adamant: "*Authentic* existence is not something which floats above falling everydayness; existentially, it is only a modified [*modifiziertes*] way in which such everydayness is seized upon" (*BT*, 224). So also when it comes to the relationship between constancies of Self and Unself: "*Authentic Being-one's-Self* does not rest upon an exceptional condition of the subject, a condition that has been detached from the 'they'; *it is rather an existentiell modification [Modifikation] of the 'they'—of the 'they' as an essential existentiale*" (*BT*, 168). And again in division 2 of *Being and Time*: "Authentic Being-one's-Self takes the definite form of an existentiell modification [*Modifikation*] of the 'they'" (*BT*, 312). Make no mistake: like Kierkegaard before him and Lacan in his wake, Heidegger sees the fallen state of average everydayness as a condition of possibility for authentic existence.

This kinship between average everydayness and authentic existence is among the most misunderstood aspects of Heidegger's early thought. Part of the problem, it seems, is that leading interpreters of the foregoing quotations have struggled to reconcile them with other passages in *Being and Time* where Heidegger appears to state the opposite. "Inauthenticity is based on the possibility of authenticity," he notes elsewhere in the book (*BT*, 303). Accordingly, "the they-self . . . is an existentiell modification [*Modifikation*] of the authentic self" (*BT*, 365). "So, which is it?" Taylor Carmen asks in his foreword to the standard English translation of *Being and Time*. "Does individual authentic selfhood consist in occupying a preestablished place in an already constituted social and historical world—or perhaps occupying it in a special *way*, with a special style and sensitivity—or is conforming to social norms necessarily a *lapsing* from a prior, more basic, more desirable form of 'authentic being-oneself'?" Which comes first, in other words, average everydayness or authentic existence? At issue here, Carmen suspects, is either "the only explicit contradiction in *Being and Time*" or a careless "mistake" on the part of its author, "simply a blunder, perhaps owing to the frenetic pace at which Heidegger was writing" (*BT*, xix–xx). Joan Stambaugh, in another prominent reading of the above statements, arrives at the same question: "Which is more 'primordial'—authenticity or inauthenticity?" Like Carmen, she concludes that Heidegger, in begging this question, leaves a "problematic contradiction" at the heart of *Being and Time*.[1]

Noticeably absent from these leading interpretations is any consideration of the key term in each of the foregoing passages: *modification*. Which is why Jean-Luc Nancy remains among the most penetrating readers of *Being and Time*. As Nancy rightly notes, Heidegger's use of "modification" is not only central to the passages cited above, but also crucial to his entire existential analytic. In service to this insight, Nancy deconstructs the much-belabored "opposition" between authentic and inauthentic modes of existence. "*There is no existentiale that is not at once, and as such, caught in the existentiell.*" Any inquiry that presupposes an opposition between these ways of being is thus destined to fail, for "an opposition of this type is specifically excluded by the existential analytic." In order to grasp the secret affinity between authentic and inauthentic modes of existence, Nancy contends, we must first grapple with Heidegger's use of the term "modification."

The *owness* of existence—its own truth, its own sense—*does not distinguish itself in any way* from what could be called *existentiell* existence except insofar as the former is a "modified grasp" of the latter. The essence of the decision in favor of the originary—and the originary essence of decision—can consist only in this "modification" of the grasp. But, reciprocally, this "modification" (change of mode: from the *Modus* of the "floating" to the *Modus* of the "decision," but without any change of the "ground," that is, "suspension"), this modification, about which the text teaches us nothing else, can be determined only as the stakes, even the act, of decision.[2]

Mode, *Modus*, Modification—these are the operative terms in Heidegger's existential analytic. The only term missing from this list is arguably the only term which was more crucial to his early thought: *Modality*. And not just any modality. As we saw in chapters 4 and 5, it was *potentiality* that most intrigued Heidegger. If authentic existence is a "modification" of average everydayness, and vice versa, as he claims in *Being and Time*, it is because each way of living serves as the other's *counter-possibility*. Implicit in our potential for inauthentic existence is its ownmost impotentiality—namely, the possibility of its incapacitation in moments of authentic existence. And implicit in our potential for authentic existence is its ownmost impotentiality—namely, the possibility of its incapacitation in moments of inauthentic existence. When Heidegger insists that authenticity and inauthenticity are both "modes" of existence, he means that they are both *modal* and even *modular* ways of being in the world. Moreover, he means to suggest that their basic modality is *potentiality* and that, as such, any instantiation of either way of being can and should be understood as a condition of possibility for its modification at a later date. In average everydayness, he sees the opportunity structure of authentic existence; and in authentic existence, he sees the opportunity structure of average everydayness.

How else are we to interpret tables 5.1, 6.1, and 6.2 above? What is ultimately at stake in the spectrum of discourse ranging from silence to babble, *Schweigen* to *Geschwätz*, is a series of existential transitions between authentic and inauthentic ways of living. When spoken discourse slips from *Rede* to *Gerede* to *Geschwätz*, everyday life slides toward inauthentic existence. But when spoken discourse proceeds from *Rede* to *Durchsprechen* to *echte Sprechen*, everyday life edges toward authentic existence. And at any point along the way, these communicative-existential trajectories can reverse course, effectively steering interlocutors in the opposite direction. Babblers can become stooges, stooges can become sophists, and sophists can become orators, thereby setting the stage for more authentic ways of speaking and, by extension, more authentic ways of being. And philosophers, much to Heidegger's frustration, can devolve into any one of these average everyday figures, becoming little more than sophists in search of stooges, stooges in search of sophists, or babblers wholly adrift in their buzzwords and catchphrases—and all at the same academic conference.

All of these possibilities, and many more, are implicit in Heidegger's use of the Latin *modus*—a term that ripples through *Being and Time*, much as it does in *History of the Concept of Time*, often alongside *Modifikation*. When he characterizes falling as a *"Modus"* of inauthenticity, he does not mean to define it as a singular way of being or fixed state of existence.[3] On the contrary, in keeping with Western music theory, where modes are musical scales coupled with specific melodic behaviors (and, according to Plato and Aristotle, particular social moods and character formations as well), Heidegger suggests that falling is a *mobile* and *multivalent* way of being that proceeds like descending notes in a musical scale. If the persuasive *Rede* of the orator is the discursive key or tonic—the first tone—of this descending scale of existence, the deceptive *Gerede* of the sophist, the deceived *Gerede* of the stooge, and the distracted *Geschwätz* of the babbler form its discursive pitches or intervals—the descending linguistic steps from everyday life into inauthentic existence. But the *Rede* of the orator also serves as the discursive key or tonic for this scale's counter-possibility, the first tone in an ascending series of increasingly authentic linguistic pitches or intervals ranging from the *Durchsprechen* of the dialectician to the *echte Sprechen* of the philosopher, to the *Schweigen* of the theorist.

When Heidegger championed *Rede* as a "*Seinsmodus des Verstehens*" in the summer of 1925, it was the *modus* of authenticity that he meant to index (*GA* 20, 366). And when he went on to characterize the fall from *Rede* to *Gerede* as a "*Seinmodus im Man*," it was the *modus* of inauthenticity that he wished to signal (*GA* 20, 373). It was not until the 1950s, however, that he realized what *modus* and its musical heritage meant for his philosophy of language. To modify average everydayness with moments of authentic existence is not just to grasp this fallen mode of existence anew, radically appropriating its latent counter-possibility, but also to speak this mode of existence anew, allowing original appropriations to emerge in ways of speaking whose average everydayness can no longer be understood, much less lived, as "average" or "everyday." For every original appropriation of the world, Heidegger suggests, there is an equally original way of addressing the world's average everyday inhabitants. "Saying is the mode in which Appropriation speaks: mode not so much in the sense of *modus* or fashion, but as the melodic mode, the song which says something in its singing. For appropriating Saying brings to light all present beings in terms of their properties—it lauds, that is, allows them into their own, their nature" (*OWL*, 135).

What Heidegger could only intuit in the mid-1920s became increasingly apparent in his later work: "the kinship between song and speech" (*OWL*, 98). And yet, even after realizing this kinship, he could not help but hearken back to his earlier thoughts on language. When saying verges on singing, language begins to actualize its potential as a medium of disclosure, he concludes, emerging from the *pseudos* of average everydayness as a genuine mode of *aletheuein*.

Fearless Flight

When coupled with tables 5.1, 6.1, and 6.2 above, the foregoing discussion lends itself to quick summary. Heidegger sees a continuum, not a contradiction, between average everydayness and authentic existence. Each way of being not only functions as the other's counter-possibility but also serves as its basic opportunity structure. And between these reciprocally conditioned ways of being, he sees a spectrum of communicative practices. At the center of this spectrum, midway between the *aletheia* of authentic existence and the *pseudos* of its inauthentic counterpart, is the *Rede* of the orator. Beneath the *Rede* of the orator are three increasingly inauthentic ways of speaking: the deceptive *Gerede* of the sophist, the deceived *Gerede* of the stooge, and the distracted *Geschwätz* of the babbler. And above the *Rede* of the orator are three increasingly authentic ways of speaking: the *Durchsprechen* of the dialectician, the *echte Sprechen* of the philosopher, and the *Schweigen* of the theorist.

Heidegger would have bristled at the use of "beneath" and "above" to describe this discursive spectrum. Evaluative terms of this sort impose an unnecessary and wholly misleading sense of linguistic hierarchy onto what is, in fact, an existential continuum determined by certain ways of speaking, he would have claimed. But it is difficult to imagine him arguing against the position of each way of speaking relative to the others on this communicative-existential continuum. And this, of course, poses its own conceptual risk. At the very least, it suggests that discursive shifts between average everydayness and authentic existence are marked by a linear, continuous, and step-by-step progression from one communicative practice to the next. Although this is often the case, there are other, more circuitous pathways between average everydayness and authentic existence.

Recall, for instance, Heidegger's notion of *Durchsprechen*, as discussed in the previous chapter. In order to arrive at the genuine speech of philosophical inquiry, this mode of discourse loops through the idle talk of common opinion. In its push toward authentic existence, *Durchsprechen* detours through average everydayness, effectively moving in the opposite direction.

But this is not the only circuitous way of speaking that captured Heidegger's attention in the mid-1920s. Another appears in *Being and Time* as *alltägliche Rede*, the best translation of which is "everyday discourse." If *Durchsprechen* approaches genuine speech by *passing through* idle talk, *alltägliche Rede* encounters it *in the midst of* idle talk. What the former achieves by way of critical inquiry, deliberately traversing average everydayness in search of authentic existence, the latter accomplishes by accident, unwittingly stumbling into authentic existence even (and especially) when its speakers struggle to avoid it.

Midway between *Rede* and *Gerede*, and irreducible to either linguistic practice, *alltägliche Rede* is the final communicative practice to be studied in this chapter—and arguably the final conceptual testament to Heidegger's early yet unwavering belief that there is always something about everyday talk that cannot itself be understood as "everyday." But the route to *alltägliche Rede*, like that of *alltägliche Rede* itself, is conceptually circuitous, requiring us to wend our way, if only cursorily, through Heidegger's imbricated discussions of falling, fleeing, fear, anxiety, and death.

To begin, consider the secret affinity between "falling" and "fleeing" that Heidegger develops in *Being and Time*. To fall into average everydayness and its worldly concerns is also to flee from their crucial alternative: authentic existence. And to flee from authentic existence is always to admit a certain familiarity with it—at least enough familiarity to know which lines of flight lead away from this way of being. In this sense, the flight away from authentic existence is always, to some extent, a flight in the face of authentic existence.

> *Dasein*'s fleeing is a fleeing *in the face of* itself. Only to the extent that *Dasein* has been brought before itself in an ontologically essential manner through whatever disclosedness belongs to it, *can* it flee *in the face of* that in the face of which it flees. To be sure, that in the face of which it flees is *not grasped* in thus turning away [*Abkehr*] in falling; nor is it experienced even in turning thither [*Hinkehr*]. Rather, in turning away *from* it, it is disclosed 'there'. This existentiell-ontical turning-away, by reason of its character as a disclosure, makes it phenomenally possible to grasp existential-ontologically that in the face of which *Dasein* flees, and to grasp it as such. (*BT*, 229)

It is tempting, but ultimately mistaken, to associate flight with fear. To experience fear is to notice and typically to flee from something in the world that is close by, fast approaching, and potentially harmful. In this sense, the experience of fear presupposes a degree of separation between fearful subjects and fearsome objects. In falling, however, *Dasein* flees from *itself*. To be sure, that in the face of which it flees is threatening; but this threat cannot also be fearsome, since "the turning-away of falling is not a fleeing that is founded upon a fear of entities within-the-world" (*BT*, 230). Just the opposite, in fact. Oddly enough, *Dasein*'s flight from itself doubles a *desire* for these entities: "What this turning-away does is precisely to *turn thither* towards entities within-the-world by absorbing itself in them" (*BT*, 230). If fear repels us from specific beings in the world, then falling, in its flight from authentic existence, drives us toward them.

The mood in which we encounter our potential for authentic existence is not fear but *anxiety*. And that in the face of which we experience anxiety is not a specific entity within-the-world but something "completely indefinite" (*völlig unbestimmt*). The contours of this experience are unmistakable: "Not only does this indefiniteness leave factically undecided which entity within-the-world is threatening us, but it also tells us that entities within-the-world are not 'relevant' at all. Nothing which is ready-to-hand or present-at-hand within the world functions as that in the face of which anxiety is anxious. Here the totality of involvements of the ready-to-hand and the present-at-hand discovered within-the-world, is, as such, of no consequence; it collapses into itself; the world has the character of completely lacking significance [*völliger Unbedeutsamkeit*]" (*BT*, 231).

The operative terms in this passage are *unbestimmt* and *Unbedeutsamkeit*. If something is *unbestimmt*, it is not only "indefinite" but also "unsettled" and, to this extent, *nowhere in particular*. If something is *Unbedeutsamkeit*, it is not just insignificant in the sense of "meaningless" and "senseless" but also insignificant in the sense of "irrelevant" and "unimportant," to the point of seeming like *nothing at all*. To experience anxiety is to encounter an aspect of the world that is at once something and nothing, there beside us and nowhere at all.

In that in the face of which one has anxiety, the "It is nothing and nowhere" becomes manifest. The obstinacy of the "nothing and nowhere within-the-world" means as a phenomenon that *the world as such is that in the face of which one has anxiety*. The utter insignificance [*völlige Unbedeutsamkeit*] which makes itself known in the "nothing and nowhere," does not signify [*bedeutet nicht*] that the world is absent, but tells us that entities within-the-world are of so little importance in themselves [*ihm selbst so völlig belanglos*] that on the basis of this *insignificance* [*Unbedeutsamkeit*] of what is within-the-world, the world in its worldhood is all that still obtrudes itself. (*BT*, 231)

As significance, importance, and relevance drain from familiar entities within-the-world, the condition of possibility for these worldly attributes becomes increasingly discernible, until it is only the *possibility* of worldliness itself—"the *possibility* of the ready-to-hand in general"—that returns our anxious gaze (*BT*, 231). And because this possibility is detached from any specific entity in the world, it fails to provide us with any relief. On the contrary, encountering the possibility of worldliness only increases our anxiety, widening its already awkward gyre to include not only objects and others, but also *ourselves*. As the world of meaningful objects and others recedes, so also does our familiar sense of self—the sense of self in terms of which we have learned to frame our identities, in whose likeness we have come to see ourselves as other-selves, nonselves, unselves—in short, *das Man-selbst*. "The 'world' can offer nothing more, and neither can the *Dasein*-with of Others. Anxiety thus takes away from *Dasein* the possibility of understanding itself, as it falls, in terms of the 'world' and the way things have been publicly interpreted" (*BT*, 232). Neither *Gerede, Geschreibe,* nor *Geschwätz* elude its grasp.

"It Was Really Nothing"

What anxiety leaves behind, much to Heidegger's delight, is an individualized and uncanny mix of *"Being-possible"* and *"Being-free"* in which our "authentic [*eigentliches*] potentiality-for-Being-in-the-world" becomes at once apparent and attainable. "Anxiety makes manifest in *Dasein* its *Being towards* its ownmost [*eigensten*] potentiality-for-Being—that is, its *Being-free for* the freedom of choosing itself and taking hold of itself," he writes in a crucial section of *Being and Time*. "Anxiety brings *Dasein* face to face with its *Being-free for* (*propensio in* . . .) the authenticity [*Eigentlichkeit*] of its Being, and for this authenticity as a possibility which it always is" (*BT*, 232).

Clearly, "authenticity" is not the only word for *Eigentlichkeit*. Another option, well suggested by the above translation of *eigensten*, is "ownedness." According to William Blattner, this is the best translation of *die Eigentlichkeit*, for "the phenomenon Heidegger is trying to capture with this language is not a matter of being true to anything, but rather of owning who and how one is."[4] If our average, everyday lives are characteristically *unowned*, anxiety provides us with an opportunity to modify our grasp of this wayward condition. To embrace anxiety is to refuse to remain "at-home" in the world, and thus to *own* our potential for something other than average everydayness. To flee from anxiety, however, is to avoid feeling "not-at-home" in the world, and thus to *disown* the very same potential.

How, then, does our ownmost potentiality-for-Being, with its existential mix of "Being-possible" and "Being-free," appear to us in moments of anxiety? According to Heidegger, we experience it as *anticipation of the end of human being*, specifically "*the possibility of the impossibility of any existence at all*" (*BT*, 307). He goes on to characterize this state of anxious anticipation as *being-towards-death*. "In this state-of-mind, *Dasein* finds itself *face to face* with the 'nothing' of the possible impossibility of its existence" (*BT*, 310).

Like so many breakthroughs in *Being and Time*, Heidegger had been preparing for this one for years. In his summer 1924 lecture, "The Concept of Time," delivered toward the end of his famous 1924 lecture course on Aristotle, for instance, he described the experience of being-towards-death as a *having* of one's own death. "What is it *to have one's own death in each case?*" he asked his audience. *"Dasein's running ahead to its past, to an extreme possibility of itself that stands before it in certainty and utter indeterminacy"* (*CT*, 12). Even and especially when *Dasein* "shrinks back" from the certain yet indeterminate prospect of its own death, retreating to the "busyness [*Betriebsamkeit*]" of everyday life we discussed in chapter 4, with all of its "babbling [*Geschwätzigkeit*]" and "idle talk [*Gerede*]," it remains profoundly if only implicitly aware of its own mortality (*CT*, 12; trans. modified).

For Heidegger, death has less to do with the end of human life as a biological event than the end of human being in its average everydayness. As a mode of existence, being-towards-death does not mean dwelling on the end of all human life, nor even on our own eventual demise. Rather, it means *reflecting on the outer limits of our own ability to be*, ever watchful for any and all experiences that prevent us from pressing forward into preexisting and culturally circumscribed forms of self-understanding. In this sense, being-towards-death inverts the line of flight implicit in falling. Instead of fleeing from authentic existence, we now move toward it, unfettered by the bustling loquacity of average everydayness, with all of its *Gerede*, *Geschreibe*, and *Geschwätz*. When Heidegger insists that being-towards-death is always also *freedom towards death*, this is what he means. Being-towards-death is an authentic mode of existence because it enjoys *"a freedom which has been released from the Illusions of the 'they'"* (*BT*, 311).

But narrow is the gate and difficult the road from anxiety to authenticity. More often than not, we welcome any detour from death, brushing off the experience of anxious anticipation with chatty regressions into average everydayness. And it is here, in consideration of these chatty regressions, that Heidegger introduces readers to "everyday discourse" (*alltägliche Rede*). "When anxiety has subsided, then in our everyday way of talking [*alltägliche Rede*] we are accustomed to say that 'it was really nothing' [*es war eigentlich nichts'*]" (*BT*, 231). Although variations on *alltägliche Rede* recur throughout Heidegger's early work, it was not until this crucial passage at the heart of *Being and Time*, just after his renowned discussion of idle talk, that he began to conceptualize this average, everyday mode of discourse. What are we to make of this communicative practice, especially given its close proximity to Heidegger's account of idle talk?

Heidegger anticipates this question in *Being and Time*, but he never answers it. The closest he comes to defining *alltägliche Rede* is when attempting to distinguish it from idle talk. And not just in *Being and Time*. Well into the 1930s, Heidegger struggled to differentiate these ways of speaking. In the summer of 1935, for instance, he separated the "at-homeness" of idle talk, with all of its concealing "glibness" and closures by "ready tongue," from the uncanny use of *alltägliche Rede* to tame the overwhelming experience of the uncanny—a strangely operative practice that he allusively describes as "the happening of what is most uncanny, in which, through doing violence, the overwhelming comes to appearance and is brought to stand."[5] The following summer, he referred students to the *alltäglichen Rede* of the ancient Greeks, where ordinary, prephilosophical ways of speaking often turned out to be extraordinarily philosophical modes of discourse. If the Greeks were the first to speak the language of philosophy, Heidegger concludes, it is because there was something in their everyday discourse that could not be heard as idle talk, something which "philosophizes in its basic structure and formation."[6]

In *Being and Time*, however, *alltägliche Rede* remains focused on the topic of death. If there is something in everyday discourse that cannot itself be understood as "everyday," it is readily apparent in "the everyday manner in which the 'they' talks about death [*der alltäglichen Rede des Man über den Tod*]" (*BT*, 302). Proximally and for the most part, however, talk of death in moments of *alltägliche Rede* sounds a lot like talk of death in the *Gerede* of *das Man*. "If idle talk [*Gerede*] is always ambiguous, so is this manner of talking about death," Heidegger freely admits (*BT*, 297). But this is as far as their likeness goes. When speakers use *Gerede* to talk about death, they often resort to vacuous statements, examples of which abound in *Being and Time*. "One of these days one will die too, in the end; but right now it has nothing to do with us" (*BT*, 297). "One dies too, sometime, but not right away" (*BT*, 299). "Death is certain" (*BT*, 301). "It is certain that 'Death' is coming" (*BT*, 301). "Death certainly comes, but not right away" (*BT*, 302). All of these pronouncements, in keeping with their function as idle talk, are ambiguous, indefinite, assigned to no one in particular, and thus guilty of misunderstanding death as "an event of public occurrence which the 'they' encounters" (*BT*, 297).

By contrast, Heidegger's illustration of *alltägliche Rede*—"it was really nothing"—is referentially pointed. So pointed, in fact, that *"what it was, indeed, does get reached ontically by such a way of talking"* (*BT*, 231). Hence the appearance of *"eigentlich nichts"* in this anxiety-avoiding expression. Miss the connection between *eigentlich nichts* and Heidegger's term for "authenticity"—*Eigentlichkeit*—and we miss the crucial function of *alltägliche Rede* in moments of anxiety. When someone attempts to shirk being-towards-death by brushing off anxiety with the expression "it was really nothing," he cannot help but achieve the opposite effect, inadvertently giving voice to this impossible mode of being (death) and its unbearable underlying mood (anxiety). Indeed, when someone says, "it was really nothing," he means just that: it was truly, genuinely, authentically *nothing* that he just experienced, and it is precisely this nothingness that now finds unambiguous expression in his speech. If *Gerede* has nothing to say, then *alltägliche Rede* finds a way *to say nothing*. As a species of discourse, it reveals and reproduces, in unwitting flourishes of genuine speech, the anxious encounters with *no-thing* from which its speakers recoil.

To be sure, *alltägliche Rede* verges on idle talk. But it always manages to exceed this groundless way of speaking, if only by making groundlessness itself a point of reference in the discussion. In *alltägliche Rede*, the tendencies toward "covering up" and "closing off" implicit in idle talk double as testaments to the discovery and disclosure of an alternate, more unruly, more authentic, more *eigentlich* way of speaking—a mode of discourse that is irreducible to *Gerede* but also unintelligible as *Rede*. At once flippant and revealing, "it was really nothing" stretches tensors between average everydayness and authentic existence, suggesting that we are falling toward the former but have not yet arrived there, and fleeing from latter but have not yet lost sight of it. Heidegger did not have words for this deterritorialized way of speaking. As we shall see, however, his psychoanalytic contemporaries did.

PART THREE

Empty Speech

SEVEN

The Writing on the Wall

Missed Connections

Heidegger never cared for Freud, least of all his metapsychological works. "He simply did not want to have to accept that such a highly intelligent and gifted man as Freud could produce such artificial, inhuman, indeed absurd and purely fictitious constructions about homo sapiens," the Swiss psychiatrist Medard Boss recalls. When reading Freud's theoretical works, "Heidegger never ceased shaking his head."[1]

The philosopher's frustration was readily apparent in his *Zollikon Seminars*. "Freud's basic approach [genetic-causal explanation] is far from [providing] a phenomenological direction. It specifically neglects to determine the human being's character of being [*Seinscharakter*], the character of the human being, who radically articulates his being human with language," Heidegger remarked. "Were there even a trace of phenomenological-ontological determination present in Freud's basic approach, then it would have prevented him from the aberration of his 'theory.'"[2]

Only Freud's "Papers on Technique" appealed to Heidegger. Especially compelling to him, it seems, were Freud's reflections on anonymous group membership and its tendency to obstruct individuality, free choice, and personal responsibility. But even these insights were profoundly limiting: "Psychoanalysis glimpses from *Dasein* only the mode of fallenness and its urge. It posits this constitution as authentically human and objectifies [the human being] with his 'drives' [*Triebhaftigkeit*]," Heidegger complained. "Therefore, there should be a seminar where there is no talk about psychology and psychoanalysis—ways of representational thinking that are especially prone to becoming bungled [*verhockt*] because the whole world can be explained by reducing it to unclarified subjectivity." Psychoanalysis, Heidegger concluded, was little more than "pigheadedness."[3]

Freud was less familiar with Heidegger's work but no less critical in his response. His closest encounter with the renowned phenomenologist came in 1936, when another Swiss psychiatrist, Ludwig Binswanger, shared a copy of his recent lecture on "Freud's Conception of Man in Light of Anthropology," in which Binswanger argued that human existence is "understandable only as being-in-the-world, as the projection and disclosure of world—as Heidegger has so powerfully demonstrated." Freud commended Binswanger for his prose, erudition, and intellectual range. "But, of course," Freud added, "I don't believe a word of what you say."[4]

Heidegger was almost seventy years old when he began the *Zollikon Seminars*, and Freud was in his eightieth year when he received a copy of Binswanger's lecture. Had they encountered each other's work decades prior, at the start of their lengthy intellectual careers, they would have found much in common. In both of their path-breaking books—*The Interpretation of Dreams* (1900) and *Being and Time* (1927)—several connections are readily apparent. Crucial for our purposes is the kinship between their accounts of everyday talk. What Heidegger theorized as idle talk (*Gerede*) and everyday discourse (*alltägliche Rede*) in *Being and Time*, Freud well-illustrated in the 24 July 1895 "dream-specimen" with which he began *The Interpretation of Dreams*—a dream-specimen which would soon enter psychoanalytic lore as "the dream of Irma's injection."

More than illustrations of idle talk and everyday discourse, however, the communicative practices at work in Freud's iconic dream of Irma's injection were harbingers of a psychoanalytic approach to everyday talk whose fullest expression would not occur until Jacques Lacan, in response to Freud and Heidegger alike, began to theorize "empty speech" (*parole vide*) in the early-1950s. To begin elucidating Lacan's culminating account of everyday talk, this chapter begins by considering Freud's dream of Irma's injection and its subsequent analysis in *The Interpretation of Dreams*. It then explores Lacan's self-proclaimed "re-analysis" of this dream, the meaning Freud assigned to it, and the relevance of both to early psychoanalytic theory and technique. In so doing, this chapter attempts to set the stage for those which follow. As we shall see in chapters 8 and 9, Lacan's return to the dream of Irma's injection not only allowed him to round out his early conceptualizations of empty speech but also provided him with a unique opportunity to underscore the basic therapeutic horizon of this vacuous way of speaking—a retrospective mode of discourse he aptly dubs "full speech" (*parole pleine*).

No Matter

The dream of Irma's injection received more consideration from Freud than any other dream in his 600-page book on *The Interpretation of Dreams*. And no dream in the history of psychoanalysis has received more attention from secondary scholars in turn. All of which is especially remarkable given that the dream itself, when rendered on the page, amounts to a single paragraph:

A large hall—numerous guests, whom we were receiving.—Among them was Irma. I at once took her on one side, as though to answer her letter and to reproach her for not having accepted my 'solution' yet. I said to her: 'If you still get pains, it's really only your fault.' She replied: 'If you only knew what pains I've got now in my throat and stomach and abdomen—it's choking me'—I was alarmed and looked at her. She looked pale and puffy. I thought to myself that after all I must be missing some organic trouble. I took her to the window and looked down her throat, and she showed signs of recalcitrance, like women with artificial dentures. I thought to myself that there was really no need for her to do that.—She then opened her mouth properly and on the right I found a big white patch; at another place I saw extensive whitish grey scabs upon some remarkable curly structures which were evidently modeled on the turbinal bones of the nose.—I at once called in Dr. M., and he repeated the examination and confirmed it. . . . Dr. M. looked quite different from usual; he was very pale, he walked with a limp and his chin was clean-shaven. . . . My friend Otto was now standing beside her as well, and my friend Leopold was percussing her through her bodice and saying: 'She has a dull area low down on the left.' He also indicated that a portion of the skin on her left shoulder was infiltrated. (I noticed this, just as he did, in spite of her dress.) . . . M. said: 'There's no doubt it's an infection, but no matter [*es macht nichts*]; dysentery will supervene and the toxin will be eliminated.' . . . We were directly aware, too, of the origin of the infection. Not long before, when she was feeling unwell, my friend Otto had given her an injection of a preparation of propyl, propyls . . . propionic acid . . . trimethylamin (and I saw before me the formula for this printed in heavy type). . . . Injections of that sort ought not to be given so thoughtlessly. . . . And probably the syringe had not been clean.[5]

Freud's analysis of this dream was extensive, but also easily summarized: "The dream acquitted me of the responsibility for Irma's condition by showing that it was due to other factors" (*FR*, 140). And yet, as he goes on to explain, Irma's condition and its various causes were not the only worries that infused his dream. "Certain other themes played a part in the dream, which were not so obviously connected with my exculpation from Irma's illness," he adds. "But when I came to consider all these, they could all be collected into a simple group of ideas and labeled, as it were 'concern about my own and other people's health—professional conscientiousness'" (141). In other words, the dream of Irma's injection was a work dream—a dream in which Freud's professional identity, specifically his being-in-the-world of medicine, was at stake.

If Irma was his dream's lodestar, her mouth was its gravitational center. In his interpretation, Freud associates the *"big white patch"* on the right side of her mouth with her more attractive and compliant friend, who had recently suffered from a diphtheritic membrane. He also links it to his eldest daughter, Mathilde, who had narrowly survived a "serious illness" two years prior. More troubling to him were the *"extensive whitish grey scabs upon some remarkable curly structures which were evidently modeled on the turbinal bones of the nose."* These "recalled a worry [*Sorge*] about my own state of health," which, in turn, brought to mind several more linked memories: "I was making frequent use of cocaine at that time to reduce some troublesome nasal swellings, and I had heard a few days earlier that one of my patients who had followed my example had developed an extensive necrosis of the nasal mucous membrane. I had been the first to recommend the use of cocaine, in 1885, and this recommendation had brought serious reproaches down on me. The misuse of that drug had hastened the death of a dear friend of mine" (*FR*, 134–35). From Irma to her friend, to Mathilde, to Freud, to a woman patient, to a dearly departed friend, a spectrum of suffering begins to emerge, with illness at one end, fatality at the other, and Freud's professional identity strewn throughout. Hence, Irma's recalcitrance and its likeness to that of *"women with artificial dentures."* It was sickness, aging, and demise—all barriers to Freud's psychotherapeutic "solution," and thus also to his chosen profession— that her recalcitrance concealed. It was being-towards-death—the outer limit of his own capacity to be, beyond which he could no longer press forward into his self-understanding as a psychologist—that Freud discovered there.

What Irma was slow to reveal, Dr. M. was quick to obscure. But even Dr. M. could not shield Freud from the horrific contents of her mouth and the threat they posed to his professional identity. Even the simple fact that he called in Dr. M. *"at once"* recalled a "tragic event" in his practice: "I had on one occasion produced a severe toxic state in a woman patient by repeatedly prescribing what was at that time regarded as a harmless remedy (sulphonal), and had hurriedly turned for assistance and support to my experienced senior colleague." Her name, Freud adds, was Mathilde—the same as that of his eldest daughter. "This Mathilde for that Mathilde," he remembers thinking, "like an act of retribution on the part of destiny" (*FR*, 135).

More than a dream about "professional conscientiousness," the dream of Irma's injection was a nightmare about its repeated failure. "It seemed as if I had been collecting all the occasions which I could bring up against myself as evidence of a lack of medical conscientiousness," Freud eventually admits (*FR*, 135). This is partly why he required the assistance of Dr. M., as well as that of two more colleagues: Otto and Leopold. If Irma's opened mouth revealed traumatic images of sickness, demise, and medical negligence—images which the metonymic shift from daughter-Mathilde to deceased-Mathilde transformed into a vengeful circuit of pain—the opened mouths of Otto, Leopold, and Dr. M. suggested several ways to override these unpleasant images and, in so doing, to short this painful circuit. In place of sickness, demise, and medical negligence, Freud's imaginary colleagues offered insight, diagnosis, and, above all, expert consolation.

As Freud aptly notes, however, their speech became increasingly groundless as the dream progressed. Leopold's first statement—*"'She has a dull area low down on the left'"*—made a bit of sense to Freud. Much as idle talk, according to Heidegger, "brings what is understood to a sham clarity" (*BT*, 208), Leopold's insight into Irma's condition yielded little more than "a vague notion of something in the nature of a metastatic affection." And the "unusual phrasing" of his second finding—namely, *"that a portion of the skin on the left shoulder was infiltrated"*—was even more puzzling, especially when coupled with Freud's parenthetical response: *"I noticed this, just as he did."* Recalling the equivocality of idle talk, Freud acknowledges that "the wording in the dream was most ambiguous." Like the urgency of his call to Dr. M., however, this ambiguity proved deeply meaningful: "I saw at once that this was the rheumatism in my own shoulder, which I invariably notice if I sit up late into the night" (*FR*, 136). Just as "*at once*" returned him to the "anxious days" of his daughter's illness, so also did "*the left shoulder*" recall concerns about his own unhealthy state. Like Dr. M. before him, then, Leopold was there to distract Freud from the contents of Irma's mouth. His comments, in keeping with their function as idle talk, served to close off and cover up these horrific entities within-the-world of Freud's dream. In the final analysis, however, Leopold recalled their traumatic corporeal features.

At which point Dr. M. interjected, causing even more confusion: "'*There's no doubt it's an infection, but no matter; dysentery will supervene and the toxin will be eliminated.*'" "At first this struck me as ridiculous," Freud writes. But again, on closer inspection, the utterance made sense. "*Infection*" returned him, once more, to "the time of my daughter's illness." "*Dysentery*," in turn, brought to mind another clinical blunder, when he sent a constipated hysteric on a long sea voyage, during which the patient developed an intestinal infection—or, as Freud downplays the incident, recalling Irma's condition, "some organic trouble." Only "*no matter*" seemed to relieve his anxiety. "This was intended as a consolation," Freud concludes—a way to shift the blame for Irma's illness, and all it represented, away from himself. Her pains were not only "organic," and thus unrelated to his "psychological treatment," but also, as Dr. M. suggested, and much to Freud's liking, "an assurance that all would be well in the end," for dysentery would soon overcome her illness, eliminating it completely. Just as there was "*really no need*" for Irma to resist Freud's oral examination, so also was there really no need for Freud to dwell on its horrific results, for her illness was itself "*no matter*" at all. "It was really nothing," Dr. M. all but said, inviting Freud to shrug off his anxiety and, by extension, his being-towards-death. Even so, Freud wonders, "why was the consolation so nonsensical?" (*FR*, 136–37)

At once meaningful and ridiculous, significant and illogical, it is easy to read "*no matter*" as an instance of what Heidegger described as "everyday discourse" (*alltägliche Rede*). Although it encouraged Freud to shirk anxiety and death, it did so by giving voice to this uncomfortable existential mood and its nearly unbearable mode of being. This is abundantly clear in Freud's German. "*No matter*" is a translation of *macht nichts*, meaning "not important," "never mind," and even "forget it." But *macht nichts* also lends itself to sayings like "it makes no difference" (*es macht nichts aus*), "it's no bother for me" (*das macht mir gar nichts aus*), and, more tellingly, "that's nothing to me" (*das macht mir nichts aus*). What Freud saw in Irma's mouth was indeed *nothing* to him. And this is precisely what the nonsensical speech of Dr. M. confirms: *"no matter"* calls attention to a void, an emptiness, a nonentity, a no-thing—in short, a *Nichts*—that is uniquely, if insignificantly, addressed to Freud himself. That *Nichts* also means "cipher"—an entity of no influence, no clout, no mastery, no *macht*—makes Dr. M.'s "consolation" even more pointed. Much as *alltägliche Rede* verges on *Gerede* but ultimately eludes this groundless way of speaking by making groundlessness itself a point of discussion, *"no matter"* verges on the nonsense characteristic of Leopold's discourse but ultimately escapes its vortex by making nonsense itself, in all of its harrowing emptiness, a point of serious consideration—serious enough for Freud to interpret *"macht nichts"* as professional consolation.

But Freud did not delve this deep into Dr. M.'s consolation. Instead, he concludes that "I must have been making fun of Dr. M. with the consoling prognosis." And rightfully so, for "Dr. M. was just as little in agreement with my 'solution' as Irma herself." Thus, at this point in the dream, Freud was avenging himself against two people: "on Irma with the words 'If you still get pains, it's your own fault,' and on Dr. M. by the wording of the nonsensical consolation that I put into his mouth" (*FR*, 138). Both were given mouthfuls of nonsense by Freud. But what Irma's mouthful challenged, Dr. M.'s reaffirmed: Freud's professional identity.

Otto's Dirty Syringe

No sooner had Freud struck this tenuous balance between horror and ridicule, anxiety, and reassurance, than the origin of Irma's lingering illness presented itself: Otto's dirty syringe. Initially, Freud was content to recall Otto's history of traveling injections. But this in turn reminded him, once again, of his dearly departed friend who "poisoned himself with cocaine," specifically "cocaine *injections*." Again, Freud seemed intent on reproaching himself for professional carelessness. And again, he seemed committed to reproach in the midst of ambiguity. This time, however, it was Freud, not his bumbling colleagues, who verged on nonsense: *"propyl, propyls . . . propionic acid."*

Freud's interpretation of this alliterative sequence is curiously detailed, focusing on a foul bottle of liquor that he and his pregnant wife had recently received from Otto. "This liquor gave off such a strong smell of fusel oil that I refused to touch it," he recounts. "The smell of fusel oil (amyl . . .) evidently stirred up in my mind a recollection of the whole series—propyl, methyl, and so on—and this accounted for the propyl preparation in the dream." But even Freud sensed the inadequacy of this interpretation. "It is true that I carried out a substitution in the process: I dreamt of propyl after having smelt amyl" (*FR*, 138). How are we to account for this substitution?

In order to account for "*propyl, propyls . . . propionic acid*," we must first attend to its verbal climax: "*trimethylamin.*" Given Freud's keen memory of Otto's foul-smelling gift, it is hardly surprising that "*propyl, propyls . . . propionic acid*" culminated in this organic compound. Trimethylamine is a colorless, flammable product of decomposing plants and animals. In high concentrations, it smells like ammonia. In low concentrations, however, it smells like rotting fish and is often associated with infections, bad breath, and vaginal odor, especially as a symptom of *bacterial vaginosis*—an infection that may result from sex with new or multiple partners. Freud was quick to note the connection between trimethylamine and "the chemistry of sexual processes," recalling a conversation with his close friend Wilhelm Fliess, who, in another context, had made "some remarkable connections between the turbinal bones and the female organs of sex." Which in turn reminded Freud of the scabby turbinal bones he discovered in Irma's mouth, if only by way of comparison: "Cf. the three curly structures in Irma's throat," he adds parenthetically (*FR*, 139). Even in this moment of startling medical clarity, when he finally arrives at the word "*trimethylamin,*" with its formula appearing before him "*printed in heavy type,*" Freud was unable to forget the unsettling image of his own poor health, specifically his "nasal swellings," which he was treating with cocaine at the time, and the adverse effects of such treatment on his self-understanding as a medical professional (134).

To be sure, "*propyl, propyls . . . propionic acid*" was linked to the ghastly image in Irma's mouth by way of smell, specifically by way of Freud's memory of Otto's foul-smelling gift (an issue to which we will return later). But it was also connected to this image by way of Freud's ongoing attempt to relieve anxiety about his professional identity and, in so doing, to evade being-towards-death. What Irma was hesitant to reveal (but eventually disclosed) during her oral examination and Dr. M. was quick to obscure (but inadvertently conveyed) during his prompt reassessment is precisely what Freud was determined but ultimately unable to resist with "*propyl, propyls . . . propionic acid.*" More than a sputtering yet successful start toward "*trimethylamin,*" Freud suggests in his analysis, this alliterative sequence was a repeated yet ultimately futile effort to avoid this flammable organic compound, with all of its oral, sexual, infectious, and repulsive connotations—the collective meaning of which could only return him, once more, to the jarring contents of Irma's mouth.

All of this was Otto's fault. It was Otto, not Freud, who gave Irma the injection. It was Otto's syringe, not Freud's "solution," that prolonged her illness. It was Otto's "thoughtlessness," not a "lack of medical conscientiousness" on Freud's part, that the dream revealed. In keeping with the structure of his analysis up to this point, which Freud summarizes as "a comparison between the content of the dream and the concealed thoughts lying behind it," these accusations recalled several well-worn memories. Otto's thoughtlessness reminded Freud, again, of his dear friend who overdosed on cocaine injections, as well as his unfortunate patient Mathilde who suffered an equally toxic fate. Both fatalities, Freud laments, "gave grounds for the same accusation against myself" (FR, 139–40).

But these were not the only memories evoked by Otto's apparent thoughtlessness. Freud also was reminded of his last conversation with Otto, which occurred the day before he dreamt of Irma's illness:

I had a visit from a junior colleague, one of my oldest friends, who had been staying with my patient, Irma, and her family at their country resort. I asked him how he had found her and he answered: 'She's better, but not quite well.' I was conscious that my friend Otto's words, or the tone in which he spoke them, annoyed me. I fancied I detected a reproof in them, such as to the effect that I had promised the patient too much; and, whether rightly or wrongly, I attributed the supposed fact of Otto's siding against me to the influence of my patient's relatives, who, as it seemed to me, had never looked with favor on the treatment. However, my disagreeable impression was not clear to me and I gave no outward sign of it. (FR, 131)

In his dream and its subsequent analysis, the accusation of "thoughtlessness" allowed Freud to resume and legitimate his earlier annoyance with Otto, providing him with a metonymic justification for his "disagreeable impression" of the previous day. "I seemed to remember thinking something of the same kind that afternoon when his words and looks had appeared to show that he was siding against me," Freud notes in the final section of his analysis. "It had been some such notion as: 'How easily his thoughts are influenced! How thoughtlessly he jumps to conclusions!'" (FR, 139)

Moreover, the accusation of "thoughtlessness" allowed Freud to crystalize his "obscure, disagreeable impression" of the previous day, when Otto had claimed that Irma was "better, but not quite well." With the other memories evoked by his dream still fresh in his mind—memories of sickness and fatality, all tinged with suggestions of professional negligence—Freud was even able to caption his earlier annoyance: "This group of thoughts that played a part in the dream enabled me retrospectively [*nachträglich*] to put this transient impression into words. It was as though he had said to me: 'You don't take your medical duties seriously enough. You're not conscientious; you don't carry out what you've undertaken." Thus, Freud summarizes, "The dream gave me my revenge by throwing the reproach back on to him" (*FR*, 140–42).

Irma, Dr. M., and Otto—all wrongly questioned Freud's "solution," and all got what they deserved in his dream. "*I* was not to blame for Irma's pains, since she herself was to blame for them by refusing to accept my solution," he inferred from her recalcitrance. "*I* was not concerned with Irma's pains, since they were of an organic nature and quite incurable by psychological treatment," he realized in response to Dr. M.'s nonsense. "Irma's pains had been caused by Otto giving her an incautious injection of an unsuitable drug—a thing *I* should never have done," he surmised from Otto's thoughtlessness. And all the other "disagreeable memories" evoked by his dream—memories which initially seemed to support Otto's reproach rather than Freud's vindication—were made to follow suit. "This group of thoughts," Freud concludes, inverting many of his foregoing insights, was in fact "evidence of how highly conscientious I was, of how deeply I was concerned about the health of my relations, my friends, and my patients" (*FR*, 142). In this sense, Freud was not only acquitted in the end, but also wrongfully accused at the start—or so he told himself.

Menē, Menē, Tekēl, Upharsin

Lacan deeply admired Freud and Heidegger, and he won much of his early celebrity in praise of their work. The earliest of his renowned public seminars were dedicated to rereading Freud's technical writings. In seminar one, he explored *Freud's Papers on Technique* (1953–1954). In seminar two, he considered *The Ego in Freud's Theory and the Technique of Psychoanalysis* (1954–1955). And by seminar three, he was already trumpeting this stage of his career as "the return to Freud" (1955–1956).

Along the way, Lacan was also meeting with Heidegger. In the spring of 1955, he visited the aging philosopher in Freiburg; and a few months later, Heidegger returned the favor, joining Lacan at his country house in Guitrancourt. Then, in a 1956 issue of *La Psychanalyse*, alongside his bold psychoanalytic manifesto, "The Function and Field of Speech and Language in Psychoanalysis," which pays tribute to Freud and Heidegger alike, Lacan published a daring yet devoted translation of Heidegger's essay on "Logos."[6]

Speech was the conceptual centerpiece around which Lacan arranged the works of Freud and Heidegger. And not just any kind of speech: It was *empty speech* (*parole vide*), and its ability to occasion moments of *full speech* (*parole pleine*), that captured his attention. From Freud, Lacan borrowed the analytic technique of free association, the attendant laws of non-omission and non-systematization, and, ultimately, the therapeutic horizon of "psychoanalytic anamnesis." From Heidegger, he gleaned additional insights into the social functions of idle talk, curiosity, and ambiguity, especially as these functions intersect in the discourse of *das Man*. Together, these Heideggerian insights steered Lacan toward the outer existential limit of everyday life, in all of its historical complexity: *being-towards-death*. If "speech reveals truth and truth is fundamentally historical," Lacan notes in his 1956 manifesto, then the function of being-towards-death is in keeping with the therapeutic goal of psychoanalytic anamnesis. In addition to showing how human subjects are defined by their "historicity" as theorized by Heidegger, Lacan aimed to empower them with the analytic technique of "retrospection" as practiced by Freud.

It was against this intellectual backdrop, and in service to his emerging theory of empty speech, that Lacan returned to Freud's dream of Irma's injection. He had much to say about this historic dream and Freud's subsequent analysis—enough, he quips in his second seminar, to qualify his account as a "re-analysis" of both texts.[7] At stake in this re-analysis, Lacan argues, is a crucial piece of evidence in his career-long argument that "the essence of the Freudian discovery [is] the decentering of the subject in relation to the *ego*" (*S 2*, 148). Much of Lacan's early work on "empty speech" is indebted to this discovery and, as we shall see, connected to the very dream in which Freud made it.

Lacan begins by dividing the dream of Irma's injection into two parts. The first part centers on Freud's exchange with Irma and culminates in the startling contents of her mouth. What begins as an imaginary dialogue between the ego (Freud) and one its objects (Irma) ends in a traumatic revelation of its ghastly corporeal underpinnings, specifically a "revelation of that which is least penetrable in the real, of the real lacking any possible mediation, of the ultimate real, of the essential object which isn't an object any longer, but this something faced with which all words cease and all categories fail, the object of anxiety *par excellence"*—in short, "the revelation of this something which properly speaking is unnamable" (*S* 2, 164).

But name it Freud did: *"I saw extensive whitish grey scabs upon some remarkable curly structures which were evidently modeled on the turbinal bones of the nose."* He even went so far as to interpret this apalling image as self-addressed. As we have seen, the scabby turbinal bones in Irma's throat recalled his own health issues, specifically his "troublesome nasal swellings," which he was attempting to reduce with cocaine at the time—a treatment which, in turn, recalled a series of related medical debacles. None of this was lost on Lacan: "There's a horrendous discovery here, that of the flesh one never sees, the foundation of things, the other side of the head, of the face, the secretory glands *par excellence*, the flesh from which everything exudes, at the very heart of the mystery, the flesh in as much as it is suffering, is formless, in as much as its form in itself is something which provokes anxiety." The result was nothing short of an "identification of anxiety" addressed to Freud: *"You are this, which is so far from you, this which is the ultimate formlessness"* (*S* 2, 154–55). In sum, Lacan tells members of his second seminar, "Freud comes upon a revelation of the type, *Mene, Tekel, Peres* at the height of his need to see, to know, which was until then expressed in the dialogue of the *ego* with the object" (154–55).

If *"You are this, which is so far from you, this which is the ultimate formlessness"* adds captions to the jarring contents of Irma's mouth, *"Mene, Tekel, Peres"* invites us to interpret these captions alongside the biblical event of Belshazzar's feast (Daniel 5:1–30). Not content with the tableware at his feast, King Belshazzar ordered his servants to fetch the sacred gold and silver vessels that his father Nebuchadnezzar had taken from Solomon's temple, so that he and his guests could drink wine from them as they praised the gods of gold, silver, bronze, iron, wood, and stone. Just as this sacrilegious meal was beginning, however, a disembodied hand appeared and began scrawling on the dining room wall. "Menē, Menē, Tekēl, Upharsin," the hand wrote. Flabbergasted, Belshazzar summoned his conjurers, diviners, astrologers, and wise men to help him decipher this text. When all failed to do so, he sent for the visionary Daniel, who offered the following interpretation: "'Menē'—God has numbered [*menah*] your kingdom and put an end to it. 'Tekēl'—you have been weighed [*teqiltah*] on the scales and found deficient. 'Perēs'—your kingdom has been divided [*perisat*] and given over to the Medes and Persians [*paras*]." Later that night, the king was slain, and soon thereafter his kingdom fell—all as Daniel had predicted.

It is easy to mark the parallels between this biblical event and the first part of Freud's dream. Just as *"Menē, Menē, Tekēl, Upharsin"* disrupted Belshazzar's drunken feast and sent the king reeling, so also did the appearance of scabby turbinate bones in Irma's throat disrupt Freud's dialogue with his patient, confounding their phantasmatic exchange. And just as the writing on the wall predicted the demise of Belshazzar and the downfall of his kingdom, so also did the ghastly contents of Irma's mouth allude to Freud's own failing health, several related missteps in his medical practice, and, by extension, his being-towards-death as a psychoanalyst. Add to this Freud's recollection of his seriously ill daughter, as well as the metonymic shift from this Mathilde to his poisoned patient of the same name, and the resonance becomes even stronger: Just as *"Menē, Menē, Tekēl, Upharsin"* was a foreboding message from God, whom "you have not glorified" (Daniel 5:23), so also were the contents of Irma's mouth powerful reminders of this morbid Mathilde swap—a swap which Freud suspected was "an act of retribution on the part of destiny," or, as Lacan further specifies, "some mysterious sort of divine retribution for his professional negligence" (*S* 2, 164).

All of this, according to Lacan, makes the horrific contents of Irma's mouth a "turning point in the dream" (*S* 2, 165). If Irma's oral examination begins as a phantasmatic dialogue between the ego (Freud) and one of its objects (Irma), it ends in a "fundamental destructuration" of this imaginary relationship. The object of Freud's ego becomes an "object which isn't an object any longer"—a becoming which, in turn, initiates "a spectral decomposition of the function of the ego" (164–65). When Freud encounters the ghastly contents of Irma's mouth, his professional identity, like Belshazzar's kingdom, is at once *numbered*, *weighed*, and *divided* into several distinct yet constitutive identifications, each of which, at its most basic level, is a component of his narcissistic relation to the perceptual world:

To the extent that a dream may get to the point of entering the order of anxiety, and that a drawing nigh of the ultimate real is experienced, we find ourselves present at this imaginary decomposition which is only the revelation of the normal components of perception. For perception is a total relation to a given picture, in which man always recognizes himself somewhere, and sometimes even sees himself in several places. If the picture of the relation to the world is not made unreal by the subject, it is because it contains elements representing the diversified images of his ego, and these are so many points of anchorage, of stabilization, of inertia. (*S* 2, 167)

But the significance of this imaginary decomposition is more pointed than this passage suggests. In the wake of his horrific discovery in Irma's mouth, Freud suffers "the experience of his being torn apart, of his isolation in relation to the world" (*S* 2, 167). On this point, Lacan is outspoken: "He becomes something totally different, there's no Freud any longer, there is no longer anyone who can say *I*." Where his ego was, a "series of egos" appears instead (164–65). Three egos, to be exact—Dr. M., Otto, and Leopold: "Dr. M. represents the ideal character constituted by the paternal pseudo-image, the imaginary father. Otto corresponds to the character who played a perennial role in Freud's life, the intimate, close friend who is both friend and enemy, who from one hour to the next changes from being a friend to being an enemy. And Leopold plays the role of the character who is always useful to counter the character of the friend-enemy, of the beloved enemy" (*S* 2, 156). "All these characters are significant, in that each of them is the site of an identification whereby the *ego* is formed," Lacan goes on to explain (156). But all of them are also ridiculous. "This is the moment I've called the entry of the fool, since that is more or less the role played by the subjects on whom Freud calls" (164–65). And this, Lacan claims, is where the second part of Freud's dream begins. If part one centers on Freud's competent, conscientious interaction with Irma but culminates in the traumatic disintegration of this professional identity, part two focuses on the bumbling, nonsensical discourse of his colleagues in the wake of this traumatic breakdown. And yet, as we shall see, the second part of Freud's dream culminates in the resurgence of his professional identity—a resurgence which, in turn, belies the formation of another sense of self, a sense of self paradoxically beyond that of his ego.

Much as Belshazzar summoned his conjurers, diviners, astrologers, and wise men to help him read the writing on the wall, Freud appealed to Dr. M., Leopold, and Otto for assistance in diagnosing Irma's ongoing illness. And much as Belshazzar's interpreters failed to read the writing on the wall, and thus also to anticipate the imminent destruction of his kingdom, Freud's colleagues failed to provide a coherent, compelling diagnosis of Irma's condition, and thus also a convincing response to her mouth's apalling contents. Their collective insights reminded Freud of "the defense put forward by the man who was charged by one of his neighbors with having given him back a borrowed kettle in a damaged condition. The defendant asserted first, that he had given it back undamaged; secondly that the kettle had a hole in it when he borrowed it; and thirdly that he had never borrowed the kettle from his neighbor at all" (*FR*, 141). Any of these defenses, if accepted, would have been sufficient to acquit the man, Freud quips. And so it was in his dream—or so he made it seem in his dream's analysis.

Mixing Subjects

If their insights amount to kettle logic, Dr. M., Leopold, and Otto themselves constitute a *crowd*. "But it is a structured crowd, like the Freudian crowd," Lacan specifies, recalling Freud's book on group psychology and his earlier essay on narcissism. "That is why I would prefer to introduce another term, which I will leave to your reflection with all the double meanings it contains—the inmixing of subjects [*l'immixtion des sujets*]," he goes on to allude. "The subject enters and mixes in [*mêlent*] with things—that may be the first meaning. The other one is this—an unconscious phenomenon which takes place on the symbolic level, as such decentered in relation to the *ego*, always takes place between two subjects" (*S* 2, 160). Let us consider each of these meanings in turn, for each, in its own way, puts us on the path to Lacan's theory of empty speech.

The first meaning of *immixtion* refers to the spectral decomposition of Freud's ego at the beginning of his dream's second part, when his professional identity (ego) splinters into images of Dr. M., Otto, and Leopold (identifications). Initially, these images are defensive. By appealing to "the consensus of his fellow-beings, of his equals, of his colleagues, of his superiors," Freud is able to shield himself from the ghastly contents of Irma's mouth, offsetting his own anxiety and being-towards-death as a psychoanalyst with "the congress of all those who know" (*S* 2, 164, 159). But this protection comes at a price, for it marks the disappearance of Freud himself. The cost of professional absolution, it would seem, is his absorption into the crowd. "We see the subject substituted by the polycephalic subject," Lacan summarizes, a many-headed figure composed "of the imaginary plurality of the subject, of the fanning out, the blossoming of the different identifications of the *ego*" (167).

Of central importance here is the *speech* of this many-headed figure. As we have seen, Freud found the words of his colleagues "unusual," "ambiguous," "ridiculous," and, in the case of Dr. M., utterly "nonsensical." Lacan also notes their apparent insignificance: "The discourse of the multiple *ego* makes itself heard in a great cacophony," in "senseless discourse," in "the hubbub of speech" (*S* 2, 167–68, 170, 157). At most, "it plays with speech, with decisive and adjudicating speech," taunting Freud's dislocated ego with the professional reassurance it craves (156).

Freud knew his analysis of the dream was egocentric. Over and against the senseless speech of Dr. M., Otto, and Leopold, which effectively abolished his ego, thereby divesting the dream of "anyone who can say *I*," Freud's careful interpretation of their idiotic remarks in the analysis of his dream allowed him to restore this subject position, gradually yet forcefully reclaiming his ego's ability to speak. Hence, all of the emphatic I-statements in his concluding account of the dream's relevance to his professional identity: "*I* was not to blame for Irma's pains, since she herself was to blame for them by refusing to accept my solution. *I* was not concerned with Irma's pains, since they were of an organic nature and quite incurable by psychological treatment. Irma's pains could be satisfactorily explained by her widowhood (cf. the trimethylamin) which *I* had no means of altering. Irma's pains had been caused by Otto giving her an incautious injection of an unsuitable drug—a thing *I* should never have done" (*FR*, 141).

Freud also realized that his egocentric interpretation of the dream was incomplete. "I will not pretend that I have completely uncovered the meaning of this dream and that its interpretation is without a gap," he admits. Even so, Lacan observes, Freud seemed a little too content with this concluding self-awareness. "How is it that Freud, who later on will develop the function of unconscious desire, is here content, for the first step in his demonstration, to present a dream which is entirely explained by the satisfaction of a desire which one cannot but call preconscious, and even entirely conscious?" (*S* 2, 151) Surely there is more at work in the dream's second part than the restoration of Freud's ego.

The second meaning of *l'immixtion des sujets* certainly suggests as much. "An unconscious phenomenon which takes place on the symbolic level, as such decentered in relation to the *ego*, always takes place between two subjects," Lacan elaborates, alluding to the basic discovery of Freudian psychoanalysis—namely, the decentered relation of the unconscious subject to the self-conscious ego. But he also ties this Freudian discovery to the dream from which it is noticeably removed: "What is at stake in the function of the dream is beyond the *ego*, what in the subject is of the subject and not of the subject, that is the unconscious" (*S* 2, 159). In particular, Lacan attempts to anchor the discovery of the unconscious in the dream's second part, where the spectral decomposition of Freud's ego gives way to a rambling dialogue between his ego identifications. If the first meaning of *l'immixtion des sujets* recalls the opening of the second part of the dream, where Freud's ego begins to decompose, the second meaning refers to the senseless discourse that emerges in the wake of this decomposition.

In the midst of this rambling dialogue—in the *immixtion* constituted by its kettle logic—Lacan hears another voice, a voice which belongs to Freud but also exceeds him, indexing his professional identity but only by traversing it. Lacan refers to this excessive, extrinsic speaking subject as "Nemo," the Greek word for "no one." If Dr. M., Otto, and Leopold constitute a polycephaic crowd, Nemo is their acephalic counterpart—not the headstrong Freud who regains himself as a self-conscious ego in the dream's analysis, but the headless Freud who loses himself as the dream proceeds, disappearing as an unconscious subject behind the senseless discourse of his egomorphic peers. "If there is an image which could represent for us the Freudian notion of the unconscious, it is indeed that of the acephalic subject, of the subject who is no longer an *ego*, who doesn't belong to the *ego*," Lacan plainly states. "And yet he is the subject who speaks, for that's who gives all the characters in the dream their nonsensical lines" (*S* 2, 167). If Freud's ego was the beneficiary of these characters' senseless speech, his unconscious was its secret underwriter. It was Freud, as an acephalic subject, who presented his colleagues as a cacophonous, polycephalic crowd. And it was Freud, as *no one*, who filled their mouths with nonsense.

It was also he who caused the dream to stutter on *"propyl, propylene . . . proprionic acid,"* and he who halted the progression of this alliterative sequence with *"trimethylamin"* and its chemical formula. With each *"prop,"* Freud's unconscious, acephalic self gains momentum, overcoming each of his egomorphic peers in turn. Then, with the emergence of *"trimethylamin,"* this acephalic self surges forth with a voice of its own. No longer mediated through Dr. M, Leopold, and Otto—and no longer subordinate to Freud's account of his mind's metonymic drift from the "fusel oil" stench of Otto's gift, to "the chemistry of sexual processes" according to Fliess, to "the three curly structures in Irma's throat"—it is the voice of Nemo, of no one, of Freud's unconscious, of the Freudian unconscious itself. In *"trimethylamin,"* this lone voice becomes clearly audible; but with the addition of trimethylamine's chemical formula, it is no longer a voice alone. Instead, it is a voice echoing at the outer limits of vocalization itself, a voice whose echo is neither vocal nor verbal, but graphic, glyphic, and even hieroglyphic. At the height of his dream's second part, when the chemical formula of tri-methylamine appears (fig. 7.1), Freud encounters an alluring, honorific, symbolic-real counterpart to the repulsive, horrifying, imaginary-real contents of Irma's mouth:

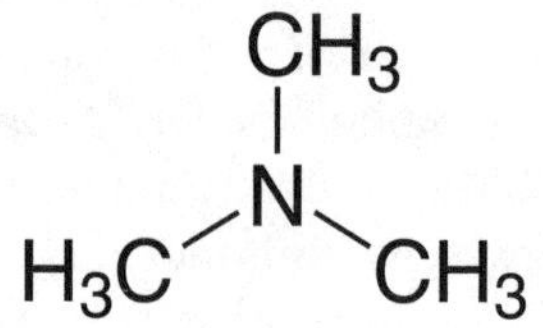

$$
\begin{array}{c}
CH_3 \\
| \\
H_3C {\diagup} N {\diagdown} CH_3
\end{array}
$$

FIGURE 7.1. The chemical formula of trimethylamine.

When Lacan, in his second definition of *l'immixtion des sujets*, suggests that the unconscious phenomena of Freud's dream take place on "the symbolic level," this is precisely what he means. "Just when the hydra has lost its heads, a voice which is nothing more than *the voice of no one* causes the trimethylamine formula to emerge, as the last word on the matter, the word for everything. And this word means nothing except that it is a word" (*S* 2, 170).

Later, in his third seminar, Lacan would limit his explanation of this purely symbolic aspect of Freud's dream to issues of signification: "It's a question of signifiers, of signifiers as such, handled by a subject for signifying aims, signifying so purely that the meaning very often remains problematic."[8] Here, however, in seminar two, he is content to recall, once more, the biblical event of Belshazzar's feast: "What emerges, printed in heavy type, beyond the hubbub of speech, like the *Mene, Mene, Tekel, Upharsin* of the Bible, is the formula of trimethyl-amine." And to repeat himself for good measure: "The dream, which culminated a first time, when the *ego* was there, with the horrific image I mentioned, culminates a second time at the end with a formula, with its *Mene, Mene, Tekel, Upharsin* aspect, on the wall, beyond what we cannot but identify as speech, universal rumor" (*S* 2, 158).

Ludicrous Talk, Encrypted Text

From the senseless speech of Freud's egomorphic peers to the *"prop . . . prop . . . prop"* of their unconscious animator, to the appearance of *"tri-methylamin,"* to the emergence of its chemical formula, Lacan interprets the second part of Freud's dream as a progressive, linguistic advancement from ludicrous talk to encrypted text. Although it is Freud, as Nemo, who underwrites this linguistic progression, gradually yet effectively offsetting meaningless words with the mystical Word as such, it is Lacan who lays claim to its final esoteric achievement: "Like my oracle, the formula gives no reply whatsoever to anything. But the very manner in which it is spelt out, its enigmatic, hermetic nature, is in fact the answer to the question of the meaning of the dream. One can model it closely on the Islamic formula—*There is no God but God*. There is no other word, no other solution to your problem, than the word" (*S* 2, 158).

To be sure, this reading of trimethylamine's chemical formula has "a delirious air about it." And if Freud had attempted to perform this reading on his own, the analysis of his dream would have succumbed to such delirium. It would have spelled disaster for his egocentric account if Freud, "all by himself, analyzing his dream, [had] tried to find in it, proceeding as an occultist might, the secret designation of the point where as a matter of fact the solution to the mystery of the subject and the world lies" (*S* 2, 170). By publishing his analysis instead, and thus addressing himself to a broader scientific community, Freud was able to stave off such delirium. "Once he communicates the secret of this Luciferian mystery to us, Freud is not confronted with this dream by himself," Lacan concludes. "And that is why seeing the word in the absurd final word of the dream isn't to reduce it to a delirium, since Freud, by means of this dream, makes himself heard by us, and effectively puts us on the road toward his object, which is the understanding of the dream" (*S* 2, 170).

Hence, the return to Belshazzar's feast. Like the disembodied hand of God, which interrupted this irreverent bacchanal to inscribe the palace wall for all to see, Freud's incorporeal, acephalic, unconscious self interrupts the rambling dialogue of his peers to deliver a cryptic text addressed to us. And like Daniel—conveyor of godly visions, interpreter of kingly dreams, master of all conjurers, diviners, astrologers, and wise men—Lacan presents himself as the exclusive interpreter of this cryptic text. With characteristic bravado, he identifies himself as the chosen translator of the chosen text in the chosen dream of psychoanalysis—the dream which inaugurated Freud's work as a psychoanalyst and in which his greatest discovery—the function of the unconscious—could only appear as "something which is both him and not him," in "speech which is in the subject without being the speech of the subject," saying in effect:

I [je] am he who wants to be forgiven for having dared to begin to cure these patients, who until now no one wanted to understand and whose cure was forbidden. I [je] am the one who wants to be forgiven for that. I [je] am he who wants not to be guilty of it, for to transgress any limit imposed up to now on human activity is always to be guilty. I want to not be (born) that [je veux n'être pas cela]. In place of me [A la place de moi], there are all the others [autres]. I [je] am only the representative of this vast, vague movement, the quest for truth, in which I efface myself [où moi, je m'efface]. I am no longer anything [je ne suis plus rien]. My [Mon] ambition was greater than me [moi]. No doubt the syringe was dirty. And precisely to the extent that I [je] desired it too much, that I [j'ai] partook in this action, that I [j'ai] wanted to be, myself [moi], the creator, I [je] am not the creator. The creator is someone greater than me [moi]. It is my [mon] unconscious, it is the word which speaks in me [moi], beyond me [moi]. (S 2, 170–71; trans. modified)

And "*voilà,*" Lacan concludes, "the meaning of this dream" (*S* 2, 171).

Not surprisingly, there is more to this paraphrastic conclusion than meets the eye, especially when we consider Lacan's original French. Consider, for instance, the play of *I* and *me—je* and *moi—*in the above passage. *Je* is a Lacanian watchword for the subject and here refers to Freud's unconscious, acephalic self; *moi* is among his key terms for the ego and here refers to Freud's conscious, polycephalic self. Behind the dream's *moi*-driven first part, in which Freud (as ego) interacts with Irma (as object), Lacan detects a *je* in search of forgiveness, acquittal, and redemption—a *je* who, when Freud's *moi* encounters the horrific contents of Irma's mouth, wishes never even to have begun treating patients beyond the limits of "organic" medicine, and, more dramatically, never to have become someone capable of such treatment. Hence, the ambiguity of "*je veux n'être pas cela*" in the foregoing passage: It can mean "I want it not to be" but also "I want to not be that" and even, as the foregoing translation suggests, "I want to not be born that."

And there's more. Just as the ghastly discovery in Irma's mouth splinters Freud's professional identity into several ego identifications, so also does Lacan's paraphrastic summary of the dream dissolve Freud's *moi* into a "vast, vague movement." But with an additional twist: It is a vast, vague movement in and as which a specific agential force—Freud's *je*—does the dissolving. Hence, the subtlety of "*moi, je m'efface*" above, which can mean "*I*, as me, disappear" but also, more directly, "I delete myself" and, more suggestively still, "I move myself aside," and thus "I stand aside from myself." After not wanting to be *that*, not wanting to have become *that*, not wanting to have been born *that*, Freud's unconscious, acephalic self finds an opportunity to annihilate this *that*, reducing his *moi* to ruins. Hence, *je ne suis plus rein*, the precise translation of which is not "I am no longer anything" but instead, as Heidegger would have been eager to point out, "I am nothing." These are Freud's first words as Nemo, the first words of his acephalic subject, and the first words of the Freudian unconscious—words en route to what Lacan understands as the dream's final Word.

EIGHT

First and Final Words

Where I Was

Recall the spectral decomposition of Freud's ego at the beginning of his dream's second part. In his summative account of this decomposition, Lacan suggests that Freud's *je* dissolves his *moi* into a vast intellectual movement, representatives of which include Dr. M., Leopold, and Otto. Again, the original French is revealing: "*je ne suis là que le représentant de ce vaste, vague mouvement qui est la recherche de la vérité où, moi, je m'efface.*" In addition to "*moi, je m'efface*" at the end of this sentence, we must attend to its preceding "*où*"—the French adverb for "where"—especially as it ripples through the rest of Lacan's summative remarks on the dream. Where Freud's ego was (*A la place de moi*), Freud's polycephalic self becomes (*il y a tous les autres*), and where his polycephalic self becomes (*ce vaste, vague mouvement*), his acephalic self annihilates, laying waste to Freud's ego (*où, moi, je m'efface*). All of which is well captured in the more literal, and certainly more Lacanian, translation of this crucial sentence: "I am just a representative of this vast, vague movement that is looking for the truth where I efface myself" (*S* 2, 170; trans. modified).

This "where" resurfaces a few lines later in the same passage, where Lacan, still paraphrasing Freud, insists that "*justement dans la mesure où je l'ai trop désiré, où j'ai participé à cette action, où j'ai voulu être, moi, le créateur, je ne suis pas le créateur.*" The standard English translation of this sentence completely obscures its spatial dimensions: *"Precisely to the extent that I desired it too much, that I partook in this action, that I wanted to be, myself, the creator, I am not the creator"* (170–71). Another, sharper, and again more Lacanian translation would read: *"Precisely in the position where I desired it too much, where I partook of this action, where I wanted to be, myself, the creator, I am not the creator."*

Although *dans la mesure* is the French equivalent of "insofar" and "to the extent," this phrase, when read to the letter, suggests something far more nuanced. *Dans* is the French preposition for "in" and "among," but it can also mean "during." And *la mesure* can mean "measure" in several different senses, including quantity (how much), action (by what means), and moderation (to what extent). But it can also mean "measure" in the sense of musical notation (textual spacing) and musical rhythm (temporal pacing), both of which find expression when *la mesure* designates a specific "step" or "pace" or, put a bit more archly, "cadence"—from the Latin verb *cadere*, meaning "to fall." All of which further suggests that the crucial question in Freud's analysis and Lacan's re-analysis of this iconic dream is not *when* but, instead, *where*. Where, exactly, does the *moi* fall and the *je* rise in the dream of Irma's injection?

An answer arrives in the second definition of *l'immixtion des sujets* we discussed in the previous chapter: "An unconscious phenomenon which takes place on the symbolic level, as such decentered in relation to the *ego*, always takes place between two subjects." As Freud's *moi* dissolves into Dr. M., Leopold, and Otto, his *je* begins to emerge *in between* these interlocutors—first in the ridiculous form of their senseless discourse, then in the sputtering shape of *"prop . . . prop . . . prop,"* then in the crystalizing figure of *"trimethylamin,"* and finally in the enigmatic text of trimethylamine's chemical formula. As we have seen, this final enigmatic text marks the emergence of something in and beyond Freud himself, specifically a discourse which is at once a part of and apart from his ego—or, as Lacan puts it, again paraphrasing Freud, *"the word which speaks in me [moi], beyond me [moi]."* In this sense, the two subjects between whom the chemical formula of trimethylamine "takes place" might be Freud's acephalic and polycephalic selves. Or they might be the dreaming Freud and the analyzing Freud, or either of these speaking subjects and the broader readership of *The Interpretation of Dreams*.

Lacan does not further specify this "where." But Freud, in his original presentation of the dream, does. Recall the position—*la mesure par excellence*—of *"prop . . . prop . . . prop,"* *"trimethylamin,"* and the chemical formula in his 1895 dream: "*We were directly aware, too, of the origin of the infection. Not long before, when she was feeling unwell, my friend Otto had given her an injection of a preparation of propyl, propyls . . . propionic acid . . . trimethylamin (and I saw before me the formula for this printed in heavy type). . . . Injections of that sort ought not to be given so thoughtlessly. . . . And probably the syringe had not been clean*" (*FR*, 132). If "*prop . . . prop . . . prop,*" "*trimethylamin,*" and its chemical formula are all unconscious phenomena, and all unconscious phenomena take place "between two subjects," the subjects between whom these utterances occur would seem to be Otto and Nemo—a someone then and there who probably caused Irma's illness (Otto as a dyslogistic stand-in for Freud's battered ego) and a no one here and now emerging in the former's thoughtless wake (Nemo as an insightful figure of Freud's bolstered unconscious).

Freud does not explore this Otto-Nemo relation, but he does allude to its basic symbolic function. As we saw in chapter 7, the final moments of his dream recalled his earlier conversation with Otto. When asked how Irma was feeling, Otto had replied, "'She's better, but not quite well,'" leaving Freud with a vague yet memorable sense of indignation—not only because Otto seemed to be reproaching his "solution" but also because he appeared to be siding with Irma's family against Freud. In his dream, Freud simply reversed this accusation, projecting blame for Irma's illness back onto Otto. Only in his subsequent analysis, after dredging up several painful memories of sickness and fatality, all tinged with suggestions of medical carelessness, was Freud able to clarify the motive for this projection, adding captions to his previously "obscure" and "transient" sense of indignation toward Otto: "'How easily his thoughts are influenced! How thoughtlessly he jumps to conclusions!'" (*FR*, 139). And only in view of this previously obscure motive could Freud return to Otto's initial remark about Irma's lingering illness, "retrospectively" (*nachträglich*) clarifying his earlier sense of indignation: "It was as though he had said to me: 'You don't take your medical duties seriously enough. You're not conscientious; you don't carry out what you've undertaken'" (141–42).

This retrospective conclusion was implicit in Freud's telling of the dream. Between Dr. M's absolution of Freud and Freud's indictment of Otto, the tense of the original German text shifts from present to past. In this sense, the transition from "*prop . . . prop . . . prop,*" to "*trimethylamin,*" to the chemical formula of trimethylamine is not just *agential*, allowing Freud's unconscious (*je*) to displace his ego (*moi*), but also *tem-*

poral, suggesting that the perspective afforded by this transition is specifically *historical*.[1] At stake in Freud's retrospective account of Otto's earlier remark, then, is a *resubjectivization* of this past event, the effect of which is a transformation of Freud's relation to Otto and, by extension, a transformation of Freud's relation to himself. That both of these transformations take place in *The Interpretation of Dreams* is equally significant. By addressing this resubjectivization to his readers, Freud was able to illuminate the basic methodological challenge of psychoanalytic technique and, in so doing, to set the stage for its theorization in Lacan's early work: "This assumption by the subject of his history, insofar as it is constituted by speech addressed to another, is clearly the basis of the new method Freud called psychoanalysis."[2]

I Was This

Lacan refers to this retrospective, resubjectivizing form of address as "true speech" (*parole vraie*). In the dream of Irma's injection, true speech initially appears in the linguistic shift from "*prop . . . prop . . . prop*" to "*trimethylamin*" to the chemical formula of this compound. But it is not until Freud's analysis of this dream, when he discovers the connection between this linguistic shift and his earlier conversation with Otto, that its retrospective, resubjectivizing effects become fully apparent. Only then does the transformation of Freud and Otto occur, allowing them to become "two very different subjects from what they were prior to [this] speech" (*S* 2, 160).

To this extent, true speech resembles symbolic transference. "Each time a man speaks to another in an authentic and full manner, there is, in the true sense, transference, symbolic transference—something takes place which changes the nature of the two beings present."[3] Like true speech, symbolic transference also has a historical dimension. But Lacan does not specify its retrospective, resubjectivizing function—at least not explicitly. Instead, he shifts his attention to the opposite of symbolic transference—imaginary transference—and the problematic, pseudo-historical obstacles it poses to intersubjective transformation. When imaginary transference occurs, the past becomes an obstacle to change, hindering expressions of true speech with various historical misrecognitions: "the repetition of prehistoric situations, unconscious repetition, the putting into effect of a reintegration of history—history in the opposite sense to the one I once put forward, since it is a question of an imaginary reintegration, the past situation only being experienced in the present, without the knowledge of the subject, in so far as its historical dimension is misrecognized [*méconnue*] by him" (*S* 1, 109). None of which, Lacan adds, permits the subject to engage in a retrospective resubjectivization of the past.

Even more suggestive in this context is the conceptual affinity between "true speech" and Lacan's early notion of "full speech" (*parole pleine*). Nowhere in his work is the transformative, historicizing function of true speech more apparent. Like true speech, full speech reconceives of past events and, in so doing, resubjectivizes their participants. And like Freud's reassessment of his earlier conversation with Otto, it often emerges as retrospective captions to personal narratives addressed to one's contemporaries. Not unlike the Greek *epos*: "The recitation of the *epos* may include a discourse of earlier days in its own archaic, even foreign tongue, or may even be carried out in the present with all the vivacity of an actor; but it is like indirect speech, isolated in quotation marks in the thread of the narrative, and, if the speech is performed, it is on a stage implying the presence not only of a chorus, but of spectators as well" (*E*, 212). The keyword here is *recitation*. And all the more so in light of Freud's retrospective account of Otto's earlier insult: "It was as though he had said to me: 'You don't take your medical duties seriously enough. You're not conscientious; you don't carry out what you've undertaken'" (*FR*, 141–42). How are we to understand recitations of this sort, where the archaic, foreign discourse of past events finds expression in transformative discourse addressed to one's contemporaries? "To Freud's mind, it is not a question of biological memory, nor of its intuitionist mystification, nor of the paramnesia of the symptom, but of remembering, that is, of history," Lacan replies (*E*, 213). In remembering, Freud discovered "the index and mainspring of therapeutic progress," an interpretive horizon against which to measure the completion of his increasingly refined talking cure: *anamnesis* (211, 213).

But let's make no mistake. In suggesting that full speech operates as a curative anamnesis, Lacan does not mean to equate psychoanalytic technique with the Platonic practice of deep memory recall. On the contrary, the work of psychoanalysis consists in helping patients reconceptualize past events of which they are already, to some extent, aware. "We help [the subject] complete the current historicization of the facts that have already determined a certain number of the historical 'turning points' in his existence," Lacan explains. "But if they have played this role, it is already as historical facts, that is, as recognized in a certain sense or censored in a certain order" (*E*, 217). To this extent, psychoanalytic anamnesis marks a significant advancement over its Platonic ancestor. "Psychoanalysis alone allows us to differentiate in memory the function of remembering. The latter, rooted in the signifier, resolves the Platonic aporias of reminiscence through the ascendency of history in man" (431). At stake in therapeutic remembering, then, is not the reminiscent recovery of forgotten pasts in service to innate bits of human knowledge (Platonic anamnesis) but, instead, the historical reconfiguration of existing memories in service to intimate, intersubjective moments of truth (psychoanalytic anamnesis). "In psychoanalytic anamnesis, what is at stake is not reality, but truth, because the effect of full speech is to reorder past contingencies by conferring on them the sense of necessities to come, such as they are constituted by the scant freedom through which the subject makes them present" (213).

When Freud uses the German *nachträglich* to describe his reassessment of Otto's earlier comments, this is what he means. Their conversation about Irma's lingering illness may have seemed insignificant at the time, little more than a contingent event culminating in "transient" and "obscure" impressions. But from the vantage point of *The Interpretation of Dreams*, this exchange could be seen for what it was—namely, the catalyst for a dream in which Freud not only discovered the royal road to the unconscious but also, in his interpretation of this dream, lit the way for all to see. "It isn't just for himself that he finds the *Nemo* or the alpha and omega of the acephalic subject, which represents his unconscious," Lacan insists. "On the contrary, by means of this dream it's him to who speaks, and who realizes that he is telling us—without having wanted to, without having recognized it at first, and only recognizing it in his analysis of the dream, that is to say while speaking to us—something which is both him and no longer him" (*S* 2, 170).

In this sense, psychoanalytic anamnesis is more Pauline than Platonic, recalling Paul of Tarsus' use of the Greek *typos*, meaning both "figure" and "prefiguration." For Paul, "each event of the past—once it becomes a figure—announces a future event and is fulfilled in it."[4] To recite important past events in discourse addressed to one's contemporaries is to dislocate these events from the continuum of past experience, typifying or figuring them as historical pronouncements of future events in which their potential to serve as defining moments in the speaker's life will have been realized. In this sense, the past is not something whose meaning resides in previous experience but "the effaced signal of something which only takes on its value in the future, through its symbolic realization, its integration into the history of the subject. Literally, it will only ever be a thing which, at the given moment of its occurrence, will have been" (*S* 1, 159). At issue here, Lacan argues, stretching tensors through Freud's notion of developmental history (*Entwicklungsgeschichte*), is "not the *Entwicklung*, the development, but the *Geschichte*, that is, that within which the subject recognizes himself, correlatively in the past and in the future" (157).

If speech can be "full," it is precisely for this reason: It allows us to fill the present with traces of our past and, in so doing, to discover the meaning of these traces here and now, in moments of historical consciousness—moments which also double as opportunities for personal growth. "What is realized in my history is neither the past definite as what was, since it is no more, nor even the perfect as what has been in what I am, but the future anterior as what I will have been, given what I am in the process of becoming" (*E*, 247). To assume our history is to alter our present, offsetting both the knowledge of what we *were* and the experience of what we *are* in order to arrive at the far more precarious truth of *what we must now become*. And arrive at this truth we must, "for the point is to take up our place in it." Like any *mesure* worth its while, where textual spacing and temporal pacing alike make for new forms of experience, the truth of what we must now become "requires us to go out of our way" (433). In moments of full speech, when psychoanalytic anamnesis erupts in discourse addressed to our peers, we go *out of our way*, and in more ways than one, to realize the moral imperative implicit in the Freudian motto *Wo Es war, soll Ich werden*: "I was this only in order to become what I can be" (209).

The Opening Song of Analysis

In full speech, the past neither overrides nor overwhelms the present but instead reveals the secret affinity between these two moments; and the present neither recovers nor repeats the past but instead discovers its origin there. Together, these revelations and discoveries constitute the history of the subject, and with it the truth of his past—and all in the here and now of concrete discourse. When Lacan claims that "history constitutes the emergence of truth in reality," this is what he means. "For it is present speech that bears witness to the truth of this revelation in current reality and grounds it in the name of this reality" (*E*, 212–14).

But present speech is not always full speech, and current reality is not always pocked with emergent truth. Full speech is the exception,

not the rule, of everyday talk. The symbolic, historical truth it promises to reveal about the subject's cryptic past often remains shrouded in
imaginary rhetorics of error, misrecognition, and inauthenticity. More
than barriers to psychoanalysis, however, these fallen ways of speaking
are its primary points of departure. "The analytic method, if it aims at
attaining full speech, starts off on a path leading in the diametrically
opposed direction, in so far as it instructs the subject to delineate a
speech as devoid as possible of any assumption of responsibility and
that it even frees him from any expectation of authenticity" (S 1, 108).
Lacan refers to this barren, inauthentic mode of discourse as "empty
speech" (*parole vide*). If full speech is the final word of psychoanalysis,
empty speech is its opening song. Indeed, as Lacan well notes, "emptiness is the first thing to make itself heard in analysis" (*E*, 206).

This is not to suggest that empty speech is insignificant. Even when
empty, speech remains meaningful: "However empty his discourse
may seem, it is so only if taken at face value—the value that justifies
Mallarmé's remark, in which he compares the common use of language
to the exchange of a coin whose obverse and reverse no longer bear but
eroded faces, and which people pass from hand to hand "in silence."
This metaphor suffices to remind us that speech, even when almost
completely worn out, retains its value as a *tessera*" (*E*, 209).

How are we to understand this comparison of empty speech to
a *tessera*? A *tessera* is a small, square tile of glass or stone used in the
construction of mosaics. In the ancient world, however, *tesserae* also
served as tallies, tickets, tokens, vouchers, permits, passwords, and
other forms of identification. In the mystery religions of antiquity, for
instance, *tesserae* were used to distinguish initiates from non-initiates.
Pieces of pottery would be broken in half, the halves distributed, and
these halves, when brought together at a later date, would allow for
mutual recognition among the faithful.[5] Even speech that is broken,
useless, and apparently insignificant—like a shard of pottery or an effaced coin—allows for self-identification and mutual recognition. In
this sense, the function of empty speech is nothing other than "the
pure function of language, which is to assure us that we are, and nothing more" (S 1, 157).

Not coincidentally, ancient Greeks also understood the *tessera* as a
symbolon. Like a *tessera*, a *symbolon* could be a ticket, a token, a mark, a
watchword, a permit, and even a license—any sign by which to make
inferences. More literally, though, a *symbolon* was something *thrown
or cast together* (from the prefix *syn-* meaning "together" and the verb
ballein meaning "to throw"). If *tesserae*, when brought together, could

allow for self-identification and mutual recognition, the etymology of the Greek *symbolon* allows us to isolate their basic sociological function: *bringing people together*. "Symbol means pact," Lacan reminds his readers, and the strongest pact-forming symbols in the ancient world were *gifts*, especially *useless gifts*. "The objects of symbolic exchange—vases made to remain empty, shields too heavy to be carried, sheaves that will dry out, lances that are thrust into the ground—are all destined to be useless, if not superfluous by their very abundance." The primary purpose of such gifts is not to transfer use-value but, instead, to form a community. "They are first and foremost signifiers of the pact they constitute as the signified" (*E*, 225). Symbolic commerce, not commodity exchange, is their basic function. So also with empty speech: Its utility as a means of community formation often coincides with its uselessness as a means of information exchange.

Hence, Lacan's turn to *communication* immediately after likening empty speech to a *tessera*. "Even if it communicates nothing, discourse represents the existence of communication," he writes (*E*, 209). As John Durham Peters has shown, "communication" descends from the Latin noun *communicatio*, which had nothing to do with union or unity, but instead meant a "sharing" or "imparting."[6] And not just any kind of sharing or imparting. In keeping with its verbal sibling *communicare*, meaning "to make common"—and in anticipation of the German *Mitteilung* on which Heidegger would later draw—*communicatio* referred to an act of sharing or imparting resulting in *commonality*. To communicate was at once to share something with others (commonality as "the common") but also, in so doing, to run the risk of making it ordinary, vulgar, polluted, and even profane (commonality as "the commons"). Communication was a *munus*—a service, a favor, a tribute, or, crucially, a gift—whose effect was always to some extent *communis*—not only shared and thus public but also contaminated and to this extent inferior. More than an amiable gift to the community, it was the ambiguous gift of community itself—at once the origin of human togetherness and, paradoxically, its greatest risk.

Empty speech functions similarly. Even as it traffics in error, misrecognition, and inauthenticity (contaminated forms), it tills the soil of human togetherness, provoking new forms of collective life (community formations). Like the collectivities evoked by chatter, idle talk, and the like, however, these new forms of collective life often come with additional forums for empty speech, allowing this vacuous way of speaking to extend its reach into any given community. Understanding how this occurs, especially in the midst of psychoanalytic technique, is the task to which we now turn.

Hollowed, Stuffed, and Leaning Together

If empty speech is "the first thing to make itself heard in analysis," then the first occurrence in any therapeutic session is not the transmission of information from patient to doctor but, instead, the establishment of doctor-patient relationship. In keeping with its irreducible status as communication, empty speech constitutes a profound, if polluted, sense of human togetherness. Lacan refers to this foundational sense of community as *intersubjectivity*. "When the subject begins an analysis, he accepts a position that is more constitutive in itself than all the orders by which he allows himself to be more or less taken in—the position of interlocution—and I see no disadvantage in the fact that this remark may leave the listener dumbfounded [*interloqué*]. For I shall take this opportunity to stress that the subject's act of addressing [*allocution*] brings with it an addressee [*allocutaire*]—in other words, that the speaker [*locuteur*] is constituted in it as intersubjectivity" (*E*, 214).

At first, this intersubjectivity is problematic. Instead of revealing the truth of the subject, empty speech allows the subject to resist this truth by "hooking on to the other," offsetting the transformative potential of intersubjectivity with an imaginary investment in "the system of the ego and the other." "The resistance in question projects its effects on the system of the ego, in as much as the system of the ego isn't even conceivable without the system, if one can put it this way, of the other. The ego has a reference to the other. The ego is constituted in relation to the other. It is correlative. The level on which the other is experienced locates exactly the level on which, quite literally, the ego exists for the subject" (*S* 1, 50).

If this dual relation persists, it is because the analyst fails to realize that she is complicit, and all too often mired, in the patient's resistance. "The patient's resistance is always your own," Lacan chides his colleagues, "and when a resistance succeeds it is because you are in it up to your neck" (*S* 3, 48). That empty speech is the medium—or, as Lacan would have it, the "agency" (*instance*)—of the patient's resistance only makes matters worse. When emptiness finds expression in a patient's discourse, the analyst often searches for "a reality beyond speech to fill the emptiness," Lacan explains. "This leads the analyst to analyze the subject's behavior in order to find in it what the subject is not saying. Yet for him to get the subject to admit to the latter, he obviously has to talk about it" (*E*, 206). Thus, even when "sounding the depths" of the patient's speech, in search of something "beyond the emptiness of his words," the analyst has only one medium on which to rely: *speech*. And the emptier the patient's speech becomes, the more inquisitive talk it tends to provoke from the analyst. Indeed, as Lacan is careful to remind fellow analysts, empty speech is "discourse that says nothing merely to make us speak" (*E*, 349). When acted upon, this compulsion to speak only serves to redouble the patient's ego-other relation, all the while tempting the analyst, once more, with the illusory hope of discovering something beyond the patient's speech to break its imaginary spell. "The emptier his discourse is, the more I too am led to catch hold of the other, that is to say, led into doing what one does all the time, in this famous analysis of the resistances, led into seeking out the beyond of his discourse—a beyond, you'll be careful to note, which is nowhere" (*S* 1, 51). Few circuits of analytic experience are more intransigent than this interpsychological play of egos and alter egos.

And this is just the beginning, for empty speech also invites patients and doctors alike to mediate their imaginary dyad through a "third party"—namely, the object. More specifically, it goads them with the prospect of verbal agreement on the object in question—an object which both of them mistakenly perceive as external to, expressed in, and ultimately at stake in their discourse (*S* 1, 108). In this sense, the system of the ego is not only the system of the other but also a "system of objects" (*système objectal*) or, as Lacan further specifies, a system determined by its "objective" (*objectif*).

In optical engineering, an objective is a visual medium (e.g., a lens or a mirror) that gathers light from an observed object and focuses it into a distinct image. In much the same way, the objective system which mediates the ego and its other is not a world of material objects but *a way of seeing this world* or, more to point, an *ideology*. Lacan does not use the word "ideology" here, but he certainly suggests as much, defining the objective system as "the accumulated prejudices which make up a cultural community, up to and including the hypotheses, the psychological prejudices even, from the most sophisticated generated by scientific work to the most naïve and spontaneous, which most certainly do not fail considerably to influence scientific references, to the point of impregnating them" (*S* 1, 108). In this "enormous objectification," Lacan worries that the truth of the subject will be entirely forgotten: "He will make an effective contribution to the collective undertaking in his daily work and will be able to occupy his leisure time with all the pleasures of a profuse culture which—providing everything from detective novels to historical memoirs and from educational lectures to the orthopedics of group relations—will give him the wherewithal to forget his own existence and his death, as well as to misrecognize the particular meaning of his life in false communication" (*E*, 233).

If full speech is true communication, empty speech is *false communication*. While the former "realizes the truth of the subject," the latter reveals "the subject's impotence to end up in the domain in which his truth is realized." At best, empty speech is communication in which the truth of the subject is left unsaid. At worst, it is communication in which the expression of this truth has become "fundamentally impossible." Instead of discovering himself anew in the transformative, historicizing effects of true speech, "the subject loses himself in the machinations of the system of language [*les machinations du système du langage*], in the labyrinth of referential systems made available to him by the state of cultural affairs to which he is a more or less interested party" (*S* 1, 49–50). In moments of empty speech, the ego hooks on to the other, and both set off in search of something beyond their discourse to fill its emptiness. Analytic experience becomes little more than an ideological state apparatus.

So much the worse for intersubjectivity. When emptiness prevails, "the plane of recognition in so far as speech links the subjects together into this pact which transforms them, and sets them up as human subjects communicating [*communiquant*]," gives way to "the plane of the *communiqué*, in which one can distinguish all sorts of levels, the call, discussion, knowledge, information, but which, in the final analysis, involves a tendency to reach an agreement on the objective [*l'objet*]" (*S* 1, 108; trans. modified). To be sure, both are planes of communication. But the *communiquant* which occurs on the plane of recognition rarely doubles as a *communiqué*. In English and French alike, a *communiqué* is an official report or announcement, usually sent in haste, typically addressed to a mass audience, and often appearing as a press release. Empty speech operates in much the same way. It reduces communication to informatics, intersubjectivity to image management, and the ultimate prospect of analytic experience—transformative revelation—to a recursive play of egos, alter egos, and ideological objectives. In moments of empty speech, interlocutors become hollow men, stuffed men, headpieces full of straw, leaning together, groping together, in hollow valleys of false communication (*E*, 234). In short, they become *das Man*.

Tessellations of Empty Speech

More than a community, the egos, alter egos, and ideological objectives of empty speech constitute a *crowd*. But again, as we saw in the dream of Irma's injection, it is "a structured crowd, like the Freudian crowd." In *Group Psychology and the Analysis of the Ego*, Freud argues that individual psychology is always, to some extent, social psychology. "In the individual's mental life someone else is invariably involved, as a model, as an object, as a helper, as an opponent" (*FR*, 627). Not coincidentally, all four of these egomorophic figures are present in Freud's iconic dream of Irma's injection, notably in the dream's second part, when his professional identity undergoes its spectral decomposition. Dr. M. serves as Freud's model, Leopold as his helper, Otto as his opponent, and Irma as the object of their pseudoscientific examination. As we have seen, this spectral decomposition comes at a high price, for it marks the disappearance of Freud himself. The cost of his professional absolution is his disappearance into an egomorphic crowd—a polycephalic figure composed of rigid yet brittle identifications.

As we also have seen, the speech of this many-headed figure is crucial to the meaning of Freud's dream. Like *Gerede*, Leopold's discourse is vague, ambiguous, equivocal, distracting, and groundless throughout. It is a botched attempt to close off and cover up the horrific, imaginary-real interiors of Irma's mouth. And, like *alltägliche Rede*, Dr. M.'s professional consolation is ridiculous yet oddly significant, nonsensical yet strangely effective. Although his "no matter" verges on idle talk, it ultimately eludes this vacuous way of speaking by making vacuity itself—the *Nichts* of "*macht nichts*"—a meaningful expression of solace, allowing Freud to shirk anxiety and being-towards-death, but only by disclosing the emptiness at the center of these worrisome states.

Taken together, the words of Freud's egomorphic peers form a cacophonous hubbub of senseless discourse. "With this trio of clowns, we see a rambling dialogue [*un dialogue à bâtons rompus*] built up around little Irma, closer in fact to a game of interrupted conversations [*jeu des propos interrompus*], and even to the well-known dialogue of the deaf [*dialogue bien connu de sourds*]," Lacan concludes. "The three of them are so ridiculous that anyone would seem like a god beside such absurd automata [*machines à absurdité*]" (*S 2*, 156). With each turn in this highly figurative, metonymic conclusion, Lacan brings us one step closer to the basic communicative structure of empty speech. Let us consider each of these figurative descriptions in turn.

To characterize the imaginary discourse in Freud's dream as *"un dialogue à bâtons rompus"* is not merely to describe it as "a rambling dialogue." To converse *à bâtons rompus* is speak freely, casually, and continuously about a wide range of topics, without ever allowing the conversation to settle on a single topic, much as old friends, when reunited after years apart, talk for hours on end, flitting from topic to topic without ever running out of things to discuss. In this sense, we might say that conversation *à bâtons rompus* is temporally constant yet topically discontinuous, much like the interjections of Holberg's talkative barber, the sermonizing of Kierkegaard's prattling priests, and the babbling of Heidegger's *Schwätzer*.

The literal meaning of this expression, "broken sticks," certainly suggests as much. In music, masonry, parquetry, textiles, and other visual arts, *bâtons rompus* refers to staggered, zigzagging lines and patterns. Note, for instance, the difference between chevron and herringbone designs. Unlike a simple chevron, where zigging and zagging shapes meet along perfectly straight axes, resulting in a fixed and orderly zigzag pattern (fig. 8.1), a herringbone design—also known as *bâtons rompus* in French—occurs when the zigging and zagging shapes break at reversal, resulting in a sharply stepped and seemingly restless zigzag pattern (fig. 8.2). If there is a pattern to the rambling dialogue of Freud's egomorphic peers, it is almost certainly that of a herringbone.

The metonymic shift from *"rompus"* to *"interrompus"* in Lacan's description above further supports this insight. If the discourse of Freud's egomorphic peers resembles a *"jeu des propos interrompus,"* it is because their statements *break into, break off,* and effectively *break apart* the very conversation they purport to sustain. Leopold begins by revealing "a

FIGURE 8.1. Chevron (*Point de Hongrie*). Figure 53 from the *Dictionnaire encyclopédique et biographique de l'industrie et des arts industriels*, vol. 7, ed. Eugène-Oscar Lami (Paris: Librairie des dictionnaires, 1887), 97.

FIGURE 8.2. Herringbone (*Bâtons Rompus*). Figure 54 from the *Dictionnaire encyclopédique et biographique de l'industrie et des arts industriels*, vol. 7, ed. Eugène-Oscar Lami (Paris: Librairie des dictionnaires, 1887), 97.

dull area low down on the left" of Irma's back, then quickly interjects with another discovery, hurtling the discussion in a new direction: "a portion of the skin on her left shoulder was infiltrated." At which point Dr. M. chimes in, addressing Leopold's latest discovery only in order to send their conversation in another new direction: "There's no doubt it's an infection, but no matter; dysentery will supervene and the toxin will be eliminated." From Irma's dull back to her infiltrated shoulder, to her infected skin, to her impending dysentery, the hurried zigs and harried zags of her examination are nothing if not *interrompu*. In keeping with the French expression on which Lacan is improvising—*jouer aux propos interrompus*—Leopold and Dr. M. are *talking at cross purposes*, unwittingly opposing each other's aims and insights. Like orthogonal shapes in a herringbone design, Leopold zigs one way then zags in another direction, and Dr. M. replies in turn, zigging in response Leopold's zag, but only to zag again in a new direction. Much to Lacan's amusement, their statements are as perpendicular to themselves as they are to each another. So much so, he quips, that their exchange of words, if indeed it functions as a dialogue at all, can be easily mistaken for a *dialogue de sourds*—a dialogue of the deaf.

It is tempting to interpret this quip as an extension Kierkegaard's earlier critique of ancient sophistic approaches to dialogue, which he likens to "eccentric antiphonal singing, in which everyone sings his part without regard to the other and there is a resemblance to conversation only because they do not all talk at once" (*CI*, 34). But there is nothing songlike—antiphonal or otherwise—about the dialogue which occurs between Freud's phantasmatic peers. Much as *rompus* gives way to *interrompus* in Lacan's description of their herringbone exchange, the *sourds* at work in their *dialogue de sourds* quickly morphs into the *absurdité* of his final comment on these egomorphic figures: "The three of them are so ridiculous that anyone would seem like a god beside such absurd automata [*machines à absurdité*]." In order to understand this final metonymic shift, we must read it to the letter. Between *les sourds* and *l'absurde* is a lineage of terms extending from the Latin *surdus*, meaning "inattentive" and "unresponsive." *Absurdus* is one of these terms, with meanings ranging from "silly," "stupid," and "senseless" (all of which suggest breakdowns of reason) to "incongruous," "dissonant," and, more figuratively, "out of tune" (all of which suggest breakdowns of rhyme). That *surdus* itself is a translation of the Arabic *assam*, and *assam* a translation of the Greek *alogos*, only strengthens this interpretation. Freud's colleagues are as a dumb as they are deaf, Lacan suggests. As *alogos*, their examination of Irma is at once senseless and, paradoxically, speechless.

Again, the herringbone structure of their discourse is instructive. Herringbone patterns operate according to the principle of periodic tiling known as *tessellation*. To tessellate a flat surface is to overlay it with a repeating geometric design, each iteration of which tightly adjoins several others (e.g., the illusion of cubes in fig. 8.3). This organizing principle also applies to the iterations themselves: Each repetition of this geometric design is itself a closed set of tightly fitted individual shapes known as *tessellae* (e.g., the diamonds of which the illusory cubes in figure 8.3 appear to be composed).

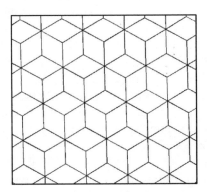

FIGURE 8.3. Tessellation. Source: https://geometricolor.wordpress.com/2012/08/22/doubling-the-tessellation-of-hexagons-and-triangles/.

That *tessella* is the diminutive form of the Latin *tessera*—the same word which, as we have seen, Lacan uses to describe empty speech—is essential here. If the discourse of Freud's egomorphic peers is *alogos*, it is because their individual words and the adjoining utterances into which they are tightly fitted form *a tessellation of empty speech*. The collective effect of their pronouncements is not a sophisticated medical account of Irma's lingering illness but, instead, the *illusion* of such an account—a semblance of intellectual depth, complexity, and resolve structured atop a restless, almost robotic repetition of patterned nonsense regarding her condition.

More than insightful peers, Freud's colleagues are "absurd automata" (*machines à absurdité*). Yet another reason to read Lacan's concluding description of their speech to the letter. Beneath *absurdus* and its Latin origin *surdus* is the Proto-Indo-European root *swer-*, meaning "to buzz." For better and for worse, the discourse of Leopold and Dr. M. hums along like a smooth-running, self-regulating, and remarkably senseless machine. Empty speech functions similarly. As we have seen, it subjects interlocutors to "the machinations of the system of language," fragmenting them into buzzing imaginary crowds of egos, alter egos, and ideological objectives. When these crowds intermingle, tessellations of empty speech begin to emerge. Communication becomes little more than a "mechanical movement" and thus "entirely analyzable in terms of mechanics" (*S* 1, 240).

To study the mechanics of empty speech, as Lacan would have us do, is to study "the automatic scraps of everyday discourse: rote-learning and delusional refrain, modes of communication perfectly reproduced by objects scarcely more complicated than this lectern, a feed-back construction for the former, a gramophone record, preferably perfectly scratched in the right places, for the latter" (*E*, 356–57). If empty speech has the visual appearance of a tessellated surface, in which tightly fitted geometric shapes repeat throughout, it has the sonic properties of an echo, a feedback loop, a skipping record—and usually all at once—the recursive mechanical racket of which can only be described as "a great cacophony." Indeed, what Lacan says about the discourse of Freud's colleagues is also true of empty speech more broadly: It is always, to some extent, a "hubbub of speech."

To further illustrate this cacophonous way of speaking, Lacan invites members of his canonical first seminar to consider the inarticulate yet all-engulfing sounds of a mill wheel in motion. Empty speech is "the mill-wheel whereby human desire is ceaselessly mediated by re-entering the system of language," he explains. "What we go on and on about, often in a confused, scarcely articulate fashion, are the subject's imaginary relations to the constructions of his ego" (*S* 1, 179). Elsewhere, notably in "The Function and Field of Speech and Language in Psychoanalysis," he likens his attempt to reposition spoken discourse at the center of analytic theory and technique to an exercise in incremental lifting, "as if a heavy mill wheel had fallen on speech" (*E*, 211). In empty speech, this cumbersome mill wheel continues to turn, despite its fallen state—and is all the noisier as a result.

All of which further suggests that Leopold and Dr. M. are *motor mouths*. Like teeth rattling against teeth—molar against molar in service to the mill of empty speech (all from the Latin *molere*, meaning "to grind")—their utterances grate against the animality of spoken discourse implicit in Aristotle's *zoon echon logon*, suggesting that we are neither rational animals nor speaking beasts but, instead, *senseless speech machines*. And yet, as Lacan well notes, again and again, mindless mechanical utterances like those of Freud's egomorphic peers are the warp and woof of analytic technique. But how, exactly, are we to understand this refrain, especially given the foregoing discussion?

Truth from Behind

According to Lacan, the pathway of analytic technique has always been "the pathway of chatter [*le voie de bavardage*]" (*E*, 573; trans. modified). And the pathway of chatter, he goes on to argue, echoing Kierkegaard and Heidegger before him, stretches back to ancient notions of *adoleschia*. In Plato's endorsement of "an art which seems to be useless and is called by most people mere loquacity [*adoleschias*]," Lacan sees "the foreshadowing of what we call in our crude language . . . free associations."[7] And in the free associations generated by the patient's "constant 'chatting' [«*jaspinage*» *sans répit*]," he claims that psychoanalysis finds "its means of action and even its modes of examination" (370).

If errant chatter fuels analytic technique, the latter, in turn, tills the soil for true speech. "The subject's discourse normally unfolds—this is a genuine bit of Freud—within the order of error, of misrecognition, even of negation," Lacan explains at the end of his first seminar. "But—this is the novelty—during analysis, within this discourse which unfolds in the register of error, something happens whereby the truth irrupts" (*S* 1, 265). For it is "neither simply the obtuse pressure nor the static-like noise of the unconscious tendency that makes itself heard in this discourse, but the interferences of its voice" (*E*, 370).

We have heard this voice before. Recall the "prop . . . prop . . . prop" of *"propyl, propyls . . . propionic acid"* in the second part of Freud's dream, following his colleagues' absurd examination of Irma. That Freud traced these "props" to his memory of the foul-smelling gift delivered by Otto the day before is not surprising. *Tagesreste*—the day-residues of which dreams are often made—are often just as vacuous as empty utterances. They are "the stray forms which have become, for the subject, of minimal importance—and are emptied of their meaning" (S 1, 245). But in the emptiness of these forms, another discourse, the discourse of the unconscious, begins to speak. "It is within this vacuum, within this hollow, with what thus becomes working materials, that the deep secret discourse gains expression. We see it in the dream, but we also rediscover it in the slip of the tongue and throughout the psychopathology of everyday life" (S 1, 247).

Just as dreams often begin with day-residues but rarely end there, so also does analysis begin with the patient's empty speech, but only in order help them fill it with intersubjective truth. "That is our starting-point for listening to the person who speaks to us," Lacan soberly concludes. "And we only have to refer back to our definition of the discourse of the unconscious, which is that it is the discourse of the other, to understand how it authentically links up again with intersubjectivity in the dialogue, that full realization of speech" (S 1, 247).

This is not to suggest that the transition from empty speech to full speech is smooth, fluid, or eloquent in the least. On the contrary, when full speech begins to find expression in empty speech, it usually does so by way of mistake, in turbulent moments of disfluency. "In analysis, truth emerges in the most clearcut representative of the mistake—the slip, the action which one, improperly, calls *manquée* [missed, failed, abortive]." "Improperly" because, as Lacan goes on to show, "abortive actions are actions which succeed, those of our words which come to grief are words which own up. These acts, these words reveal a truth from behind. Within what we call free associations, dream images, symptoms, a word bearing the truth is revealed. If Freud's discovery has any meaning, it is that—truth grabs error by the scruff of the neck in the mistake" (S 1, 265). Hesitations, repairs, awkward pauses, interruptions of every sort—these are not barriers to truth but, instead, its conditions of possibility. On this point, Lacan is insistent: "The moment when the subject interrupts himself is usually the most significant moment in his approach towards the truth" (52). Even when it stumbles—especially when it stumbles—empty speech paves the way for full speech.

Clearly, Freud understood *"propyl, propyls . . . propionic acid"* as an error. "I dreamt of propyl after having smelt amyl," he admits. And as we have seen, this error doubled as an interruption, at once cutting off and breaking away from his colleagues' empty speech, effectively shifting the course of the dream toward *"trimethylamin"* and its chemical formula, with all of their oral, sexual, infectious, and repulsive connotations. Although the collective meaning of these connotations returned Freud, once more, to the horrific contents of Irma's mouth, they did so from the vantage point of "organic chemistry," thereby inviting a retrospective account of his earlier conversation with Otto. More than a mistaken, failed, or abortive utterance, then, *"propyl, propyls . . . propionic acid"* was a stammering yet successful catalyst in this analytic remembrance. In its repetitive, mechanical "props," the gears of empty speech are beginning to grind out another discourse, the discourse of an other, the discourse of the unconscious—and with it the first few murmurs of full speech. Where the register of error once prevailed, subjugating Freud to the misrecognitions of his ego, the discourse of truth begins to find expression, conditioning the possibility of his resubjectivization. It is to this expression, and each of its "props," that we now turn.

NINE

A Play of Props

A Guessing Game

According to Lacan, the discourse of Freud's egomorphic peers is like a rambling dialogue, a game of interrupted conversations, a dialogue of the deaf, and a ridiculous interaction between absurd automata. As we saw in chapter 8, each of these descriptors sheds a unique light on the communicative practice of empty speech. Their sequential relation also bears mention. The order in which these descriptors appear suggests that empty speech ranges from spoken discourse to mechanical noise, even and especially as it approaches full speech.

Not surprisingly, this shift from speech to noise is well represented in Freud's iconic dream. What begins as an articulate yet nonsensical discussion of Irma's condition ends with the repetitive mechanical clamor of *prop . . . prop . . . prop* in *"propyl, propyls . . . propionic acid."* And this clamor, in turn, sets the stage for *"trimethylamin,"* its chemical formula, and ultimately Freud's retrospective account of his earlier conversation with Otto—an account which, however mundane, can be shown to operate as full speech. How are we to understand this strange progression from empty speech to its full counterpart?

To be sure, there is more to *"propyl, propyls . . . propionic acid"* than a sputtering start toward full speech. As we have seen, it also marks a failed attempt to avoid the organic compound and chemical formula that precipitated Freud's retrospective discourse. If the metonymic shift from *propyl* to *propyls* to *propionic acid* has a stuttering sonic shape—*prop . . . prop . . . prop*—it is precisely for this reason: Freud's polycephalic self, as embodied in the ego identifications of Leopold, Dr. M., and Otto, is eager to repress and avoid any return of the ghastly contents of Irma's mouth; but his acephalic self, initially hidden behind this egomorphic crowd, cannot help but interject, returning the dream to this horrific centerpiece—albeit from the safe, sublimated distance of "organic chemistry."

And this is where things get interesting, for in place of his ego's traumatic encounter with the imaginary-real in Irma's mouth, and the spectral decomposition of his professional identity immediately thereafter, Freud's unconscious delivers a sequence of chemical signifiers, transforming the dream into a pseudo-scientific inquiry of sorts: The amyl stench of Otto's liquor bottle leads to the propyl preparation of his dirty syringe, which leads to the sexual chemistry of trimethylamine as revealed by Fliess, which leads to the sterile image of trimethylamine's chemical formula. No longer the passive subject of a traumatic encounter with the imaginary-real, Freud reemerges in the dream's conclusion as the active agent of a pseudo-scientific guessing game, the master and commander of an allusive play of signifiers—"propyl, methyl, and so on"—in the field of organic chemistry.

Freud did not make much of this guessing game in July 1895. From amyl to propyl to propyls to propionic acid to trimethylamine, "substitutions of this kind are perhaps legitimate in organic chemistry," he concluded, all but dismissing this strange sequence of chemical signifiers. Only the first term in this signifying chain—amyl—caught his attention at the time, and only in connection to Otto's fetid gift of the previous day: "The smell of fusel oil (amyl . . .) evidently stirred up in my mind a recollection of the whole series." Curiously, Lacan paid even less attention to this chain of signifiers in his re-analysis of the dream, limiting his discussion of this series to its final term: trimethylamine. What are we to make of the alliterative sequence of "props" that occurs between the day-residue of "amyl" that intrigued Freud and the dream work of "*trimethylamin*" that interested Lacan?

Crucial to the interpretation of "*propyl, propyls . . . propionic acid*," as we shall see, is the concept of *repetition*, especially as understood by Freud and retheorized by Lacan. With this final conceptual turn, I hope to reveal a long-standing yet largely untraversed bridge between their otherwise distinct accounts of this canonical dream. Between Freud's analysis and Lacan's re-analysis, this chapter considers an object of critical inquiry that on first glance seems to be little more than a passing stutter in the dream's conclusion, but on second glance presents itself as the quilting point of the entire dream—a quilting point that well illustrates the therapeutic shift from empty speech to full speech that Lacan, during his "return to Freud," found integral to analytic theory and technique.

Medical Drama

In keeping with chapters 7 and 8, we should begin by reading Freud's "props" to the letter. In Middle Low German, a *prop* was a "plug." By the nineteenth-century, *prop* had become *Pfropf,* meaning "stopper" or, more precisely, "cork." Hence, the substitution of "propyl" for "amyl" in Freud's dream. When his pregnant wife opened Otto's fetid bottle of liquor the evening before, it released a disgusting smell of "fusel oil (amyl . . .)"—so disgusting, in fact, that Freud "refused to touch it," much less allow anyone in his household to drink from it. Just as someone should have stopped Otto from giving injections with a dirty syringe, so also did his rancid bottle of liquor require a stopper, a cork, a *Pfropf.* That *Pfropf* is also the medical term for a clot, specifically a thrombus—a clot of coagulated blood formed in a blood vessel and attached to its site of origin—is also telling in this context. Otto's dirty syringe reminded Freud of a former patient who was currently suffering from "phlebitis" (*Venenentzündung*), almost certainly "caused by a dirty syringe." And this, in turn, reminded him of his wife, "who had suffered from thrombosis [*Venenstauungen*] during one of her pregnancies." In this sense, the *Pfropf* required to protect Freud's pregnant wife from Otto's fetid gift was also the *Pfropf* from which she once suffered.

Yet another reason to read *"propyl, propyls . . . propionic acid"* as a divided, stop-and-go expression. If its "props" are torn between motives of avoidance and approach, repulsion and attraction, it is partly because the network of *Pfropfen* implicit in Freud's dream is similarly split. Consider, for instance, the subtle yet important semantic gap between the *Venenentzündung* of his former patient and the *Venenstauungen* of his pregnant wife. Again, Freud's original German is revealing. An *Entzündung* is an "inflammation," but it can also mean "ignition," verging on terms like *Zündfunken,* meaning "ignition spark," and, even more suggestively, *Anlasszündkerze,* meaning "spark plug." An *Entzündung* is a *Pfropf* that starts the engine of a machine, usually in anticipation of the machine's movement. In sharp contrast, the *Stauung* in *Venenstauungen* suggests images of "congestion," "stasis," "jamming," and even "choking."[1] A *Stauung* is a *Pfropf* in which mechanical movement grinds to an idling halt, usually in anticipation of resumed motion—not unlike the handkerchief Gert Westphaler stuffs into his mouth at the end of Holberg's play, briefly jamming the oral machinery on which his chatter depends. In light of these semantic differences, we might say that the *Venenentzündung* of Freud's former patient indexes the motive of approach in *"propyl, propyls . . . propionic acid,"* while the *Venenstauungen* of his pregnant wife indexes its motive of avoidance. The former designates the "go" while the latter designates the "stop" in this overtly stop-and-go expression.

The *Pfropfen* of *"propyl, propyls . . . propionic acid"* are also connected by way of scent. Between the amyl aroma of Otto's rancid gift and the fishy stench of trimethylamine, we find propionic acid—a translucent liquid with an equally unpleasant odor, produced by the metabolic breakdown of fatty acids. The bacteria that produce propionic acid are often found in the stomachs of cud-chewing animals like cattle, goats, sheep, and the like. But they are also present in human sweat glands, providing human body odor with its uniquely pungent scent. Other species of *Propionibacteria* live elsewhere in the human body, and some are indicated by visual more than olfactory signs. *Propionibacterium acnes*, for instance, lives mainly in the oil glands of the human face and contributes to the development of its English namesake. With puberty, it would seem, come the smells as well as the sights of propionic acid.

All of this points to Freud's relationship with the colleague mentioned in his dream's analysis: Wilhelm Fliess. As commenters have often noted, "Irma" was a stand-in for Emma Eckstein, an early patient of Freud's who suffered from severe nasal pains, often accompanied by bloody secretions.[2] Freud suspected that her nosebleeds were psychogenic but encouraged her to contact Fliess for a second opinion. Fliess decided that nasal surgery was required and traveled to Vienna in February 1895 to perform the procedure. And this is where the trouble began, as Freud informed Fliess in their correspondence the following spring, adding captions to a series of events that would eventually culminate in the dream of Irma's injection.

Two weeks after her surgery, Eckstein was still experiencing painful nosebleeds. Moreover, "a bone chip the size of a heller" had emerged from her surgical wound, accompanied by "two bowlfuls of pus," Freud wrote to Fliess, initiating what would soon become an about-face in their close friendship. At the same time, her surgical wound had begun to swell, "going up and down 'like an avalanche'" (a play on the German expression, "life is like an avalanche, up and down"). Then, while attempting to irrigate her wound, Freud met with considerable "resistance," encountering "an obstacle" of some kind—probably from another bone chip. So he requested the assistance of another surgeon, Robert Gersuny, who installed "a drainage tube" in Eckstein's wound and threatened to "break it open" if this tube did not reduce her swelling and reestablish regular "discharge."

Freud also noticed a "fetid odor" coming from Eckstein's nose and mouth. So he called upon another specialist, Ignaz Rosanes. While cleaning Eckstein's wound, Rosanes "removed some sticky blood clots" (*zog Blutgerinnsel heraus*). Then, all of a sudden, he "pulled at something like a thread" (*zog er an etwas wie einem Faden*)—and he "kept on pulling" (*zog weiter an*). "Before either of us had time to think, at least half a meter of gauze had been removed [*herausbefördert*] from the cavity," Freud reports to Fliess. "The next moment came a flood of blood [*Blutstrom*]. The patient turned white, her eyes bulged, and she had no pulse." In less than a minute, Eckstein was flat on her back, covered with blood, and "beyond recognition" (trans. modified). This was more than a massive hemorrhage. From clots to thread to fetid gauze—with each *Zug* came another, more extreme *Herausziehen*, from the German verb of the same name, meaning "to unplug." And with each *Herausziehen*, Eckstein veered closer to death. So close, in fact, that Freud went on to describe her *Blutstrom* as a *Verblutungsszene*—"a scene of bleeding to death."

Freud's response to this horrific turn of events was nearly as dramatic. But it was not the surge of blood that sent him reeling. Instead, it was the gauze itself. He refers to it as a *Fremdkörper*, a "foreign body," but also, more precisely, an "impurity," a "contamination," a "piece of debris." "At the moment the foreign body came out [*herauskam*] and everything became clear to me—and I immediately afterward was confronted by the sight of the patient—I felt sick." And not just sick: As Freud later confessed to Fliess, he felt completely "overwhelmed" by the sight of Eckstein—colorless, flat on her back, eyes bulging, and covered in blood. "Strong emotions [*Affekte*] were welling up in me," he recounts. So many, so fast, that once Rosanes had finished packing her nasal cavity with fresh gauze, Freud "fled to the next room, drank a bottle of water, and [still] felt miserable." Only after downing a glass of cognac did he regain some semblance of his former self. By the time he returned to Eckstein's side, still "somewhat shaky," she had regained conscious and enough of her former self to quip, "So this is the strong sex."

At first, Freud blamed Rosanes. Just as his wife should not have uncorked Otto's contaminated bottle of liquor, threatening to poison everyone in their household, Rosanes should not have tugged on the thread he found in Eckstein's nasal cavity, effectively uncorking Fliess' fetid patient, with near-fatal consequences as well. "He should immediately have thought, There is something inside; I shall not pull it out [*ich zieh es nicht heraus*] lest there be a hemorrhage." In fact, Rosanes should have done just the opposite: "stuff it some more." By packing additional gauze into her wound, he could have plugged it further, thereby guarding against any surprise hemorrhages, and thus allowing for Eckstein's safe transport to a better-equipped medical facility. But this would have been asking too much, Freud admits, for Rosanes was "just as surprised as I was" when the thread appeared.

To be sure, Rosanes played a part in this medical tragedy. And Freud himself was even willing to share the blame. But it was Fliess, more than either of them, who set the stage for Eckstein's near fatality. Though it pained Freud to admit this, admit it he did—and in no uncertain terms. "She was not at all abnormal," he wrote to Fliess. But the cause of her near-death experience certainly was: "A piece of iodoform gauze had gotten torn off as you were removing it and stayed in for fourteen days, preventing healing; at the end it tore off and provoked the bleeding."

This medical drama of packed gauze versus profuse blood continued for months after Eckstein's operation. "Gloomy times, unbelievably gloomy," Freud informed Fliess later that spring. Even when stuffed with fresh gauze, her nose continued to swell and hemorrhage. "New packing, renewed perplexity," Freud laments. So much perplexity that Eckstein nearly bled to death again on two separate occasions. Once in March: "When they lifted the packing to examine her, renewed hemorrhage, so that she almost died." And again in April: "As soon as the packing was partly removed [*halb heraus was*], there was a new, life-threatening hemorrhage which I witnessed. It did not spurt, it surged. Something like a [fluid] level rising extraordinarily rapidly, and then overflowing everything." Again, Freud found himself "very shaken," and much as before, he blamed Fliess: "to think that such a mishap could have arisen from the operation, which was purported to be harmless." In the end, Freud could only grieve for Eckstein: "I have given up hope for the poor girl and am inconsolable."[3]

If Otto was to blame for Irma's lingering illness in the dream, Fliess was to blame for the lingering illness of her counterpart in reality. Hence, the easy shift from propionic acid to trimethylamine in Freud's dream. If the pubescent undertones of the propionic acid contained in Otto's dirty syringe could give way to the sexual chemistry of trimethylamine as observed by Fleiss—an otherwise abrupt transition from the apparent thoughtlessness of one colleague to the seeming brilliance of another—it is because Fliess' reflections on trimethylamine were intimately connected to his purported expertise on the human nose—expertise which Freud could not help but question, again and again, in the wake of Eckstein's botched surgery, much as his dream casts repeated doubts on Otto's skill as a physician.

Add to this the dramatic play of *Pfropfen* in Eckstein's medical history, and the stuttering series of "props" leading up to *"trimethylamin"* shows itself, once more, to be a defining moment in Freud's dream. From start to finish, the Eckstein tragedy was a dialectic of plugged openings resulting in the buildup of fluids and unplugged openings allowing for their escape. And like most complex dialectics, it also yielded hybrid, intermediate phenomena like plugged openings with unplugging effects and unplugged openings with plugging effects. All are on display in Freud's account of Eckstein's medical history. It was in hopes of preventing future nosebleeds (a plugging intention) that Fliess removed part of one of Eckstein's turbinate bones (an unplugging procedure). But he left a large piece of surgical gauze in her nasal cavity, along with several bone chips (a series of plugs). One of these bone chips subsequently emerged from the wound, accompanied by secretions of pus (an unplugging sequence), but other bone chips presumably remained inside, causing her surgical wound to swell and preventing its irrigation (a plugging effect). So Gersuny inserted a drainage tube (another plug of sorts) in hopes of allowing the fluid to escape (an unplugging function). Later, while removing blood clots from her wound (another unplugging procedure), Rosanes discovered a thread (yet another plug). When he tugged on the thread, Fliess' forgotten gauze emerged, followed by a surge of blood (another, even more dramatic unplugging sequence, underwritten, once again, by the German verb *herausziehen*, meaning "to unplug"). While Rosanes packed her gaping wound with fresh gauze, Freud welled-up with affect, then water, and finally cognac (an equally dramatic plugging sequence). And as we have seen, this plug-unplug dialectic continued for months: fresh packing to stop Eckstein's bleeding (additional plugs) followed by renewed hemorrhaging once this packing was removed (further unplugging), followed by fresh packing to stop her bleeding (additional plugs) . . . and so on.

If Irma represents Eckstein and Otto represents Fliess, as scholars have suggested for years, then we can no longer afford to ignore the connection between *"propyl, propyls . . . propionic acid"* and the dramatic play of *Pfropfen* from which Eckstein continually suffered.[4] More than a stop-and-go advance toward *"trimethylamin,"* the "prop . . . prop . . . prop" of this fitful expression is a recurring testament to the fact that the founding dream of Freudian psychoanalysis was itself premised on the near-fatal treatment of one of its first patients. With each "prop," we hear a pointed reference to the traumatic play of *Pfropfen* in which Eckstein repeatedly verged on death—a ghastly matrix of bones, tubes, clots, threads, and gauze, some of which held back while others gave way to blood, pus, infection, stench, and the like.

Insistent Trauma

What Freud sees in Irma's throat, sidesteps in the discourse of his ego-morphic peers, returns to in the expression *"propyl, propyls . . . propionic acid,"* and eventually sublimates in the chemical formula of trimethyl-amine is a ghastly representation of his esteemed colleague's near-fatal malpractice. This recursive sequence of dream events—trauma, resis-tance, return, sublimation—can be shown to operate at three different registers of analytic repetition. Taken together, these three conceptual registers allow us to account for the progression of Freud's dream from the imaginary-real contained in Irma's mouth to the symbolic-real outlined in the chemical formula of trimethylamine. Moreover, they provide us with a final, summative series of insights into the linguis-tic structures and communicative effects of empty speech and its full counterpart.

The first form of analytic repetition at work in Freud's dream is also the most obvious. As we have seen, the dream of Irma's injection was a phantasmatic reprise of several traumatic events in Eckstein's medical history—events which Freud was clearly struggling to forget, as indi-cated by his failure to mention Eckstein at any point in his otherwise extensive analysis of the dream. Lacan borrows a term from Aristotle to describe traumatic events of his sort: *tuché.* In his eleventh seminar, he translates *tuché* as an *"encounter with the real . . . as if by chance."*[5] As *tuché,* the real emerges as a radical, unassimilable, apparently acciden-tal, and, for all these reasons, traumatic life event. Experiences of the real as *tuché* can range from painful past events (like Freud's struggle to help Eckstein) to phantasmatic representations of these events in dreams (like his subsequent dream of Irma's injection).

Lacan even goes so far as to suggest that fantasy operates in strict correspondence with the real: "The real supports the phantasy, the phantasy protects the real" (*S* 11, 41). In particular, he claims they are connected by way of *repetition*, the traumatic imagery of the dream being but a veiled recurrence of traumatic-real events from the past. "The phantasy is never anything more than the screen that conceals something quite primary, something determinant in the function of repetition," he explains (60). "At the very heart of the primary processes, we see preserved the insistence of the trauma in making us aware of its existence." In the illusory present of the dream, traumatic past events "emerge repeatedly" (55).

Freud's dream was no exception. The appalling image he beholds in Irma's mouth is the "very face" of his traumatic experience of Eckstein's postoperative suffering—namely, "the screen that shows us that it is still there behind" (*S* 11, 55). In Irma's mouth, Freud finds a condensed, phantasmatic representation of Eckstein's near-death experiences, each of which, as a radical point in the real, could not help but shock, overwhelm, and traumatize him anew. Specifically, he finds an imaginary-real amalgam of the various *Pfropfen* around which her near-death experiences were structured. Implicit in the scabs and curly structures he discovered in Irma's mouth were all of the bones, tubes, clots, threads, pus, and gauze he discovered in Eckstein's nasal cavity. Much of his dream and most its subsequent analysis orbits this horrific amalgam, adhering to its repetitive logic.

Like the whitish grey scabs atop bits of turbinal bone inside Irma's mouth, several other key images in Freud's dream are connected to her lingering illness and, by extension, to that of Eckstein as well. The hall, Irma's pale and puffy appearance, Freud's reproach, his fear of missing an organic illness, Dr. M.'s appearance, Otto's injection—all refer to the contents of Irma's mouth and thus repeat, once again, traumatic moments in Eckstein's medical history. Even Irma's complaint—"it's choking me"—reinforces this connection, if only making use of the German verb *schnüren*, from the noun *Schnur*, meaning "cord," "twine," and, crucially, "string"—a glaring allusion to the thread Rosanes discovered in Eckstein's mouth.

Some of these images also point elsewhere. The scabby turbinal bones in Irma's mouth, for instance, gesture beyond Freud's traumatic encounters with Eckstein's suffering, recalling other stricken figures from his past: another female patient who followed Freud's example in her use of cocaine and developed extensive necrosis; his dearly departed friend who went even further in his emulation, overdosing on cocaine injections; and even Freud himself, whose "cocaine treatments" had resulted in troublesome nasal swellings of his own (swellings on which Fliess also operated while in Vienna for Eckstein's surgery). Likewise, the white patch in Irma's mouth points beyond Eckstein's medical plight to that of Freud's eldest daughter, Mathilde. Other images follow suit, rehashing separate yet similarly traumatic events in Freud's medical practice. Dr. M's diagnosis recalls the "toxic state" of another female patient and, again, the illness of Freud's eldest daughter. Irma's infiltrated left shoulder, in turn, refers Freud to his own struggle with rheumatism. Dysentery, meanwhile, reminds him of the constipated young man whom he sent on a tragic sea voyage. And Otto's injection, beyond its reference to Eckstein's botched surgery, directs Freud, once more, to the death of his dear friend. We could go on tracing these images, but the point seems clear enough: Like the horrific representation in Irma's mouth, each of these images is an anxious repetition of one or more traumatic mishaps in Freud's medical practice—mishaps resulting in the prolonged suffering of other patients, close friends, family members, and even Freud himself.

"An Other Scene"

As a therapeutic technique, psychoanalysis attempts to perforate the phantasmatic imagery of our dreams, exposing the traumatic encounters with the real that lurk within—and behind—this imagery. "The real has to be sought beyond the dream—in what the dream has enveloped, hidden from us, behind the lack of representation of which there is only one representative," Lacan insists. "This is the real that governs our activities more than any other and it is psychoanalysis that designates it for us" (S 11, 60). Although it punctures the phantasms of our dreams, exposing their traumatic-real origins, psychoanalysis does not discard these images. On the contrary, much as empty speech simultaneously evades and conditions moments of full speech, and thus warrants careful consideration in analytic experience, the phantasmatic imagery of our dreams is at once an unwitting repetition of traumatic past experience and the condition of possibility for the therapeutic remembering of this painful experience.

Freud seems to have known as much. In his 1914 essay "Remembering, Repeating, and Working-Through," he not only distinguishes between repetition and remembering, but also claims that the compulsion to repeat can become a motive for remembering.[6] Later, in *Beyond the Pleasure Principle*, he underscores the difficulty of this shift from repetition to remembering, especially when preceded by repeated encounters with the traumatic-real. We have a tendency to repress painful past events, he explains, only to have them return at a later date as similarly traumatic specters, effectively repeating these events in the present instead of remembering them for what they are—namely, moments in our past. "What appears to be reality," Freud concludes, "is in fact only a reflection of a forgotten past" (*FR*, 602).

Clearly, dreams were on his mind (*FR*, 598). But he also realized that repetitions of this sort can occur in our waking lives—and often at our own behest. To illustrate this strangely willful phenomenon, Freud recalls his grandson Ernst, who often had a curious response to his mother's departure. Instead of crying when she left the room, he would throw toys and other small objects into corners, under beds, and so on. "As he did this he gave vent to a loud, long-drawn-out 'o-o-o-o', accompanied by an expression of interest and satisfaction" (*FR*, 599). Freud and the boy's mother both suspected that his "o-o-o-o" was a garbled expression of the German word *fort*, meaning "gone." One day, while visiting his grandson, Freud was able to confirm this suspicion:

The child had a wooden reel with a piece of string tied round it. It never occurred to him to pull it along the floor behind him, for instance, and play at its being a carriage. What he did was to hold the reel by the string and very skillfully throw it over the edge of his curtained cot, so that it disappeared into it, at the same time uttering his expressive "o-o-o-o." He then pulled the reel out of the cot again by the string and hailed its reappearance with a joyful "*da*" [meaning "there" but also, in this context, "here"]. This, then, was the complete game—disappearance and return. (*FR*, 599)

In Freud's view, Ernst was repeating at the level of a game the distressing experience of his mother's frequent absence. What he was unable to prevent in his everyday life (traumatic-real object loss) became an occasion for his overt control at the level of the game (phantasmatic representation). "At the outset he was in a *passive* situation—he was overpowered by the experience; but, by repeating it, unpleasurable though it was, as a game, he took on an *active* part" (*FR*, 600). In playing *fort-da*, Ernst was able to offset his passive experience of the real with an active mastery in the realm of the symbolic. With each *fort*, he avenged, anticipated, and even willed his mother's departure; and with each *da*, he determined, controlled, and celebrated her eventual return anew. "We can now see that the subject here does not simply master his deprivation by assuming it," Lacan summarizes. "For his action destroys the object that it causes to appear and disappear by *bringing about* its absence and presence in advance." If indeed *fort-da* is a game, as Freud suggests, it is a game of "banishing summons" (*E*, 262).

This brings us to second form of analytic repetition at work in Freud's dream. What the discourse of his egomorphic peers banishes is also what the expression *"propyl, propyls . . . propionic acid"* summons— namely, the horrendous phantasm contained in Irma's mouth, a ghastly representation of Freud's traumatic-real experience of Eckstein's pro- longed suffering. Whether the discourse of Dr. M., Leopold, and Otto is a rambling dialogue, a game of interrupted conversations, a dialogue of the deaf, or a ridiculous exchange between absurd automata, its pur- pose remains the same: distracting Freud from the ghastly image in Irma's mouth and the traumatic-real events figured therein. That their senseless examination of Irma quickly shifts from her mouth to her torso to her shoulder, interspersed with images of Dr. M.'s poor health, is in strict keeping with this rhetorical purpose. With each of these metonymic shifts, Freud's egomorphic peers exclaim *"fort,"* and with each of its alliterations, *"propyl, propyls . . . propionic acid,"* replies *"da."*

Irma's torso, Irma's shoulder, Dr. M's poor health—each receives its own "prop." This sequence of "props" marks a significant interven- tion in his colleagues' ridiculous examination of Irma. So significant, in fact, that it begins to reverse the diversionary flow of their empty speech, threatening to redirect the dreaming Freud to the horrendous pile of *Pfropfen* he initially discovered in Irma's mouth (a phantasmatic representation) and, by extension, to the series of *Pfropfen* in which Eckstein's real-world suffering found repeated expression (a repressed trauma). What the empty speech of his colleagues allows him to re- sist, the *Pfropfen* implicit in *"propyl, propyls . . . propionic acid"* attempts to recall from another location, the location of an other, or, as Freud specifies in his theory of the unconscious, "an other scene" (*ein anderer Schauplatz*).

From *Tuché* to *Automaton*

To be sure, the *Pfropfen* implicit in *"propyl, propyls . . . propionic acid"* are closely connected to the *Pfropfen* Freud discovered in Irma's mouth, as well as the *Pfropfen* he endured alongside Eckstein. But they are not equivalent. As we have seen, the *Pfropfen* of Eckstein's prolonged suf- fering and the *Pfropfen* in Irma's mouth are all anchored in the real. Indeed, as Lacan is careful to insist, "The place of the real . . . stretches from the trauma to the phantasy" (*S* 11, 60). In stark contrast, the *Pfropfen* at work in *"propyl, propyls . . . propionic acid"* are all anchored in the symbolic. More precisely, they are anchored in a *fort-da* game, the very game in which Freud, according to Lacan, discovered how "the child is born into language" (*E*, 262).

More precisely still, the *Pfropfen* of *"propyl, propyls . . . propionic acid"* are anchored in a *fort-da* guessing game. In the first part of this guessing game—the *fort* part—Freud's polycephalic self flits from symptom to symptom in search of what ails poor Irma, avoiding the ghastly contents of her mouth by venturing a series of guesses on the underlying cause of her illness instead. In the second part of this guessing game—the *da* part—Freud's acephalic self commandeers this play of symptoms, shifting the game's objective from the enigmatic cause of Irma's lingering illness to the obvious origin of Eckstein's prolonged suffering—namely, Wilhelm Fliess.

Instead of culminating in an indictment of his illustrious colleague, however, the second part of Freud's guessing game ranges from *"propyl, propyls . . . propionic acid"* to *"trimethylamin"* and its chemical formula, traversing a "whole series" of chemical substitutions ("propyl, methyl, and so on"), only to end, at the height of his dream's analysis, in praise of Fliess' keen insights regarding "the chemistry of sexual processes." Indeed, by the time Freud arrives at the chemical formula of trimethylamine in his analysis of the dream, the ghastly amalgam of *Pfropfen* he initially encountered in Irma's mouth—a phantasmatic representation of the traumatic-real events for which Fliess was clearly responsible—has become little more than a passing, parenthetical note: "(Cf. the three curly structures in Irma's throat.)" How are we to account for this mitigating turn of events?

Again, much depends on our reading of *"propyl, propyls . . . propionic acid."* From the vantage point of Freud's analysis, notably his analysis of trimethylamine and its chemical formula, this alliterative sequence of "props" appears to be the final word of his polycephalic self, rather than first pronouncement of his acephalic self. While the *fort* of his colleagues' empty speech allows for a repetitive, metonymic escape from his traumatic encounters with the real (as *tuché*), the *da* of *"propyl, propyls . . . propionic acid"* paves the way for what is arguably the most common, and certainly the most hazardous, effect of this ordinary way of speaking: not the recollection of traumatic past events in moments of full speech (a retrospective, resubjectivization of the *tuché*) but, instead, the repressive desublimation of these events in more empty speech, allowing traumatic encounters with the real to be at once indexed, abstracted, and further forgotten (a repetitive, desubjectivization of the *tuché*).

Clearly, the shift from *"propyl, propyls . . . propionic acid"* to *"trimethylamin"* and its chemical formula recalls the horrific contents of Irma's mouth and, by extension, those of Eckstein's medical history. But it does so from the safe, sterile, and thoroughly symbolic distance of "organic chemistry." What begins as an acutely personal dream, with Freud "collecting all the occasions which I could bring up against myself as evidence of lack of medical conscientiousness" (*FR*, 135), ends as little more than "a question of signifiers, of signifiers as such, handled by a subject for signifying aims, signifying so purely that the meaning very often remains problematic" (*S* 3, 193). And yet, as we have seen, the meaning of these signifiers remains problematic *only at the level of a guessing game*, in a diversionary flourish of *fort* and *da*, where the primal scene of Freud's dream, as well as its subsequent analysis, has given way to an abstract, pseudo-scientific inquiry limited to the realm of chemical signifiers.

Not coincidentally, this abstract, pseudo-scientific inquiry also proceeds by way of repetition. Just as "prop" recurs in *"propyl, propyls . . . propionic acid,"* so also does trimethylamine recur—first as word, then as formula—at the end of Freud's dream. This recurrence of recurrence— the likes of which we have not seen since chapter 2, in the matheme we assigned to Kierkegaard's theory of the public—calls our attention to the third form of analytic repetition at work in Freud's dream. After the *tuché* returns as a gruesome image in the back of Irma's mouth, and after Freud recoils and steadily abstracts from this gruesome image in a *fort-da* guessing game, he encounters something more autonomous and more symbolic—something operating strictly at the level of the signifier: not the final word in the signifying chain stretching from amyl to propyl to propyls to propionic acid—namely, *"trimethylamin"*—but the recurrence of this final word as a chemical formula "printed in heavy type." In this sense, what is ultimately on display in this chemical formula is not a repetition of *"trimethylamin,"* but the "eminently symbolic form" in which this repetition takes place (*S* 2, 158). This is "the secret reality of the dream," Lacan shrewdly notes in his re-analysis. Behind Freud's search for trimethylamine and its chemical formula in a pseudo-scientific guessing game is "the quest for signification as such"—a quest whose objective is neither the discovery of trimethylamine nor the appearance of its chemical formula but, instead, the revelation of the *symbolic structure* that allows the latter to double as a recurrence of the former. In the chemical formula of trimethylamine, the meaning of Freud's dream becomes clear at last: "There is no other word of the dream than the very nature of the symbolic" (S 2, 160).

Later, in his eleventh seminar, Lacan describes repetition of this sort as *automaton*: "the return, the coming-back, the insistence of the signs, by which we see ourselves governed by the pleasure principle" (S 11, 54–55). If the return of the *tuché* stretches Freud beyond the pleasure principle by recalling Eckstein's traumatic medical history, and the subsequent *fort-da* guessing game allows Freud to begin reinstating this principle—first as distraction in his colleagues' empty speech, then as abstraction in the realm of organic chemistry—the emergence of "*trimethylamin*" and its chemical formula completes this reinstatement of the pleasure principle, returning Freud to a previous state of equilibrium, constancy, and repose. In particular, this *automaton* returns him to an earlier state of unwavering, almost reverential admiration for Wilhelm Fliess—the very state of admiration that Eckstein's prolonged suffering had recently compromised. From this perspective, the repetitive function of trimethylamin and its chemical formula can be shown to exist in tension with the repetitive function of the ghastly image in the back of Irma's mouth. In place of the *tuché*'s painful recurrence, we see the restitution of pleasure in *automaton*.

All of which suggests that the guessing game at play in Freud's dream is in fact *rigged*. In the *fort* of his colleagues' empty speech, the traumatic events of Eckstein's medical history, as figured in the ghastly contents of Irma's mouth, are placed under erasure; in the *da* of "*propyl, propyls . . . propionic acid*," these events slip deeper into oblivion; and in the insistent, automated return of trimethylamine, these traumatic events are all but forgotten in celebration of the colleague most responsible for them. What the *tuché* called into question, and what the first part of Freud's dream suggests is still in doubt, the second part of his dream and its subsequent analysis promises to restore entirely: his unwavering admiration for Fliess. As long as Freud could avoid the *tuché* and resist each of its returns, he could rest assured that his closest, most trusted friendship was not in peril.

Paralipsis

But rest and assurance were both foreign to Freud at this stage of his career, which is partly why he was in frequent correspondence with Fliess in the months between Eckstein's botched surgery and the dream of Irma's injection—and frequently in denial of his colleague's responsibility for Eckstein's profound suffering. Exploring this psychodrama, especially as it relates to the linguistic contours and interpretive aftermath of Freud's dream, is the final task of this chapter.

Initially, Freud tried to withhold blame, limiting his correspondence with Fliess to diagnostic accounts of Eckstein's condition (*CL*, 113). But then he "began to feel ashamed" for having "shied away" from the obvious cause of her near fatality, at which point, he could not help but attribute responsibility for this horrible turn of events, informing Fliess of the fetid gauze he and Rosanes discovered in her nasal cavity (118). Even then, however, in full view of this medical malpractice, Freud struggled to hold Fliess accountable. He was willing to blame himself, to blame Rosanes, and even to share the blame with Fliess. He also attempted to lessen everyone's blame for Eckstein's medical plight, reporting to Fliess that she held no one responsible for her suffering, least of all the two of them. "It does speak well of her that she did not change her attitude toward either of us," he writes. "She honors your memory beyond the undesired accident" (119). And again, later that month: "She is a very nice, decent girl who does not hold the affair against either of us and refers to you with great respect" (123).

Although Eckstein's prolonged suffering figures largely in Freud's correspondence, his letters also reveal a deep concern for Fliess' emotional well-being. Even at the height of the *tuché*, when Rosanes removed the fetid gauze, nearly killing Eckstein and all but incapacitating Freud, Fliess was on his mind. "I do not believe it was the blood that overwhelmed me," Freud writes. Instead, it was a flood of "strong emotions," most of which, he adds, surged toward Fliess: "That this mishap should have happened to you; how you will react to it when you hear about it; what others could make of it; how wrong I was to urge you to operate in a foreign city where you could not follow through on the case; how my intention to do my best for this poor girl was insidiously thwarted and resulted in endangering her life—all this came over me simultaneously" (CL, 117).

By March 1895, Freud was more concerned for Fliess than he was for Eckstein. "In my thoughts I have given up hope for the poor girl and am inconsolable that I involved you and created such a distressing affair for you" (*CL*, 121). As his care for Eckstein dwindled to little more than regret, his concern for Fliess grew into something verging on anxiety:

Now that I have thought it through, nothing remains but heartfelt compassion for my child of sorrows. I really should not have tormented you here, but I had every reason to entrust you with such a matter and more. You did it as well as one can do it. The tearing off of the iodoform gauze remains one of those accidents that happen to the most fortunate and circumspect of surgeons, as you know from the business with your little sister-in-law's broken adenotome and the anesthesia. Gersuny said that he had had a similar experience and therefore he is using iodoform wicks instead of gauze (you will remember your own case). Needless to say, no one is blaming you, nor would I know why they should. And I only hope that you will arrive as quickly as I did at feeling regret and rest assured that it was not necessary for me to reaffirm my trust in you once again. (*CL*, 118, trans. modified)

Tellingly, this passage begins and ends with a profession of trust: Freud claims to have trusted Fliess before Eckstein's operation and then insists that he retains this trust in the wake of her prolonged suffering. Between these professions of trust, he also attempts to console and reassure his colleague, carefully framing his remarks as reminders: "as you know . . . ," "you will remember. . . . ," "Needless to say . . ." Not coincidentally, each of these reminders also functions as its own expression of trust, saying in effect, *I trust you are aware that . . .* These rhetorical gestures culminate in Freud's concluding profession of trust, specifically his claim that "it was not necessary" to reaffirm his trust in Fliess after Eckstein's botched surgery. Which raises two related questions: If it was unnecessary for Freud to reaffirm his trust in Fliess, why does he go out of his way to do so in this passage, repeatedly suggesting that he remains confident in his colleague? And why does Freud feel compelled to inform Fliess, in no uncertain terms, that this reaffirmation of trust was itself unnecessary?

The Greeks had a word for talk of this sort: *paralipsis*. As a rhetorical device, *paralipsis* allows speakers to mention something by refusing to mention it. In political culture, it is often used to criticize one's opponents by refusing to criticize them. Although *paralipsis* is often used to level accusations, and with divisive rhetorical effects, it also presumes a certain amount of mutual understanding, or at least some common knowledge, between accuser and accused, as demonstrated in each of Freud's reminders to Fliess: "as you know . . . ," "you will remember . . . ," "Needless to say . . ." In this sense, *paralipsis* is a conflicted rhetorical trope, one whose persuasive artistry is always torn between motives of reciprocity and reproach, identification and division.

Not surprisingly, *paralipsis* also has a place in psychoanalytic theory and technique. Consider, for instance, Lacan's use of the French expletive *ne*, the literal meaning of which is "not," but the practical use of which often suggests "not but" (*E*, 677). *Ne* allows speakers "to introduce a certain hesitation, ambiguity, or uncertainty into the utterance in which it appears, as if to suggest that the speaker is denying the very thing he is asserting, afraid of the very thing he claims to wish, or wishing for the very thing he seems to fear," Bruce Fink explains. "In such cases, we get the impression that the speaker *both wants and does not want* the event in question to take place or the person in question to show up."[7] To illustrate this curious way of speaking, Fink refers to its English analogue: "I cannot help but . . ." Practically speaking, this expression means "I cannot stop myself from . . ." More precisely, it verges on a double negative: "I cannot not . . ." In each expression, we see a conflict between the intentional discourse of the ego and the interruptive discourse of the unconscious, where the latter intrudes upon the former, effectively interjecting "No!" in the midst of an otherwise conscious utterance.

Freud could not help but inform Fliess of his ongoing trust. Nor could he stop himself from informing Fliess that it was unnecessary for him to "reaffirm" this trust after Eckstein's botched surgery. Together, these statements suggest the opposite of what each of them on their own seems to convey: not that Freud's trust in Fliess remains unshaken but, instead, that it has now begun to waver; and not that Freud is certain of the former but, instead, that Fliess (like Freud himself) has now begun to suspect the latter. If this were not the case—if these statements of trust were not collectively tinged with doubt—why would Freud feel compelled to profess his trust in Fliess so frequently and, simultaneously, to offset these professions of trust with an even more outspoken insistence on their superfluousness?

In the wake of Eckstein's botched surgery, Freud was eager to convey his abiding confidence in Fliess. With each profession of trust, however, he also signaled its opposite, reminding Fliess as well as himself, again and again, that mutual trust was no longer an obvious, given feature in their relationship. What had gone without saying before Eckstein's operation now required frequent restatement. This alone seems to have given Freud pause—enough pause, at least, for him to add, above and beyond his repeated expressions of trust, that the trust to which these expressions lay claim was never in need of restatement in the first place, that the close friendship he seems so desperate to recover was never lost to begin with.

24 July 1895

By summer 1895, the loss Freud feared had become a reality. "Woe unto you if you do not write soon!" he warned Fliess on 13 July, playfully marking the slowdown in their correspondence and anxiously hoping to elicit a response. But Fliess did not reply. So Freud wrote to him again. Nowhere was his concern for their waning friendship, and his dread of its irretrievable loss, more pronounced than in this follow-up letter: "Daimonie [Demon], why don't you write? How are you? Don't you care at all any more about what I am doing? What is happening to the nose, menstruation, labor pains, neuroses, your dear wife, and the budding little one? True, this year I am ill and must come to you; what will happen if by chance both of us remain healthy for a whole year? Are we friends only in misfortune? Or do we also want to share the experience of calm times with each other?" (CL, 134).

It is difficult to overstate the importance of this letter. It is dated 24 July 1895—the day after Freud dreamt of Irma's injection. Years later, looking back on this monumental day, Freud could only wonder (and only half-jokingly) if "some day a marble tablet will be placed on the house [in which he was staying at the time], inscribed with these words: 'In this house on July 24, 1895, the secret of dreams was revealed to Dr. Sigmund Freud.'" In hindsight, he could see the dream of Irma's injection for what it was: the catalyst for his renowned book on *The Interpretation of Dreams* and, with it, his discovery of the most profound and utterly precarious concept in Freudian psychoanalysis: the unconscious. In July 1895, however, when this discovery was still in progress, Freud was far more trepidatious. He knew his work on the unconscious was significant, but he was wildly uncertain of its ramifications. "The experience of the fundamental discovery was, for Freud, living through the putting into question of the very foundation of the world," Lacan observes in his re-analysis of Freud's dream. "He lives in an atmosphere of anxiety with the feeling that he's making a dangerous discovery" (S 2, 162).

At no point in Freud's life was his correspondence with Fliess more needed—or more sorely missed. In the years leading up to his remarkable discovery of the function of unconscious in dreams, Fliess had become Freud's closest confidant, his most passionate interlocutor, and, more often than not, the sole addressee of his innermost thoughts on the hazards and horizons of psychoanalysis. Which is why trimethylamine and its chemical formula were of "quite special importance" to his understanding of the dream of Irma's injection and, with it, the conceptual foundation of *The Interpretation of Dreams*. Both presaged the return of Freud's newly aggravated and increasingly tense relationship with Fliess to its previous state of equilibrium, constancy, and repose.

Or, in keeping with the pleasure principle, they reminded Freud of this previous state and encouraged him to attempt its reprisal. Lacan is keen on this distinction: "The function of the pleasure principle is to make man always search for what he has to find again, but which he never will attain."[8] Hence the fervency of Freud's search for the meaning of trimethylamine and its chemical formula and his apparent satisfaction upon its discovery. Implicit in the *fort-da* guessing game leading up to these enigmatic signifiers, Freud suggests in his analysis of the dream, also dated 24 July 1895, is a dire wish for the renewed support of a "friend who had for many years been familiar with all my writings during the period of their gestation," specifically "a person whose agreement I recalled with satisfaction whenever I felt isolated in my opinions" (*CL*, 138–9).

None of Freud's writings were more uncertain, and none of his opinions more isolating, than those he was developing alongside these flattering tributes to Fliess in 1895. If indeed all dreams are wish-fulfillments, as he claims in *The Interpretation of Dreams*, the wish at the center of the dream of Irma's injection is readily apparent. Above all, Freud wished that the malpractice which yielded the *tuché* which yielded the dream which yielded the book which yielded his most startling discovery to date—the function of the unconscious—had not also simultaneously compromised his relationship to the colleague whose intellectual and emotional support was most needed in this moment of great insight. As Lacan well notes, "The very meaning of the dream of Irma's injection is related to the depth of this experience" (*S* 2, 162).

The Return of the Repressed

Even when apparently found, the traumatic object-cause of Freud's dream seemed destined to remain lost—and not just because he was desperate to redeem his friendship with Fliess. The lost-and-found circuitry at work in the second part of his dream had more to do with the function of the *tuché* as such than it did with Freud's underlying wish to avoid the painful implications of this *tuché* in particular.

Because it is experienced as a traumatic event, the *tuché* undergoes repression, specifically secondary repression: Its defining signifiers (in this case, the various *Pfropfen* in which Eckstein's suffering found expression) are expelled from the signifying chain of human memory (in this case, Freud's memory of the colleague responsible for her suffering). Like most repressed signifiers, however, those of the *tuché* frequently return in distorted form at a later date, notably in the form of dream images (hence, the horrific contents of Irma's mouth and the sequential "props" of *"propyl, propyls . . . propionic acid"*).

And yet, from the vantage point of their eventual return—a future moment of repetition relative to a previous act of repression (which is why Lacan claims that the repressed always returns from one place: the future)—the *tuché* can only appear as a *missed* encounter with the real, or, more precisely, an *avoided* encounter with the real (*S* 11, 55, 128). Missed and avoided because, when the repressed returns to us at a later date, it is always twice removed from the *tuché* at its origin. In the slip, the dream, the symptom, we see a distant and distorted representation of what is *already* the obscure trace—an unconscious vestige—of some radically unassimilable past event. When Lacan insists that analytic repetition is structured atop a "constitutive occultation," this is what he means: it is founded on "the opacity of the trauma" and, by extension, "its resistance to signification" (*S* 11, 128–29). To this extent, the return of the repressed is never a direct, unadulterated repetition of the past. On the contrary, it is always a repetition riddled with difference. What returns to us at a later date in the slip, the dream, and the symptom is not the *tuché* as such but a distorted representation of its already cryptic image.

Hence, the images of infection strewn throughout Freud's dream. From his egocentric examination of Irma to her reexamination by his egomorphic peers to Otto's thoughtless injection to the sordid recollections evoked by these events—the central theme remains one of infection. So also does the redoubled signifier in which these images of infection culminate: *"trimethylamin"* and its chemical formula. Add to this the contaminated bottle of liquor Freud received the day before, and a curious through line begins to emerge: *stench*. It is precisely here, at the olfactory register—especially as it relates to the theme of infection—that the repressed memory of Eckstein's botched surgery stages its return. What Freud encounters in Irma's mouth and subsequently disperses throughout his dream is a distorted image of his painful and increasingly complicated memory of Eckstein's near fatality, specifically his memory of its object cause—namely, the half meter of fetid gauze he and Rosanes discovered in her nasal cavity.

How else are we to account for the emphatic push toward trimethylamine as his dream progresses? In his account of *"trimethylamin"* and its chemical formula, Freud found an opportunity to redeem the very person whose expertise on the human nose the rest of the dream called into question. "Freud's reading constitutes a massive displacement,"

Peter Gay affirms in his biography of Freud. "The doctor whose conscientiousness he wished to establish with this dream was far less himself than Fliess."[9] If in fact the dream of Irma's injection was a dream about Eckstein's infection, then the "lack of medical conscientiousness" to which it referred was not that of Freud but, instead, that of his dearest friend, Wilhelm Fliess—just the opposite of what Freud's otherwise exhaustive analysis of the dream suggests.

This is partly why Freud struggled to make sense of *"propyl, propyls . . . propionic acid"* in his analysis of the dream. Although he rightly suspected that this alliterative sequence of chemicals was connected to the foul-smelling, potentially poisonous bottle of liquor he received the previous day, he failed to grasp (or at least to mention) the underlying significance of this connection—namely, its relevance to his newly troubled friendship with Fliess. Not even the peculiar shift from amyl to propyl gave him pause in July 1895. That Otto's polluted bottle of liquor had reeked of amyl, but the alliterative sequence in his dream began with propyl, was of little import, Freud concluded, for "substitutions of this kind are perhaps legitimate in organic chemistry."

Only in hindsight, hundreds of pages into *The Interpretation of Dreams*, did Freud begin to sense that there was more at stake in this shift from amyl to propyl than the substitutive practices of organic chemistry. And only then, with the personal and professional tumult of 1895 well behind him, did he also begin to suspect that the alliterative sequence enabled by this shift—*"propyl, propyls . . . propionic acid"*—was uniquely relevant to his friendship with Fliess: "When I allowed my attention to dwell for a moment longer on the word 'propyls,' it occurred to me that it sounded like 'Propylaea.' But there are Propylaea not only in Athens but in Munich. A year before the dream I had gone to Munich to visit a friend who was seriously ill at the time—the same friend who was unmistakably alluded to in the dream by the word 'trimethylamin' which occurred immediately after 'propyls'" (*SE* 4, 294). With this subsequent insight—an "addition to the analysis of the dream," as Freud portrayed it—the hidden connection between amyl and trimethylamine also begins to emerge, and with it the secret affinity between Otto and Fliess.

Notice how Freud accounts for these connections:

On the one hand we see the group of ideas attached to my friend Otto, who did not understand me, who sided against me, and who made me a present of liquor with an aroma of amyl. On the other hand, we see—linked to the former group by its very contrast—the group of ideas attached to my friend in Berlin, who *did* under-

stand me, who would take my side, and to whom I owed so much valuable information, dealing, amongst other things, with the chemistry of the sexual processes.

The recent exciting causes—the actual instigators of the dream—determined
what was to attract my attention in the "Otto" group; the amyl was among these
selected elements, which were predestined to form part of the dream-content.
The copious "Wilhelm" group was stirred up precisely through being in contrast
to "Otto," and those elements in it were emphasized which echoed those which
were already stirred up in "Otto." All through the dream, indeed, I kept on turning
from someone who annoyed me to someone else who could be agreeably contrasted with him; point by point, I called up a friend against an opponent. Thus
the amyl in the "Otto" group produced memories from the field of chemistry in
the other group; in this manner the trimethylamin, which was supported from several directions, found its way into the dream-content. "Amyls" itself might have entered the dream-content unmodified; but it came under the influence of the "Wilhelm" group. For the whole range of memories covered by that name was searched
through in order to find some element which could provide a two-sided determination for "amyls." "Propyls" was closely associated with "amyls," and Munich
from the "Wilhelm" group with its "propylaea" came half-way to meet it. The two
groups of ideas converged in "propyls-propylaea"; and, as though by an act of compromise, this intermediate element was what found its way into the dream-content.
Here an intermediate common entity had been constructed which admitted of
multiple determination. It is obvious, therefore, that multiple determination must
make it easier for an element to force its way into the dream-content. In order to
construct an intermediate link of this kind, attention is without hesitation displaced
from what is actually intended on some neighboring association. (*SE* 4, 294–95)

In his July 1895 analysis of the dream, Freud claimed that the polluted contents of Otto's liquor bottle as well as those of his dirty syringe were "united" (*vereint*) in the stammering utterance "*propyl, propyls . . . propionic acid*" (*FR*, 140). Here, however, with the addition of
"propylaea," the function of this alliterative sequence shifts from uni-
fication to *compromise*. Instead of uniting the "Otto" group, "*propyl, propyls . . . propionic acid*" now operates as a separate, intermediate element
between the "Otto" group and its opposite, the "Wilhelm" group. On
this point, Freud is adamant: "*propyl, propyls . . . propionic acid*" is not
just "an intermediate link" between amyl and trimethylamine but also,
more directly, "an intermediate common entity" whose "multiple determination" derives from the contrasting groups of ideas represented
by these two chemicals.

Interestingly, Freud returns to this topic in his 1901 essay "On
Dreams." He begins by confessing that his July 1895 account of "*propyl,*

propyls . . . propionic acid" was incomplete. "To begin with, the analysis only led me to an indifferent experience which had acted as dream-instigator, and in which a part was played by *amyl*," he admits. "I was not yet able to justify the confusion between amyl and propyl." As if to make up for this earlier confusion, he then recalls visiting Fliess in Munich and being "struck by the *Propylaea*," reiterating much of his previous "addition to the analysis of the dream." The *"propyl"* in *"propyl, propyls . . . propionic acid"* was not just "an intermediate idea between *amyl* and *Propylaea*," Freud now realized. More specifically, it was "a kind of *compromise"* between the annoying "Otto" group represented by *amyl* and the agreeable "Wilhelm" group represented by *Propylaea*. But what did he mean by this? And what does it tell us about the relationship between empty speech and its full counterpart, as illustrated in his dream and its subsequent analysis?

A Parallelogram of Forces

When Freud refers to *"propyl, propyls . . . propionic acid"* as "a kind of *compromise,"* he is not suggesting that it serves as "a composite idea, in which a relatively distinct nucleus represents what [these two contrasting groups of ideas] have in common, while indistinct subordinate details correspond to the respects in which they differ from each other." On the contrary, as he is careful to insist, again underscoring the status of this alliterative utterance as a complex multiplicity of ideas, *"propyl, propyls . . . propionic acid"* operates as "an intermediate common entity, which stands in relation to [the "Otto" group and the "Wilhelm" group] similar to that in which the resultant in a parallelogram of forces stands to its components" (*FR*, 157).

Had he pursued this similarity further, Freud would have discovered a continuum, not a contrast, between the "Otto" group and the "Wilhelm" group. As a geometric proof, a parallelogram of forces shows that when two forces are applied to a single object (A in fig. 9.1), and the magnitude and direction of these forces are represented by two sides of a parallelogram (ABC and ADC in fig. 9.1), the resultant is a diagonal line extending from that single object to the opposite corner of the parallelogram (the AC vector in fig. 9.1).

To interpret *"propyl, propyls . . . propionic acid"* as a parallelogram of forces is to suggest that the amyl stench of Otto's polluted gift (A in fig. 9.1), when acted upon by the mixed ideational forces of the "Otto" group and the "Wilhelm" group (ABC and ADC in fig. 9.1), yielded a

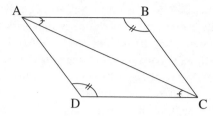

FIGURE 9.1. A parallelogram of forces. Posted by user Erez Segal on Wikimedia Commons: https://commons.wikimedia.org/wiki/File:Parallelogram_CDA_eq_BAC.svg.

rhetorically slanted and semantically oblique vector of chemical signifiers: *"propyl, propyls . . . propionic acid"* (the AC diagonal in fig. 9.1). Which begs the question, of course: If *amyl* corresponds to point A, and *"propyl, propyls . . . propionic acid"* maps onto the AC vector, how are we to account for point C at the end of this vector?

One answer clearly presents itself: *"trimethylamin."* Although Freud does not refer to this chemical compound in his 1901 account of *"propyl, propyls . . . propionic acid"*—a noticeable difference from his previous "addition to the analysis of the dream," where he mentions it several times—the analogy he draws between this alliterative sequence and a parallelogram of forces clearly suggests as much. In particular, this analogy suggests that trimethylamine not only belongs to the agreeable "Wilhelm" group, but also, oddly enough, extends from the annoying "Otto" group. As point C in the diagonal originating in point A, trimethylamine serves as the final linguistic turn in a series of chemical signifiers extending from amyl to propyl to propyls to propionic acid.

To this extent, Freud was correct: the "Wilhelm" group "echoed" the "Otto" group. But he overemphasized the contrast between these two groups—and for good reason. To have acknowledged *"trimethylamin"* as the final term in the oblique yet rather obvious signifying chain extending from amyl would have been to accept the "Wilhelm" group as a continuation, not a contradiction, of the "Otto" group. In the virulent, malodorous undertones of *"trimethylamin"* and its chemical formula, Freud would have found the crowning olfactory expression of his self-proclaimed "wrath" against Otto. And in the polluted contents of Otto's liquor bottle, as well as those of his dirty syringe, he would have found traumatic representations of the various *Pfropfen* from which Eckstein continually suffered—a gruesome slurry of bone chips, blood clots, drainage tubes, fetid gauze, and infected lesions.

The Jam

With and without the advantage of hindsight, it seems, the dream of Irma's injection remains a dream centered on the theme of infection. Crucial for our purposes, of course, is the connection between this central theme and the prevailing communicative practice of those who develop it in Freud's dream. When the empty speech of Leopold and Dr. M. gives way to *"propyl, propyls . . . propionic acid"*—a complex expression whose "multiple determination" even Freud could not deny—Irma's infection becomes symptomatic of the dream itself. And all the more so when we understand this dream as Lacan does—namely, as an encrypted message about "the very nature of the symbolic" addressed to readers of *The Interpretation of Dreams*.

As we saw in chapter 8, the etymology of *communication* suggests not just the act of sharing something with others but also, at the same time, the act of making something ordinary, vulgar, profane, and polluted. To communicate is always, to some extent, to contaminate. Which is why the eruption of *"propyl, propyls . . . propionic acid"* in the second half of Freud's dream, at the height of his colleagues' empty speech, is so revealing: *It is at once a signifier of contamination and, paradoxically, a contamination of signifiers.* In its "multiple determination," this alliterative expression not only advances the rhetoric of infection at work in the dream by tainting the agreeable images of the "Wilhelm" group with the annoying images of the "Otto" group, but also infects the empty speech in which much of this rhetoric finds expression, stretching tensors of error and confusion through the already ridiculous yet still more-or-less intelligible discourse of Freud's egomorphic peers. In *"propyl, propyls . . . propionic acid,"* the language of the unconscious *contaminates* that of Freud's already wounded ego, bringing the empty speech of his polycephalic self to the brink of unintelligibility. In keeping with the etymology of communication, this alliterative sequence reveals what Lacan, while grappling with the work of mid-century cyberneticists, would later describe as *the jam*—"this tendency there is in communication to cease being a communication, that is to say, of no longer communicating anything at all" (*S* 2, 83).

Where conscious communication suffers unconscious contamination, causing empty speech to stutter and even jam, the repressed stages its return, occasioning moments of full speech. And it is precisely here, on the verge of communication breakdown, that the analytic threshold between repetition and remembering becomes wholly apparent. Where the repetitive, evasive practice of empty speech has begun to falter—in the slip, in the dream, in the symptom—the retrospective, resubjectifying process of full speech finds a toehold. Repetition with a difference, it turns out, is the condition of possibility for recollecting ourselves.

And again, there is nothing Platonic about this. "Recollection is not Platonic reminiscence," Lacan reiterates, indexing his earlier discussion of psychoanalytic anamnesis. "It is not the return of a form, an imprint, an *eidos* of beauty and good, a supreme truth, coming to us from the beyond." Instead, "it is something that comes to us from the structural necessities, something humble, born at the level of the lowest encounters and of all the talking crowd that precedes us, at the level of the structure of the signifier, of the languages spoken in a stuttering, stumbling way"—in short, at the level of empty speech, but only when it verges on something else entirely (*S* 11, 47). If indeed the shift from repetition to recollection, resistance to remembrance, empty speech to full speech begins in the register of error, it is because our stuttering, stumbling utterances—in speech, action, and dream alike—are less communication breakdowns occurring at the level of the ego than communication breakthroughs originating in the field of the unconscious. Our repression of the *tuché* and its return at a later date in doubly distorted form is not an obstacle to self-awareness but, instead, its opportunity structure.

Did Freud miss this opportunity in July 1895? Yes and no. Yes, insofar as he failed to realize (or at least to acknowledge) any connection between Irma and Eckstein, Otto and Fliess. But also no, because he clearly sensed the importance of these missed connections, notably in his retrospective account of Otto's earlier insult: "It was as though he had said to me: 'You don't take your medical duties seriously enough. You're not conscientious; you don't carry out what you've undertaken'" (*FR*, 141–42). The key term here is "conscientious" (*gewissenhaft*), especially as it relates to the through line of his dream's analysis: "medical conscientiousness" (*ärztliche Gewissenhaftigkeit*). In Freud's view, the dream served his "wish to be innocent of Irma's illness" by providing "evidence of how highly conscientious I was, of how deeply I was concerned about the health of my relations, my friends, and my patients" (142). But this interpretation, as we have seen, only scratched the surface of his dream. Beneath it, a more troubling insight was left to fester—an insight which has captured scholarly attention ever since. "What Freud did not tell Fliess on July 24, 1895, or the readers of *The Interpretation of Dreams*," Gay explains, synthesizing decades' worth of critical-historical commentary, "was that the dream of Irma's injection was a carefully constructed, highly intricate scenario designed at least in part to rescue Freud's idealized image of Fliess in defiance of some damning evidence."[10]

To stop here, however, as readers of Freud often do, is to overlook the *motive* for his unconscious attempt to redeem Fliess. Although Fliess was clearly responsible for Eckstein's botched surgery, it was Freud who had encouraged her to contact him in the first place. If his retrospective account of Otto's earlier insult functions as full speech, it is precisely for this reason: It speaks to Freud's overwhelming feelings of guilt for subjecting Eckstein to his colleague's negligent care. All of which, in turn, suggests a crucial extension of Gay's foregoing account: By redeeming Fliess, Freud ultimately hoped to redeem himself. And by doing so in private letters and published works alike, he also hoped to resubjectivize their shared history, preserving their intense personal and professional relationship for years to come.

Whether or not Freud succeeded in this task, his effort can and should be understood as an instantiation—arguably the very first—of what would eventually become the conceptual foundation of psychoanalytic theory and technique. Indeed, as Lacan plainly states in his 1956 manifesto on the topic, "This assumption of the subject of his history, insofar as it is constituted by speech addressed to another, is clearly the basis of the new method Freud called psychoanalysis" (E, 213)—and not in the final draft of *The Interpretation of Dreams*, Lacan adds, but several years prior, in 1895, when this book began to take shape around the interpretation of a single dream, a specimen dream, the dream of Irma's injection.

Conclusion

Crowds and Publics

Twenty years ago, the Stanford Humanities Lab launched an interdisciplinary project on the social and cultural history of crowds. Initial discussions were retrospective, even funerary. "When our project team first set to work," the directors recall, "it was easy enough to see the signs that Le Bon's *era of crowds* was nearing its end, at least in the world's leading industrial/postindustrial nations." A few years later, in the project's crowning publication, they were more optimistic. "Any obituary would be premature," they acknowledged. "Online masses in chat rooms, connected only by fiber optics and a shared passion for collectables, gossip, or massively networked multiplayer games; . . . drivers hermetically sealed into an automobile container, gridlocked in roving bumper-to-bumper assemblies; . . . pedestrians milling about, each in a solipsistic entertainment cocoon of his or her own devising"—all suggested to members of the Humanities Lab that crowd culture was different, not defunct, in late-modernity.[1]

A century prior, crowd theorists were having a similar discussion. Again, Le Bon figured prominently. "The age we are about to enter will in truth be the ERA OF CROWDS," he predicted in 1895—the same year in which a cacophonous, polycephalic crowd of colleagues appeared to Freud in a momentous dream, setting him on the royal road to the unconscious.[2] And again, scholars saw signs of this era at its end. "The crowd is the social group of the past," Gabriel Tarde rejoined a few years later. "The invention of printing has caused a very different type of public to appear, one which never ceases to grow and whose indefinite extension is one of the most clearly marked traits of our period," he claimed. "I therefore cannot agree with that vigorous writer, Dr. Le Bon, that our age is the 'era of crowds.' It is the era of the public or of publics, and that is a very different thing."[3] From old technologies like the printing press to new technologies like the railway, the telegraph, and the telephone—all of which culminated in the modern, mass-circulation newspaper—Tarde saw a quickening social shift from crowd culture to public culture. Where discrete physical assemblies once thrived, vast virtual audiences now prevailed.

The French Revolution catalyzed this shift from crowds to publics. With the Revolution came the modern crowd; with the modern crowd came political journalism; and with political journalism came another, more encompassing form of collective life: the reading public. Unlike revolutionary crowds, which were inspired by orators and "incapable of extension beyond a limited area," reading publics were informed by journalists and characterized by "indefinite extension." If the modern crowd was an assemblage of "psychic connections" anchored in structures of "physical contact," the modern public was "a purely spiritual collectivity, a dispersion of individuals who are separated and whose cohesion is entirely mental." Members of reading publics "do not come into contact, do not meet or hear each other," Tarde insists. "They are all sitting in their own homes scattered over a vast territory, reading the same newspaper" (*GT*, 277–81).

The social effects of these structural differences were profound. Because they gathered in physical assemblies, members of crowds were vulnerable to suggestion, imitation, hypnosis, magnetism, and other forms of "emotional contagion"—all of which, in turn, made them equally susceptible to hysteria, hallucination, somnambulism, automatism, and other kinds of "emotional insanity." In crowds, distinct individuals were "completely taken over, irresistibly drawn along by a force with no counterbalance" (*GT*, 281). They became "a single animal, a wild beast without a name." In stark contrast, modern readers, because they were geographically dispersed and often belonged to several publics at once, could experience "intellectual freedom" and, by extension, a "civilizing transformation"—"a transformation which is always accompanied by progress in tolerance, if not in skepticism"

(283, 286, 281). If modern crowd culture was a psychosocial pathology, modern public culture was its right-minded cure. What the former spread as communicable disease, the latter combated with communicative rationality.

From Edmund Burke to Hannah Arendt, revolutionary crowds have never lacked illustrious, if pessimistic, commentators. And from Immanuel Kant to Jürgen Habermas, reading publics have never wanted for renowned, often starry-eyed theorists. At their worst, revolutionary crowds were thought to be unruly, irrational, ignorant, impulsive, intolerant, despotic, extreme, and violent. At their best, reading publics were thought to be civilized, rational, educated, reflective, tolerant, deliberative, moderate, and peaceful.

Contemporary democratic culture lies somewhere in between. Ours is neither an era of crowds, as Le Bon feared, nor an era of publics, as Tarde hoped. Instead, it is an era in which crowds and publics once more overlap. But not as they overlapped during the French Revolution. In the late-eighteenth century, revolutionary crowds were conditions of possibility for reading publics. Today their roles are typically reversed. From political uprisings like the Arab Spring to social spectacles like flash mobs, today's crowds usually begin as publics. What newspapers were to publics at the end of the *ancien régime*, social media platforms like Facebook, Twitter, YouTube, and Instagram have become to crowds in the twenty-first century.

This is not to suggest, of course, that crowds-turned-publics and publics-turned-crowds are separate historical phenomena. Just as publics continue to emerge from journalistic coverage of crowds—much as they did during the French Revolution—so also do crowds continue to emerge from publics, giving rise to more journalistic coverage, more publics, more crowds, and so on. Yet another reason to recall the Arab Spring: When self-immolation and revolutionary crowds in Tunisia found international media coverage, a vast and virtual public culture began to emerge. And when members of this public culture in Algeria, in response to another self-immolation, assembled more revolutionary crowds, another flourish of media coverage ensued, thereby expanding and emboldening this new public culture. Then the same occurred in Egypt, garnering even more international media coverage, which in turn inspired revolutionary crowds in Yemen, Lebanon, Jordan, Palestine, Libya, Iraq, Morocco, and so on.

Conversational Turns

Tarde anticipated this sociopolitical cycle of crowds-turned-publics-turned-crowds-turned-publics, but he did not conceptualize it. He did, however, provide us with a clue to its analysis. A year after his landmark essay on "The Public and the Crowd," he published a related piece on "Opinion and Conversation." His argument was simple: Orators with their crowds and journalists with their publics all participate in opinion-formation, and they all do so by occasioning ordinary conversation. "If no one conversed, they would exercise no profound influence on any minds," Tarde explains. "They would be like a string vibrating without a sounding board" (*GT*, 307). What this meant for the study of modern crowds and publics was clear—at least to Tarde. Scholarship could no longer limit itself to the study of their oratorical and journalistic origins. It now had to account for their conversational effects as well. Once "entirely neglected," casual conversation had to become the era's "highest interest."[4]

What, then, does Tarde mean by "conversation"? His definition is expansive yet precise: "By conversation, I mean any dialogue without direct and immediate utility, in which one talks primarily to talk [*parle surtout pour parler*]." More than instrumental discourse, conversation is "superfluous chatter [*bavardages superflus*]." And this, he argues, is precisely what makes it compelling: "A captivating and much applauded discussion is often less suggestive because it avows the intention of being so." But casual conversation, because it disavows this intention, is far more suggestive: "It marks the apogee of the *spontaneous attention* that men lend each other, by which they interpenetrate to a much greater depth than in any other social relationship. By making them confer, conversation makes them communicate via an action as irresistible as it is unconscious. It is, consequently, the strongest agent of imitation, of the propagation of sentiments, ideas, and modes of action" (*GT*, 308–09). What makes conversation crucial to opinion-formation, and thus to crowds and publics alike, is its remarkable ability to appear otherwise, Tarde suggests. Its utility consists in apparent uselessness.

In this sense, Tarde is less concerned with the art of conversation than the practice of everyday talk—but not as it has concerned us in this book. Note, for instance, the kinship between his account of conversation and the gradual instrumentalization of everyday talk we discussed in the opening pages of this book. Tardean conversation not only includes the means-turned-ends practice of "phatic communion," in which interpersonal communication doubles as evidence of the social bonds it also seeks to establish, but also integrates this practice into the more purposeful activity of "political talk," where phatic communion becomes one of many means to the ends of public opinion and collective will-formation.

As we have seen, however, there is often something incessant about everyday talk, particularly when it occurs as chatter, idle talk, empty speech, and the like. More than means-turned-ends or means-to-ends, these average, everyday modes of discourse frequently operate as *means without end*. Speakers regularly suspend the pursuit of attainable rhetorical advantage in order to prolong their own utterances—and for no other reason than to prolong their own utterances. If Tarde suggests that everyday talk is purposeless, and for this reason intensely persuasive, this book has shown that its motivational structure can also be intensely purposive, even purely purposive, especially when speakers forgo the act of persuasion in order to continue talking.

With this distinction comes another. Tarde's depiction of everyday talk as "the apogee of *spontaneous attention*" does not account for many of the communicative practices discussed in this book. As we have seen, chatter, idle talk, empty speech, and their garrulous kin are neither spontaneous nor attentive but, instead, *automated, involuntary, senseless*, and strangely *machinelike*. And like the dysfunctional grandfather clock we considered at the start of this book—an illustration which set the stage for several others in the chapters that followed—these motorized ways of speaking are often, to some extent, *out of order*. Chatter, idle talk, and empty speech often communicate little more than their dysfunctional status as cogent discourse. Each remains a communicative practice, but one whose primary referent has become its own disordered state, whose rhetorical purpose has devolved into the maintenance of this state, and whose questionable significance has become, like the grandfather clock, "abstractly normal."

And yet, as Kierkegaard, Heidegger, and Lacan all argued, there is always something about these average everyday ways of speaking that cannot itself be understood as "average" or "everyday." In the chatter of the gallery-public, Kierkegaard found an *"examen rigorosum"* by which to religiously educate "the single individual." In the idle talk of the they-self, Heidegger discovered an important resource for the development of *"Authentic Being-one's-Self."* And in the resistive practice of empty speech, Lacan saw an occasion for transformative personal expressions of "full speech." In each case, everyday talk was shown to serve as the proving ground, not the killing field, of genuine subjectivity.

Which brings us to what is arguably the key difference between Tardean conversation and the communicative practices discussed in this book. Unlike Tarde and his successors, most of whom were intrigued by the *collective effects* of everyday talk, Kierkegaard, Heidegger, and Lacan were all interested in its *individuating potential*. Chatter, idle talk, and empty speech were not just means of opinion-formation available to crowds and publics alike. They were also *techniques of self-cultivation*—modes of communication in and by which modern individuals could not only lose themselves in mass society but also find themselves anew in its perpetual churn. Here, in the final pages of this book, I would like to suggest that we are now uniquely poised to advance these techniques of self-cultivation, thanks in part to the network revolution of late-modernity and its most sweeping social effect: networked individualism.

Exercises in Virtualization

Recall Stanford's project on the history of crowds. If members of the Humanities Lab saw turn-of-the-century chat rooms, traffic jams, and entertainment cocoons as signs that crowd culture is different rather than defunct in late-modernity, it was in part because these technophilic forms of collective life had begun to stretch tensors through one of the basic assumptions of late-nineteenth-century crowd theory—an assumption which found initial expression in Tarde's work on "imitation" and then fuller articulation in Frankfurt School critiques of "the culture industry," Situationist assaults on "the spectacle," and social psychological theories of "deindividuation"—namely, the belief that *physical assemblies erode psychic interiors* and, more broadly, that *mass society destroys modern individuals.* "The most marvelous phenomenon is precisely this obliteration of the singular personality in a single, immense personality," the Italian criminal anthropologist Scipio Sighele mused in 1903, adding early captions to this century-long belief. "One would say that each individual loses the ability to feel and to think and becomes a blind instrument of an unknown brain and spirit."[5]

Today's collectivities challenge this assumption. Instead of erasing individuality, they extend it. German sociologist Ulrich Beck refers to this process as *individualization*. "In plain terms, 'individualization' means the disintegration of the certainties of industrial society as well as the compulsion to find and invent new certainties for oneself and others without them," he writes. "Opportunities, threats, ambivalences of the biography, which it was previously possible to overcome in a family group, in the village community or by recourse to a social class or group, must increasingly be perceived, interpreted and handled by individuals themselves." This is not to suggest, of course, that late-modern individuals are on their own. Indeed, as Beck goes on to argue, individualization "does not mean atomization, isolation, loneliness, and the end of all kinds of society, or unconnectedness."[6] On the contrary, as individuals tinker with themselves and their worlds, they become "increasingly tied to others," generating "new interdependencies, even global ones," the sum of which is not a new social order but, instead, "a paradoxical collectivity of reciprocal individualization."[7]

And when they do so using new techniques and technologies of mobile communication, these tinkering individuals generate scores of new interdependencies. More than autonomous selves, they become *networked individuals*. "In incorporating gadgets into their lives, people have changed the ways they interact with each other," Lee Ranie and Barry Wellman explain. "They have become increasingly networked as individuals, rather than embedded in groups. In the world of networked individuals, it is the person who is the focus: not the family, not the work unit, not the neighborhood, and not the social group."[8] What began as iMacs and iBooks at home, connecting us to idiosyncratic chat rooms, soon became a menagerie of iPods and iPads in transit, infotaining us through traffic jams and train delays, which in turn paved the way for generations of iPhones among strangers, cocooning our pedestrian selves in a host of distant friendships. With each contemporary social formation came a new communication technology; with each communication technology came a new technique of personalization; and with each technique of personalization came a new form of networked individualism.

But we cannot stop here, for the rise of networked individualism also marks a further imbrication of contemporary crowds and publics. With every turn of the super-connected screw, the structural gaps between crowd culture and public culture narrow toward indiscernibility. New platforms and instruments of mobile communication allow networked individuals to weave assembled crowds into absent publics (e.g., livestreaming a dinner party on Instagram) and, simultaneously, to intersperse absent publics among assembled crowds (e.g., sharing Instagram newsfeeds at a dinner party)—to the point that, as Paul Mihailidis recently demonstrated, "they find it increasingly difficult to distinguish relationships that exist in their pockets from those that exist in their physical surroundings."[9] As crowds and publics both become others to themselves, their basic structural features—proximal presence and physical absence—become reciprocally interpenetrative. Separation from the near and congregation from afar become synchronous exercises in virtualization.

A Sociology of Associations

When the distinctions between crowd culture and public culture begin to dissolve, intermingling proximal presence and physical absence in new forms of human togetherness, the modern dichotomy between self and society follows suit, becoming wholly inadequate to the task of understanding, much less improving, life in these intermingled collectivities.

Hence, the meteoric rise of actor-network theory. "Instead of THE individual versus society problem," Bruno Latour notes, "we are now faced with the multiplicity and fully reversible combinations of highly complex individual constituents and multiple and fully reversible aggregates."[10] The implications of this multiplicity, reversibility, and mounting complexity are at once conceptual, methodological, and crucial to comprehending the techniques of self-cultivation implicit in the conceptual history of everyday talk we have traced from Kierkegaard to Heidegger to Lacan—and ultimately into the algorithmic era, where small talk now doubles as a resource for big data, and big data as the lynchpin of our digital selves.[11]

To be an individual is to have been individualized, and to have been individualized is to have accepted many "offers" of individualization. "You need to subscribe to a lot of subjectifiers to become a subject and you need to download a lot of individualizers to become an individual," Latour writes. "Attachments are first, actors are second." Only by entering into relationships with "extra-psyches" is it possible secure something like an "intra-psychology." And the more extra-psychological relationships one sustains, the easier it is to see how these intra-psychological worlds are populated. Only by multiplying connections to beings outside oneself is it possible to see how one's insides are being furnished.[12] What Sherry Turkle and other techno-skeptics frequently bemoan as a self-dissipating state of "overconnection," Latour and his successors often embrace as the long-awaited empirical basis for showing how anonymous and generic bodies are made into discrete people.

At stake in this attitude toward digital communication and culture is what Latour calls "a non-individualistic grasp on the individual." With a nod to Tarde, whose neo-Leibnizian theory of monads paved the way for actor-network theory, he insists that we are no longer "self-contained atomic entities" but, instead, "long and complex individual profiles." On this point, he is adamant: "Instead of those atomic individuals of the past, we now possess individuals for whom we are allowed to assemble *profiles* made of long lists of properties. Nothing is more common on the Web than this explosion of profiles willingly or unwittingly accumulated, stored, treated, and visualized" (*NSS*, 805–6). For too long, Latour concludes, again with a nod to Tarde, theories of the self have centered on the verb "to be" and, with it, the problem of *identity*. New techniques and technologies of mobile communication suggest that the verb of our times is not "to be" but "to have," and that the dilemma we now face is not one of identity but one of *association*. "'To have' (friends, relations, profiles . . .) is quickly becoming a stronger definition of oneself than 'to be'" (801).

Methodologically, this means that whenever we wish to define social actors, we must first deploy their various networks. Or, more precisely, we must deploy them *as* their various networks. And thanks to massive datascapes like Facebook, YouTube, Twitter, WhatsApp, Reddit, and the like—users of which now number in the billions—deploying these actor-networks has become a simple procedure. "There is nothing easier now than to navigate back and forth from an individual profile to an aggregate of hundreds and thousands of profiles," Latour well notes (*NSS*, 804). Unlike yesterday's self and social strata, today's individual and collective phenomena are *fully traceable*.

With this ease of navigational movement come two more methodological insights. First: There is a reversible continuity between actors and networks. "To be self-contained—that is, to be an actor—and to be thoroughly dependent—that is, to be a network—is to say twice the same thing" (*NSS*, 801). And second: Traditional, two-tier, part-whole approaches to social life, which "start with atomic individuals and imagine a second level where the collective phenomenon takes over," are less useful to the study of these reversible actor-networks than single-tier, wholly particulate notions of human togetherness in which "a phenomenon can be said to be collective without being superior to individuals"—or, more accurately, "collective without being social" (807–8). Indeed, as Latour goes on to explain, "The true digital revolution in social theory is to open a way whereby it is possible to study the individuals and their aggregates without relying at any point on two levels, without accepting any discontinuity where the individual action disappears mysteriously into a *sui generis* structure" (809). So much for the self-versus-society problem.

But again, we cannot stop here, for self-versus-society is not the only modern dichotomy that actor-network theory has reduced to ruins. As Latour reminds his readers, the collapse of "self versus society" ontologies also signals the breakdown "rational versus irrational" epistemologies and, with them, "normal versus pathological" axiologies—all of which are well-captured in his clever merger of "fact" and "fetish," resulting in the wonderfully antimodern neologism *factish*.[13] Where these sterile and starkly tiered dichotomies once prevailed, propping up the post-Enlightenment world, flattened and crosscut star shapes have now begun to emerge, raising new questions about the order of things in the digital age. Whatever else the network revolution in social theory entails, it has enabled us to document and bring some conceptual clarity to these crosscut, starlike shapes, inviting us to trace and theorize tiny conduits, continuous trails, points of connection—and thus also lines of contamination—between self and society, rationality and irrationality, normalcy and pathology.

Modes of Circulation

Much as new techniques and technologies of mobile connection have blurred the lines between proximal presence and physical absence, allowing users to mediate assembled crowds through absent publics, and vice versa, the actor-networks sustained by these crosshatched collectivities now call our attention to communicative practices that are at once individual *and* collective, rational *and* irrational, normal *and* pathological.

Latour does not explore these communicative practices. Like Tarde before him, though, he does provide us with a clue to their conceptualization. Any rigorous theory of these communicative practices, he insists, must be able to account for "the ways in which standards circulate through the net, or fashion, buzz, epidemics—that is, just the sort of things that are now easy to detect, to follow and to visualize with the new digital tools made available" (*NSS*, 807).

Chatter, idle talk, and empty speech are among these modes of circulation. Which makes the conceptual history of these phenomena, especially as it stretches from Kierkegaard to Heidegger to Lacan, an important first step toward the history and philosophy of communication implicit in actor-network theory. In Kierkegaard's existentialist critique of chatter, Heidegger's phenomenological account of idle talk, and Lacan's psychoanalytic treatment of empty speech, we find an array of intellectual resources for understanding and explaining individual and collective life in a world where "self versus society" and "publics versus crowds" are no longer reliable ways of seeing, and their moralistic siblings—"rational versus irrational" and "normal versus pathological"—only obscure things further.

Recall, for instance, the curious psychosocial formations through which chatter, idle talk, and empty speech circulate. In the fuzzy math of modernity's chatter, Kierkegaard discovered the social arithmetic of the gallery-public, suggesting that contemporary democratic culture is, at root, a numerical entity—specifically one in which individuals count each other's statements, calculate their combined meanings, and aggregate the results (as well as themselves) in abstract social sums. By way of sorites reasoning, paralogistic rationales, epistemic probabilities, and part-whole slippages, these abstract social sums are erroneously thought to be superior to their constitutive elements, and thus fit to serve as their denominators—an error which effectively reduces shared experience to social statistics. In the repetitive clamor of idle talk, Heidegger saw the linguistic guise in which *Dasein* encounters itself as *das Man*—a phantasmatic iteration of human being that, with the aid of normative ways of being with others (e.g., distantiality, averageness, leveling-down, and publicness), encourages us to see ourselves as other-selves, non-selves, unselves, and, ultimately, they-selves. And in the machinations of empty speech, Lacan found evidence of the Freudian crowd—an imaginary order comprised of hyper-rationalized (and for this reason profoundly neurotic) attachments between specular images, egos, ego-ideals, ideal egos, superegos, and the like. Suffice it to say: In the chatter of gallery-publics, the idle talk of they-selves, and the empty speech of Freudian crowds, we see a transhistorical assemblage of communicative practices and cross-hatched identities that are at once individual *and* collective, rational *and* irrational, normative *and* pathological—and thus just as likely to thrive in reading publics comprised of educated elites as they are to flourish in revolutionary crowds made up of lay citizens. Such is the range of modernity's chattering mind.

Calculating Machines

At the risk of putting too fine a point on this summative account of the conceptual history traced in this book, I would like to conclude by suggesting that gallery-publics, they-selves, and Freudian crowds are just as senseless, involuntary, automated, and machinelike as the communicative practices that sustain them. More than actor-networks, they are *calculating machines*. And these calculating machines are just as relevant to life in the digital age as they were when Kierkegaard, Heidegger, and Lacan initially discovered of them. Marking this continued relevance is the final task of this book.

As we have seen, the conceptual history which stretches from Kierkegaard to Heidegger to Lacan is less a history of the idea of everyday talk than a study of how the modern world became anxious about this way of speaking. So it should come as no surprise that many of the cultural anxieties that piqued their interest continue to inform individual and collective life in the digital age. Kierkegaard's critique of the gallery-public's chatter was a response to many of the same anxieties of aggregation that now provoke concerns about anonymous "meta" sites like Google News, which are quickly outstripping human curations (the aggregated) with collectivity algorithms (the aggregator) in a frantic effort to encompass every other meta news site. Heidegger's interest in the idle talk of the they-self was fueled by many of the same anxieties of averageness that continue to amplify late-modern doubts about the "collective intelligence" of Web 2.0 sites like Wikipedia, whose user-generated content now threatens to reduce human creativity to crowd sourcing, individual accomplishment to information sharing, and, ultimately, the lifeworld to a database. And Lacan's treatment of empty speech in the Freudian crowd laid claim (and siege) to many of the same anxieties of alterity that repeatedly find expression in contemporary public debates about the "echo chamber" effects of social media platforms like Facebook, whose personalization features often yield "filter bubbles," effectively limiting users' exposure to difference.

Aggregation, averageness, alterity—it is difficult to imagine a more complete configuration of today's algorithmic angsts, and even more challenging to imagine a world of user-generated content where these algorithmic angsts do not figure prominently. But this is precisely what the productive, individuating potential of chatter, idle talk, and empty speech has emboldened us to do. And daringness of this sort, I would like to suggest, is crucial to the task of living well in the digital age, when many of the self-cultivating techniques implicit in these communicative practices are increasingly being outpaced, and sometimes entirely outstripped, by streams of behavioral data produced when these practices occur online. If small talk has become a resource for big data, and big data the basis for much of today's technophilic angst, it is arguably for this reason: Bits and bytes of user-generated discourse are being algorithmically transcoded into vast proprietary datasets in terms of which individual users, at the behest of pointcast newsfeeds, are then asked to compose themselves anew, thereby generating more behavioral data, further algorithmic transcoding, advanced proprietary datasets, and additional pointcasts—all of which encourage users to recompose themselves again, and again, *ad infinitum.*

The datafied worlds sustained by this recursive process clearly function as actor-networks. And like gallery-publics, they-selves, and Freudian crowds, these actor-networks clearly function as calculating machines. But there is little room in their operational structures for anything like the *"examen rigorosum"* Kierkegaard discovered in the gallery-public, the "modifications" of average everydayness Heidegger derived from the they-self, or the "psychoanalytic anamnesis" Lacan occasioned in Freudian crowds. How are we to account for this basic structural discrepancy between the calculating machines that sustain big data and those we have considered in this book? And what, if any, opportunities exist for their reconciliation in today's digital economy?

Control Society

Time is short, so let's be categorical. The datafied worlds of the twenty-first-century bear little resemblance to the disciplinary societies studied by Foucault. Instead, they mark the late-capitalist apogee of what Deleuze foresaw as *societies of control.* "The disciplinary societies have two poles: the signature that designates the *individual*, and the number or administrative numeration that indicates his or her position within a *mass*," Deleuze explains. "In societies of control, on the other hand, what is important is no longer either the signature or a number, but a code." And these codes, in turn, serve as *passwords*: "The numerical language of control is made of codes that mark access to information, or reject it. We no longer find ourselves dealing with the mass/individual pair. Individuals have become *'dividuals,'* and masses, samples, data, markets, or *'banks.'"*[14]

If the subject of disciplinary society is like a mole, ever confined to spaces of near-total enclosure, the subject of control society is like a serpent, undulating without limit in a continuously modulating "network" whose basic machinery Deleuze, writing in the early-1990s, could only describe as "computers" (*PSC*, 6). To illustrate this late-capitalist network of passwords and computers, dividuals and data banks, he then recalls the work of his longtime collaborator Félix Guattari, who imagined an urban landscape turned control society: "One would be able to leave one's apartment, one's street, one's neighborhood, thanks to one's (dividual) electronic card that raises a given barrier; but the card could just as easily be rejected on a given day or between certain hours; what counts is not the barrier but the computer that tracks each person's position—licit or illicit—and effects a universal modulation" (6). Prison systems, school systems, hospital systems, corporate systems—all the disciplinary formations that used to individualize bodies and mass them together, effectively sustaining modern dichotomies between self and society, reason and irrationality, normalcy and deviance— are thrown into varying states of institutional crisis by this "universal modulation," allowing new systems of domination to replace old systems of disciplinarity.

Which brings Deleuze, at last, to the question of resistance:

One of the most important questions will concern the ineptitude of the unions: tied to the whole of their history of struggle against the disciplines or within the spaces of enclosure, will they be able to adapt themselves or will they give way to new forms of resistance against the societies of control? Can we already grasp the rough outlines of these coming forms, capable of threatening the joys of marketing? Many young people strangely boast of being "motivated"; they re-request apprenticeships and permanent training. It's up to them to discover what they're being made to serve, just as their elders discovered, not without difficulty, the telos of the disciplines. The coils of a serpent are even more complex than the burrows of a molehill. (PSC, 7)

And this was 1992—a decade before the mass migration from Friendster to MySpace to Facebook began, when social media platforms were still limited to bulletin-board systems and internet relay chats. Is it any easier now, in the algorithmic era, to discern the rough outlines of an organized resistance to control society, specifically one on par with yesterday's unionized struggle against the disciplines?

Personal Data Unions

By way of conclusion, I would like to answer, *yes*. Many young people now realize what their tireless contributions to digital media platforms are being made to serve. And they are increasingly refusing to provide this service—at least as they have up to this point.

In the first wave of today's digital economy, personal data was willingly exchanged for free services. Google, Facebook, and Twitter could offer free services because they were (and remain) in the business of selling user data. Tech-savvy users have long been aware of this basic business model, but only recently have they begun to contest it. And their nascent resistance, in turn, has begun to power a second wave in today's digital economy. What the World Economic Forum realized in 2011, and daring technologists like Jaron Lanier have been professing ever since, is that personal data is not free information but, instead, *a new asset class*.[15] Digital media platforms, which have been collecting, aggregating, analyzing, and monetizing users' behavioral data, largely to support microsegmented service-delivery models, will soon be forced to reckon with a host of new protocols, platforms, and applications, all designed to give users greater control over how their personal data is collected, stored, shared, and, ultimately, commercialized.[16]

Many of the legal, economic, and computational infrastructures needed to develop these new services are still emerging.[17] But this has not kept a new generation of technopreneurs from advancing viable prototypes. Foremost among these prototypes are cloud-based management services known as "personal data stores," which allow individuals to consolidate and control their personal data, reclaiming it from various digital provenances and integrating it into a single, transparent, human-centered platform. Instead of monetizing user data in the form of targeted advertising, many of these personal data stores generate revenue by charging outside organizations for access to personal data that individuals have preapproved for sharing. Often absent from this business model, however, is another kind of sharing, one in which users who grant access to their personal data are also entitled to a share of the proceeds generated by its circulation. Although the revenue to be shared with users would likely be scant, personal data stores are increasingly moving in this direction, if only to incentivize further data sharing.[18]

If the first wave of the digital economy—free services in exchange for behavioral data—quickly reduced individuals to dividuals and masses to datasets, the second wave of the digital economy, at the behest of personal data stores, now promises to reconstitute dividuals as individuals, and individuals as data traders—but not in such a way that alters the basic financial structure of online collective life. Even with the rise of personal data stores, masses remain datasets, datasets remain in the hands of platform operators, and platform operators remain in the business of liaising between data producers and data purchasers. "We seem only to have shifted the problem of data storage and management onto a new set of companies by creating a marketplace in which brokers may be incentivized to play both sides," Andrew Bennett rightly suspects. In the midst of this shift, however, he also detects the beginning of another, more momentous turn in the digital economy. Instead of relying on personal data stores, users could form *personal data unions*—platform cooperatives in which personal data ownership and collective bargaining power would allow them to forgo data brokers and, in so doing, to negotiate better terms with data purchasers— and all while remaining impervious to many of the "market-based incentives" that continue to impel the digital economy.[19]

From dividuals deprived of personal data to individuals armed with personal data, to platform cooperatives with enough collective bargaining power to rival personal data stores—is this the rough outline of an emerging resistance to the control society foreseen by Deleuze? It is still too soon to say. But it is not too soon to assert that, however else tomorrow's data unions will influence today's digital economy, they are likely to do so atop vast yet fully traceable actor-networks established and sustained by communicative practices like chatter, idle talk, and empty speech. To be sure, these practices will be subject to datafication. Because the resulting datasets will be owned and governed by the same actor-networks whose everyday talk sustains them, however, they also will provide users of every stripe with unprecedented access to their own digital pasts—chatter, idle talk, and empty speech galore. Whether this will be sufficient to inspire the "psychoanalytic anamnesis" advocated by Lacan, or the "modifications" of average everydayness theorized by Heidegger, or the *"examen rigorosum"* envisioned by Kierkegaard remains to be seen. Preserving these possibilities has long been an important yet unwitting function of the chattering mind. Pursuing them in earnest, and ideally all at once, must now become the top priority of those eager to radicalize this way of speaking, thinking, and being with others.

Acknowledgments

This book has benefited from much institutional support. Codirecting a research seminar at the University of Copenhagen allowed the initial chapters to find expression. A Development of Research and Creativity Grant from San Francisco State University yielded the book's middle part. A EURIAS & Marie-Curie Fellowship at Aarhus Institute of Advanced Studies, with support from the European Institutes of Advanced Studies and the European Commission's Marie-Sklodowska-Curie Actions COFUND Program, moved the project toward completion. A research sabbatical funded by San Francisco State University culminated in the finished manuscript. And San Francisco's Golden Gate Park was a matchless setting in which to revise the book. Along the way, speaking engagements sponsored by Aarhus University, University of California–Berkeley, Università Cattolica del Sacro Cuore, University of Copenhagen, Harvard University, University of Iowa, Purdue University, San Francisco State University, University of San Francisco, University of South Carolina, and St. John's University helped to advance several of the book's core arguments.

This book has also benefited from many friends and colleagues. Correspondence and conversation with Daniel M. Gross, Robert Hariman, and John Durham Peters were invaluable throughout, as were written comments on several chapters from Young-Cheon Cho, Fatmir Haskaj, Jason Lesko, Janda Hay Sunna, Michael P. Vicaro, and dozens of graduate and undergraduate students at San Francisco State University. Feedback from two anonymous reviewers com-missioned by the University of Chicago Press proved crucial as well, as did the peerless work of the editorial trio that saw the book into print: the editorial associate who gave the manuscript book form, Dylan Montanari; the executive editor who skillfully oversaw the book's publication, Kyle Wagner; and the correspondent extraordinaire who championed the project from the start, Doug Mitchell.

More than anyone, though, I wish to thank my four-year-old daugh-ter, Iris. Conversations with her are keen reminders that there is al-ways something about everyday talk that cannot itself be understood as "everyday."

Notes

INTRODUCTION

1. Sherry Turkle, *Reclaiming Conversation: The Power of Talk in a Digital Age* (New York: Penguin, 2015).

2. On the relationship between these scholarly traditions, see Peter Burke, "Conversation," in *The Handbook of Communication History*, ed. Peter Simonson et al. (New York: Routledge, 2013), 122–32.

3. See, for instance, Stephen E. Kidd, *Nonsense and Meaning in Ancient Greek Comedy* (Cambridge: Cambridge University Press, 2014); Emily Butterworth, *The Unbridled Tongue: Babble and Gossip in Renaissance France* (Oxford: Oxford University Press, 2016); Carla Mazzio, *The Inarticulate Renaissance: Language Trouble in an Age of Eloquence* (Philadelphia: University of Pennsylvania Press, 2009).

4. Stephen Miller, *Conversation: A History of a Declining Art* (New Haven, CT: Yale University Press, 2006).

5. The nascent conceptual history of these phenomena is apparent in several recent literature reviews. See, for instance, Gunter Senft, "Phatic Communion," in *Culture and Language Use*, ed. Gunter Senft et al. (Amsterdam: John Benjamins, 2009), 226–33; Erik K. Foster, "Research on Gossip: Taxonomy, Methods, and Future Directions," *Review of General Psychology* 8, no. 2 (2004): 78–99; and Joohan Kim and Eun Joo Kim, "Theorizing Dialogic Deliberation: Everyday Political Talk as Communicative Action and Dialogue," *Communication Theory* 18, no. 1 (2008): 51–70.

6. Kenneth Burke, *A Rhetoric of Motives* (Berkeley: University of California Press, 1969), 270. See also Samuel McCormick, "Arguments from Analogy and Beyond: The Persuasive Art-

istry of Local American Civic Life," *Quarterly Journal of Speech* 100, no. 2 (2014): 186–212.

7. Søren Kierkegaard, *Two Ages*, ed. and trans. Howard V. Hong and Edna H. Hong (Princeton, NJ: Princeton University Press, 1978), 97. Hereafter abbreviated *TA*.

8. Peter Fenves, *"Chatter": Language and History in Kierkegaard* (Stanford, CA: Stanford University Press, 1993).

9. See John Heath, *The Talking Greeks: Speech, Animals, and the Other in Homer, Aeschylus, and Plato* (Cambridge: Cambridge University Press, 2005), 186; Laura McClure, *Spoken Like a Woman: Speech and Gender in Athenian Drama* (Princeton, NJ: Princeton University Press, 1999), 42–43, 95–96.

10. See John Durham Peters, "Witnessing," *Media, Culture & Society* 23, no. 6 (2001): 722.

CHAPTER ONE

1. Søren Kierkegaard, *Early Polemical Writings*, ed. and trans. Julia Watkin (Princeton, NJ: Princeton University Press, 1990), 140–41. Hereafter abbreviated *EPW*.

2. Ludvig Holberg, *Master Gert Westphaler; or, The Talkative Barber*, in *Seven One-Act Plays by Holberg*, trans. Henry Alexander (Princeton, NJ: Princeton University Press, 1950), 23; trans. modified. Hereafter abbreviated *MGW*.

3. Søren Kierkegaard, *Letters and Documents*, trans. Henrik Rosenmeier (Princeton, NJ: Princeton University Press, 1978), 264–47, 249. Hereafter abbreviated *LD*.

4. Søren Kierkegaard, *Kierkegaard's Journals and Notebooks*, vol. 1, ed. Niels Jørgen Cappelørn et al. (Princeton, NJ: Princeton University Press, 2007), 101. Hereafter abbreviated *JNB* 1.

5. Søren Kierkegaard, *Prefaces*, ed. and trans. Todd W. Nichol (Princeton, NJ: Princeton University Press, 1997), 103–4. Hereafter abbreviated *P*.

6. Søren Kierkegaard, *Christian Discourses*, ed. and trans. Howard V. Hong and Edna H. Hong (Princeton, NJ: Princeton University Press, 1997), 239. Hereafter abbreviated *CD*.

7. Søren Kierkegaard, *Concluding Unscientific Postscript to Philosophical Fragments*, vol. 1, ed. and trans. Howard V. Hong and Edna H. Hong (Princeton, NJ: Princeton University Press, 1992), 287. Hereafter abbreviated *CUP* 1.

8. Søren Kierkegaard, *Stages on Life's Way*, ed. and trans. Howard V. Hong and Edna H. Hong (Princeton, NJ: Princeton University Press, 1988), 464.

9. See, for instance, Aristophanes, *Clouds* 1476–92; Xenophon, *Economics* 11.3; Isocrates, *Against the Sophists* 13.8; Plato, *Statesman* 299b; Aristotle, *Nicomachean Ethics* 117b; Aristotle, *Rhetoric* 1390a; Theophrastus, *Characters* 3; Dio Chrysostom, *Discourses* 20.3. Existing scholarship on this ancient tradition is well-summarized in Lieve Van Hoof, *Plutarch's Practical*

Ethics: The Social Dynamics of Philosophy (Oxford: Oxford University Press, 2010), 152.

10. Plutarch, "On Talkativeness," in *Moralia*, vol. 6, trans. W. C. Helmbold (Cambridge: Loeb Classical Library, 2000), 502B. Hereafter abbreviated T.

11. Søren Kierkegaard, *Kierkegaard's Journals and Notebooks*, vol. 4, ed. Niels Jørgen Cappelørn et al. (Princeton, NJ: Princeton University Press, 2011), 380. Hereafter abbreviated *JNB* 4.

12. Søren Kierkegaard, *The Book on Adler*, ed. and trans. Howard V. Hong and Edna H. Hong (Princeton, NJ: Princeton University Press, 1998), 7. Hereafter abbreviated *BOA*.

13. Aristophanes, *Clouds*, trans. Jeffrey Henderson (Cambridge: Loeb Classical Library, 1998), 130, 792. Hereafter abbreviated *C*.

14. Søren Kierkegaard, *The Concept of Irony, with Continual Reference to Socrates*, ed. and trans. Howard V. Hong and Edna H. Hong (Princeton, NJ: Princeton University Press, 1992), 64. Hereafter abbreviated *CI*.

15. Jacob and Wilhelm Grimm, "The Elves in Scotland," in *Fairy Legends and Traditions of the South of Ireland*, trans. Thomas Crofton Croker (London: John Murray, 1827), 34.

16. Søren Kierkegaard, *Kierkegaard's Journals and Notebooks*, vol. 2, ed. Niels Jørgen Cappelørn et al. (Princeton, NJ: Princeton University Press, 2008), 105. Hereafter abbreviated *JNB* 2.

17. Søren Kierkegaard, *Kierkegaard's Journals and Notebooks*, vol. 3, ed. Niels Jørgen Cappelørn et al. (Princeton, NJ: Princeton University Press, 2010), 227. Hereafter abbreviated *JNB* 3.

18. Søren Kierkegaard, *Kierkegaard's Journals and Notebooks*, vol. 9, ed. Niels Jørgen Cappelørn et al. (Princeton, NJ: Princeton University Press, 2017), 720. Hereafter abbreviated *JNB* 9.

19. Søren Kierkegaard, *Philosophical Fragments*, ed. and trans. Howard V. Hong and Edna H. Hong (Princeton, NJ: Princeton University Press, 1985), 78. Hereafter abbreviated *PF*.

20. Søren Kierkegaard, *The Concept of Anxiety: A Simple Psychologically Orienting Deliberation on the Dogmatic Issue of Hereditary Sin*, ed. and trans. Reidar Thomte (Princeton, NJ: Princeton University Press, 1980), 134–35. Hereafter abbreviated *CA*.

21. On the increasingly tense, polemical relationship between Heiberg and Kierkegaard in the following decade, and its importance for understanding Kierkegaard's work during this period, see Samuel McCormick, *Letters to Power: Public Advocacy without Public Intellectuals* (University Park: Pennsylvania State University Press, 2011), chapter 5; and Samuel McCormick, "Inter et Inter: Between Kierkegaard and the Heibergs," *Søren Kierkegaard Newsletter* 59 (March 2012): 3–7.

22. Søren Kierkegaard, *The Corsair Affair and Articles Related to the Writings*, ed. and trans. Howard V. Hong and Edna H. Hong (Princeton, NJ: Princeton University Press, 1982), 6. Hereafter abbreviated *COR*.

23. See McCormick, *Letters to Power*, 137–141; and McCormick, "Inter et Inter," 3–7.
24. Aristotle, *Nicomachean Ethics*, rev. ed., ed. and trans. Roger Crisp (Cambridge: Cambridge University Press, 2014), 1108a. Hereafter abbreviated *EN*.

CHAPTER TWO

1. Martin Heidegger, *Being and Time*, trans. John Macquarrie and Edward Robinson (Oxford: Blackwell, 1962), 158. Hereafter abbreviated *BT*.
2. Translated from the editorial comments on *Søren Kierkegaards Skrifter*, ed. Niels Jørgen Cappelørn et al. (Copenhagen: Gad, 1997–), 8, 76. Hereafter cited as *SKS* and followed by volume number.
3. Statistical surveys of Denmark began in the second half of the eighteenth century, but it was not until 1835, with the first publication of census data compiled by the Table Commission, that social statistics became a prominent feature of Danish civic life. See Franz Rothenbacher, *Statistical Sources for Social Research on Western Europe, 1945–1995: A Guide to Social Statistics* (Oplanden: Leske + Budrich, 1998), 171–81. On the broader European tradition of nineteenth-century social statistics, in which Kierkegaard's critique of mathematical equality clearly participates, see Alain Desrosières, *The Politics of Large Numbers: A History of Statistical Reasoning*, trans. Camille Naish (Cambridge, MA: Harvard University Press, 1998); and Theodore M. Porter, *The Rise of Statistical Thinking, 1820–1900* (Princeton, NJ: Princeton University Press, 1986).
4. Bruce H. Kirmmse, *Kierkegaard in Golden Age Denmark* (Bloomington: Indiana University Press, 1990), 275.
5. A more detailed account of these intellectual and cultural tensions is provided in McCormick, *Letters to Power*, 110–16.
6. Cf. Søren Kierkegaard, *Kierkegaard's Journals and Notebooks*, vol. 10, ed. Niels Jørgen Cappelørn et al. (Princeton, NJ: Princeton University Press, 2018), 206–8. Hereafter abbreviated *JNB* 10.
7. Alfred North Whitehead and Bertrand Russell, *Principia Mathematica*, 2nd ed. (Cambridge: Cambridge University Press, 1927), 37.
8. Alain Badiou, *Being and Event*, trans. Oliver Feltham (London: Continuum, 2005), 52–69.

CHAPTER THREE

1. Søren Kierkegaard, *Kierkegaard's Journals and Notebooks*, vol. 8, ed. Niels Jørgen Cappelørn et al. (Princeton, NJ: Princeton University Press, 2015), 370. Hereafter abbreviated *JNB* 8.
2. Quoted in Joakim Garff, *Søren Kierkegaard: A Biography*, trans. Bruce H. Kirmmse (Princeton, NJ: Princeton University Press: 2005), 782–83.

3. Søren Kierkegaard, *The Moment and Late Writings*, ed. and trans. Howard V. Hong and Edna H. Hong (Princeton, NJ: Princeton University Press, 1998), 269 (trans. modified). Hereafter abbreviated *M*.

4. The conceptual basis for this affinity was established in Theophrastus, *Characters* 3 and 7, where *adoleschia* and *lalia* receive comparable treatments.

5. Søren Kierkegaard, *Eighteen Upbuilding Discourses*, ed. and trans. Howard V. Hong and Edna H. Hong (Princeton, NJ: Princeton University Press, 1990), 137–38. Hereafter abbreviated *EUD*.

6. As quoted in Carl Henrik Koch, "Adolph Peter Adler: A Stumbling-Block and an Inspiration for Kierkegaard," in *Kierkegaard and his Danish Contemporaries, Tome II: Theology*, ed. Jon Stewart (New York: Routledge, 2016), 12.

7. Peter Fenves, *"Chatter": Language and History in Kierkegaard* (Stanford, CA: Stanford University Press, 1993), 145.

8. Fenves, *"Chatter,"* 1–2.

9. Giorgio Agamben, *Means without End: Notes on Politics*, trans. Vincenzo Binetti and Cesare Casarino (Minneapolis: University of Minnesota Press, 2000), 59.

10. Fenves, *"Chatter,"* 236.

11. Søren Kierkegaard, *Kierkegaard's Journals and Notebooks*, vol. 6, ed. Niels Jørgen Cappelørn et al. (Princeton, NJ: Princeton University Press, 2012), 135. Hereafter abbreviated *JNB 6*. Cf. Søren Kierkegaard, *Kierkegaard's Journals and Notebooks*, vol. 7, ed. Niels Jørgen Cappelørn et al. (Princeton, NJ: Princeton University Press, 2014), 81–82. Hereafter abbreviated *JNB 7*. See also Søren Kierkegaard, *The Sickness Unto Death: A Christian Psychological Exposition for Upbuilding and Awakening*, ed. and trans. Howard V. Hong and Edna H. Hong (Princeton, NJ: Princeton University Press, 1980), 102. Hereafter abbreviated *SD*.

12. Søren Kierkegaard, *Practice in Christianity*, ed. and trans. Howard V. Hong and Edna H. Hong (Princeton, NJ: Princeton University Press, 1991), 107. Hereafter abbreviated *PC*.

13. Ludvig Holberg, "The Fussy Man," in *Four Plays by Holberg* (Princeton, NJ: Princeton University Press, 1946), 13.

14. On the history and theory of epistemic probability, see Ian Hacking, *The Emergence of Probability*, 2nd ed. (Cambridge: Cambridge University Press, 2006).

15. Cf. Søren Kierkegaard, *Judge for Yourself!*, in *For Self-Examination / Judge for Yourself!*, ed. and trans. Howard V. Hong and Edna H. Hong (Princeton, NJ: Princeton University Press, 1991), 98–105.

16. Søren Kierkegaard, *Kierkegaard's Journals and Notebooks*, vol. 5, ed. Niels Jørgen Cappelørn et al. (Princeton, NJ: Princeton University Press, 2011), 374; trans. modified. Hereafter abbreviated *JNB 5*. Cf. *JNB 9*, 30.

CHAPTER FOUR

1. Martin Heidegger, *Becoming Heidegger: On the Trail of His Early Occasional Writings, 1910–1927*, ed. Theodore Kisiel and Thomas Sheehan (Evanston, IL: Northwestern University Press, 2007), 367. Hereafter abbreviated *BH*.

2. Martin Heidegger and Karl Jaspers, *The Heidegger-Jaspers Correspondence (1920–1963)*, ed. Walter Biemel and Hans Saner, trans. Gary E. Aylesworth (Amherst, MA: Humanity Books, 2003), 224. Hereafter abbreviated *HJC*.

3. Martin Heidegger, *Towards the Definition of Philosophy*, trans. Ted Sadler (London: Athlone Press, 2000), 3–4. Hereafter abbreviated *WES* 1919.

4. Fritz K. Ringer, *The Decline of the German Mandarins: The German Academic Community, 1890–1933* (Cambridge, MA: Harvard University Press, 1969), 385, 392–93.

5. Ringer, *Decline*, 384.

6. Ringer, *Decline*, 393–94, 402.

7. As quoted in Ringer, *Decline*, 391.

8. Martin Heidegger, *Letters to His Wife: 1915–1970*, ed. Gertrud Heidegger, trans. R. D. V. Glasgow (Cambridge: Polity, 2008), 70; trans. modified. Hereafter abbreviated *LHW*.

9. Martin Heidegger, *The Phenomenology of Religious Life*, trans Matthias Fritsch and Jennifer Anna Gosetti-Ferencei (Bloomington: Indiana University Press, 2010), 236; trans. modified. Hereafter abbreviated *WS* 1920–21.

10. Martin Heidegger, *Phenomenology of Intuition and Expression: Theory of Philosophical Concept Formation*, trans. Tracy Colony (London: Continuum, 2010), 11.

11. Martin Heidegger, *Phenomenological Interpretations of Aristotle: Initiation into Phenomenological Research*, trans. Richard Rojcewicz (Bloomington: Indiana University Press, 2001), 53. Hereafter abbreviated *WS* 1921–22.

12. Martin Heidegger, *Ontology—The Hermeneutics of Facticity*, trans. John van Buren (Bloomington: Indiana University Press, 1999), 24–25. Hereafter abbreviated *SS* 1923.

13. Vincent van Gogh to Theo van Gogh, Cuesmes, August 1879. Available online at http://vangoghletters.org/vg/letters/let154/letter.html.

14. Martin Heidegger, "Why Do I Stay in the Provinces?" trans. Thomas J. Sheehan, in *Philosophical and Political Writings*, ed. Manfred Stassen (New York: Continuum, 2003), 18; trans. modified. Hereafter abbreviated *PPW*.

15. Eduard Spranger, "Rickerts System," *Logos: Internationale Zeitschrift für Philosophie der Kultur* 12 (1923–24), 198, quoted in *SS* 1923, 33.

16. Also worth mentioning here, especially given Heidegger's use of *Bewegtheit* above, is his occasional reliance on the watery verb, *plätschern*—meaning "to splash," "to burble," and, tellingly, "to purl"—in his early letters to Jaspers. When Heidegger spoke of *Dasein*'s peculiar *Bewegtheit*,

it was the wider *Plätschern* of the present age that he often meant to bemoan.

17. The summer of 1922 was Heidegger's first at the cabin, and he quickly came to feel more at home there than anywhere else. Which makes his use of *aufhalten* and its German siblings in the summer of 1923 all the more interesting. As John van Buren notes, *Aufenthalt* lends itself to homey translations like "residence," "dwelling place," and "home." As does the expression *sich aufhalten*, which can mean "to dwell," "to abide," and "to reside" (*SS* 1923, 10, n. 9).

18. Martin Heidegger, *On the Way to Language*, trans. Peter D. Hertz (New York: Harper & Row, 1971), 122. Hereafter abbreviated *OWL*. See also Martin Heidegger, *History of the Concept of Time: Prolegomena*, trans. Theodore Kisiel (Bloomington: Indiana University Press, 1985), 267–68. Hereafter abbreviated *SS* 1925. Cf. *BT*, 208.

CHAPTER FIVE

1. Martin Heidegger, *Basic Concepts of Aristotelian Philosophy*, trans. Robert D. Metcalf and Mark B. Tanzer (Bloomington: Indiana University Press, 2009), 71. Hereafter abbreviated *SS* 1924.

2. Giorgio Agamben, *Potentialities: Collected Essays in Philosophy* (Stanford, CA: Stanford University Press, 1999), 215.

3. For more on Heidegger's treatment of truth as *aletheia*, as well as some of the scholarly resistance with which his treatment met, see Michael Inwood, *A Heidegger Dictionary* (Oxford: Blackwell, 1999), 13–15.

4. Martin Heidegger, *The Essence of Human Freedom: An Introduction to Philosophy*, trans. Ted Sadler (London: Continuum, 2004), 34; trans. modified. Hereafter abbreviated *SS* 1930.

5. Hannah Arendt, "Martin Heidegger at Eighty," trans. Albert Hofstadter, *New York Review of Books*, 21 October 1971.

6. Martin Heidegger, *Plato's Sophist*, trans. Richard Rojcewicz and André Schuwer (Bloomington: Indiana University Press, 1997), 212. Hereafter abbreviated *WS* 1924–25.

7. Martin Heidegger, *Basic Concepts of Ancient Philosophy*, trans. Richard Rojcewicz (Bloomington: Indiana University Press, 2007), 192. Hereafter abbreviated *SS* 1926.

8. Martin Heidegger, *The Concept of Time*, trans. William McNeill (Oxford: Blackwell, 1992), 17. Hereafter abbreviated *CT*.

9. Heidegger went on to summarize the distinction between *nous* and *Gerede* as follows: "The first: *nous*, conceptual determination; the One, the Whole, Being. What beings are in themselves undistorted; truth, Being. The other: *doxa*, 'semblance,' idle talk [*Gerede*]; the multifarious in what is otherwise, the equivocal [?], opposition, nonbeing. Semblance distorts, since the many individuals are not the One." Philosophical inquiry, he

tells his students, should aim for the former and avoid the latter: "openness to the things and not mere idle talk [*Gerede*]" (*SS* 1926, 54–55; trans. modified).

10. Heidegger would later implicate *Geschwätz* in this discussion as well: "In philosophy one should not babble on and on [*schwätze*] but should speak of and from the things themselves. That is easy to demand, but hard to live up to" (*WS* 1925–26, 232; trans. modified).

CHAPTER SIX

1. Joan Stambaugh, *Thoughts on Heidegger* (Lanham, MD: Center for Advanced Research in Phenomenology & University Press of America, 1991), 16.

2. Jean-Luc Nancy, *The Birth of Presence*, trans. Brian Holmes et al. (Stanford, CA: Stanford University Press, 1993), 99–100.

3. Martin Heidegger, *Gesamtausgabe, Band 2* (Frankfurt: Klostermann, 1979), 238. Hereafter abbreviated *GA* and followed by volume number; cf. *BT*, 224.

4. William Blattner, *Heidegger's Being and Time: A Reader's Guide* (London: Continuum, 2006), 15.

5. Martin Heidegger, *Introduction to Metaphysics*, trans. Gregory Fried and Richard Polt (New Haven, CT: Yale University Press, 2000), 180–84. Hereafter abbreviated *SS* 1935.

6. Martin Heidegger, *The Essence of Human Freedom: An Introduction to Philosophy*, trans. Ted Sadler (London: Continuum, 2002), 35. Hereafter abbreviated *SS* 1936.

CHAPTER SEVEN

1. Quoted in Richard Askay, "Heidegger's Philosophy and Its Implications for Psychology, Freud, and Existential Psychoanalysis," in Martin Heidegger, *Zollikon Seminars: Protocols—Conversations—Letters*, trans. Franz Mayr and Richard Askay, ed. Medard Boss (Evanston, IL: Northwestern University Press, 2001), 309.

2. Heidegger, *Zollikon Seminars*, 224.

3. Heidegger, *Zollikon Seminars*, 174, 267–68.

4. As quoted in Askay, "Heidegger's Philosophy," 308.

5. Sigmund Freud, *The Freud Reader*, ed. Peter Gay (New York: W. W. Norton, 1989), 131–32. Hereafter abbreviated *FR*.

6. A more detailed account of these events is provided in Elisabeth Roudinesco, *Jacques Lacan*, trans. Barbara Bray (New York: Columbia University Press, 1997), 231.

7. Jacques Lacan, *The Ego in Freud's Theory and in the Technique of Psychoanalysis, 1954–1955*, ed. Jacques-Alain Miller, trans. Sylvana Tomaselli (New York: W. W. Norton, 1991), 148. Hereafter abbreviated *S* 2.

8. Jacques Lacan, *The Psychoses, 1955–1956*, ed. Jacques-Alain Miller, trans. Russell Grigg (New York: W. W. Norton, 1993), 193. Hereafter abbreviated *S* 3.

CHAPTER EIGHT

1. The standard English translation of Freud's work fails to account for this temporal subtlety, mistakenly rendering the entire dream of Irma's injection in the imperfect tense. See Patrick J. Mahony, "Towards a Formalist Approach to Dreams," *International Review of Psycho-Analysis* 4, no. 1 (1977): 83–98.
2. Jacques Lacan, *Écrits*, trans. Bruce Fink (New York: W. W. Norton, 2006), 213. Hereafter abbreviated *E*.
3. Jacques Lacan, *Freud's Papers on Technique, 1953–1954*, ed. Jacques-Alain Miller, trans. John Forrester (New York: W. W. Norton, 1991), 109. Hereafter abbreviated *S* 1.
4. Giorgio Agamben, *The Time That Remains: A Commentary on the Letter to the Romans*, trans. Patricia Dailey (Stanford, CA: Stanford University Press, 2005), 74. This temporal logic is developed more fully in McCormick, *Letters to Power*, 52–80.
5. See Bruce Fink, "Translator's Endnotes," in *E*, 786.
6. John Durham Peters, "Communication, History of the Idea," in *The International Encyclopedia of Communication*, ed. Wolfgang Donsbach (Oxford: Blackwell, 2008), 689–93.
7. Plato, *Parmenides*, 135d. Cf. *Phaedrus*, 269e. Jacques Lacan, . . . *ou pire* (Paris: Seuil, 2011), 94. Hereafter abbreviated *S* 19.

CHAPTER NINE

1. Cf. Irma's complaint at the beginning of the dream: "it's choking me." This complaint may have functioned, at least in part, as a phantasmatic representation of the thrombosis from which Freud's wife previously suffered, as well as Freud's ongoing concern that his wife, who was pregnant again at the time of his dream, might develop another thrombosis.
2. See, for instance, Jeffrey M. Masson, "Freud and the Seduction Theory: A Challenge to the Foundations of Psychoanalysis," *Atlantic*, February 1984.
3. Freud to Fliess, 4 March, 8 March, 13 March, and 11 April 1895, in *The Complete Letters of Sigmund Freud to Wilhelm Fliess, 1887–1904*, ed. and trans. Jeffrey Moussaieff Masson (Cambridge, MA: Belknap, 1985), 113–24. Hereafter abbreviated *CL*.
4. More precisely, Peter Gay suggests, Otto represents Fliess, as mediated through Freud's friend and family physician, Oskar Rie; and Irma represents Eckstein, as mediated through one of his other patients, Anna Lichtheim. See Peter Gay, *Freud: A Life for Our Time* (New York: W. W. Norton, 1998), 82–84.

5. Jacques Lacan, *The Four Fundamental Concepts of Psychoanalysis*, ed. Jacques-Alain Miller, trans. Alan Sheridan (New York: W. W. Norton, 1981), 53–54. Hereafter abbreviated *S* 11.

6. Sigmund Freud, *The Standard Edition of the Complete Psychological Works of Sigmund Freud*, vol. 12, ed. and trans. James Strachey (London: Hogarth, 1958), 154. Hereafter abbreviated *SE* and followed by volume and page numbers.

7. Bruce Fink, *The Lacanian Subject: Between Language and Jouissance* (Princeton, NJ: Princeton University Press, 1995), 39.

8. Jacques Lacan, *The Ethics of Psychoanalysis, 1959–1960*, ed. Jacques-Alain Miller, trans. Dennis Porter (New York: W. W. Norton, 1992), 68. Hereafter abbreviated *S* 7.

9. Gay, *Freud*, 83.

10. Gay, *Freud*, 82.

CONCLUSION

1. Jeffrey T. Schnapp and Matthew Tiews, eds., *Crowds* (Stanford, CA: Stanford University Press, 2006), xvi.

2. Gustave Le Bon, *The Crowd: A Study of the Popular Mind* (New York: Macmillan, 1896), xv.

3. Gabriel Tarde, "The Public and the Crowd" (1901), in *Gabriel Tarde: On Communication and Social Influence*, ed. Terry N. Clark (Chicago: University of Chicago Press, 1969), 277, 281. Hereafter abbreviated *GT*.

4. Gabriel Tarde, *L'Opinion et la foule*, 3rd ed. (Paris: Alcan, 1910), vi.

5. As quoted in Christine Poggi, "Mass, Pack, and Mob: Art in the Age of the Crowd," in Schnapp and Tiews, *Crowds*, 160.

6. Ulrich Beck, "The Reinvention of Politics: Toward a Theory of Reflexive Modernization," in Ulrich Beck et al., *Reflexive Modernization: Politics, Tradition and Aesthetics in the Modern Social Order* (Stanford, CA: Stanford University Press, 1994), 14, 8, 13. See also Ulrich Beck and Elisabeth Beck-Gernsheim, *Individualization: Institutionalized Individualism and its Social and Political Consequences*, trans. Patrick Camiller (London: Sage, 2001).

7. Beck and Beck, *Individualization*, xxi; Beck, "Reinvention of Politics," 14.

8. Lee Rainie and Barry Wellman, *Networked: The New Social Operating System* (Cambridge, MA: MIT Press, 2012), 6.

9. Paul Mihailidis, "A Tethered Generation: Exploring the Role of Mobile Phones in the Daily Life of Young People," *Mobile Media & Communication* 2, no. 1 (2014): 59. See also Keith N. Hampton et al., "The Social Life of Wireless Urban Spaces: Internet Use, Social Networks, and the Public Realm," *Journal of Communication* 60 (2010): 701–22. For a broader reading of this social phenomenon, in which online public culture (the digital) and offline crowd culture (the physical) are not dichotomous but dialectical, part and parcel of a new "augmented reality," see Nathan Jurgenson,

"When Atoms Meet Bits: Social Media, the Mobile Web and Augmented Revolution," *Future Internet* 4, no. 1 (2012): 83–91.

10. Bruno Latour, "Networks, Societies, Spheres: Reflections of an Actor-Network Theorist," *International Journal of Communication* 5 (2011): 804–5. Hereafter abbreviated *NSS*.

11. See, for instance, John Cheny-Lippold, *We Are Data: Algorithms and the Making of our Digital Selves* (New York: New York University Press, 2017).

12. Bruno Latour, *Reassembling the Social: An Introduction to Actor-Network Theory* (Oxford: Oxford University Press, 2005), 216–17.

13. Bruno Latour, *On the Modern Cult of the Factish Gods* (Durham: Duke University Press, 2010).

14. Gilles Deleuze, "Postscript on the Societies of Control," *October* 59 (Winter 1992): 5. Hereafter abbreviated *PSC*.

15. World Economic Forum, *Personal Data: The Emergence of a New Asset Class*, January 2011; Jaron Lanier, *Who Owns the Future?* (New York: Simon & Schuster, 2013).

16. See Andy Crabtree et al., "Enabling the New Economic Actor: Data Protection, the Digital Economy, and the Databox," *Personal and Ubiquitous Computing* 20 (2016): 947–57.

17. See, for instance, Václav Janeček, "Ownership of Personal Data in the Internet of Things," *Computer Law & Security Review: The International Journal of Technology Law and Practice* 34, no. 5 (2018): 1–14; and Pantelis Koutroumpis et al., "The (Unfulfilled) Potential of Data Marketplaces," *ETLA Working Papers* 53 (2017): http://pub.etla.fi/ETLA-Working-Papers-53.pdf.

18. See, for instance, Laura Kemppainen et al., "Revenue Models of Personal Data Platform Operators," paper delivered at the 24th Nordic Academy of Management Conference in Bodø, Norway (2017) online at https://www.researchgate.net/profile/Laura_Kemppainen/publication/ 317687549_Revenue_Models_of_Personal_Data_Platform_Operators/links/ 5948eb28a6fdcc70635d3f2e/Revenue-Models-of-Personal-Data-Platform -Operators.pdf; Crabtree et al., "Enabling the New Economic Actor," 947; Mark van Rijmenam, "From Data Ownership to Data Usage: How Consumers Will Monetize Their Personal Data" (2015), online at https://datafloq .com/read/data-ownership-data-usage-consumers-monetize-data/68.

19. Andrew Bennett, "Sketching a Model of Data Ownership," *Medium*, 1 March 2018, online at https://medium.com/@andrewjb/sketching-a -model-of-data-ownership-85ab38037ca3. On the growing movement toward "platform cooperativism," see Nathan Schneider, "An Internet of Ownership: Democratic Design for the Online Economy," *Sociological Review Monographs* 66 (2018): 320–40.

Index

Note: Page numbers followed by a *t* refer to a table and those followed by an *f* refer to a figure.

298; deviation from itself, 200; and discoveredness and understanding, 195; flight from itself, 211; in historical consciousness, 147; and "idle talk," 148, 155–56, 182; *Jeweiligkeit* of, 153; in philosophy, 147, 158; potentiality for being, 206; and *Rede*, 201, 203; and rhetoric, 161; scattering, 204; as they-self, 205; understanding itself, 213. *See also* being-towards-death

data sharing, 302

data unions, 301–3

deception, 18, 39, 45, 167, 175, 176, 189t, 195

deindividuation, 293

Deleuze, Gilles, 300–301, 303

delusions of grandeur, 17, 26–27, 29, 31, 42, 45, 141

Denmark, 57

Descartes, René, 7

dialectic, 189–90, 192

dialectician, 181, 185, 188, 189t, 193, 209, 210

dialegesthai (speaking-through), 185–88, 189t, 192. See also *Durchsprechen* (speaking-through)

dialogue: and the *adoleschos*, 179; compared to antiphonal singing, 18, 35, 254; conversation as, 72, 291; of ego with object, 230; in Freud's dream, 229, 231, 235, 237, 252–55, 258, 260, 271; in Holberg's play, 19–20; Platonic, 185; Socratic, 33–35, 45

dianoein (thinking-through), 189t

digital communication, 3, 295

digital economy, 302–3

digital media, 3, 301, 302; overconnection to, 9

Dilthey, Wilhelm, 148

Dio Chrysostom, 30

disclosive knowledge. See *aletheuein* (to uncover)

dissimulation, 166–68, 175, 189t

distraction, 27–29, 40, 141, 143, 189t, 274. See also *adoleschia* (aimless speech)

doxa, 161–67, 169, 199–200; and *endoxa*, 162; *Ja-Sagen* in, 163–64. See also *endoxa* (reputable opinions)

Durchsprechen (speaking-through), 181, 185–88, 189t, 192–94, 193t, 199, 202t, 208–10. See also *dialegesthai* (speaking-through)

echte Sprechen (genuine speech), 181, 185, 188, 189t, 192, 193t, 199, 202t, 208–10. See also *logos*

Eckstein, Emma, 263–66, 268, 275, 286–87

education in Germany, 131–34, 147–48

Eftersnakken (parroting), 40–42, 47–48

egalitarianism, 56–58

ego, 229–38, 240–42, 249–53, 257, 259, 261, 277, 285, 286, 298

eiron (mock-modest person), 45, 48, 174–75

eironeia (mock modesty), 45–46

elitism, 58

empty set, 77–81, 83

empty speech: in analysis, 249–50, 258, 285–86, 298; compared to *tessera*, 247; and everyday talk, 4–5, 10, 292, 303; as false communication, 251; in Freud's dream, 259, 267, 271, 272, 274, 283, 285; function of, 247–48; individuating potential of, 299; Lacan's thoughts on, 3, 8, 11, 21, 24, 220–21, 229, 233, 247–50, 260, 262, 269, 292–93, 297–98, 299; as mode of circulation, 297–98; online, 8; tessellations of, 252–57

endoxa (reputable opinions), 162, 164, 169, 172, 175, 176. See also *doxa*

episteme, 164–65

Eubulides of Miletus, 68

everyday talk, 123, 192, 210–11, 220, 224, 225, 252, 291, 292–93, 295, 299; defined, 4–5; and everyday thought, 10–11; features of, 8–9; as a means without end, 5–6

everyday thought, 10–11

extra-psyches and intra-psychology, 295

factish, 297

falsehood. See *pseudos* (falsehood)

Fenves, Peter, 6–7, 96–97

Fichte, Johann Gottlieb, 36

Fink, Bruce, 277

flash mobs, 290

Fliess, Wilhelm, 263, 265–66, 281, 286–87; Freud's correspondence with, 274–78

Foucault, Michel, 300

free association, 257

freedom of the press, 15–16

French Revolution, 289, 290

Freud, Sigmund: cocaine treatments, 268; correspondence with Fliess, 274–78; drama of Emma Eckstein, 263–66;